Newcomers, Outsiders, & Insiders

THE POLITICS OF RACE AND ETHNICITY

Series Editors Rodney E. Hero, University of Notre Dame
Katherine Tate, University of California, Irvine

Politics of Race and Ethnicity is premised on the view that understanding race and ethnicity is integral to a fuller, more complete understanding of the American political system. The goal is to provide the scholarly community at all levels with accessible texts that will introduce them to, and stimulate their thinking on, fundamental questions in this field. We are interested in books that creatively examine the meaning of American democracy for racial and ethnic groups and, conversely, what racial and ethnic groups mean and have meant for American democracy.

The Urban Voter: Group Conflict and Mayoral Voting Behavior in American Cities
Karen M. Kaufmann

Democracy's Promise: Immigrants and American Civic Institutions
Janelle S. Wong

Mark One or More: Civil Rights in Multiracial America
Kim M. Williams

Race, Republicans, and the Return of the Party of Lincoln
Tasha S. Philpot

The Price of Racial Reconciliation
Ronald W. Walters

Politics in the Pews: The Political Mobilization of Black Churches
Eric L. McDaniel

Newcomers, Outsiders, and Insiders: Immigrants and American Racial Politics in the Early Twenty-first Century
Ronald Schmidt Sr., Yvette M. Alex-Assensoh,
Andrew L. Aoki, and Rodney E. Hero

Newcomers, Outsiders, & Insiders

Immigrants and American Racial Politics in the Early Twenty-first Century

Ronald Schmidt Sr., Yvette M. Alex-Assensoh, Andrew L. Aoki, and Rodney E. Hero

THE UNIVERSITY OF MICHIGAN PRESS

Ann Arbor

Copyright © by the University of Michigan 2010
All rights reserved
Published in the United States of America by
The University of Michigan Press
Manufactured in the United States of America
♾ Printed on acid-free paper

2013   2012   2011   2010   4   3   2   1

A CIP catalog record for this book is available from the British Library.

Library of Congress Cataloging-in-Publication Data

Newcomers, outsiders, and insiders : immigrants and American racial
    politics in the early twenty-first century / Ronald Schmidt Sr. . . .
    [et al.].
        p.   cm. — (The politics of race and ethnicity)
    Includes bibliographical references and index.
        ISBN 978-0-472-11703-1 (cloth : alk. paper) — ISBN 978-0-472-
    03376-8 (pbk. : alk. paper) — ISBN 978-0-472-02219-9 (e-book)
        1. Immigrants—United States—Political activity.
    2. Americanization.   3. Cultural pluralism—United States.   4. United
    States—Race relations.   5. United States—Ethnic relations.
    I. Schmidt, Ronald, 1943–

    JV6477.N149   2009
    305.9'069120973—dc22   2009024951

        ISBN13 978-0-472-02219-9 (electronic)

Preface and Acknowledgments

Throughout the history of the United States, multiple racial and ethnic minority outsider groups have struggled to overcome stigmatization, discrimination, and exclusion in order to become equal insiders in the country's political, social, and economic spheres. In recent decades, the political efforts of three particular such outsider groups—Blacks, Latinos, and Asian Americans—to gain greater presence and power in American society and politics have been among the most widely recognized and written about by the country's political media, and by many social scientists as well. For many members of these groups, these efforts continue into the early decades of the twenty-first century, despite multiple improvements in the past fifty years.

For nearly a century, however, most mainstream political scientists and American politics textbooks ignored the roles of race and racial inequality in the country's politics, describing and analyzing the institutions of government and politics, as well as the behavior and political preferences of individual voters, as though ethnic and racial divisions and inequalities played little part in the grand drama of American democracy. This remains too true even today.

This pattern of scholarly neglect has begun to change, however, and that change was most significantly marked by the creation in 1995 of an Organized Section on Race, Ethnicity, and Politics (REP) in the American Political Science Association. The coauthors of this book met as members of REP, and with the help of one of the section's key founders—Anthony Affigne—we proposed a scholarly paper on the subject of the book for a theme panel at the 2002 Annual Meeting of the APSA. The proposal was accepted, and we coauthored and presented a paper, asking what political scientists know about the impacts of recent immigrants on American racial politics, and what the discipline still needs to learn. After presenting the paper, we tried to publish it in a scholarly journal, but it was too lengthy for such a venue, and we could not find a way to shorten it without seeming to take the life and vitality out of our inquiry. Frustrated, we decided to turn the project into a book, and the result of our subsequent work is in your hands.

Any book is a collaborative effort, but that may be more true of this book than most. Accordingly, we would like to acknowledge the support and encouragement of a large number of (sometimes unwitting) collaborators. To begin, we need to thank our families, and our colleagues in the respective higher education institutions that employed us during our work, for their support during the years in which we have worked on this book. We especially want to thank the members of the Organized Section on Race, Ethnicity, and Politics of the American Political Science Association for sponsoring the initial 2002 theme panel paper that led to this book, and for listening to—and commenting on—various parts of the work as it made its way toward a book. We also want to especially thank the Department of Political Science at the University of Notre Dame for enabling us to gather there for several days in both 2003 and 2005 to work out our approach to the inquiry contained herein. And we thank our employers—California State University, Long Beach; Indiana University, Bloomington; Augsburg College; and the University of Notre Dame—for furnishing us with places to work while we wrote, and for other forms of material research support. We are grateful, too, for the American Political Science Association, whose annual conferences provided an important space in which we could meet annually and talk through our collective work face-to-face. We also thank both Jim Reische and Melody Herr—our editors at the University of Michigan Press—for believing so strongly in our project, and for their patience and support in helping us see it through to completion. And we are grateful to the three anonymous readers who supported the project and recommended several important ways to improve it. Finally, we thank each other for the opportunity to work together in this way—it has been a journey of discovery both challenging and joyful.

We dedicate this book to those immigrants and their children who have been transforming our politics and society even while we have sought to understand their impacts on the efforts to make the United States a genuine racial democracy in the fullest sense: may your efforts result in a better democracy for us all.

Contents

Introduction: Focus, Framework, Benchmarks   1

Part 1 | Immigrants and the New Racial Politics

1 | The "New Immigration" and U.S. Ethnoracial Politics   9

2 | Analytical Framework for Studying Political Incorporation   37

Part 2 | Historical and Social Contexts

3 | The Historical Context of U.S. Ethnoracial Politics   67

4 | The Persistence of Racial Segregation in a Diverse America   104

Part 3 | Political Incorporation in an Era of Immigration

5 | Political Participation, Descriptive Representation, and
the Quest for Political Power   131

6 | Political Incorporation, Governing Coalitions, and
Public Policy   194

Part 4 | Conclusions

7 | Immigrants and the Future of American Ethnoracial Politics   249

Notes   269
References   275
Index   297

Introduction: Focus, Framework, Benchmarks

This book explores the political consequences of the intersection of two highly controversial social phenomena: the continuing efforts of racial minority outsider groups to gain greater presence and power in American politics and society, and the arrival of an extraordinary number of immigrant newcomers from countries other than Europe to the United States in the last four decades, an influx that is dramatically changing the ethnic and racial composition of the U.S. population. Indeed, the vast majority of newcomers—and their children—soon learn after arriving here that they are perceived by most Americans as members of long-standing racial "minorities," are perceived as "persons of color," in their new social and political environment. So, we asked, how is immigration's immense increase in the size of this country's "minority" populations affecting the efforts of Blacks, Latinos, and Asian Americans to become equal insiders in the country's politics, society, and economy? This book is our attempt to answer this central question, incomplete though it remains.

To frame our inquiry, we drew upon studies by other scholars to suggest four alternative trajectories for the future of ethnoracial[1] politics in the United States, trajectories that the arrival of large numbers of recent immigrant newcomers may directly influence. The following are the four alternative futures for American ethnoracial politics that we outline and assess.

Individual assimilation. In this scenario, racial identities become a thing of the past in American society; increasingly all Americans would become free to choose whether or not to identify as members of an ethnic or panethnic group, but in politics and in public policy—as signified by the color-blind ideal—racial and ethnic identities will play no significant role. Thus, in our political and public roles, we are all unique *individuals* and *Americans,* but not hyphenated Americans. In this scenario the influx of new immigrants from Africa, Latin America, and Asia—peoples with no real experiences in, or attachments to, the racial identities of the American past—will help (in conjunction with all the progress the country has made in removing racial discrimination in recent decades) all Americans get past racialization, so that the country will finally be able to put the divisions and hierarchies of racial inequality into the history books.

Political pluralism. A second scenario has ethnoracial identities continuing to play a role in political organization and mobilization so that many Americans see these identities as linked in important ways to their political aims and aspirations. At the same time, pluralism assumes a relatively even playing field in political and social life, so that ethnoracial groups (along with a huge range of other interest groups such as economic, professional, so-called values groups, etc.) are free to associate, to form alliances, and to influence the outcome of elections, governmental appointments, and public policy decisions through various forms of political persuasion and pressure. In the pluralist scenario no important racial barriers to such political influence remain for long-standing American ethnoracial minorities, and all such interest groups are assumed to have a fair chance at affecting political outcomes. In this scenario of the American future, the incorporation of the large influx of immigrants who are perceived as "peoples of color" may take several forms. These may include the formation of new political identity groups but may also lead to a substantial increase in the size and political clout of organizations that have long sought to represent the interests of ethnoracial minority groups, particularly those of Latinos and Asian Americans, since these groups have experienced the greatest growth during the contemporary period of high immigration.

Biracial hierarchy. Our third scenario for the future of American ethnoracial politics suggests that over a relatively brief period of time most immigrant newcomers, particularly those from Asia and Latin America, will be successfully assimilated politically as individuals and/or will be represented by increasingly successful and powerful pluralist political organizations. On the other hand, Blacks (as well as dark-skinned immigrants from Latin America) will remain highly disadvantaged in comparison with other groups, excluded from increasing their political power and social positions through the ongoing workings of a continuing White/Black biracial hierarchy. In this scenario, the large influx of new immigrants from Asia and Latin America (and particularly the light-skinned among them) will be integrated successfully into American society in a fashion similar to that of most eastern and southern European immigrants in the aftermath of the huge arrival of immigrants that occurred in the late nineteenth and early twentieth centuries. Most Blacks (and dark-skinned immigrants), meanwhile, will remain in the lower rungs of the economy, will continue to be racially stigmatized, and will continue to see their political power insufficient for ensuring that most political appointments and public policy positions reflect their interests and preferences. In part, this will be *because* many new immigrants will have taken over jobs, neighborhoods, and political interests that American Blacks continue to struggle to hold and/or to attain.

Multiracial hierarchy. Our fourth scenario suggests that the multiracial pattern of racial hierarchy prevalent since at least the mid–nineteenth century in the American West and Southwest will be nationalized by contemporary immigration. Accordingly, the racial hierarchy of the United States will be more complex and multifaceted, but systematic ethnoracial inequality will continue to exist in the country's economy, society, and politics for the foreseeable future. This scenario, in short, sees the large influx of immigrants from Latin America and Asia as engendering the spread of a pattern of multiracial hierarchy—a pattern that includes triangulation among multiple racialized groups and that stigmatizes, excludes, and/or pits minority groups in opposition to each other in multiple ways, but that systematically supports various forms of political, social, and economic advantage for a steadily decreasing White, European-origin population.

We should note here that the first two of these future trajectories are indicative of a high degree of ethnoracial equality in the United States and, accordingly, a high degree of ethnoracial democracy as well. The latter two scenarios, however, indicate either biracial or multiracial hierarchy, and continuing obstructions to ethnoracial democratization in the United States.

In order to further frame our inquiry to make sense of the multitude of changes occurring in relation to the political efforts of outsider minority groups to become equal insiders in American politics and society, we employ four benchmarks of political incorporation toward ethnoracial democracy:[2] (1) increased *political participation,* leading to (2) increased *political representation,* making possible (3) *effective influence* over governmental decisions through memberships in "governing coalitions," and (4) the *adoption of public policies* favored by minority group members and thought to advance toward greater ethnoracial equality in the country.

voting is only the beginning!

Each of these benchmarks is important in the struggle for ethnoracial democracy in the United States. Adherents of democracy believe that *political participation* is important because without it, government decision makers are much less likely to think about or represent the interests of groups that are not involved. Black Americans in the American South were excluded from most forms of political participation for many decades, as were many Latinos and Asian Americans in other parts of the country. In collecting information for our study, therefore, we sought to determine how recent immigrants have affected the degree to which Blacks, Latinos, and Asian Americans participate in the political processes of the United States.

Political representation is important to ethnoracial democracy for the same reasons that participation is important. That is, if there are no members of ethnoracial minority groups sitting at the table through memberships in legislative and executive governmental bodies, those representatives are less likely to think about or to reflect the interests of those missing groups in their decisions as governmental agents. In recent decades, a substantial amount of work has been done by political activists from ethnoracial minority communities aimed at increasing the descriptive representation of these groups in public office. Again, therefore, we framed our inquiry here by asking how recent immigration has affected these efforts at greater descriptive representation.

Our third benchmark of political incorporation, *effective influence* over governmental decisions through membership in "governing coalitions," is important because it is all too possible to gain some measure of descriptive representation in public office without being able to substantially influence the decisions of governing institutions. Particularly if a polity is racially polarized, it is not unusual to be on the losing side of every decision that is believed to affect the interests of ethnoracial minority communities in important ways. If such a pattern of decision making is systematic or continuous, then ethnoracial hierarchy will be prevalent despite token representation. Thus minority group political leaders have sought membership in those political coalitions that tend to dominate the governing institutions of the society. In respect to this benchmark, then, we have sought information on how the large increases from immigration have affected the capacity of ethnoracial minority group members to gain membership in the dominant coalitions of governing institutions at various levels of the U.S. government.

Finally, our fourth benchmark of political incorporation for ethnoracial democracy is the successful *adoption of egalitarian public policies* favored by minority communities and thought to advance ethnoracial equality in American society, politics, and economics. This is believed to be the ultimate goal for many political activists and leaders seeking greater presence and power in the political system for Blacks, Latinos, and Asian Americans. This is because it is through public policy that government acts directly to change the workings and outcomes of the country's society and economy. In the face of such efforts, failure to adopt such policies is seen as indicative of a continuation of those social forces that perpetuate ethnoracial inequality and undermine democratization of the United States. Our research work asked how the recent influx of immigrants has affected the public policy agenda in the United States in respect to ethnoracial equality.

Using these benchmarks of political incorporation and racial democracy, we sought in this book to determine the nature and degree of political integration of long-standing outsider ethnoracial groups, as affected by the new immigrants, in relation to the four scenarios for the future as sketched here. In the end, we found evidence favoring all four of our future scenarios for ethnoracial politics in the United States. That is, we found—and presented—evidence that might convince conscientious readers that it is possible to be optimistic regarding the future of ethnoracial democracy in the United States as a result of high levels of individual assimilation and greater political involvement through pluralistic ethnoracial identity groups, and that recent immigration has enhanced these developments. However, we also found—and presented—evidence that leads to a more pessimistic conclusion, a conclusion that supports continued racial hierarchy, not only for American Blacks, but also for the enlarged Latino and Asian American populations.

This more pessimistic conclusion is reached, we believe, if one applies consistently all four of the benchmarks for political incorporation sketched here. There is little doubt that increased immigration is increasing the political participation and representation of Latinos and Asian Americans in American politics, and that Black participation and representation continues to be relatively robust in comparison with the past. Those realities can be persuasive to some as indicative of the arrival of ethnoracial equality and democracy in the United States. However, if one believes—as we do—that increased political participation and simple descriptive representation are insufficient for the realization of ethnoracial democracy, that democracy requires that outsider groups have real influence in the governing institutions of American politics, and that democratization requires the adoption of egalitarian public policies that will reverse the long-standing patterns of ethnoracial inequality in American society, then it is more difficult to be optimistic about the elimination of racial hierarchy from the U.S. political system. Indeed, we find that the influx of new immigrants has made the realization of ethnoracial democracy in the United States both more complex and more important, but this important demographic change has *not* reduced the likely continuation of ethnoracial hierarchy in American politics.

Before we reach these conclusions, however, we have much information to present, to analyze, and to digest. We turn to those tasks in chapter 1, beginning with an overview narrative comparing racial politics in the 1960s and in the present decade, and an overview of the demographic changes to the United States as a whole, particularly the changes immigrants have brought—and continue to bring—to the country's ethnoracial minority groups.

Part I | Immigrants and the
New Racial Politics

1 | The "New Immigration" and U.S. Ethnoracial Politics

Prologue: Then and Now

On August 28, 1963, in one of the largest public demonstrations of political engagement in U.S. history, more than two hundred thousand people—most, but by no means all, of them with dark skins—gathered before the Lincoln Memorial in Washington, D.C., to demand freedom and justice for America's Black population. Covered live by the national television news media, the highlight of the mass demonstration was a speech by the Reverend Martin Luther King Jr. Now known as his "I have a dream" speech, Dr. King's oration would be heard generations later by millions of American schoolchildren on his birthday, now a national holiday. In that speech, the Rev. King crystallized the issues at the heart of the struggle for racial equality in the United States in 1963.

> But one hundred years later [after the Emancipation Proclamation of President Abraham Lincoln], the Negro still is not free; one hundred years later, the life of the Negro is still sadly crippled by the manacles of segregation and the chains of discrimination; one hundred years later, the Negro lives on a lonely island of poverty in the midst of a vast ocean of material prosperity; one hundred years later, the Negro is still languishing in the corners of American society and finds himself an exile in his own land.
>
> ... Now is the time to make real the promises of democracy; now is the time to rise from the dark and desolate valley of segregation to the sunlit path of racial justice; now is the time to lift our nation from the quicksands of racial injustice to the solid rock of brotherhood; now is the time to make justice a reality for all God's children. ... There will be neither rest nor tranquility in America until the Negro is granted his citizenship rights. (King 1986, 217–18)

9

Now, fast-forward a little more than four decades, to May 1, 2006, when a coordinated series of public demonstrations took place in more than 150 cities and towns all across the United States—from Anchorage, Alaska, to Miami, Florida; from Seattle and Los Angeles to New York City and Washington, D.C.—politically engaging more than three million people, thought to be the largest number of people to participate in a single protest event in American history (Woodrow Wilson International Center 2007). As in 1963's March on Washington, most of the faces in the crowds of demonstrators were dark faces, people of color, and they too were demanding an end to discrimination and prejudice, demanding freedom and justice from the U.S. government.

Despite its immense size and scope, however, this more recent series of political marches and demonstrations caught most Americans by surprise, as they had not been prepared by the news media through ongoing coverage of public confrontations between marchers and Southern law enforcement officers with fire hoses and attack dogs. There had been much public discussion of the 2006 marches leading up to the May 1 events, but most of that discussion occurred in the Spanish language and was covered mainly by Spanish language media, many of whose newscasters' broadcasts encouraged more people to turn out for the demonstrations. Indeed, while their faces were similarly dark, most of the 2006 demonstrators were not only racial outsiders but also immigrant newcomers to the United States.

The juxtaposition of these two political events spanning more than four decades marks the focus of our inquiry in this book. We seek to understand how the political struggle for racial equality in the United States has been affected by four decades of large-scale immigration, most of it from countries whose populations are viewed as non-White by most Americans. Because of this massive immigration, the size and diversity of U.S. racial minority populations have increased dramatically in these four decades. How has this international migration of newcomers affected the efforts of long-standing racialized outsider minority groups' efforts to gain political equality, full access to their citizenship rights? That is the central question that we will address in this book.

At the time of the 1963 March on Washington, the civil rights movement and the struggle for racial equality occupied the political limelight much of the time in the United States. Working on behalf of Black Americans in the Southern states, the civil rights movement worked in a variety of venues: *in the streets*, as in the case of the March on Washington and hundreds of other more localized protest demonstrations (e.g., picketing, marches, rallies, sit-ins, community organizing); *in the courts* through litigation; *in the legislative processes* of Congress and the White House through intense lobbying; and *in the court of public opinion* through capturing extensive coverage by the news media (especially the relatively new medium of television). The original target of this massive political mobilization was the legal system of racial domination and exclusion known at the time as Jim Crow. This system of domination and exclusion—established in the South following the demise of the Reconstruction policy after the Civil War (but not entirely confined to that region)—had spawned and maintained involuntary racially segregated housing, educational institutions, public facilities (e.g., restrooms, water fountains, swimming pools), public accommodations (e.g., restaurants, hotels, motels), public transportation (e.g., buses, trains), and employment and other forms of economic activity. It included also a variety of obstacles to political participation by African Americans, ranging from poll taxes and literacy tests for voter registration to economic reprisals, intimidation, and threats of physical violence intended to prevent and/or discourage Blacks from voting.

Following a lengthy campaign of litigation led by the NAACP's Legal Defense and Education Fund, in 1954 the U.S. Supreme Court had overturned the constitutional foundation for the South's apartheid system in the case of *Brown v. Board of Education of Topeka*. Soon after the 1963 March on Washington, moreover, the political mobilizations of the civil rights movement resulted in several key victories in public policy. The Twenty-fourth Amendment to the Constitution, for example, outlawed the poll tax in 1964. Even more important, the Civil Rights Act of 1964 was adopted by Congress, outlawing the system of involuntary racial segregation in public facilities, accommodations, transportation, and educational institutions, as well as racial discrimination in most places of employment. In 1965, moreover, the Voting Rights Act was passed, creating a structure of intervention through which the federal government could supervise—and, if necessary, directly operate—local electoral systems to ensure that African Americans could exercise their right to vote. A few years later, in 1968, Congress passed another law banning racial discrimination in the sale or rental of housing.

Despite these public policy victories in the 1960s, most of the activists in the campaign for racial democracy in the United States believed they still had a distance to go before seeing their goals fully realized. Though it did not take long after passage of the Voting Rights Act for African Americans in the South to reach voting percentages equal to those of Whites, the social and political inequalities that had accompanied several centuries of racial domination and exclusion were not to be easily excised through the adoption of a few laws against racial discrimination. By the end of the 1960s, for example, few African Americans had been elected to public office at federal, state, or local levels anywhere in the country, and political activists began intensive efforts to increase the descriptive representation of Blacks in public office. With the formal demise of the legal system of domination and exclusion in the South, many of the movement's leaders (e.g., Martin Luther King Jr., Jesse Jackson) sought to expand their mobilization campaigns for racial equality—particularly for equal access to housing, employment, and educational opportunities—by joining local activists in cities in the North and West (e.g., Chicago, Detroit, New York City, Boston, Philadelphia, Los Angeles, San Francisco), where many Blacks remained ghettoized, underemployed, and lacking in relative educational attainment.

As the civil rights movement took on a national rather than sectional character, it was joined by similar efforts for ethnoracial equality on behalf of other U.S. peoples of color in other parts of the country. By the middle 1960s, for example, Mexican American activists had begun to mobilize a Chicano movement in the West and Southwest; Puerto Rican activists similarly mobilized in the Northeast; and Japanese and Chinese American activists increased their efforts to combat racial stereotyping and exclusion, and to seek justice for historical wrongs. As was true of the African American movement of the time, these mobilizations (among other goals) worked to increase the political participation and representation of these specific racialized minority groups, they aimed at gaining greater power and influence on behalf of these groups in government, and they sought the adoption of a variety of public policies they believed would be helpful for attaining greater social and economic equality for their group members.

Among the policies sought in this wider campaign for ethnoracial equality were antidiscrimination policies, equal educational opportunities (through, e.g., desegregation of schools, equalization of school funding formulas, greater sensitivity to racial and cultural differences on the part of schoolteachers and counselors, greater access to higher education, public school integration in metropolitan areas, bilingual and bicultural education for Chicano and Puerto Rican students), expanded job training and opportunities in minority and low-income communities, affirmative action in public and private employment, open housing legislation and assistance, and expansion of government contracts to minority business firms. By the end of the 1960s, in short, ethnoracial minorities in the

United States were pressing a variety of claims for political inclusion and representation in hopes of gaining policies and institutional actions that would substantially increase the degree of racial equality in the country.

Four decades have now passed since these political events of the 1960s. How do these mobilizations appear to us now? In some respects, the ethnoracial mobilizations of the 1960s and early 1970s seem to belong to the remote past. Despite the 1992 "uprising" in Los Angeles following the acquittal verdict in the trial of the police officers seen beating Rodney King on national television, the urgency and centrality of racial justice as a political issue seem to have passed off the radar screen of most Americans long ago.

Most Black Americans no longer have to stir up their courage—for fear of losing their jobs, their homes, or even their physical safety—before casting their votes in political elections. Most large cities in the United States—in all parts of the country, including the South—routinely see Blacks, Latinos, and/or Asian Americans elected to city councils, county commissions, and school boards. Many state legislatures and the U.S. Congress have enough Black and Latino members to support caucuses of legislators from their groups to operate extensively on behalf of these ethnoracial minority group interests. A number of large and small American cities, moreover, have elected Black, Latino, and/or Asian American mayors over the past 40 years. Even those involved in presidential elections have witnessed serious campaigns mounted by Black and Latino candidates. Indeed, the most recent presidential election, in 2008, saw the nomination and election of an African American candidate—Senator Barack Obama—to the highest office in the land.

In addition to these improvements in the political status of these ethnoracial groups, many of their members have also dramatically improved their socioeconomic standing in the United States. The educational and economic successes of Asian Americans have led to their widespread description as America's "model minority," and both the Black and Latino populations now have substantial middle classes whose members have college degrees, live in comfortable homes, and work at relatively well-paid professional or managerial jobs or own their own businesses. Public opinion polls routinely and consistently show that a majority of Americans believe that racial justice is an accomplished fact in the United States, and racial inequality is not viewed by the majority as a public problem requiring corrective action by government. Four decades after the 1960s, as we have seen, immigration seems to be a much more pressing issue for the American political agenda than is the struggle for racial equality.

Yet race remains a vexing and unsettled issue in American public and social life: virtually all Americans are conscious of racial differences among racial groups in the national population, and most remain unsure, unconfident, and/or defensive when it comes to discussions about the subject of race in "mixed company." Moreover, despite the measures of progress over the past four decades, there are still important areas of systematic inequality between ethnoracial groups in the United States.

While the U.S. Black population is now much closer to parity in political representation in many parts of the country, it is still substantially below the national average in educational attainment, income, wealth, and job security, and a disproportionate share of African Americans still live, as King said, "on a lonely island of poverty." Further, Black Americans are much more likely to live in segregated residential neighborhoods, attend segregated schools, and be the victims of violent crime than are most other Americans. Similarly, Latinos are about as likely as Blacks to be poor, to live in segregated neighborhoods, to attend segregated schools, and to be victims of violent crime. Latinos are greatly underrepresented in the ranks of both voters and public officials at all levels of government. While Asian Americans—lumped together as a group—enjoy relatively high incomes and high levels of educational attainment in the United States, they are also underrepresented politically, and they frequently encounter others' perceptions of their foreignness no matter how many generations their forebears may have lived in this country. Some Asian American subgroups (particularly those groups containing large numbers of refugees), moreover, experience disproportionate levels of failure in the country's public schools, have great difficulty integrating into the social and cultural fabric of American society, and experience high levels of poverty. A number of studies indicate that even the best educated and most talented Asian Americans may face glass ceiling barriers of prejudice and discrimination in the workplace and in the public spaces of civil society.

Thus, more than four decades after the famous 1963 March on Washington, many Blacks, Latinos, and Asian Americans continue to experience life in the United States as racialized outsiders, despite the successes of some members of their groups. Black, Latino, and Asian American political activists and public officials continue seeking ways to increase the political presence and power of ethnoracial minorities in U.S. politics, and they continue seeking adoption of public policies that would generate greater equality among all ethnoracial groups in the American polity. Despite goals similar to those of the 1960s, however, we believe it is likely that ethnoracial politics in the United States has been changed in important ways as a result of the demographic transformation of the country generated by the large-scale immigration of the past four decades. For one thing, the complex subject of immigration has virtually eclipsed discussions of racial equality on the national political and public policy agenda. For another, the groups in focus in this discussion—Blacks, Latinos, Asian Americans—have themselves been transformed by the recent arrival of millions of newcomer immigrant members of their groups. Accordingly, in the rest of this chapter we will begin our work by describing the ways in which the new immigration has changed the demographic face of the nation, and, more specifically, each of these ethnoracial minority groups.

The New Immigration and the Changing Face of the U.S. Population

As most Americans know, the United States has experienced a period of sustained large-scale immigration since the 1960s. Indeed, by the 2000 census there were more foreign-born people living in the United States than at any previous time in its history. The year 1965 is usually cited by scholars as the beginning point of the "new immigration," mainly because it was then that Congress approved a new immigration law eliminating a 40-year-old national-origins quota system for allocating immigration authorizations. The old law, adopted by Congress in 1924, was widely perceived as racially discriminatory in that it gave first priority to applicants from the British Isles, and northern and western Europe. The new immigration law gave priority to family reunification and to admitting those with skills needed for the American economy (see, e.g., Glazer 1985; Tichenor 2002).

How has immigration changed the demographic face of the United States in the past four decades? What are the political implications? Tables 1.1, 1.2, and 1.3 summarize the major changes in the country's demographic makeup during the past 40-plus years.

What do these numbers mean? For one thing, beginning in the late 1960s there was a sharp increase in the *number of immigrants* coming to the United States. From the beginning of 1966 through 2007, U.S. government immigration statistics show that almost 30 million international migrants have established authorized permanent residency in the United States.[1] Largely as a result, the *2007 American Community Survey* conducted by U.S. Census Bureau[2] found that 12.6 percent of the U.S. population, more than 38 million residents, declared themselves to be "foreign

TABLE 1.1.   2007 Demographic Comparisons (in percentages)

Ethnoracial Group	U.S. Population	U.S. Foreign Born	Group Foreign Born	Group Non–U.S. Citizens
White, Non-Hispanic[a]	65.8	20.5	3.9	1.6
Hispanic/Latino	15.1	48.0	39.8	28.6
Black[b]	12.4	7.9	8.0	4.5
Asian American[b]	4.4	23.7	67.3	29.5

Source: U.S. Census Bureau 2007.

[a]For those choosing only one race.

[b]For those choosing only one race. Includes those who identified as Hispanic, as well as those who did not identify as Hispanic.

TABLE 1.2.   Percentage Foreign Born and Noncitizens, 1970 vs. 2007

Ethnoracial Group	Group Foreign Born, 1970	Group Foreign Born, 2007	Group Non–U.S. Citizens, 1970	Group Non–U.S. Citizens, 2007
White, Non-Hispanic	4.2	3.9	1.1	1.6
Hispanic/Latino	19.9	39.8	15.2	28.6
Black	1.1	8.0	0.7	4.5
Asian American	35.7	67.3	21.8	29.5

Source: U.S. Census Bureau, 1970 Census, U.S. Census Bureau 2007. Data for 1970 Group Non–U.S. Citizens from IPUMS: Steven Ruggles, Matthew Sobek, Trent Alexander, Catherine A. Fitch, Ronald Goeken, Patricia Kelly Hall, Miriam King, and Chad Ronnander, *Integrated Public Use Microdata Series: Version 3.0* (machine-readable database) (Minneapolis, Minn.: Minnesota Population Center [producer and distributor], 2004), http://usa.ipums.org/usa/.

TABLE 1.3.   Percentage Change, 1970–2007

Ethnoracial Group	Increase in Numbers (in thousands)	Change in Group % of U.S. Population	Group % Increase, 1970–2007
White, Non-Hispanic	28,900	−17.7	17.0
Hispanic/Latino	36,355	10.6	400.7
Black	14,795	1.3	65.6
APIA[a]	12,142	3.8	795.4

Source: U.S. Census Bureau, Historical Census Statistics on Population Totals by Race, 1790 to 1990, and by Hispanic Origin, 1970 to 1990, for the United States, Regions, Divisions, and States, table 1, ("United States—Race and Hispanic Origin: 1790 to 1990"; U.S. Census Bureau 2007. Decennial census data from 100 percent counts, except 1970 Hispanic and non-Hispanic White data from 15% sample.

[a]APIA includes both Asian Americans and Native Hawaiian and Other Pacific Islanders. Black and Asian American data include Black Latinos and Asian American Latinos, respectively. The 2007 data are for those reporting one race only.

born," an increase from 4.7 percent (9.6 million) in the 1970 census. As noted earlier, this is the largest number (not percentage) of foreign-born residents in U.S. history, and it means that the period since 1965 may be characterized accurately as one of the three peak periods of in-migration in U.S. history (the first having been in the mid-1800s, the second in the late nineteenth and early twentieth centuries).

As was true during previous periods of large-scale immigration, some states and cities have received a disproportionate share of immigrants in the past four decades. Thus, the *2007 American Community Survey* shows that the major immigrant-receiving centers in the United States in the current immigration era have been six states—California, New York, Texas, Florida, Illinois, and New Jersey—which, taken together, contained two-thirds (65.7 percent) of the foreign-born population of the country in 2007 (U.S. Census Bureau 2007d). California alone had over one-quarter (26.3 percent) of the U.S. foreign-born population in 2007. As a result, most of these same states contain the largest percentage of foreign-born residents as well: California again leads with a population that was 27.4 percent foreign-born in 2007, followed by New York (21.8 percent), New Jersey (19.9 percent), Nevada (19.4 percent), Florida (18.9 percent), Hawaii (17.3 percent), Texas (16.0 percent), Arizona (15.6 percent), Massachusetts (14.2 percent), and Illinois (13.8 percent) (U.S. Census Bureau 2007d).

As a result of these patterns of concentration in immigrant destinations, some American cities contain large percentages of foreign-born residents, as reported in a 2006 press release from the Census Bureau accompanying the *2005 American Community Survey.*

> According to the ACS, more than 1-in-3 residents living in Los Angeles (40.3 percent), San Jose (37.9), and New York (36.6) were not U.S. citizens at birth. Conversely, Detroit (6.3 percent) and Indianapolis (6.7) were large cities where the percent of foreign born was half that of the national average. Among smaller cities, East Orange, N.J. (25.9 percent); Missouri City, Texas (22.2); and Boynton Beach, Fla. (20.5), had some of the higher percentages of residents who were foreign born. (U.S. Census Bureau 2006)

Despite this continuing concentration in immigrant destination states, recent Census Bureau data indicate that a growing number of immigrants are moving to other parts of the country, and some previously low-immigration states have experienced substantial increases in the number of immigrants in recent years. An analysis of Census Bureau data from 1992 to

2004 by researchers at the Pew Hispanic Center, for example, found that during that period the share of immigrants going to the traditional settlement states, such as California and New York, dropped from about 37 percent in the early 1990s to about 30 percent in 2000. Meanwhile, immigrant settlement patterns have spread out, shifting toward 22 so-called new growth states in the Southeast (i.e., Delaware, North Carolina, South Carolina, Georgia, Kentucky, Tennessee, Alabama, Mississippi, Arkansas, Oklahoma); Midwest (Indiana, Minnesota, Iowa, Nebraska, Kansas); and Mountain/West (Idaho, Colorado, Arizona, Utah, Nevada, Washington, Oregon) (Passel and Suro 2005, 9). Overall, these new growth states have seen the most dramatic changes in their population makeup over the past 15 years, with relatively large percentage increases of immigrants living in their midst, as have suburban and outlying areas in both the traditional immigrant states and in the new growth states as well. In short, the experience of living near immigrants is no longer confined to a relatively few central cities or to traditional gateway states but has spread throughout much of the country.

For our purposes, even more striking than the sheer number of new immigrants is their *ethnoracial demographic composition*. Whereas immigrants in the earlier peak periods came mostly from Europe,[3] the current peak period of immigration has been numerically dominated by migrants whose origins lie in Latin America and Asia, and has also witnessed a significant growth in immigration among African and Middle Eastern origin peoples. As tables 1.1 through 1.3 demonstrate, the last three decades of immigration have substantially increased the U.S. populations of Latinos and Asian Pacific Americans, which in turn has dramatically increased the size and potential political significance of U.S. peoples of color. As those figures indicate, nearly 80 percent of the foreign-born people arriving after 1965 have come from Latin America and the Caribbean, Asia, Africa, or the Middle East. During this same four-decade period, the White (non-Hispanic) population of the United States dropped from nearly 88 percent of the total in 1960 to under 66 percent in the Census Bureau's 2007 *American Community Survey*. Most demographers believe that the non-Hispanic White population will drop below 50 percent nationally sometime before the midpoint of this century, thus giving the United States no ethnoracial majority population group. And the major driving force behind this politically important shift is immigration from non-European regions. In short, these sharp demographic changes heighten the political importance of the questions addressed in this book.

We will turn later to a closer examination of how immigration has changed the demography and ethnic composition of the U.S. Black, Latino, and Asian American populations, but to understand the potential political significance of these sweeping demographic changes, it is worthwhile to pause and consider several key facts that emerge from the *2007 American Community Survey* Census Bureau data.

- By 2007, Latinos/Hispanics (15.1% of the U.S. population) had substantially surpassed the Black population (12.4%) as the largest ethnoracial minority group in the United States.
- 40% of Latinos, 67% of Asian Americans, and 8% of African Americans were foreign born in 2007, compared to less than 4% of those identified as "White, Non-Hispanic" and 12.6% of the total U.S. population.
- Nearly 29% of Latinos were not U.S. citizens in 2007, as were nearly 30% of Asian Americans, and 4.5% of African Americans. In comparison, only 1.6% of the White, Non-Hispanic population were non-U.S. citizens and 7.3% of the total U.S. population.
- Mexico alone accounted for more than 30% of all foreign-born residents, and the number of Latinos/Hispanics in the United States (over 45 million) is 11 million more than the entire population of Canada. Among Latinos/Hispanics, Mexicans are the largest national-origin group (64.2%), followed by Puerto Ricans (9.1%), Cubans (3.5%) and Dominicans (2.7%) from the Caribbean, and Central (7.8%) and South (5.5%) Americans.
- Between 1990 and 2005, Asian immigration grew at more than five times the national rate, and Asians now make up 4.4% of the U.S. population, up from 2.8% in 1990.[4] There was also a change in the ranking of Asian ethnic groups by size. Although Chinese Americans remain the most populous, 2004 census numbers indicate that Japanese Americans have dropped from the second largest Asian-origin group to sixth place, behind Asian Indians, Filipinos, Koreans, and Vietnamese (U.S. Census Bureau 2007a).
- Recent immigration has changed the racial balance of many U.S. cities. As a result, almost half of America's 100 largest cities are now home to more minorities than Whites. Still, the places of fastest immigrant population growth are the suburbs, portending significant political change there as well.

To sum up this overview, it is apparent that recent immigration has changed, and continues to change, the demographic face of the American population, particularly by changing its ethnoracial composition in significant ways. In order to better understand this phenomenon, we turn now to a discussion of important demographic changes that have occurred in each of the three ethnoracial minority groups at the heart of this study. How has the surge in immigration in recent decades changed the demographic composition of the Black, Latino, and Asian American communities in the United States?

Immigration and the U.S. Black Community

The African American population in the United States is the paradigmatic case of an American "racial minority," so we will begin our discussion with this group. Demographically, Blacks have been affected by immigration in several important ways, not least being its recent displacement by Latinos as the country's largest ethnoracial minority group. Further, both groups are overrepresented among the poor, so that Blacks and Latinos often find themselves living in close proximity in low-income neighborhoods in the cities and/or suburbs of the immigrant gateway states, especially California, New York, New Jersey, and Texas. This has important political implications, especially in relation to political representation and efforts to build ethnoracial minority group coalitions. Another potentially important, and as yet unstudied, phenomenon is the impact of increasing Latino immigrant populations in the South, where a growing number of Blacks have settled in recent decades (see, e.g., Pew Hispanic Center 2005).

Immigrants from Asia also have had important repercussions for Black communities, especially (again) in immigrant gateway states and communities where a significant percentage of small businesses have been purchased by Asian immigrants. This niche economic phenomenon has received a great amount of public attention in relation to interethnic relations, with most of the emphasis in news articles and scholarly works placed on friction between native Blacks and immigrant Asians in some low-income communities. This has had political repercussions affecting both Asian and Black political leaders and organizations (see, e.g., Kim 2000). Again, we will be returning to this aspect of the impact of immigration on the Black political community in later chapters.

But how has the Black community been changed by the addition of new African-origin immigrants? Historically, there was little immigration of African-origin people to the United States, due in part to the racially discriminatory pre-1965 immigration policy but also, perhaps, in recognition of the treatment of Blacks under this country's regime of racial hierarchy. Even now, in comparison with both Latinos and Asian Americans, a relatively small percentage of African Americans are foreign born, some 8 percent. It should be noted, however, that this is about twice the percentage of foreign-born in the White population. And the numbers are steadily increasing, diversifying the African American population. According to the U.S. Census, two-thirds of foreign-born Blacks came from Latin American "African diaspora" countries (including the Caribbean), while 30 percent migrated directly from countries in Africa (U.S. Census Bureau 2007b, 15).

One of the most striking demographic facts about the African-origin immigrants in relation to the total U.S. Black population is that immigrants tend to be concentrated in a relatively few states where they make up sizable portions of the Black population, and most of these high-Black-immigration states are not where most U.S.-born Blacks reside. Thus, seven states have Black populations in which the foreign-born portion of the group's population is larger than 14 percent: New York (28.4 percent), Massachusetts (28.4 percent), Minnesota (25.5 percent), Florida (19.3 percent), Connecticut (17.2 percent), Washington (17.2 percent), and New Jersey (14.4 percent) (U.S. Census Bureau 2007b, fig. 9, p. 13). As can be seen in table 1.4, only 2 of these states (New York and Florida) are among the 10 states that, together, contained nearly 60 percent of the U.S. Black population in 2004 (U.S. Census Bureau 2007a, fig. 1, p. 5). It is also noteworthy that Florida was the only high-Black-immigration state that is in the South, at a time when the trend toward Blacks returning to the South from points north and west (in an apparent slow but steady reversal of the Great Migration) is not only continuing but is undergoing moderate acceleration (see, e.g., Frye 2006, 7).

What are the political implications of African-origin immigration for the U.S. Black community? It seems likely that the greatest impacts will be in those places (e.g., states such as New York and Florida; cities such as New York, Boston, Miami, Minneapolis, Seattle, Atlanta) with the highest concentrations of African-origin immigrants. Based on previous research, it seems advisable to watch for political implications such as the following.

• Diversification of the Black population may bring increased economically based divisions between native Blacks and immigrant Blacks. For example, previous studies have found such tension between native-born U.S. Blacks and Caribbean-origin Blacks (who emphasized their ethnic characteristics, such as West Indian–accented English, in an apparent effort to distance themselves for economic advantage; see, e.g., Sowell 1978; Kasinitz 1992; Woldemikael 1989; Waters 1999).

- Some research indicates that Blacks from the Caribbean are much more likely to have significant ties to their home countries than do Black immigrants from sub-Saharan Africa, which may make their participation in American politics less intense as compared with both African Americans and other Black immigrants (Rogers 2006).

- On the other hand, others have found that Caribbean Blacks have had a more consistent and sizable pattern of immigration, indicating that their political organizations may be comparatively more developed than immigrants from Africa, who increasingly desire to make the United States their personal home (Takougang 2004).[5]

- Finally, research has begun to emerge showing that the presence of Black immigrants in high Black-empowerment cities such as New York can provide opportunities for both competition and cooperation among Black groups, with circumstances stimulating either racial or distinctly ethnic political identities. That is, under some circumstances (e.g., the highly publicized brutalization and killing of two Black immigrants in New York City in the early 1990s), racial identity stimulates a strong sense of linked fate with African Americans leading to joint campaigns against police brutality, and to a shared affinity for the Democratic Party (see, e.g., Waters 1990; Tak-

TABLE 1.4. Afro-Origin Immigrants and Black Settlement—State Concentrations of Foreign-Born and Native Blacks

States with Highest Concentrations of Foreign-Born Blacks, 2004		States with Highest Percentage of Total U.S. Black Population, 2004	
New York	(28.4%)	New York	(8.5%)
Massachusetts	(28.4%)	Florida	(7.4%)
Minnesota	(25.5%)	Georgia	(7.1%)
Florida	(19.3%)	Texas	(6.9%)
Connecticut	(17.2%)	California	(6.2%)
Washington	(17.2%)	Illinois	(5.2%)
New Jersey	(14.4%)	North Carolina	(5.0%)
Colorado	(9.8%)	Maryland	(4.4%)
Arizona	(9.1%)	Louisiana	(4.1%)
Nevada	(7.1%)	Virginia	(4.0%)

Source: U.S. Census Bureau 2007b.

ougang 2004; Rogers 2004). Under other circumstances, however, Caribbean Blacks worked to distinguish themselves from African American Blacks in an effort to secure descriptive representation for Caribbeans as such, often in opposition to African American candidates (Rogers 2006).

In any case, despite the relatively small percentage of the foreign born among the U.S. Black population, immigrants *are* diversifying that population, and it is apparent that in some states and cities, Black politics has already been affected by African-origin immigrants. Black politics certainly has been affected by immigration from Latin America and Asia, as will be discussed in more detail in later sections of the book.

The Latino/Hispanic U.S. Population: Immigration and Change

Immigration has had a dramatic impact on the U.S. Latino or Hispanic population in recent decades, as has been widely discussed by the media and by social scientists. We believe it is helpful to describe these impacts in terms of four primary dimensions to the changing demography of the U.S. Latino population.

First, the Latino population has experienced a sharp increase in numbers and every year represents a larger share of the national population, as noted previously. In 1966, according to an analysis by the Pew Hispanic Center (2006a), the Latino population accounted for 4 percent of the total U.S. population, some 8.5 million people. By 2006, there were 44.7 million U.S. Hispanics, making up about 15 percent of the U.S. population as a whole. Indeed, the Pew Hispanic Center's analysis indicates that Latinos accounted for 36 percent of the population growth of the United States between 1966 and 2006 (a growth of 100 million people, from 200 million to 300 million) (Pew Hispanic Center 2006a). As table 1.5 indicates, moreover, there has been consistent and steady growth of the U.S. Latino population throughout the past four and a half decades. As a consequence of that steady growth rate, many demographers expect that Latinos will make up about 25 percent of the U.S. population by 2050 (see, e.g., U.S. Census Bureau 2007e).

A second dimension of Latino population change is that of the *factors driving that growth,* which include both continued immigration and native birthrates. According to the Pew Hispanic Center's analysis of Census data, 66 percent of the Hispanic growth from 1966 to 2006 can be attributed to immigration (Pew Hispanic Center 2006a).[6] Further, census data indicate that U.S. Latinos (both native and foreign-born) have relatively high birthrates in comparison with the birthrates of the White, Black, and Asian American populations. Thus, while there were some 50.3 births per 1,000 women aged 15 to 50 in the White population in 2004, there were 75.3 per 1,000 comparable women among Hispanics, 56.1 per 1,000 Black women, and 58.7 births per 1,000 Asian American women (U.S. Census Bureau 2007a,b,c). As others have claimed, therefore, it appears true that even if all immigration somehow were stopped now, the Latino population would continue to grow rapidly in comparison to other U.S. ethnoracial groups.

It should be noted here also that a significant proportion of Latino population growth in recent decades has come from *unauthorized immigrants*. A widely cited analysis of census data by a researcher at the Pew Hispanic Center (Passel 2006) estimates that the population of unauthorized immigrants living in the United States surged rapidly in the decade from 1995–2005, to nearly 12 million people, making up some 30 percent of the foreign-born population in the United States in 2005. Moreover, about 78 percent of the unauthorized population comes from Latin America, more than half (56 percent) of the unauthorized population from Mexico alone (Passel 2006, i–ii). Passel estimates that some 8.7 million Latinos (6.2 million Mexicans), or about 20 percent of the Latino population in 2005, were living in the United States without authorization.

The third dimension of Latino demographic change is that of its *ethnic, national-origins composition*. Prior to the 1960s, as will be elaborated

TABLE 1.5. Latino Population Growth, 1966–2007

Demographic Measure	1966	1970	1980	1990	2000	2007
Number of U.S. Latinos (in thousands)	8,500	9,073	14,609	22,345	35,306	45,427
Latinos as percentage of U.S. population	4	4.5	6.4	9.9	12.5	15.1
Numerical increase in Latinos since previous date (in thousands)	N.A.	573[a]	5,536	7,736	12,961	10,121[a]
Percentage increase in Latinos since previous date	N.A.	6.76[a]	61.0	53.0	58.0	28.7[a]

Source: U.S. Census Bureau 2007d; Pew Hispanic Center 2006a; Garcia 2003.
Note: N.A. = not applicable.
[a]These numbers are for less than a full decade.

in chapter 3, most U.S. Latinos were Mexican and Puerto Rican in origin, supplemented by a surge of Cuban refugees in the 1960s. The census data reported in table 1.6 indicate that, while the Mexican-origin portion of the U.S. Latino population has increased slightly over the past 40 years, the Puerto Rican and Cuban portions have declined due to sharp relative increases in immigration from the Dominican Republic, and from Central and South America. As a consequence, the data in table 1.6 demonstrate, there has been a significant increase in the national-origins diversity of the U.S. Latino population over the past 40 years. The U.S. Latino population can no longer be described in terms of three national-origin groups (Mexican, Puerto Rican, Cuban) without seriously distorting the realities of this panethnic group through the omission of so many others.

The fourth important dimension of Latino population change is that this ethnoracial population is *no longer confined to its traditional geographic concentrations* in the southwestern states, Florida, New York City, and Chicago. Indeed, both the 2000 census and the *2007 American Community Survey* show that Latinos now have a clear national presence. In 1990, Latinos were the largest minority group in only 16 of the 50 states, and their share of the population exceeded 5 percent in only 15 states. By 2000, Latinos outnumbered all other minorities in 23 states, and their population exceeded 5 percent in almost half the states (Fraga, Garcia, Hero, Jones-Correa, Martinez, and Segura 2003). As these figures indicate, there are areas of significant growth in the Latino population where this ethnoracial group has not lived previously in appreciable numbers. This includes the central and upper Midwest, and especially the South. With

TABLE 1.6.   Latino Ethnic Diversification, 1970–2007 (in percentages)

National-Origin Group	Hispanic Population, 1970	Hispanic Population, 1980	Hispanic Population, 1990	Hispanic Population, 2000	Hispanic Population, 2007
Mexican	50.0	59.8	60.4	58.5	64.2
Puerto Rican	15.8	13.8	12.2	9.6	9.1
Cuban	6.0	5.5	4.7	3.5	3.5
Dominican	N.A.	N.A.	2.3	2.2	2.7
Central American	N.A.	N.A.	5.9	4.8	7.8
South American	N.A.	N.A.	4.6	3.8	5.5
Other Hispanic[a]	28.3	20.9	9.9	17.6	7.2

Source: Garcia 2003, 34, table 3.1 for census data 1970, 1980, 1990, 2000, U.S. Census Bureau 2007d.

Note: N.A. = not available.

[a]"Other Hispanic" is a residual category, reporting percentage those not in other cells.

the exception of Florida, few Hispanics had settled in the South until the 1990s, but this is changing, as noted in a recent report.

> The Hispanic population is growing faster in much of the South than anywhere else in the United States. Across a broad swath of the region stretching westward from North Carolina on the Atlantic seaboard to Arkansas across the Mississippi River and south to Alabama on the Gulf of Mexico, sizeable Hispanic populations have emerged suddenly in communities where Latinos were a sparse presence just a decade or two ago. (Pew Hispanic Center 2005)

Other scholars with a focus on demographic change in U.S. metropolitan areas have noted a similar shift toward "new growth" areas by the Latino population (see, e.g., Frye 2006). As table 1.7 indicates, the U.S. metropolitan areas with the highest Latino growth rates over the past 14 years have been mostly in the Southern states.

TABLE 1.7.   Latino Metropolitan Diversification—Top 10 Metro Areas

Hispanic Growth Rates, 2000–2004			Hispanic Growth Rates, 1990–2000		
Rank	Metropolitan Area	Growth %	Rank	Metropolitan Area	Growth %
1	Cape Coral–Fort Myers, FL	55.4	1	Charlotte-Gastonia-Concord, NC-SC	605.9
2	Charlotte-Gastonia-Concord, NC-SC	49.8	2	Raleigh-Cary, NC	541.7
3	Raleigh-Cary, NC	46.7	3	Nashville-Davidson-Murfreesboro, TN	422.5
4	Nashville-Davidson-Murfreesboro, TN	44.9	4	Atlanta–Sandy Springs–Marietta, GA	355.0
5	Indianapolis, IN	44.3	5	Indianapolis, IN	263.3
6	Atlanta–Sandy Springs–Marietta, GA	41.0	6	Las Vegas–Paradise, NV	259.1
7	Naples-Marco, FL	38.7	7	Portland-Vancouver-Beaverton, OR-WA	178.7
8	Lakeland, FL	38.3	8	Cape Coral–Fort Myers, FL	173.7
9	Sarasota-Bradenton-Venice, FL	38.0	9	Lakeland, FL	172.1
10	Las Vegas–Paradise, NV	35.1	10	Orlando, FL	165.3

Source: U.S. Census Bureau 2006.

Despite these rapid rates of growth in new areas of Latino settlement, however, it must not be forgotten that most Latinos continue to live in the traditional areas of concentration. This is evident in the facts that in 2004 the Los Angeles–Long Beach–Santa Ana metropolitan area, the second most populous in the United States, had a population of 12.7 million in 2005, of whom 5.6 million (43.9 percent) were Hispanic; and the New York–northern New Jersey–Long Island metropolitan area had an overall population of 18.4 million, of whom 3.9 million (21.1 percent) were Hispanic (U.S. Census Bureau 2006). Indeed, over 80 percent of the Hispanic population in 2004 lived in nine states, most of which were states with long-standing Latino populations: California (30.3 percent of the U.S. Hispanic population), Texas (18.9 percent), Florida (8.0 percent), New York (7.4 percent), Illinois (4.3 percent), Arizona (3.9 percent), New Jersey (3.2 percent), Colorado (2.1 percent), and New Mexico (2.0 percent) (U.S. Census Bureau 2007c, 5).

It is equally significant for ethnoracial politics in the United States that those states with long-standing Latino populations have experienced continuing growth in their Latino populations, so that Hispanics make up an increasing share of these states' residents. Among the most significant of these are the following: New Mexico (43.4 percent Hispanic population in 2004), California (34.9 percent), Texas (34.9 percent), Arizona (28.1 percent), Nevada (22.9 percent), Florida (19.1 percent), New York (16.1 percent), New Jersey (15.0 percent), Illinois (14.0 percent), Connecticut (10.6 percent), and Rhode Island (10.5 percent) (U.S. Census 2007c, 6). Thus, while it is striking that the U.S. Hispanic population is now national in scope, it is in these states with large percentages of Latinos that we might most expect to see this ethnoracial group gaining the most prominent levels of political presence and power.

In sum, the Latino/Hispanic population of the United States is increasing rapidly in size and becoming ever more complex in national origin, it is dispersing throughout the nation at a fast pace, and—while its growth is driven by high levels of immigration—its continued rapid growth would be assured even if all immigration were to stop tomorrow.

The Latino population's rapid growth, geographic dispersal, and increasing ethnic complexity raise a host of perplexing questions for political scientists seeking to track the impact of recent immigration on this group's politics and on ethnoracial politics in the United States more generally. We will focus on the most significant of those questions in the chapters to follow; here we note a few of the most striking political implications of these immigration-driven demographic realities.

- Both the increased national-origin diversity and the increased geographic dispersal of Latinos mean that generalizations regarding this panethnic group become ever more hazardous. There is every reason to expect that the political experiences of Latinos will vary widely across geographic and institutional contexts. For example, Latinos living in areas with comparatively small Latino populations are likely to have significantly different social and political experiences than those living in high-density Latino areas. Similarly, we would expect the experiences of Latinos living in areas where one national-origin Latino group remains overwhelmingly dominant numerically would be quite different than where there is a much greater mixture of Latino national-origin groups.

- The ethno-*racial* self-identity of Latino/Hispanic-national-origin peoples appears to be undergoing change as well. According to one recent study, for example, "only about half of Hispanics in Census 2000 identified themselves in standard racial categories such as White, Black, or Asian on their census form. Nearly as many people instead wrote in their own term, most often 'Latino,' 'Hispanic,' or a similar word. Many of these people might be perceived by non-Hispanics as 'White'—but apparently they do not see themselves in that way" (Logan 2003b). The report calls those in this category "Hispanic Hispanics." While the "white Hispanic" category was still the largest reported by the 2000 Census, in 1980 it included nearly two-thirds of Hispanics, declining to 54% in 1990, and in 2000 to just below half, at 49.9%. The share of the group referred to as Hispanic Hispanics ("some other race") rose from about a third in 1980, to 44% in 1990 and 47% in 2000 (Logan 2003b). Given the overall rise in Latino population, the actual numbers are quite notable—from just under 5 million in 1980 to over 16.7 million in 2000. A small but steady share of Hispanics identified racially as Black in all three census years, just below 3%.

  A 2002 survey of the U.S. Latino population by the Pew Hispanic Center and the Kaiser Family Foundation yielded even more striking results: when asked how they thought of themselves in specifically *racial* terms, 56% of the respondents indicated that they thought of Latinos/Hispanics as a "racial" category of its own in U.S. society, to which they belong, while only 20% said they thought of themselves as racially "White" (Pew Hispanic Center/ Kaiser Family Foundation 2002, 31). The causes and political implications of these changes in self-identity remain to be seen, and represent a continuing and major challenge to political science inquiry.

- The rapid growth of the Latino/Hispanic population across the country raises important questions regarding the implications for existing or prospective political coalitions or conflicts between this group and other ethnoracial groups. For example, how is the rapid increase in Latinos/Hispanics in certain parts of the South interacting with preexisting Black-White political relationships? How is the rapid increase in Latinos/Hispanics in urban areas—reaching majority status in some cases, plurality status in others—affecting the political status of African Americans, as well as other groups? These are only a few of the important political issues raised by the changing demographics of U.S. Latinos/Hispanics. We will return to these questions in later chapters, but for now it is sufficient to note that the immigration-driven changes in the U.S. Latino/Hispanic population raise a host of important questions for political scientists to address.

The Asian Pacific American U.S. Population: Immigration and Change

Like the Latino/Hispanic population, the first important demographic fact about the Asian American ethnoracial group is its *rapid expansion* because of immigration. Indeed, the percentage growth rate of Asian Americans, generated largely by immigration from Asia and the Pacific, has been the highest of any U.S. ethnoracial group for several decades. Table 1.8 documents this rapid rate of growth in several ways, demonstrating that from only 1.4 million Asian Americans in 1970, the APIA population increased to 15.8 million in 2007, an expansion from 0.7 percent of the U.S. population to 5.5 percent.[7] Immigration has been an even more important growth factor among Asian Americans than among Latinos, accounting for 85 percent of the group's growth from 1966 to 2006, according to the Pew Hispanic Center's analysis of the sources of U.S. population growth (2006a). Moreover, with a birthrate higher than that of either the U.S. White or Black populations, native-born Asian Americans will almost certainly emerge as a much more important population component in coming decades. Given the relatively small Asian American population in 1970, the new immigration easily overwhelmed the native-born in recent decades, producing the predominantly foreign-born population of today.

This means that the Asian American population of tomorrow will likely be quite different than that of today.

A second important demographic change in the Asian American community of the United States, and perhaps the single most politically important aspect about Asian Pacific American demography, is the group's *tremendous internal diversity.* In fact, Asian Americans are the most diverse of the Census Bureau racial groups.[8] Hailing from a vast area home to over half the world's population, Asian Americans have in their backgrounds a wide range of cultures, languages, religions, ethnic identities, and histories. The changing composition of Asian immigration has contributed to the diversity. While Latinos in the United States continue to be predominantly of Mexican ancestry, Japanese Americans (the most numerous Asian ethnic group in 1970) are now only the sixth most numerous of Asian ancestry groups (as noted earlier), dropping from 41 percent of the Asian American population to 7 percent in just 35 years. Other long-term and traditionally large national-origin Asian heritage groups (e.g., Chinese, Filipinos) have not seen their share of the Asian American population decline as much, but they have experienced a relative decline because of large-scale immigration from "newer" Asian immigrant groups.

TABLE 1.8.   Growth of Asian American and Pacific Islander (APIA) Population, 1970–2007[a]

Aspect of APIA growth	1970	1980	1990	2000	2007
Number of APIA (in thousands)	1,426	3,446	6,909	12,773	15,781
APIA as percentage of U.S. population	0.7	1.5	2.8	4.4	5.2
Numerical increase in APIA since previous date (in thousands)	N.A.	2,020	3,463	5,864	2,708
Percentage increase in APIA since previous date	N.A.	141.7	100.5	84.9	21.2[b]

Source: U.S. Census Bureau, 1970, 1980, 1990, 2000 Decennial Census; U.S. Census Bureau 2007.

Note: The 2000 and 2007 figures are for all Asian Americans and Native Hawaiians and Other Pacific Islanders (NHPI)—that is, those who identified with one race or chose one or more races, producing slightly different figures than in tables 1.1. and 1.3. N.A. = not applicable.

[a]When discussing only data from Census 2000 and later, we cite figures for the Asian American population and do not include NHPIs. However, census data from prior to 2000 did not separate Asian Americans from NHPIs, and so we use the combined figure for all years in this table, for better comparability. Therefore, the 2000 and 2007 numbers in table 1.8 include figures for both Asian Americans and NHPIs, leading to slightly different totals than reported in table 1.1.

[b]These numbers are for less than a full decade.

Table 1.9 demonstrates the growing ethnic diversity of the Asian American population, showing substantial increases in the population shares of several national-origin groups, especially Asian Indians, Vietnamese, and Koreans. In addition to coming from different areas of Asia, immigrants also come out of very different immigration circumstances, which have helped produce enormous socioeconomic differences within the Asian American population. We believe these demographic facts produce important political repercussions for political actors trying to increase the political presence and power of the Asian American community in the United States.

A third important demographic reality for Asian Americans is that, even though their growth has been dramatically high in percentage terms, they still represent a relatively small share (4.3 percent) of the U.S. population. Accordingly, unlike Latinos, who have surpassed Blacks as the largest ethnoracial minority group in the United States, Asian Americans find it relatively more difficult to have a substantial effect on elections and on other factors influencing the politics of recognition and distribution.

TABLE 1.9. Ethnic Diversification of Asian Americans, 1970–2007 (in percentages)

Asian American National-Origin Group	Asian American Population, 1970	Asian American Population, 1980	Asian American Population, 1990	Asian American Population, 2000	Asian American Population, 2007
Chinese (including Taiwanese)	30.3	23.6	23.9	23.9	23.0
Asian Indian	N.A.	11.2	11.8	16.5	19.4
Filipino	23.6	22.7	20.4	18.2	18.2
Vietnamese	N.A.	7.1	8.9	11.0	11.4
Korean	4.9	10.4	11.6	10.6	10.2
Japanese	41.3	20.8	12.3	7.8	6.1
Cambodian	N.A.	0.5	2.1	1.7	1.7
Laotian	N.A.	1.4	2.2	1.7	1.5
Pakistani	N.A.	0.5	1.2	1.5	1.5
Hmong	N.A.	0.2	1.3	1.7	1.5
Thai	N.A.	1.3	1.3	1.1	1.2

Source: Data for 1970 and 1980 are from U.S. Census Bureau, *The Nation's Asian and Pacific Islanders—1994,* statistical brief (Washington, D.C., November 1995). Data for 1990 are from Asian American Justice Center and Asian Pacific American Legal Center of Southern California, *A Community of Contrasts: Asian Pacific Americans and Pacific Islanders in the United States* (2006). Data for 2000 are from U.S. Census Bureau, *The Asian Population 2000,* statistical brief (2000 census) (Washington, D.C., February 2000). Data for 2007 are from U.S. Census Bureau 2007d.

Note: The 2000 and 2007 figures are for Asian alone population. The 1980–2007 percentage calculation is based on totals that include "other Asians," which include some Asian Americans not tabulated separately. The 1970 total Asian American count includes only the groups listed separately, and so it is not strictly comparable to the other years. N.A. = not available.

This difficulty is exacerbated, of course, by the immense internal diversity of the Asian American community.

A fourth factor that poses a challenge for those working to increase the political presence and power of Asian Americans is their *relative concentration* in a few geographic locations in the United States. According to the Census Bureau's portrait of the Asian American community in 2004, for example, more than three-fourths of Asian Americans live in just 10 states, all but one of them bordering either the Pacific or Atlantic oceans: California (35 percent of the Asian American population in 2004), New York (10.0 percent), Texas (5.8 percent), New Jersey (5.0 percent), Hawaii (4.3 percent), Illinois (4.2 percent), Washington (3.2 percent), Florida (2.9 percent), Virginia (2.7 percent), and Massachusetts (2.3 percent) (U.S. Census Bureau 2007a, 5). Like Latinos, Asian immigrants are spreading out geographically, but in much smaller numbers.

Among the most important potential political implications of these demographic changes in the Asian American population are the following.

- The tremendous internal diversity makes it unclear whether Asian Americans will develop into a coherent panethnic political entity. The best available evidence (e.g., Lien 2004) suggests that Asian immigrants identify primarily with their national-origin ethnic group (e.g., "Chinese American," or "Chinese"), although a majority may identify as Asian American at some times. Evidence for bloc voting by Asian Americans is similarly inconclusive. However, the potential for greater panethnic (i.e., Asian American) unity may be increasing, as the second and third generations grow larger as a proportion of the overall group. The Asian immigration of the late nineteenth and early twentieth centuries also saw deep divisions between nationality groups; for example, Chinese and Japanese immigrants formed their own institutions, with little desire to combine forces. By the third generation, however, older distinctions had lost much meaning, and college-age youth banded together to form a panethnic Asian American movement.

- Asian American political influence will be geographically limited, as noted earlier, because they continue to be concentrated in a few states, such as California. The tremendous importance of California in presidential elections, however, may magnify the influence of Asian Americans, much as Jewish influence has been heightened by the importance of New York. Where Asian American populations are growing elsewhere, they are usually still sufficiently small that their voting impact will be felt primarily in state legislative or local races.

- The enormous internal diversity of Asian Americans makes larger coalition-building (e.g., with African Americans or Latinos) very difficult to predict. Many Asian Americans are relatively prosperous and might not be attracted to campaigns focusing on poverty or economic opportunity, although some college-educated Asian Americans are very liberal and supportive of such efforts. It is possible that there will be friction over limited resources. For instance, Chinese American families have clashed with African American and Latino groups over admission policies to San Francisco's prestigious Lowell High School, with the Chinese American parents opposing practices that sought to reserve spaces for underrepresented groups (Asian Americans are overrepresented there). In addition, some evidence suggests that Blacks and Latinos hold negative views of Asian Americans (Committee of 100 2001). There are substantial numbers of low-income Asian Americans—for example, many Southeast Asians are still moderate or low income—but it is not yet clear whether, and under what circumstances, they will align with other communities of color, or develop more conflictual relationships with them. We will be examining these and other questions in the chapters to follow.

In sum, it should be clear by now that the United States has undergone a rapid demographic change in its ethnoracial composition that almost certainly will have important political implications for the whole country, and especially for the efforts of the country's minority groups to gain greater racial equality. However, there has been little systematic examination of these phenomena by political scientists.

This book aims to begin filling that gap in our understanding of contemporary—and future—U.S. ethnoracial politics. It seeks to demonstrate the importance of recent immigration for understanding U.S. ethnoracial politics specifically, as well as for understanding U.S. politics more generally. Using an analytical framework that melds the insights of several different approaches to political analysis, the book aims to enhance understanding of how the influx of large numbers of non-White newcomers is affecting the long-standing efforts of ethnoracial minority outsider groups to gain full and equal political incorporation as insiders in the United States. Finally, the book will sketch out where all this may be heading. How might immigration's transformation of America's political minority groups into a collective majority of the U.S. population change American politics as a whole? What would it take, politically, for the United States to become a more racially egalitarian society?

These are large and difficult questions to answer, and we do not claim to have found definitive answers to them. However, we believe the evidence we have collected, distilled, and analyzed is clear in several respects. First, it should be clear that recent immigration is indeed transforming U.S. racial politics in ways unprecedented in our national history. Second, it should be clear as well that—because of recent immigration—the efforts of U.S. ethnoracial minority outsider groups to gain full and equal political incorporation have become both *more important* and *more challenging* to our long-standing national project of realizing our core democratic values as a country. After sketching out the evidence for these assertions, we conclude our survey with a discussion of the alternative political futures our country may face as a consequence of recent immigration.

The Plan of the Book

Perhaps more than most, this book stands on the shoulders of a large number of other researchers and political analysts who have laid the groundwork that made it possible for us to write. Accordingly, we have had to be especially mindful of the importance of contextualizing and focusing our work so that it integrates and melds the work of others into a coherent analysis. Part 1 introduces and frames our inquiry. We began, in this chapter, with an overview portrait of the immigrant newcomers who are at the heart of our work, focusing especially on the demographic effects of post-1965 immigration. This overview demonstrates the important changes in the magnitude and countries-of-origin of recent immigration in comparison with past periods of U.S. immigration. Next, in chapter 2 we turn to an exposition of the organizing questions of our book, its intellectual and analytical framework. This is presented in terms of four possible answers to the question of how the contemporary era of immigration might transform the racial politics of the United States. Drawing on the work of several schools of social and political analysis—assimilation theory, pluralism, biracial and multiracial hierarchy—we develop a framework of inquiry that will guide the remainder of the description and analysis of our subject.

Part 2 of the book will provide important contextual information that we believe is crucial for understanding the specifically political issues on which we will focus in the following section. Thus, in chapter 3 we provide the important historical context for our analysis by summarizing the experiences that both created and shaped the ethnoracial outsider groups that constitute the other core focus of our inquiry. How did these ethnoracial minority groups become part of the American people? Historically, what challenges have they faced, and how have they responded to these challenges, in seeking full and equal membership as insiders in the American polity?

Chapter 4 will examine the contemporary social and economic context of continuing efforts by Black, Latino, and Asian American political leaders and activists in relation to ethnoracial equality. Since we cannot examine all the social and economic contextual factors that are important for understanding contemporary ethnoracial politics, we focus primarily on continuing patterns of segregation—both in residential areas and in public schools—as well as economic measures of inequality. Again, we believe that contemporary efforts by outsiders to gain equality in the American polity cannot be understood apart from these important parts of the context in which these efforts take place.

Part 3 of the book is the political heart of our descriptive and analytical efforts. Here we will examine the impact of recent immigration on four core political aspects of the struggle for greater ethnoracial equality in the United States: participation, representation, political influence and power, and egalitarian public policies. That is, we believe that most (not all) of the minority political activists who have worked for greater racial equality in the United States have measured their own accomplishments—and have been judged similarly by others—in terms of these four aspects of American politics. Chapter 5 begins that description and analysis by focusing on the impacts of recent immigration on ethnoracial minority efforts to gain access to political participation and representation in the political system. Chapter 6 continues that inquiry by examining the effects of recent immigration on the efforts of our outsider groups to gain greater political influence and power in American politics by gaining membership in key governing coalitions in the U.S. governments, and to use those memberships to facilitate the adoption of egalitarian public policies designed to secure and enhance the status of these groups as equal insiders in American society.

Finally, part 4 of our book presents the conclusions toward which our findings point. In chapter 7, then, we will attempt to put the descriptive and analytical work of the previous chapters into an overall perspective that enables us to say something meaningful about the ways in which immigration in the contemporary era has affected the efforts of Blacks, Latinos, and Asian Americans to become equal insiders in American politics and society. To anticipate, we will suggest that while it is possible to convince oneself that immigrants will rather smoothly meld into an already progressing development of American racial democracy, there are strong reasons for believing that many of the new immigrants are being trapped in continuing and evolving patterns of racial hierarchy that remain obstacles to genuine racial democracy in the United States.

2 | Analytical Framework for Studying Political Incorporation

Chapter 1 described the extent to which immigration has transformed the demographic composition of ethnoracial minority communities in the United States. In this chapter, we come to the central question with which this book is concerned: how is this demographic transformation affecting the politics of ethnoracial minority groups in the United States? What patterns might we expect to see in the future political development of the three primary panethnic communities, given the large-scale influx of immigrants in the past four decades? Here we sketch out four alternative futures for U.S. ethnoracial politics that have been suggested most often by other scholars, and we describe the organization of the book's inquiry in the chapters that follow.

Immigrants and Ethnoracial Politics in the United States: Four Possible Directions

What are the most likely trajectories for the future development of ethnoracial politics in the United States, and how will recent immigrants affect those trajectories? Given the importance of race in American society and public life, it should occasion no surprise that many scholars have weighed in on these questions, generating lively controversy. Drawing on the writings of the most prominent social and political scientists involved in this discourse, here we outline four major possibilities, each of which has been hypothesized as the most likely scenario for the future of ethnoracial identities in U.S. society and public life: individual assimilation, pluralism, biracial hierarchy, and multiracial hierarchy.

The first two scenarios, *individual assimilation* and *pluralism,* both suggest that racial barriers—which we term *racial hierarchy*—have been sufficiently diminished and altered in the United States that they will not prevent Blacks, Latinos, or Asian Americans from being incorporated into the political and governmental structures of American politics as equal members of the political order. Accordingly, these scenarios also predict a rather straightforward integration of most immigrants into the existing political system, individually and/or via ethnic political groups. In the language of social science, these scenarios depict a relatively high level of agency for ethnoracial minority groups, and relatively low levels of structure. Put differently, these scenarios depict relatively fluid social and political structures in the United States, structures relatively accessible to upward and inside mobility on the part of groups and individuals beginning from outside and/or at the bottom in relation to political influence.

In contrast, the other two hypotheses—biracial hierarchy and multiracial hierarchy—depict less flexible, relatively rigid structures and social formations generating relatively impervious constraints on the efforts of outsider groups for greater political influence or a redistribution of political power. Thus, implicitly or explicitly, each scenario gives an account of how social and political power is structured in the U.S. polity, and posits a preferred way to understand the processes by which outsider and newcomer groups typically come to terms with those structures and the meanings of membership in the polity.

In addition to outlining these four alternative futures for ethnoracial politics in the United States during and after a new age of immigration, we will also discuss the relationship of these alternative political futures to another potential development, *transnationalism*. A number of scholars have articulated the possibility that under new conditions of transnational mobility and communications, and a legal order altered to facilitate dual nationality, many of the new immigrants will retain important political, social, and economic ties with their homelands, even beyond the first generation in the United States, and even after they have been incorporated into U.S. politics. Our query here will concern whether this phenomenon should be considered a fifth possible scenario for the future of U.S. ethnoracial politics. In the end, however, we do not see transnationalism as a fifth alternative future, but rather as a potential development that might alter the course of each of our four scenarios in varying ways. Nevertheless, we do try to assess the ways in which transnational political behavior affects the incorporation of newcomers and outsiders into the political life of the United States.

In developing the scenarios, we draw upon and integrate the writings of social scientists focusing primarily on the role of ethnoracial identities in U.S. politics, as well as the writings of those who have focused mainly on immigrant incorporation into U.S. society. Our discussion, moreover, also draws upon models developed by political scientists for understanding the political incorporation of outsiders—both racial minorities and immigrant ethnics—in the United States. By melding these scholarly writings, we articulate the most likely scenarios for understanding how recent immigrants may change the dynamics of ethnoracial politics in the United States.

We want to emphasize at the outset of this discussion that each of the alternative scenarios is based on the premise that race is a social construct, and that distinct human races do not exist in nature. That is, while scholars disagree as to whether racial identities will or will not continue to play a significant role in U.S. politics in the future, virtually all of these scholars agree that racial identities are not a matter of biology but are established, maintained, and/or changed through the social constructs of human beings. Like nations, then, human races are *imagined* in the minds and hearts of persons, and the distinctions between them are subject to discursive and political conflict. This fact, of course, makes races no less (or more) real than nations—they have real effects on the lives of human beings so long as people believe in their significance for their own lives and for the lives of others.

Individual Assimilation

Our first scenario, *individual assimilation,* suggests that racialized identities will become a thing of the past for U.S. ethnoracial groups. In this scenario, the racial or ethnic identity of any given individual will no longer affect their socioeconomic or political well-being in any significant way, so that it will cease to play a role in the identification or realization of that individual's political interests. While individuals may retain a sense of membership in their ethnic or racial group of origin, and they may continue to value aspects of their cultural heritage, they will not have cause to see their ethnic or racial identity as connected in any significant way to their roles as political agents in the body politic.

This appears to describe the dynamics of identity politics for Americans of European ancestry in recent decades. Many European immigrants initially faced hostility from native-born Americans, who often perceived the newcomers to be fundamentally different—so much so that many considered them separate races. Irish, Italians, and Jews are examples of immigrant groups whose "Whiteness" was often questioned in the past.

Over time, however, these and other marginalized European immigrant groups came to be accepted as White, albeit in an inferior shade (e.g., Ignatiev 1995; Brodkin 1998; Jacobson 1998; Guglielmo and Salerno 2003). By the middle of the twentieth century, observers marveled at the way that ethnic barriers had largely disappeared, leaving only religious divisions to demarcate White Americans (e.g., Kennedy 1944; Herberg 1960), and even those remaining barriers fell soon thereafter.

Today, the deracialization of European Americans seems to be complete. Ethnicity is no longer an ascribed identity but a lifestyle choice. Most Americans of European ancestry can pick and choose their sense of ethnicity, and their choices are not always limited to ancestral ones. Most important, they are able to choose whether they want to be ethnic at all (e.g., Alba 1990; Waters 1990). Ethnic identity, to use Herbert Gans's term, has become symbolic (1979).

Stephan and Abigail Thernstrom are among those who argue that current understandings of racial classification can also lose power in just this way. Although they are careful to note reasons for pessimism over the possibility of achieving racial equality, the Thernstroms contend that the importance of race will continue to diminish so long as we resist the race-based policies supported by those on the political left. Like many conservative and neoconservative thinkers, Thernstrom and Thernstrom cite the "striking success" of Asian Americans as evidence of the waning importance of race.

> For the most part, they [Asian Americans] are still recognizably members of a "race" other than white . . . But it is hard to find anyone who cares much what their "race" is, and it has become anachronistic for the Census Bureau to continue (as it does) to put a racial label on people of Asian descent. (1997, 536)

Eric Liu agrees, suggesting that second- and later-generation Asian Americans are highly assimilated into an "omniculture" created by the interaction of many peoples (1999).

Similar arguments have been made for Hispanics. According to Linda Chavez (1991), the social separation of Latinos is the product of recent immigration, public policy, and misguided efforts by Hispanic activists, and not of racialization practices by non-Hispanic White Americans. A particularly optimistic view is that of Gregory Rodriguez, who believes that the surge of Mexican immigration can create a more multicultural and assimilated society. Mexicans, argues Rodriguez, have never had strong proscriptions against out-marriage, "because Mexican identity has always been more fluid and comfortable with hybridity" (2004, 132). Rodriguez sees Mexican assimilation as inevitable, although he defines assimilation in ways similar to Alba and Nee (2003), with borrowing occurring in both directions, and newcomers able to retain substantial amounts of their cultural heritage. According to Rodriguez, Mexicans will not simply assimilate through Anglo-conformity but will change America in fundamental ways.

> Instead of simply adding one more color to the multicultural rainbow, Mexican-Americans are helping to forge a unifying vision. With a history that reveals an ability to accept racial and cultural ambiguity, Mexican-Americans are broadening the definition of America unlike any earlier immigrants. (2004, 126)

Rodriguez focuses on Mexican immigrants, but his argument highlights the essential point for the assimilationist perspective: immigrants hold the potential to fundamentally change the meaning of race. By crossing the color line more easily, this view holds, immigrants can help to wear it down to the point of insignificance. The power of the color line lies in its psychological hold on the American mind, but the state has provided critical support. Jim Crow laws, for example, helped to highlight the color line, even though the physical distance between Black and White was often negligible. In the view of many advocates of deracialized assimilation, attitudes have changed sufficiently that the color line will fade away if it is no longer renewed and maintained by government policies. Immigrants, not socialized to the importance of the U.S. Black-White divide, would naturally ignore it if advocates of policies such as affirmative action and multiculturalism will stop calling attention to it.

But what about Blacks? Many of the arguments for deracialized assimilation focus on Asian and Hispanic immigrants, with guarded optimism about the prospects for native-born African Americans. For instance, although they acknowledge the tremendous prejudice that has existed toward African Americans, Thernstrom and Thernstrom point to the discrimination faced by southern and eastern Europeans in the late nineteenth century, suggesting that the experiences of the latter demonstrate that even very powerful prejudices can dissipate over time (1997, 535).

To many observers, immigrants seem already to be disrupting the definition of racial politics as Black versus White. A century ago, in the previous era of mass immigration, many Americans had perceived a multiracial world, but over time, race in America increasingly came to mean Black or White (Guterl 2001). Today, however, with the Latino population surpassing African Americans, and Asian Americans becoming a much larger segment of the population, the inadequacy of the biracial model is increasingly apparent.

Although one could hypothesize a society that simply marginalized and subordinated everyone considered as non-White, advocates of assimilation argue that this is not happening, and could not happen without substantial assistance from government policies. For example, Alba and Nee's extensive review of available data suggests that immigrants are assimilating, although they neither expect nor wish for full assimilation to occur. They argue that the evidence strongly suggests that immigrants no longer encounter powerful barriers to entry into the societal mainstream. Furthermore, they suggest, even the most powerfully marginalized group—African Americans—may benefit from the immigration of individuals of African ancestry, since those immigrants appear to be more likely to cross the color line in their social life, helping to bridge the Black-White divide.

> The more black Americans appear in the mainstream—work in middle-class jobs alongside whites and participate in core institutional structures—and take part in social life in integrated neighborhoods and intermarry with whites, the more whites' assumptions about the social meanings attached to skin color will be eroded. (2003, 291)

In short, the deracialized assimilation hypothesis predicts that the racial identities of Asian Americans, Latinos, and Blacks are on their way to the dustbin of history, that insofar as these group identities remain part of U.S. society they will be voluntary ethnic or panethnic identities, and that the highly diverse origins of recent immigrants will help push the country toward going beyond the racialization that has characterized so much of the country's history.

Assimilation and Political Incorporation

What are the political implications of this hypothesized scenario for the future of U.S. racial politics, and the impacts of recent immigrants thereon? The assimilation scenario anticipates that an increasing number of Americans from communities of color, as well as most immigrant individuals, will find steadily decreasing resonance between their personal interests and their ethnoracial and/or panethnic identity.

This model assumes that individual political interests and activities are influenced by a wide array of personal and social factors—ranging from age, sex, organizational memberships, income, educational background, to parents' political beliefs—*one* of which might be the individual's ethnic and/or panethnic identity, but in which ethnoracial identity does not play a leading structural role. Because race diminishes as a defining social cleavage, the many other potential bases of social identity will crosscut, further eroding the centrality of race.

The individual assimilation model reflects a research tradition in political science that posits a gradual (and virtually inevitable) assimilation of individual outsiders into mainstream American society.[1] Individual immigrants are seen as coming to this country with relatively thick or thin ethnic boundaries marking their differences from various norms of American life—language, religious traditions, modes of dress, social customs, and so forth—but over time, and especially over generations, nearly all immigrants and their offspring tend to assimilate as individuals into the mainstream society and culture. Accordingly, their ethnoracial identities become increasingly less important to their political behavior, and certainly a matter of personal choice rather than an ascriptive identity assigned by others.

The individual assimilation model was originally fashioned to understand (and channel) the incorporation of European-origin ethnic groups into American society and politics, and not that of racial minority groups (and especially Blacks). Still, many political activists and scholarly advocates have urged that this model is appropriate for understanding the potential incorporation of individuals historically defined as non-White (see again, e.g., Alba and Nee 2003), and normative articulations of the model have been abundant in recent decades. Most of these normative articulations call for a color-blind understanding of the U.S. polity in which most individuals do not see their political interests as being structured by ethnoracial identities (see, e.g., Chavez 1991; Liu 1999; Rodriguez 1982; Sowell 1981; Steele 1990; Thernstrom and Thernstrom 1997).

Using this model to understand the dynamics of U.S. ethnoracial politics, then, would lead us to expect that recent immigrants (with all varieties of racial characteristics) will be working to embrace American society and culture, even though this might initially involve difficult sacrifices and challenges for those coming from significantly different societies and cultures. Despite the personal sacrifices and challenges, they would also encourage their children to assimilate to the mainstream culture and society because this is the key to successful upward mobility in the American polity. The children, moreover, will be eager to do so in order to fit in to American ways. Accordingly, the model predicts that these individuals will understand their political interests, and approach their political involvements, in ways that do not emphasize their ethnic or racial identities as *political* identities. Over time, therefore, we would expect to see both recent immigrants, and individuals from ethnoracial minority group backgrounds, increasingly acting politically in ways that would be virtually indistinguishable from the political behavior of White or Euro-Americans. In calculating the effects of racial and ethnic group membership on their political behavior, political researchers would be able to find no statistically significant variation along ethnoracial lines.

As noted previously, the individual assimilation model posits a high degree of agency on the part of individuals and a relatively low level of racial or socioeconomic structure that might interfere with or obstruct the efforts of individuals to participate in politics and/or to increase their individual political power. That is, the model assumes that ethnoracial difference is not a significant long-term obstacle to individual assimilation, upward social mobility, and increased political influence. Accordingly, viewing our subject matter through its lens will direct us toward questions that center on the political opinions, attitudes, and behaviors of individual members of the U.S. polity.

Drawing on public opinion and voter behavior studies, this scenario asks about the degree to which recent immigrants and their progeny are, in fact, coming to adopt an individualistic perceptual framework and personal political identity. Thus, researchers in this tradition will try to discern the degree to which, politically, recent immigrants (and their children and grandchildren) do not think of themselves in relation to their national-origin ethnicity and/or ethnoracial identity. A further question is, are there significant differences on these questions between the incorporation experiences of individuals from various ethnoracial and recent immigrant groups? Are individuals from some groups (e.g., "model minorities") assimilating as individuals more readily than those from other recent immigrant groups? To what extent has the influx of recent immigrants facilitated and/or hindered the assimilation of native-born Blacks, Latinos, and/or Asian Americans? These are the kinds of questions toward which this alternative scenario, and its research tradition in political science, directs inquiry, and we will search for any available results along these lines.

Pluralism

Our second scenario for the future of U.S. ethnoracial politics, *pluralism*, is similar to that of individual assimilation in that it assumes few structural barriers to political incorporation on an equal footing for those groups—even previously racialized groups—that organize to participate in the political process. In this sense, ethnoracial groups are recognized as one of many forms of association into which people organize to promote their well-being and their interests.

There is a long tradition in social science of viewing human beings as naturally inclined to organize into groups in order to promote their individual welfare. Perhaps the classic depiction of the United States in these terms was that of James Madison, who in Federalist No. 10 articulated the view that human beings "by nature" divide themselves into varying groups that differ from each other politically in a multitude of ways.

> The latent causes of faction are thus sown in the nature of man; and we see them everywhere brought into different degrees of activity, according to the different circumstances of civil society. A zeal for different opinions concerning religion, concerning government, and many other points, as well of speculation as of practice; an attachment to different leaders ambitiously contending for pre-eminence and power; or to persons of other descriptions whose fortunes have been interesting to the human passions, have, in turn, divided mankind into parties, inflamed them with mutual animosity, and rendered them much more disposed to vex and oppress each other than to co-operate for their common good. So strong is this propensity of mankind to fall into mutual animosities, that where no substantial occasion presents itself, the most frivolous and fanciful distinctions have been sufficient to kindle their unfriendly passions and excite their most violent conflicts. But the most common and durable source of factions has been the various and unequal distribution of property. Those who hold and those who are without property have ever formed distinct interests in society. Those who are creditors, and those who are debtors, fall under a like discrimination. A landed interest, a manufacturing interest, a mercantile interest, a moneyed interest, with many lesser interests, grow up of necessity in civilized nations, and divide them into different classes, actuated by different sentiments and views. The regulation of these various and interfering interests forms the

principal task of modern legislation, and involves the spirit of party and faction in the necessary and ordinary operations of the government. (Madison 1787)

Madison believed that in a society embracing freedom, these differing factions cannot be suppressed or eliminated, though no one of them should be allowed to dominate the rest either. Though Madison did not cite ethnicity or race as among the primary fault lines for social and political division, certainly these are among the most important ways in which Americans have grouped themselves to discern and promote their political interests. Even though racial and ethnic identities are ascriptive in the sense that they are assigned to us by virtue of our ancestry, organizations created to maintain, reproduce, and promote the well-being of such collective identities have long been a feature of American social and political life. Thus, there are countless stories and studies of immigrant, ethnoracial, and ethnosectarian communities that have organized a diverse array of groups to bring their members together for purposes of remembrance, reproduction, and political representation (see, e.g., Archdeacon 1983; Banfield and Wilson 1963; Harding 1983; Higham 1984; Howe 1976; Kloss 1977; Lissak 1989; Sterne 2001).

Some commentators have suggested that even racial divisions in U.S. society will become increasingly like ethnic identities in that they will become increasingly voluntary bases for political association because such identities will find fewer and fewer structural obstacles to incorporation. Jennifer Hochschild and Reuel Rogers, for example, have described one possible future (which they term "deracialization") for U.S. racial politics in an era of large-scale immigration as one in which "conventional racial and ethnic identities are dissolving, at least around the edges, as groups come into close and complicated contact with each other. . . . Groups will not dissolve into an anodyne melting pot, but individuals will have considerable leeway in deciding how and how much group identity matters to their lives" (2000, 45). In their view of this scenario for the future, then, ethnoracial groups—enlarged and transformed by immigration—will operate politically along the lines of interest groups similar to the plethora of other organizations created to advance the interests of their members. Thus, they will seek political incorporation through the cooperative and competitive processes of coalition building in order to share in making authoritative decisions on behalf of the body politic, and to ensure that these decisions are to the greatest possible advantage to themselves. This scenario depicted by Hochschild and Rogers operates within a rich literature in U.S. political science that describes and analyzes the political incorporation of outsider groups in precisely this way, and it has traditionally been described as *pluralism* or "interest-group pluralism." Indeed, pluralism has been one of, and probably *the* dominant understanding of U.S. politics for several generations.

Pluralism and Political Incorporation

In relation to the political incorporation of outsider groups, the pluralist model was initially most powerfully articulated by Robert Dahl in *Who Governs?* (1961), a pathbreaking study of the organization and exercise of political power in New Haven, Connecticut. Pluralism employs political groups, rather than individual persons, as the primary units of political agency and of political analysis. The underlying assumption is that individuals have the capacity and the motivation to define their own political interests and that, in doing so, they typically act in concert with other individuals sharing similar interests to form political groups to seek representation in government and to secure governmental decisions that further those interests. In this conception, ethnic and panethnic political groups are formed by individuals who believe their personal interests are well-served through political action and representation on behalf of their ethnic and panethnic identities. Within this context, Dahl described previously marginal European-origin ethnic immigrant groups as having been able to make their way into positions of effective influence in political institutions by organizing cohesively, acting strategically, and eventually becoming effective members of governing coalitions in those policy arenas most relevant to their interests.

They could do so because, contrary to the findings of scholars of the power elite school, Dahl (and other pluralists)[2] found a political system with multiple access and decision points that was relatively open to groups seeking influence, including ethnic immigrant groups. The political dynamic within this system, in turn, could be characterized as one of competition, bargaining, and cooperation between self-generating political groups in which no single group or interest could dominate the whole. In this sense, the pluralist ethnoracial model is relatively fluid, relatively open to new political organizations seeking influence. The model, in short, is high in agency and relatively low in structure. Moreover, to the degree that governmental structure exists in this model, that structure is perceived as more a boon than an obstacle to group efforts at gaining access to political influence because government, especially the *federal* government structure in the United States, provides the relatively accessible arenas in which groups compete, bargain, and cooperate with each other to allocate the benefits and burdens of government.

How has this model been applied to the three ethnoracial groups in focus in this study? Dahl's *Who Governs?* focused only briefly on Black efforts at political incorporation (1961, 293–95; apparently there were no significant numbers of Latinos or Asian Americans in New Haven at the time of his study). However, a subsequent generation of scholars, led by Browning, Marshall, and Tabb's (1984) study of 10 Northern California cities, focused primarily on the political incorporation of Blacks and Latinos and found a similar pattern of fluidity and openness to inclusion in the post–civil rights movement era.

Despite these cities' previous records of racial exclusion, Browning, Marshall, and Tabb found that by the end of the 1960s they were relatively open to Black and Latino empowerment efforts, particularly where these groups organized cohesively and worked to become part of dominant coalitions of elected officials. Titled *Protest Is Not Enough,* this study argued that opportunities exist in electoral politics for previously excluded minority groups to join the ranks of White immigrant ethnics as insiders in a political system providing both symbolic and material benefits to organized political interests.[3]

A subsequent study by Sonenshein (1993) found a similar pattern of openness to political change benefiting Blacks in Los Angeles, as demonstrated by the electoral and policy success of former Mayor Tom Bradley's biracial governing coalition. In short, the key to successful political incorporation and empowerment for both ethnic *and* racial groups, according to this model, is an electoral strategy in which a previously excluded or outsider group organizes politically with strong leadership, seeks multiracial/multiethnic coalition with other groups sharing similar ideologies and interests, with the aim of becoming part of a dominant governing coalition that controls enough public offices to provide meaningful symbolic and material benefits to the group.

A similar argument has been made in relation to Hispanics by Peter Skerry (1993), suggesting that contemporary Latino politics is better understood as analogous to that of earlier immigrant ethnic groups (e.g., Italians, Greeks) trying to transform themselves from newcomers into insiders, rather than in terms of the racialized exclusion or racial hierarchy experienced by Blacks. And in a major survey of political science literature on the political incorporation of Latinos, Rodolfo de la Garza (2004) also concluded that pluralism, rather than racial hierarchy, best characterizes the place of Latinos in U.S. society in that "as a result of long and bitter struggles, Latinos are now part of the mainstream and have attained the clout to influence the system from within as well as from without" (de la Garza 2004, 116).[4]

Some scholars anticipate that the growing diversity and increasing size of ethnoracial communities occurring as a result of immigration will lead to the development of panethnic coalitions that will become pervasive features of American political life. Although the ethnoracial categories widely used in the United States (e.g., Latino/Hispanic, Asian American) are foreign to most immigrants, there are sometimes instrumental reasons to join in coalitions tied together by a common panethnic identity (e.g., Padilla 1985; Itzigsohn 2004). Coalition building is an enduring feature of American politics, and panethnic or racial identities provide a convenient basis for forming alliances. Government or foundation funding may be more likely when groups build substantial panethnic coalitions. Although immigrants may join for purely pragmatic reasons, such efforts help expose them to and familiarize them with groups that may be allies in other causes.

The pluralist model, then, anticipates that many recent immigrants, and especially their offspring, will gradually become aware of the group-based dynamics and stakes of pluralist political power, leading them to organize (or join previously existing) political groups seeking coalition with other groups sharing similar interests and ideologies, and aiming to become part of the governing coalitions that exist in local, state, and national political institutions. Further, the pluralist model anticipates that previously existing ethnoracial minority political groups will react to these developments in accordance with their perceptions of how their own interests are affected by them. Some preexisting political groups, for example, will seek to recruit and incorporate recent immigrants from "their" ethnic and panethnic communities of origin so as to enlarge and enhance the political clout of those groups. Other preexisting ethnoracial groups, however, may perceive a large influx of recent immigrants into their community as a threat to their interests (e.g., hard-won power positions in public institutions) and seek to curtail the influence of recent immigrants accordingly.

The logic of the pluralist integration model, in any case, leads us to anticipate a period of continuing adjustment in which ethnoracial group and immigrant political activists would negotiate and renegotiate their understandings of their shared (and conflicting) political interests, the terms on which they might work together (e.g., the degree to which a panethnic identity may serve their collective interests), the allocation of leadership positions, and the policy agendas most relevant to the groups' political efforts.

Ultimately, however, the expectation of this model is that significant numbers of recent immigrants will be incorporated into the ethnic and panethnic groups playing important political roles at the several levels of government in the United States. In addition, the model anticipates that those immigrants who do not find a political home in one of the preexisting ethnoracial political communities may form new political groups and seek power and influence through an alternative identity formation that better matches their own conception of their interests. In our inquiry in the chapters that follow, therefore, we will pay close attention to the degree to which these developments are taking place among recent immigrants and the political activists seeking to represent previously existing ethnoracial minority communities in the United States.

Biracial Hierarchy

Taking sharp issue with the first two scenarios for America's ethnoracial political future are those scholars who believe that *racial* obstacles to political incorporation continue to have a powerful influence in American public life and politics, that race-based attitudes and behaviors continue to play an important role in structuring the lives and opportunities of Americans in a wide range of private and public arenas in U.S. society. These scholars argue that while "old-fashioned" or Jim Crow racism—consisting of overt assertions of minority group inferiority and opposition to interracial "mixing" and equal rights—may have diminished greatly since the 1960s, nevertheless racial animosity continues to be a powerful force in American politics (Sears 1988; Carmines and Stimson 1989; Hero 1992, 2007; Kinder and Sanders 1996; Mendelberg 2001). A number of scholars have described and analyzed the continuing role of racial divisions and animosities in relation to residential segregation, school busing, public welfare, crime and punishment, affirmative action policy, and immigration policy, among other issue areas (see, e.g., Sears, Hensler, and Speer 1979; Massey and Denton 1993; Bobo and Zubrinsky 1996; Bobo and Johnson 2000; Massey 2001; Neubeck and Cazenave 2001; Santa Ana 2002; Hancock 2004; Brown, Carnoy, Currie, Duster, Oppenheimer, Shultz, and Wellman 2005). In a major study, moreover, Hero

(1998) found that the racial and ethnic composition in the U.S. states has a major impact on the state's politics and public policy.

Insofar as racialization continues to play a significant role in American life and its politics, it is hypothesized by numerous scholars that the large numbers of immigrants coming from non-European origins, particularly those from Latin America, Asia, the Middle East, and Africa, will enlarge and/or reshape—rather than help eliminate—the racial hierarchies that have divided Americans and structured their opportunities throughout the country's history. Here scholars are divided, however, as to the most likely form of racial categorization into which recent immigrants will be integrated. That is, some scholars predict a strengthening of the biracial pattern that has dominated characterizations of race in the U.S. East and South, whereas others predict that the multiracial pattern of racialization more common in the U.S. West and Southwest will become a more national pattern for the U.S. racial order. Thus, we turn now to outline these predictions and their hypothesized political implications.

The first, *biracial*, pattern of continued racialization has been described by Hochschild and Rogers as "black exceptionalism," where through assimilation "Anglos, Asian Americans, and Latinos are slowly becoming a single, intermingled population that will generally not include blacks. The exclusion could be voluntary, or forced onto African Americans, or the result of an interaction between exclusion and separatist preferences" (2000).

To a certain degree, this would replicate a previously experienced pattern in American history in the East and South, one that led to the incorporation and assimilation of previously racialized European Americans. At least some European immigrants, such as the Irish, Italians, and East European Jews, faced intense levels of bigotry and were considered to be inherently inferior to Americans of western or northern European ancestry. Over time, however, they gradually melted into a largely undistinguishable White category by the late 1960s (Jacobson 1998; Waters 1990). This is the pattern described here as individual assimilation or pluralism, but one in which African Americans continued to find themselves on the margins of society, racialized as the prototypical out-group that made the "whiteness" of all the others possible.

In this context, Alba and Nee's (2003) reformulation of assimilation as the most likely pattern for the incorporation of (most) recent immigrants into U.S. society is striking for its sensitivity to the continuation of a biracial pattern for some.

As many descendants of new immigrant groups come to be included in the mainstream, the nature of the distinction between blacks and the majority could simply change without losing its social salience or its import for the distribution of social goods and statuses: instead of a division between blacks and whites, the fundamental social chasm would evolve into a distinction between blacks, a category that could expand to include Afro-Caribbeans and dark-skinned Hispanics, and everyone else. (290)

Thus, some scholars believe that most recent immigrants—including those from Latin America and Asia—are once again enjoying opportunities not always available to African Americans. Perhaps the most striking example of this is found in housing patterns. Several studies have shown that African Americans remain more segregated than Asians or Latinos, even though the latter two groups have seen surges in immigration that we would expect would lead to greater residential segregation, as the newcomers initially settle in immigrant enclaves (see, e.g., Logan, Stults, and Farley 2004). Immigrants of African ancestry are also highly segregated from whites, although they tend to be segregated from U.S.-born African Americans as well, leaving the picture somewhat unclear (Logan and Deane 2003). As Massey and Denton have noted, segregation has varied not so much by ethnoracial category as by skin color: the darker the skin color the greater the level of segregation (1993).

Biracial Hierarchy and Political Incorporation

What are the political implications of a continued and expanded biracial pattern of racial hierarchy in the United States? The key notion is that most recent immigrants from Latin America and Asia would politically incorporate along the lines of pluralist integration and individual assimilation sketched here, while African-origin immigrants (and possibly dark-skinned immigrants from Latin America and the Caribbean) would be aligned with Black Americans, largely excluded from meaningful political power.

Once again, there is a literature in political science that reflects this conception of biracial exclusion of Black Americans from political power. A prominent early political science articulation of this model is Dianne Pinderhughes's (1987) study of ethnic and racial politics in Chicago. Pinderhughes described Chicago's political system as relatively open for White ethnic immigrant groups from Europe, but functioning in a decidedly exclusive way to diminish the political influence of African Americans. Finding a sharp contrast between political *ethnicity* among White ethnics and *racial* hierarchy between Whites and Blacks, Pinderhughes's model depicted White ethnic immigrants as relatively quickly overcoming initial prejudice and political opposition to attain political incorporation, while African Americans continued to operate politically under severe constraints over two hundred years after their arrival in the country. And this occurred in a city far removed from the U.S. South. The racial hierarchy described by Pinderhughes functioned through the combined effects of discrimination across "political, economic, and social spheres in the United States" (1987, 121). While Pinderhughes's analysis acknowledged the electoral success of Harold Washington's mayoralty victories over the remnants of the original Daley machine in Chicago, she argued that African American political power continued to suffer dilution and diminution through the ongoing exclusionary effects of racial hierarchy. In short, Pinderhughes's study makes a case for a "Black exceptionalist" understanding of ethnoracial politics in the United States, asserting that ethnic politics (exclusive to European-origin Whites) operates in a fundamentally different way than does racial politics in relation to the interests of Black Americans.

Studies by other political scientists have generated support for the Black exceptionalist argument in other ways. One influential example is Michael Dawson's *Behind the Mule* (1994), in which he analyzes national public opinion data to explain a striking anomaly among Black voters: unlike virtually every other ethnoracial group in the United States, increased income, wealth, and years of schooling have *not* led Black voters to shift their partisan allegiance from the Democratic to the Republican Party in recent decades. That is, Blacks at all economic and educational levels have consistently and overwhelmingly voted Democratic rather than Republican, so there is no class divide among Blacks voting in national elections as is true of other ethnoracial groups. Dawson explains this anomaly through what he terms the Black Utility Heuristic, in which Blacks' perception that their personal well-being is politically connected to that of the Black community as a whole leads them to perceive their political interests in terms of this "linked fate" rather than in relation to their strictly individual life chances. Dawson's analysis, in short, indicates that most Blacks in the United States do not experience their lives as being susceptible to individual assimilation, and their individual political calculations are made accordingly.

Other scholars have found that even when Blacks have attained a relatively high level of formal political incorporation in public offices, they may still be excluded from genuine empowerment due to the concentration of power over the future of a city's development and its people's opportunities in the hands of a relatively small and exclusive (and mostly White) social and economic elite. A leading example of this scholarly tradition is found in the work of Clarence Stone, articulated most fully in his *Regime Politics* (1989). Stone's analysis, based on his study of Black political incorporation in Atlanta, emphasized that capturing most of the key political offices in a polity does not necessarily make an ethnoracial minority group a fully incorporated partner in the polity's governing coalition. This is because many important decisions governing key aspects of the polity's allocation of resources and future development lie outside the confines of formal governmental institutions, and this is particularly true in a polity that combines a market-based economic system with the relatively limited authority granted to local governing institutions as is typical in the United States. Accordingly, Stone found that most of Atlanta's large Black population did not significantly benefit from the occupation of key political offices in city government by members of the Black middle class. While the political process may be relatively open to participation from outsider groups, then, it does not follow that significant increases in their political efficacy will result. This is so, it is argued, because the political and governmental institutions in a polity are not autonomous but are embedded in a wider network of racially stratified socioeconomic forces.

While the studies by Pinderhughes, Dawson, and Stone did not address the question of the political incorporation of Latinos and Asian Americans, other scholars have argued that both groups appear to be politically incorporating more along the lines of European-origin ethnics than the racialized African Americans, as we noted earlier. Evidence in support of this scenario in relation to the political incorporation of immigrants would indicate that Asian American and light-skinned Hispanic immigrants would be incorporating politically along pluralist or individual assimilationist lines, while African-origin immigrants and perhaps darkskinned Hispanic immigrants would find themselves transformed from immigrant newcomers to racialized Black outsiders in American politics. These latter immigrants and their offspring would increasingly align themselves politically with Blacks and with a Black political and policy agenda aimed at overturning the effects of the biracial hierarchy in the United States.

Multiracial Hierarchy

If racialization continues to exert considerable influence on American politics, the other possible pattern for the country's ethnoracial future is a multiracial hierarchy. As noted earlier, this pattern might emerge if the multiracial conception of race that has been prevalent in the U.S. West and Southwest (see chap. 3, this vol.) becomes a dominant pattern throughout the country. As with the biracial pattern, a multiracial pattern could become national in scope if multiple groups throughout the country experience forms of racialization that separate them from, and subordinate them to, others along racial lines. This could happen, however, in several different ways.

Perhaps the most obvious possibility is that immigrants could be assimilated into what David Hollinger has called the "ethno-racial pentagon" of the United States (1995). As we have noted previously there is today a widespread perception, perhaps derived from the federal government's data-gathering practices, that Americans fall into one (or more) of five ethnoracial groups: White (European), African American, American Indian, Asian American, or Hispanic/Latino. A sign of the extensive diffusion of these categories is the way that many Americans assume them to reflect some natural order, rather than the product of the administrative procedures and other social discourses that produced them (Wright 1994; Espiritu and Omi 2000; Yanow 2003). Thus, insofar as this pattern is perceived as the "natural" ethnoracial makeup of a multiracial United States, it is likely that recent immigrants will be assimilated into one (or more) of the five groups, and that such integration will be reflected in continuing patterns of ethnoracial exclusion and hierarchy. One of the central questions for scholars, then, is the extent to which the integration of immigrant newcomers will either reinforce or disrupt these dominant ethnoracial categories over the long term.

Taking this ethnoracial pentagon as a given, one possible pattern of multiracialism hypothesized by some (see, e.g., Walters 1992) anticipates a bifurcation of Asian and Latin American immigrants, in which a relatively wealthy and highly educated Asian American immigrant population will join European-origin Americans to form the upper and middle classes of the country while most Latino immigrants (undereducated and in low-paying jobs) will be relegated to the lower classes along with many Blacks. Unlike the previously described scenarios for the future, this conception does not anticipate the transformation of either Asian or Latin American origin immigrants into "voluntary" and fully incorporated ethnic or panethnic interest groups, nor does it anticipate their being assimilated into either the White or Black racial groups of the country. Rather, their racial identities are expected to be preserved in ways that will continue to work to their disadvantage whether or not they are highly successful educationally and economically.

While the concept of an ethnoracial pentagon is a generalized perception of continuing multiracialism in the United States, other scholars have articulated a more analytical conception of multiracialism, with specific reference to recent immigrants. One group of scholars, for example, has developed the concept of *segmented assimilation* to characterize the ongoing integration of recent immigrants into U.S. society (Zhou 1997; Portes and Rumbaut 2001). *Segmented assimilation* describes a complex pattern of immigrant integration that varies according to both the characteristics of recent immigrants *and* the social context into which they are integrated. Thus, some recent immigrants with high levels of human capital (e.g., educational certification, relevant employment experience, English language facility) and favorable social contexts for integration (e.g., residence in upper-income neighborhoods) may well experience the straightline assimilation pattern often assumed by supporters of the individual assimilation scenario.

These scholars note, however, that many recent immigrants possess little in the way of marketable human capital and find themselves in social contexts much less supportive of upward social mobility (e.g., impoverished and racially divided central cities or rural areas). For these migrants, the process of intergenerational integration into U.S. society may well lead toward a severely disadvantaged set of life opportunities as well as acculturation into highly racialized social identities. A critical aspect of the social context for immigrant integration, Portes and Rumbaut assert, is the "racial gradient" that "continues to exist in U.S. culture," such that "race is a paramount criterion of social acceptance that can overwhelm the influence of class background, religion, or language" (2001, 47). Accordingly, these scholars suggest that the second generation of recent immigrants includes many from Latin American and Asian origins who are being acculturated into racialized identities that do not bode well for their social standing or social mobility in the United States.

This discussion leads to an important analytical question regarding the relationship between race and class that cannot be avoided in dealing with the subject of multiracialism. We believe that racialization is a socially constructed process in which some people perceived as sharing common origins are identified and treated as "less than" others because of group characteristics perceived as essential or natural to group membership (see chap. 3, this vol.). The markers for such identification in the contemporary period usually include both perceived physical and cultural differences. But the processes through which these racialized identities operate may be highly complex as well as contested, and we believe they are always contingent on the social and political contexts within which they occur (Omi and Winant 1994).

With respect to the relationship between racial identities and economic class, then, is racialization always accompanied by economic or class domination and subordination? Or can economically successful groups be said to have been racialized as well? Some scholars have stressed the degree to which the experience of racialization is deeply intertwined with lower-class economic standing and various social formations through which social mobility is constrained and/or blocked. Others argue that racial and class domination are separate phenomena, although both may affect some groups in certain circumstances.

In the contemporary period in the United States, this question arises particularly in reference to the Asian American group. While there is enormous variation in the economic standing and educational attainment of those identified as Asian American, as we will see in chapter 3, the perception among most non-Asian origin Americans is that this is a model minority that should be emulated by other so-called racial minority groups, and some observers have offered the evident success of Asian Americans as proof that racialization (of *any* group, but certainly of this one) no longer exists in the United States.

One prominent multiracialist response to this position is that by Claire Jean Kim (2000), in which she articulates a "triangulation" conception of racialization as existing in the United States. That is, rather than conceiving of racialization on only one dimension—that of inferior and superior—Kim argues for a second dimension in contemporary understandings of racial difference in the United States: foreigner versus insider (2000, 10). In the racial order of the United States, Kim argues, racial groups are continually compared with each other in relation to both of these dimensions or axes, recreating and perpetuating a structure of White supremacy. Thus, while Asian Americans might be perceived as superior to Blacks and at least equal to Whites in economic and educational performance, they are also perceived as inherently foreign in relation to both Blacks and Whites, thus perpetuating the White supremacist racial order. Native-born Asian Americans who speak only English, for example, often are asked where they are from, the implication being that they must have been born somewhere other than the United States. This triangulated racial ordering manages to pit groups against each other, while maintaining White dominance in the overall society. The perceived unassimilable foreignness attributed to Asian Americans, in turn, is accompanied by racialized exclusion and manipulation through the deployment of "racial power" (Kim 2000, chap. 1).

Other scholars of the Asian American experience have reached similar conclusions (see, e.g., Okihiro 1994; Dhingra 2003). Continuing waves of Asian immigrants, then, may work to reinforce the image of Asian American as "forever foreigners" (Tuan 1998). In sum, these conceptions of the U.S. racial order perceive the country as having a complex but hierarchical racial order in which the European-origin White population stands above multiple peoples of color who are forever contesting and measuring their standings in relation to each other as well as in relation to the dominant group. Moreover, at least some scholars adhering to this position believe that racialization occurs apart from economic class domination, though it always works to discriminate against and disadvantage those racialized as "less than" the dominant group.

Political Implications of Multiracialism

As in the case of the three previous scenarios regarding the ethnoracial future of the United States, here too there is a literature in political science that has described and analyzed the politics of a multiracial conception of the U.S. racial order.

In a seminal work, for example, Barrera (1979) claimed that the Chicano experience in the U.S. Southwest (along with the experiences of indigenous peoples, African Americans, and several Asian American groups) in the late nineteenth and early twentieth centuries is best understood as one in which both racial hierarchy and class stratification operated together in a structured way to block Chicano efforts for social, economic, political, and cultural advancement. Hero (1992), in turn, argued that the historical experiences documented by Barrera (and others) continue to structure the political experiences of Chicanos and other U.S. Latino groups so that the operation of the U.S. political system is best understood as one of "two-tiered pluralism." Hero's analysis suggested that Latinos (along with African Americans) operate politically in the face of racial structural barriers to political empowerment, while White Americans have easier access through processes of pluralism and/or individual assimilation. More recently, Hero (1998, 2007) has provided systematic evidence showing that ethnoracial diversity operates as a significant structural obstacle to various forms of political equality in state- and substate-level governments in the United States in ways that affect not only African Americans but Latinos and Asian/Pacific Americans as well.

Kim's (2000) triangulated analysis of racial ordering in the United States focused specifically on Korean and Black *political* conflict in New York City during the late 1980s and early 1990s.

> Racial power is the key to understanding why Black-Korean conflict occurs, why it looks the way it does, and why it gets resolved in the way that it does. More specifically, racial power (1) helps to generate Black-Korean conflict by reproducing a racial order that juxtaposes the two groups and renders conflict between them highly probable; (2) shapes the form of Black collective action against Korean merchants by defining both the ideational and physical parameters within which such action unfolds; and (3) manages Black resistance by delegitimating and even criminalizing it with reference to the dominant racial discourse. (10–11)

In short, Kim asserts that racial politics in the United States cannot be properly understood or explained through a biracial conception of race, nor can we expect that the large-scale incorporation of new immigrants from Asia (and, by extension, from Latin America) will result in a deracialized future for the United States. Rather, the country's politics is thoroughly intertwined with an ongoing and evolving racial ordering that employs racialized conceptions of multiple groups in the polity to their detriment, and this process shows no signs of being abandoned in the near future.

As with the other hypothesized directions for U.S. ethnoracial politics sketched previously, examining the impact of recent immigration on these politics through the lens of the multiracial hierarchy scenario raises a host of important questions for political science research. In the chapters that follow, accordingly, we will be inquiring whether the large influx of recent immigrants is changing the nature, political significance, and/or scope of racial ordering in the U.S. polity. For example, are significant numbers of recent immigrants being "segmentally" assimilated (as per Portes and Rumbaut 2001) into multiple non-White groups blocked from equal political incorporation by barriers of racial hierarchy? Is a racially ordered hierarchy of groups being reinforced politically as a consequence of recent immigration? If so, is such a pattern emerging throughout the country, or is it largely confined to the Western and Southwestern regions of the country, where this sort of pattern has been predominant in the past? Are there significant differences between national-origin immigrant and re-gional-origin groups in relation to these questions?

Moreover, to what degree does *class difference* within and among im-migrant groups have an impact on the answers to these questions? To the degree that recent immigrants *have* been integrated into long-standing multiple ethnoracial subaltern groups, what have been the impacts of these developments on the efforts of these groups to overcome or alter the structure of racial hierarchy in the American polity? To what extent, and in what ways, has the influx of recent immigrants made efforts to disman-tle or redefine the U.S. racial hierarchy more or less difficult, more or less complex, more or less successful?

Transnationalism and Ethnoracial Identity: A Newly Emerging Pattern?

Most studies of ethnoracial politics in the United States can be fit into our four possible scenarios for the U.S. future. However, we believe that it is necessary to sketch out another possible scenario, that of *transnational-ism*. This potential development has been discussed increasingly by schol-ars of immigrant political incorporation (see, e.g., Guarnizo 2001; Jones-Correa 1998, 2007; Vélez-Ibáñez and Sampaio 2002). As a result, we think it is important for us to discuss the relationship of this phenomenon to our four scenarios for the future development of U.S. ethnoracial politics.

The attention being given to this potential mode of political incorpo-ration of immigrants derives in part from the sheer numerical expansion of the foreign-born population in the United States, as described in chap-ter 1, plus technological changes enabling individuals to live deeply em-bedded social, economic, and political lives simultaneously in multiple political communities. New technologies, for example, make it possible for individuals to commute frequently back and forth between far-distant locations; to remain in virtual constant touch with family, friends, and working colleagues located throughout the world (via cell phone, e-mail, and internet communication); to maintain in-depth knowledge of the economic, political, and social affairs of organizations and communities that may be widely dispersed geographically (via, e.g., satellite television, internet access to news sources, and the speed and ease of transmitting documents through cyberspace); and thereby simultaneously to conduct business, to maintain interpersonal relationships, and to actively participate in the political life of multiple communities.

At the same time that these technological developments have gained wider notice, an ever-growing number of countries in the world (particularly immigrant-sending states) have enacted laws recognizing and authorizing dual nationality or dual citizenship. This has enabled a steadily increasing number of emigrant individuals (and, in many cases, their offspring) to retain both legal membership and active citizenship in their country of origin, even after acquiring citizenship in their new country.

To the degree that this phenomenon is growing in size and significance in the contemporary United States, does this constitute a fifth possible scenario for the future of U.S. ethnoracial politics? What are its political implications for the future? We see several possible ways in which the transnational loyalties and political behavior of immigrants might have significant impacts on the future development of ethnoracial politics in U.S. political life. Nevertheless, since our book's focus is on the impact of new immigrants on U.S. ethnoracial politics, we do not believe that transnationalism is best conceived as a fifth alternative possible scenario for such politics. It is largely a question of perspective and focus, and we believe that analyzing transnational political behavior as a fifth distinct form of U.S. ethnoracial politics would distort the focus of our inquiry in ways that are better explored in a different scholarly work. Still, it is worthwhile exploring some of the implications of transnational political behavior for U.S. ethnoracial politics, and here we sketch out some of the things we will look for in our inquiry in later chapters in the book.

There are multiple ways in which international migrants might act transnationally in their politics. Some worry that transnationalism among international migrants will prevent them from fully assimilating into American political life (e.g., Renshon 2005), while others fear that Latin American immigrants, in particular, will serve as agents of *reconquista*, helping their homelands (especially Mexico) transform the culture and politics of the United States into that of a foreign country (e.g., Huntington 2004). On the other hand, it is fully possible that many dual nationality immigrants might continue their involvements—social, economic, political—in their homelands to the degree possible, while also becoming active in various American political activities as U.S. citizens. In relation to our four scenarios for future U.S. ethnoracial politics, for example, it is possible that some dual-nationality individuals in the United States will assimilate individually into participation in the political system in this country without any significant political connections with their coethnics who are politically involved here as well.

It is also possible, however, that the group-based pluralistic politics of some U.S. ethnoracial groups could be dramatically changed by the political involvements of transnational immigrants. The case of U.S. Jews' political activities in relation to the interests of Israel is often referenced as a prototype that might be emulated by other ethnic communities in which much stronger ties to the homeland might be wrought by immigrants. In some cases, again partly emulating the case of Israel and U.S. Jews, homeland governments might foster such activities through careful cultivation of emigrants who have settled in the United States. Such countries might have an interest in influencing not only U.S. foreign policy but U.S. immigration policy as well (as, say, in the case of countries dependent on the remittances of emigrants living in the United States). At the same time, it seems equally possible to us that most immigrant-sending countries will continue to largely ignore their expatriates, or would be mostly unsuccessful in any effort to organize a concerted action plan to affect the outcomes of U.S. politics. Whatever the case may be, our focus in later chapters will be on the effects of any such transnational political behavior on the nature of U.S. ethnoracial politics.

There are also ways in which transnational immigrants might affect U.S. ethnoracial politics by helping to transform the understanding of the meanings and significance of race in U.S. politics. In relation to our racial hierarchy scenarios, for example, some commentators have suggested that the biracial understanding of racial politics in much of the United States might undergo a transformation to something much more complex due to the very different understandings of race in Latin America and the Caribbean being brought to the United States, and expanded over time, through the influence of transnational migrants (see, e.g., Bonilla-Silva 2004). To the extent that this is true, the understanding and dynamics of racial hierarchy in the United States might well be affected. Again, however, we believe this important potential influence is best understood in this book as an impact on U.S. racial formations, and not as a fifth, transnational form of U.S. ethnoracial politics. In short, then, while we believe there are multiple ways that an increase in transnational political behaviors and activities could have important impacts on politics in the United States, we will not be examining a possible expansion of this phenomenon as a new form of U.S. ethnoracial politics.

In the chapters that follow, our aim will be to articulate and focus information on the ways in which contemporary immigration is transforming ethnoracial politics in the United States. We hope that we will ultimately be able to draw some preliminary conclusions on the degree to which of the scenarios of future ethnoracial politics in the United States seem to be coming about. Whether or not that will be possible, we believe the focus of our inquiry will yield illuminating results for those concerned about the future of ethnoracial politics in this country. In the next part of the book, then, we continue our inquiry by examining the historical and social contexts within which the political intersection of immigrant newcomers and racial minority outsiders is taking place.

Part 2 | Historical and Social Contexts

Before we move to the heart of our inquiry, we believe it is important to set the stage for that inquiry by examining several important aspects of the *contexts* within which these changes in U.S. politics are taking place. First, we believe that all political events take place within a context in which history plays an important role in shaping contemporary political action. Accordingly, it is crucial to understand that contemporary U.S. ethnoracial politics is shaped by its history. Unless one understands the history that led to the present, it is impossible to understand contemporary events. With respect to ethnoracial politics in the United States, it is necessary to understand the dynamics and structures of racialization that have played such central roles in the creation and maintenance of ethnoracial hierarchy in American life. In chapter 3, therefore, we provide a brief outline of our understanding of the workings of racialization in U.S. history, as well as brief sketches of how racialization has affected the historical development of the three ethnoracial communities in focus in this book. Without this contextual framework, it will be impossible to understand the ways in which recent immigration is changing the shape and political dynamics of these three communities.

Our second contextual inquiry is into the social context in which immigrants are becoming members of previously existing U.S. ethnoracial groups. More specifically, we believe that segregation has played a major underpinning role in the development and maintenance of racialization in American life. Accordingly, in chapter 4 we inquire into the degree to which patterns of segregation (in both residential areas and public schooling) have been affected during the high immigration period of the past four decades. We focus on segregation because we believe that both residential neighborhoods and public schools provide important foundations for subsequent opportunities for social mobility in U.S. society, and the degree to which ethnoracial minorities remain excluded from opportunities for upward social mobility through segregation will play a large role in determining the extent to which the members of such groups will prosper as insiders in the American public order. So our central questions in chapter 4 will be the degree to which ethnoracial segregation remains a significant fact in the contemporary period and the ways in which recent immigration has had an impact on that degree of segregation.

3 | The Historical Context of
U.S. Ethnoracial Politics

The new immigrants find themselves in an old ethnoracial order. In this chapter, we describe the development of this ethnoracial order in the United States. This ethnoracial system is a key contextual factor shaping the way that immigrants are incorporated into American politics. After presenting an overview of racialization, we look at the ways in which specific subpopulations have been racialized in the United States. Because we are concerned with the new immigrants, we focus on the history of the groups that are seen as ethnically or racially similar to the majority of recent immigrants: African Americans, Latinos, and Asian Americans. The newcomers have the potential to change—and perhaps even transform—that order, or they could find themselves absorbed into the existing ethnoracial system, one that is foreign to them when they first arrive in the United States.

Race and Racialization in American Public Life

Most immigrants did not—and do not—arrive in the United States with identities that fit easily into the ethnoracial categories most prevalent in this country (Higham 1984; Portes and Rumbaut 1996).[1] Instead immigrants are situated by others, and usually eventually situate themselves, in relation to the ethnoracial categories that have been constructed in the United States.

The social construction of "races" takes place through evolving historical processes in which contemporary perceptions are partly shaped by yesterday's categories of understanding. The way we understand race is shaped by discourses that occur in a wide variety of social institutions (e.g., families, laws, the media, political parties, city councils, administrative agencies, workplaces, and civil society organizations), as well as by the consciousness and actions of individual human beings. The conjunction of these various institutional and personal forces, finally, constructs an ever-changing but more or less stable "racial order" (Kim 2000) that structures the lives and life chances of individuals who are thereby categorized into that racial order's groupings. Because racial identity is so heavily influenced by a society's particular social and political institutions (see, e.g., Appiah and Gutmann 1996; Frederickson 2002; Goldberg 1993; Jacobson 1998; Omi and Winant 1994; Rodriguez 2002), it is not surprising that racial categories vary from nation to nation.[2]

While the specific boundaries of races have varied across time and place, the underlying dynamic of racialization has remained very consistent, at least in Western societies. The enduring core of the racialization process, as Frederickson has recently reiterated (2002, Introduction), includes essentialist understandings of social difference, coupled with the exercise of power to create hierarchical relationships between the groups so differentiated. Thus, the differences between social groups deemed races are understood as "essential"—that is, as so fundamental to the "natures" of group members that successfully assimilating across these racial boundaries seems highly unlikely, if not inconceivable. At times, these differences have been considered to be biological, but in recent decades ethnoracial differences are usually described as cultural.[3]

As Barth (1969) has observed, however, to consider ethnic groups to be defined by a distinctive culture begs the question: with the high level of interaction between members of different ethnic groups, how is any distinctiveness maintained? The key defining factor is not a shared culture—which may be a result rather than a cause of ethnic distinctiveness—but rather the *boundaries* that define the group. This is particularly relevant for any investigation of the ethnoracial identities of immigrants, because they often find that the identities ascribed to them do not match the identities they themselves would choose. How are these ethnoracial boundaries imposed on immigrants?

This highlights the second part of the enduring core of the racialization process, the exercise of power to create hierarchical relationships between groups. That is, no group is deemed fundamentally and essentially different along racial lines absent the use of that designation to demean, exclude, diminish, dominate, obstruct, oppress, inhibit, or otherwise subordinate a relatively less powerful group by a more powerful group. In this sense, we understand racialization to be a structured process that works to the systematic advantage of members of a dominant group and entails the subordination of another group defined as racially different through the creation, maintenance, and/or justification of a hierarchical relationship between the groups (see, e.g., Lipsitz 1998). This understanding is not meant to imply that agency in the process of racialization is exclusively in the hands of the dominant group. Indeed, because they are social constructions, racialized distinctions between human beings are inherently contestable, and because they involve the social construction of systematic inequalities, they are typically contested as well.

Public policy both reflects and reinforces racialization. Denial of civil rights, for instance, emerged in a society where belief in racial inequality was deep and wide. However, discriminatory public policies at minimum help to maintain views that support racialization, and they provide symbolic confirmation for those who endorse racial hierarchy. In addition, public policy can help perpetuate racialization, by making incorporation less likely. Statutory racialization can be seen as early as 1790, when the new Congress passed legislation limiting naturalization to "free white persons" (Jacobson 1998). In the wake of the Civil War, this was modified to allow African Americans to be citizens, but Congress resoundingly rejected efforts to allow Asian immigrants to naturalize (Chan 1991, 47).

Much of the most significant racialization in public policy has occurred at the state level. For example, one of the most fundamental efforts at racialization—laws regulating marriage—were carried out by the states. Seeking to preserve "the integrity of the white race," Louisiana went so far as to require that White patients be allowed to reject blood transfusions from Blacks (Sickels 1972, 65). Over three dozen states at one time had laws prohibiting interracial sex and marriage: all of those states forbade Black-White marriages, while 15 of them outlawed marriages between Whites and Asians or American Indians (Moran 2001, 17; Spickard 1989, 374–75).[4] As Rachel Moran has observed, "For blacks, the laws identified them as diminished persons," while for Asians, the laws "confirmed their status as unassimilable foreigners" (2001, 18).

Advocates of racial inequality also gave attention to the private sphere. One of the most striking measures was a law providing that an American woman who married "a foreigner" would "take the nationality of her husband" (Hing 1993, 206). Although this was repealed by the Cable Act of 1922, the repeal declared that "any woman citizen who marries an alien ineligible to citizenship"—that is, any women who married an Asian immigrant—"shall cease to be a citizen of the United States" (213).

For much of the country's history, racialization was openly used for exclusion and privilege: policing the boundaries of Whiteness enabled those within to enjoy benefits denied to those excluded. Racialization occurs in all spheres of life, but its effectiveness is often threatened. As a result, advocates of racialization often turned to the state to enforce the divisions. For example, even when social prescriptions against interracial marriage were very strong, some were willing to violate societal norms. To guard against such transgressions, advocates of racialization won passage of so-called antimiscegenation laws. Racialization occurs without governmental support, to be sure, but the state has played an important role in defining and limiting the benefits of Whiteness.

To be White was to gain access to a wide range of opportunities, so a critical step for immigrants was gaining acceptance as White (e.g., Ignatiev 1995; Brodkin 1998; Jacobson 1998; Guglielmo and Salerno 2003). Those who were classified as non-White found themselves at enormous disadvantage. It was not so much that "being" non-White conferred disadvantage; rather, those who were seen to be at the bottom of the sociopolitical hierarchy were thereby classified as non-White. A subpopulation lacking power and held in low esteem by the larger society would be racialized—that is, considered to be non-White. If that subpopulation managed to improve its image sufficiently, it would come to be considered White.

During the years of its peak influence, from roughly the mid-nineteenth to mid-twentieth centuries, racist ideology supported racialization by portraying groups as separated by essential differences rooted in biology, in physical differences between racial groups that were also necessarily reflected in cultural practices, in social mores, and in "natural" inequalities between the groups. White privilege gained scientific endorsement, with racial segregation and discrimination defended as a reflection of the natural order (Smith 1997; Graves 2004). "Race was perceived to be a biological category, a natural phenomenon unaffected by social forces. . . . [E]ven for self-proclaimed egalitarians, the inferiority of certain races was no more to be contested than the law of gravity to be regarded as immoral" (Barkan 1992, 3–4). At various times, Native Americans, Latinos, Asian Pacific Americans, Irish Americans, eastern and southern European-origin Americans, Jewish Americans, and Arab Americans were defined as essentially different from White Americans, defined as inherently inferior (biologically and/or culturally), and subject to legal and extralegal forms of discrimination.

By the early twentieth century, however, scientists such as Franz Boas had begun to question the nature of racial categories, and, by the 1940s, anti-Nazi efforts had helped to advance a successful assault on the idea of fundamental differences between so-called races (Barkan 1992). A vigorous political assault on racial discrimination in the 1950s and 1960s helped to undermine legal endorsement of racial superiority. However, after being politically and scientifically discredited, the biological foundation of racial essentialism (still used for purposes of marking boundaries between groups) gave way to greater emphasis on essentialist views of cultural differences between groups, so that different racial groups are perceived as invidiously and enduringly different along cultural lines that are understood as relatively impervious to change or large-scale assimilation between groups (Frederickson 2002; Solomos and Back 1995).

We consider the central meaning of "racial politics" to involve public conflicts over claims of racialization in respect to behaviors, actions, institutions, and/or social structures. Further, we understand the primary *agenda* of "racial politics" in the United States during the past 50 years to be centered on efforts by peoples of color to gain full incorporation into all segments of the U.S. political system, and to gain greater equality in the broader society and economy.

Race and the Census

The constructed nature of race can be clearly seen in the decennial census. Although there is still some debate over whether racial categories can be based on genetic differences, there is little question that the racial categories in practice have been based on social and political factors. Even the strongest advocates of the view that race is rooted in genetic differences do not suggest that such differences can develop in a decade or two—and yet, census racial categories change that quickly.

Whether census categories contribute to racialization or merely reflect it is a matter of disagreement. The primary goal is usually to reflect the categories that others have created, but the depth and breadth of census data ensure that it will also shape the way that we look at a population. William Petersen argues that the earliest censuses helped to highlight racial differences in the population. "The two categories—Negroes and Indians—that the Republic distinguished during the first half-century or so were counted differently mainly because of their anomalous civil status; but this distinction helped set the contrast among races as the fundamental ethnic characteristic in the censuses and eventually also in other works" (Petersen 1987, 201; see also Anderson 1988, 12). What is clear is that racial classification in the census has undergone constant change, almost certainly reflecting changing notions of race and changing patterns of racialization.

As Melissa Nobles has pointed out, the existence of racial categories in the earliest censuses cannot be fully explained by the "three-fifths compromise," which counted slaves as three-fifths of a person for purposes of representation. The only necessary information to calculate representation was whether a person was a slave or not and, if not, whether one was taxed or not. "The race question was included . . . because race was a salient social and political category" (2000, 27).

From 1790 to 1840, there were essentially three census categories: free White persons—sometimes divided into males and females; slaves; and other free persons—sometimes labeled "free colored persons," sometimes labeled "all other free persons except Indians not taxed" (Nobles 2000, 28). By 1850, the category Mulatto appeared, and in 1870 Chinese was added. There were eight categories by 1890—White, Black, Mulatto, Quadroon, Octoroon, Chinese, Japanese, and Indian—but the Mulatto, Quadroon, and Octoroon categories disappeared by the next census (Mulatto reappeared in 1910 and 1920, before disappearing for good). By 1930, the census racial categories increasingly resembled those used today, but there continued to be changes every ten years.

The one constant throughout the first century or so was that the census reflected racialization. The census helped to create and maintain the categories that defined some as non-White, although it took other forces to create the social and political inequality that is fundamental to racialization. In each racialized group, however, there were many who vigorously resisted these efforts, despite the overwhelming odds against them.

To understand this more thoroughly, it is helpful to examine the dynamics of racialization and oppression for specific subpopulations. The story of racialization prior to 1965 is the story of the creation of political and social inequality, a legacy that haunts the United States to this day.

African Americans: Historical Racialization Experiences

Prior to the onset of post-1965 Black immigration from the Caribbean and Africa, African Americans were considered to be a relatively stable and self-identified political group, whose members perceived themselves as having a "linked fate" (Dawson 1994). This sense of linked fate tended to trump other factors like socioeconomic class differences in influencing their political behavior. Contemporary immigrants from Africa and the West Indies, however, have brought these understandings into question, and social scientists have begun to chart the ways in which West Indian and African-origin Black immigrants have sought to avoid being trapped in the lowest rungs of the American racial order (Vickerman 1999; Rogers 2001, 2006; Assensoh 2000).

Although Blacks initially came to North America as explorers and indentured servants, they were ultimately racialized as slaves, primarily for economic reasons (Williams 1994). Slavery eventually eclipsed the system of indentured servitude because the British colonial leaders realized that indentured servitude based principally on European labor was riddled with insurmountable problems. The supply of White indentured servants was insufficient, and indentured White servants often disagreed with the terms of their services. In many instances, these Whites were able to sue their masters for better conditions of service. White servants insisted on an increase in the monetary payments that they earned, and some unhappy indentured servants ran away to parts of the country that were still being settled, where it was difficult and expensive to find them (Franklin and Moss 1998, 32; Hanks 1994). In addition, the population of young workers began to decline in the later seventeenth century, further constricting the supply of White workers willing to migrate to the colonies (Parent 2003, 58–59).

Faced with the challenges of this system of indentured servitude, colonial leaders recognized the need for a more reliable source of labor for their farms and household jobs, and they found that source in the trading of Africans as slaves. Gradually, an economic system dependent on slaves emerged. Although Blacks were being treated as slaves from the early years of Virginia colonization (McColley 1986), "not until the 1660's [did] Maryland and Virginia make the first important legal distinctions between white and Negro servants" (Stampp 1956, 22). As planters searched for sources of labor other than British immigrants, the number of enslaved Blacks grew. By the last years of the seventeenth century, independent slave traders had emerged to supply captured Africans to planters looking for labor, and by the first decade of the eighteenth century, "Virginia had become a slave society" (Parent 2003, 79). This race-based bondage was enforced through a rigid system of legally sanctioned discrimination that set in motion long-term social, economic, and political inequalities, which are still evident today. This process of enslavement was the genesis of Black racialization in North America, although Blacks had been racialized by Europeans long before that time.

Racialization of African Americans began so long ago that there is sometimes insufficient attention to the diversity of the early, involuntary immigrants. Although some of the differences are now difficult to trace, the early migrants brought with them a wide variety of linguistic, cultural, and ethnic backgrounds.

> The Africans who were to become Americans came from a region of West Africa that fanned from its westernmost tip, around the Senegal River, south and east, along the Bight of Benin, and south again below the Congo River to include a region we now call Angola. Hardly a people living within this vast region, stretching inland for two to three hundred miles, was unrepresented in the creation of the Afro-American people. Bambara, Fulani, Mandinka, and Wolof from the Senegambia, the collection of peoples from Dahomey called Whydahs, the Ashanti, Coromantees, Fanti, Ga, Hausa, Ibo, Yoruba, Angola—they all came, like migrants from Europe and later from Asia, to mix their seed and substance in the making of the American and his civilization. (Huggins 1977, 3)

Slave trade practices played a direct role in eroding this diversity, by mixing together men and women of previously separated ethnic groups. Given the lack of freedom of movement, it became impossible for the involuntary African immigrants to cluster into ethnic enclaves, as European, Latino, and Asian immigrants have often done. So, for Blacks whose families have been in the United States for generations, ethnic ties have long been blurred, having been severed on the slave ships, or shortly after arrival on American shores.

Since the 1960s, however, many Black immigrants have arrived under very different circumstances. These immigrants, from countries in Africa, the Caribbean, Canada, Europe, Latin America, and Asia, find it vastly easier to preserve ethnic distinctions. Not only do African ancestry immigrants differ from each other in ethnicity, language, culture, nationality, and political orientations, but they also often differ in significant ways from native-born American Blacks. However, these differences are sometimes obscured by an emphasis on Blackness.

Historically, the weight given to Blackness was an important part of racialization. The boundaries between Blackness and Whiteness were constantly policed, and the fiction of a color line was constructed on the "one drop" of blood concept: any person who possessed even "one drop" of African blood would be defined as Black, even if most of that person's ancestors came from Europe. This measure determined whether individuals were excluded from opportunities and access to resources in American society.

Efforts to define Blackness legally did not end with the abolition of slavery. At the end of the twentieth century, Susie Guillary Phipps filed suit against the State of Louisiana claiming that she was inaccurately classified as Black. During the civil suit, Phipps learned that one of her ancestors was a slave and, under the one-drop rule, she was considered a Black. For Phipps, who had lived her life as a White woman, the realization that she was legally Black made her "ill," given the reality that Blacks have historically occupied the bottom tier of America's socioeconomic hierarchy.

Legal discrimination was long an important part of racialization. For example, shortly after Americans fought the War of Independence to win their freedom from the British—with the assistance of enslaved Blacks—legislatures in several Southern colonies enacted the Slave Codes for the purpose of regulating every aspect of the slaves' behavior, in order to keep them subservient as well as performing at optimal levels (Bell 2002, 516). While Slave Codes varied from state to state, most of them stipulated that slaves could not own any property; that they had no standing in a court of law; that a slave could not strike a White person; and, above all, that the rape of a female slave was only to be considered trespassing, since she was deemed as property but not as a human being (Franklin and Moss 1998, 124).

These legal measures were given powerful reinforcement by violence and psychological intimidation, which were utilized to control Blacks. For example, former South Carolina Senator James Hammond, who owned more than 300 slaves, observed, "We have to rely more and more on the power of fear. We are determined to continue masters, and to do so we have to draw the reign [sic] tighter and tighter day by day to be assured that we hold them in complete check" (Takaki 1993, 111). Invariably, slave masters used psychological tactics to convince slaves that they were racially inferior and incapable of being anything else but mere slaves, who were helplessly dependent upon their masters (111).

After the abolition of slavery, lynching was a particularly repugnant and widely used tactic to keep Blacks under control and was considered a ritual in the South and in many places in the North and West, including Oklahoma, Indiana, Illinois, Ohio, and Wyoming. Often, lynchings were announced in advance and attended by families, including women and children. Lynching was widespread in America, and it occurred nonstop from 1881 to 1952 (Madison 2003).

Violence has continued to be an important mechanism of Black racialization. During the 1950s and 1960s, state-sanctioned violence operated primarily to prevent Blacks from agitating for political rights. Since then, many Blacks believe that violence in the form of police brutality, the war on drugs, and profiling have been primary ways of "keeping Blacks in their place."

Science, too, has been an invaluable tool in the process of Black racialization. Although negative and stereotypical views about Africans existed in Europe before the colonies were established, the development of full-blown racist ideologies—based on skin color—did not develop until the late 1700s when Blackness was inextricably linked with mental, biological, cultural, and moral inferiority that was later legitimated by the scientific racism of the nineteenth and twentieth centuries (Graves 2004, 20; Omi and Winant 1994, 61–69; Williams 1994). Science continues to be used as the servant of Black racialization. In the 1990s, authors of *The Bell Curve* argued that Blacks were biologically inferior to Whites and other racial groups. In contemporary racial parlance, the so-called innate inferiority of Blacks is utilized to explain differences in educational attainment. The argument is that Blacks are less educated because they are innately inferior, not because of unequal resources or unsupportive learning environments (Herrnstein and Murray 1996; but see Bell 2005).

Even though legal discrimination has been outlawed, and violence is no longer tolerated (or celebrated), the legacy of these efforts lives on in things such as racial segregation. Segregation, in turn, helps perpetuate racialization. Not only have Blacks been physically separated from others, but they have also been excluded from opportunity structures that facilitate socioeconomic mobility. For example, the development of low-interest mortgages, backed by the federal government, marked a crucial opportunity for the average American family to generate wealth. Indeed, the purchase of a home has been the primary mechanism for generating wealth and passing it across generations. However the Federal Housing Administration's conscious decision to channel loans away from the central city and to the suburbs had a powerful effect on the creation of segregated housing in post–World War II America. The FHA's official handbook even went so far as to provide a model "restrictive covenant" that would pass court scrutiny to prospective White homebuyers (Oliver and Shapiro 1997). Restrictive covenants and other segregation markers have been ruled unconstitutional in a number of important court cases. Yet, the legacy of the FHA's contribution to racial residential segregation lives on in the wide gap between Black assets and those of Whites.

Other measures also help fuel inequality, which, in turn, gives support to racialization. In a publication entitled *America: Who Really Pays the Taxes?* Donald Bartlett (2004) shows that consequences of historical racial discrimination, which were crucial to the process of Black racialization, continue to contribute to the racialization of Blacks as impoverished and disadvantaged. He demonstrates that the most generous tax benefits are often given to Americans who own assets, especially homes, other real estate, stocks, and bonds. In turn, tax breaks directly help in the accumulation of financial and real assets. Since Blacks were denied access to home mortgages as well as homes in upwardly mobile neighborhoods, the tax code works to reinforce the discrimination of the past and maintain the racialization of Blacks as disadvantaged. In this respect, the seemingly race-neutral tax code generates a racial effect that deepens rather than equalizes the economic gulf between Blacks and Whites (Oliver and Shapiro 1997, 38–41).

Black racialization has also been aided and abetted by the historical and contemporary process of racial school segregation. In some respects, the 1954 *Brown v. Board of Education* decision went a long way to begin the process of equal educational opportunity, but the slow implementation of the *Brown* decision, coupled with court decisions in the 1970s and 1980s that undermined *Brown*'s potency, has either delayed or postponed the reality of truly integrated as well as equal educational opportunities for Black and White children. As a result, the reality for most Black children is one of separate and unequal education that perpetuates Black racialization in economic and social terms.

Renewed Black immigration to the United States provides other opportunities for assessing racialization. Since the 1960s, there has been considerable growth in African-ancestry immigration from many parts of the world. Like other immigrants, the Black immigrants from the Caribbean and Africa identify most strongly with their countries of origin (e.g., Jamaica, Ghana) rather than with the racial group identity often imposed upon them in this country. Since most of these first-generation immigrants left their countries as adults, it is understandable that they have rejected the idea that they are only Black, which assigns them to an inferior racial category that denies their national and linguistic origins (Foner 1987; Assensoh 2000). Instead, these more recent immigrants have sometimes emphasized signs of their differences from native-born Blacks, such as dialects and speech patterns that distinguish them as immigrants.

Try though they might, Black immigrants find it difficult to escape the forces of racialization. By the second generation, researchers have identified two different tendencies in terms of racial identification. On the one hand, a majority of second-generation Black immigrants from the Caribbean and Africa had merged into the African American population

(Bryce-Laporte 1972). In a study of second-generation Haitian immigrants in Evanston, Illinois, researchers emphasized that second-generation Haitians increasingly conform to "racial expectations of American society rather than those of the Haitian community" (Woldemikael 1989). On the other hand, researchers also have identified a pattern of segmented assimilation, especially among immigrants with more social and economic resources, where immigrants and their children identify themselves as hyphenated Americans: for example, Trinidadian Americans or Jamaican Americans (Waters 1994).

Some scholars have suggested that recent Black immigrants may face less pressure to shed their ethnic identities and adopt traditional American racial identities as a result of changes in the nature of race relations in the United States, as well as language differences between native-born Blacks and some groups of recent Black immigrants, for whom English is not the native language. For example, recent studies of second-generation Dominicans have demonstrated a steadfast hold on the Dominican identity or in some situations, alternative use of Dominican, Spanish, or Latino (Bailey 2001).

For these second-generation Dominican immigrants, there is neither the straightforward acceptance of the Black racial identity nor the segmented assimilation that has occurred among upwardly mobile Black immigrants. That is because Dominican immigrants range in phenotype from typically White to typically Black features as well as everything in between. Moreover, unlike other Black immigrants from Africa and the Caribbean, Dominicans speak Spanish. In the Dominican Republic, Blackness is looked down upon and associated with Haitians, who are seen as racial outsiders (Bailey 2001). To some extent, these background context factors explain Dominicans' reluctance to accept the racial identity of Black in the U.S. context, especially given its negative connotation at home (Bailey 2001).

Among second-generation Dominican high school students, thus, researchers have found a pattern of speaking Spanish as a way of distinguishing themselves from other Blacks and identifying themselves as Hispanic or Dominican (Bailey 2001). In this way, the Dominicans—many of whom have an African American appearance—may have the freedom to define themselves as something other than Black. Among Dominicans with African American phenotype, this racial self-identification is important because it contravenes the traditional expectation of racial assimilation by the second generation, and it conflicts sharply with traditional understandings of how people who look Black identify themselves in

American contexts. Moreover, since Dominicans have a larger Spanish linguistic community with which to identify, they have an additional layer of distinctiveness that Jamaicans and the smaller subset of French-speaking Haitians lack (Portes and Zhou 1993).

While first- and second-generation Dominicans are similar in their tendency to shun the traditional Black label, they are different in attitudes toward Whites and Blacks. Among first-generation Dominicans, there is a tendency to admire Whites and attempt to align themselves with them, while simultaneously distancing themselves from African Americans. However, researchers have reported that second-generation Dominicans are more likely than first-generation Dominicans to associate with Blacks, who are often their peers at school and work, and they are often puzzled by parental prejudices against Blacks (Bailey 2001). These generational conflicts are the result of differences in social contexts in which first- and second-generation immigrants are reared. To be sure, the issue of racial prejudice is not a one-way street, as African Americans are not always welcoming toward Black immigrants, whom they sometimes describe as either "not black enough" or "black, but not like us" (Chude-Sokei 2007).

In some instances, Black immigrants generally report that native-born Blacks (or African Americans) have a narrow conception of themselves as African Americans, and that they tend to define issues of public policy in ways that alienate as well as exclude Black immigrants (Swarnes 2004). These tensions are evident in attitudes toward immigration policy and higher education policy, in response, for example, to reports that Ivy League institutions are recruiting much more heavily among Black immigrant populations than among native-born or mainstream Blacks (Page 2007).

Conflict with immigrants has helped to perpetuate Black racialization in American society. Given the negative stereotypes of African Americans, immigrants have often tried to avoid being associated with them. Non-African immigrants have historically used a variety of mechanisms to distance themselves from Blacks, perpetuating racial stereotypes in their efforts to demonstrate either their Whiteness or their non-Blackness. A striking example is the Irish, who initially thought of themselves as similar to Blacks because of their common history of suffering oppression. However, the Irish soon realized that in order to succeed in the United States, it was necessary to distinguish themselves from Blacks so that they could carve out higher-level social, economic, and political niches (Ignatiev 1995). Similarly, prior to the 1960s, Asian and Latino political activists made efforts to distinguish themselves from Blacks in an effort to avoid the implications of the 1896 *Plessy v. Ferguson* ruling, in which the U.S. Supreme Court endorsed state government enforcement of separate public accommodations for Blacks and Whites.

While immigrant groups have generally succeeded in avoiding the harshest discrimination that has fallen on Blacks, this has come at a price. The achievements of non-Black immigrants are used by some to argue that barriers to advancement are fictional, and that Blacks therefore have only themselves to blame for their socioeconomic difficulties.

Meanwhile, fierce competition between poor Blacks and recently arrived immigrants continues in many areas where these groups interact and compete over scarce housing, employment, and educational resources. While no group is necessarily innocent in intergroup conflict, the media have often cast Blacks as the perpetrators or bullies of newcomers, who are merely trying to attain the American dream (Kim 1999). Here, Blacks are often racialized as the permanent underclass, invariably bypassed by successive generations of immigrants.

It should be emphasized that Black racialization has not occurred without a struggle. In the earliest years, Black slaves rebelled against their oppressors. After the Civil War, Blacks became politically active during Reconstruction, when Northern troops occupied the South and forced the states of the former Confederacy to grant some political rights to African Americans. During that brief period after the Civil War, some Blacks were able to hold political office. Although the ending of Reconstruction brought new waves of political oppression, Blacks—along with some Whites as well as Latino, Asian, and Native American allies on occasion—fought against policies and processes that led to racial inequality, discrimination, and exclusion. When possible, Blacks utilized the courts, and, in the twentieth century, were able to win court cases dealing with school desegregation, voting rights, interracial marriage, and racial covenants in housing. In addition to gaining legal support for their efforts, African American activists also served as role models for the civil rights efforts of other racially stigmatized and marginalized groups.

While these efforts have gone a long way toward undermining some benchmarks of political inequality, the wide gap in social and economic measures persists, seemingly immune to the many efforts to eliminate it. Consequently, the racialization of African Americans remains powerful, despite the heroic efforts of civil rights activists to bring about changes and equity. The continuation of conditions that have left disproportionate percentages of Blacks in poverty has meant that African Americans are increasingly likely to be racialized in a nonracial fashion, whereby social class is ostensibly the critical difference, rather than race as such. Some have referred to this as an "ethno-class," which is the combination of social class and ethnicity or race (Fuchs 1990, 482). The continuing high poverty levels and other socioeconomic struggles of many Blacks can be used to justify negative racial images but can also now be justified as "not about race," since they are ostensibly based on nonracial measures. In reality, however, we believe that past discrimination continues to be an important influence on the continuing high levels of poverty, poor education conditions, and other challenges facing Blacks. The consequence is a powerful reinforcement of racialization. To a large extent, whether Whites avoid living in heavily Black neighborhoods because of the overt racial prejudice or because of other factors—such as the poverty of the residents—the result is still that large groups of African Americans continue to be marked as different and undesirable.

Latinos, Group Identity, and Racialization

In some respects, Latinos have experienced race quite differently than U.S. Blacks. Like African Americans, though, the racialization of Latinos cannot be understood apart from the historical evolution of relationships with the dominant ethnic groups in U.S. society. Indeed, the very categories of Latino or Hispanic are relatively recent developments, having come into common usage only since 1970. Prior to that time, people referred to today as Latinos and/or Hispanics were routinely categorized by national origin. The experiences of these ethnoracial groups varied by location and circumstances of incorporation, so our discussion will emphasize the differing responses to specific national-origin groups. Still, a potential panethnic Hispanic identity had roots back to the Spanish conquest and settlement in the so-called New World. Spanish conquest and settlement brought some of the features of Latin American culture and life—the Spanish language, Roman Catholicism, the creation of mestizo populations in most parts of the region—that would figure prominently as key markers for Latino racialization by Anglo-dominant Americans (Moore and Pachon 1985).

As with Asian Americans, moreover, the racialization experiences of U.S. Latinos can be partly understood in the international context—for Latinos, the competition between imperial powers (i.e., England and Spain), and subsequently between the "new world" offspring of those imperial powers. Latino populations in Florida, Texas, New Mexico, California, and other parts of the Southwest were perceived as obstacles to American expansionist aspirations.

Mexican Americans

The first significant group of Latinos to be incorporated into the U.S. population was Mexican. The United States had annexed Texas in 1845, but the Mexican government resisted, leading to war in 1846 and Mexico's humiliating defeat. Mexico was forced to "sell" nearly one half of its territory (including not only Texas, but also the areas that became the states of California, New Mexico, Arizona, Nevada, and Utah, most of Colorado, and small parts of Oklahoma, Kansas, and Wyoming), at a bargain price.

The racialization of Mexicans began in the crucible of that conflict. While there was a bitter fight between U.S. Whigs and Democrats over the wisdom of the war against Mexico, both parties agreed that the Mexicans were an "inferior race."

> Congressional Whigs pointed out the impossibility of integrating the Mexican population within the United States as citizens. Speaker after speaker attacked the Mexicans as unassimilable, [as] ". . . of a race totally different from ourselves." . . . Even those who in 1847 and 1848 argued that all of Mexico should be annexed gave practically no support to the idea of allowing the Mexicans to enter the union as equal citizens. (Horsman 1981, 242–43)

The 1848 Treaty of Guadalupe Hidalgo ending the U.S. war with Mexico stipulated that those Mexicans who remained in the annexed territory would enjoy "all the rights of citizens" (quoted in Menchaca 2001, 215), but this did not prevent Mexican Americans from being racialized in a variety of ways. "Tragically, within a year of the treaty's ratification, the United States government began a process of racialization that categorized most Mexicans as inferiors in all domains of life" (Menchaca 2001, 215).

The story of that racialization is too complex to be described here, but we give a few examples. First, within a year of the treaty's adoption, the U.S. Congress allowed the state governments of the annexed areas to interpret citizenship rights and claims (as was the case in areas previously part of the United States). The states and territories decided that most Mexicans would not enjoy full citizenship rights, since *mestizos* were not considered to be Whites.

In California, for example, a statute adopted in 1851 determined that any individual with at least one-quarter Indian ancestry would be excluded from the White category, thereby excluding them from many citizenship rights, including the right to vote. This law, which remained in effect into the twentieth century, racialized the vast majority of Mexican Californians as non-White, thereby limiting their U.S. citizenship rights (Menchaca 2001, 221). Similar laws were adopted in Texas and Arizona, and—after 1870—in New Mexico (Menchaca 2001, chap. 8). Even after these laws had been repealed, hundreds of thousands of "Mexicans" (both U.S. citizens and noncitizens) were forcibly removed to Mexico by public officials during the Great Depression of the 1930s and in the federal government's Operation Wetback during the 1950s (Haney López 1996, 38).

A second example was the transfer of Mexican-held land to Anglos. Before Mexican independence in 1821, the Spanish government had granted title to large tracts of land to both individual families and communal entities. These land grants provided a potential foundation for economic and, hence, political power. However, in varying ways (including legal subterfuge and direct violence), and over the course of only a few decades, most of the land grant titles had passed into the hands of Anglo Americans (Acuña 2006; Barrera 1979; Menchaca 2001). Even previously privileged Mexican/Spanish families were stripped of their economic foundations.

A third example was the "colonial labor system" (Barrera 1979, 34). Chicanos became important sources of wage labor, working in a system with racially segmented features such as (1) "*labor repression,* . . .the use of non-market sanctions such as coercion and legal restrictions to limit the degree of freedom of Chicanos as compared to non-minority workers"; (2) "*the dual wage system,*" which paid "one wage to minority workers and another to nonminority workers who perform the same task"; (3) "*occupational stratification,* . . . the practice of classifying certain kinds of jobs as suited for minorities [e.g., field labor] and others as suited for nonminorities [e.g., skilled work]"; and (4) the use of Chicanos as a "*reserve labor force,*" in which employers recruit potential workers far in excess of the number to be offered full-time employment, a practice particularly common among agricultural employers (Barrera 1979, 41–48).

> The system of colonial labor appears to have been based on racial rather than ethnic distinctions. On the subordinate side were all the racial minorities in the Southwest at that time: Native Americans, Asians, Blacks, and Chicanos and other Latinos. On the other side were all the White groups. (1979, 49)

Thus, when large-scale immigration from Mexico began in the early twentieth century, new *Mexicanos* came into a racially segmented and stratified socioeconomic and political system. Mexican American subordination and marginalization was justified by the perceived "essential" difference in character and talent between the dominant Anglo populations and Mexican Americans in the Southwest.

Fourth, social and geographic *segregation* for Chicanos was the dominant pattern throughout the Southwest until after World War II. Details varied, but there were certain common features, including residential segregation (based on discriminatory housing practices), educational segregation, systematic disparities in schooling practices, and segregation of public facilities (movie theaters, restaurants, public beaches and swimming pools, etc.).

A fifth example was anti-Mexican violence and physical intimidation by law enforcement personnel and Anglo civilians. Prior to the 1960s, this helped to remind residents of *barrios* and *colonias* of their subordinated status. Justifying these practices was an ideology claiming a "natural" hierarchy between the "superior" White U.S. population and the "inferior" Mexicans (e.g., Acuña 2006; Barrera 1979; Camarillo 1984; Montejano 1987; Menchaca 2001).

Some resisted these patterns of domination, of course, and their efforts gave birth to ethnoracial political frames of reference that remain relevant. Efforts included attempts at ethnoracial community control (see, e.g., Barrera 1988), pluralistic integration (see, e.g., Garcia and de la Garza 1977; Hero 1992; Marquez 1993), and individual assimilation (see, e.g., Chavez 1991; Rodriguez 1982). In the early years following annexation, violent resistance to Anglo domination was both an ideal celebrated in *corridos* and folklore (e.g., "The Ballad of Gregorio Cortéz") and a reality. Las Gorras Blancas (the White Caps) opposed the systematic loss of land by *Mexicanos* and "resorted to direct action . . . by cutting down fences and burning the property" of those Anglo ranchers who had "acquired" Mexican land in New Mexico, and they seem to have had broad support among the Mexican American population (Barrera 1985). To some degree, these early actions served as a model for Reies Tijerina's Alianza Federal de Mercedes in northern New Mexico in the 1960s, whose actions, in turn, served as an inspiration for many Chicano nationalist activists during the Chicano Movement of the 1960s and 1970s (see, e.g., Muñoz 1989).

Many agricultural and urban working-class Mexican Americans sought to improve their circumstances through the labor movement. Chicano farm workers in the Southwest participated in large numbers in agricultural strikes in the 1920s, 1930s, and 1950s and were the major component of the United Farm Workers organizing efforts led by Cesar Chavez in the 1960s (Acuña 2006). Urban Mexican American workers participated in unions that have engaged in political education and in political mobilization of their members, as well as in leadership development (Muñoz 1988; Milkman 2006).

Politically moderate Mexican American business, professional, and civic elites sought inclusion into business and professional associations (chamber of commerce, bar associations, etc.) and also formed associations aiming to facilitate the inclusion of Mexican Americans into the mainstream. Among the most important of these have been the League of United Latin American Citizens (LULAC), the American G.I. Forum, the Community Service Organization (CSO), the Mexican American Political Association (MAPA), and the Political Association of Spanish Speaking Organizations (PASSO). These groups worked for inclusion of Mexican Americans into U.S. political institutions through the encouragement of "good citizenship," individual assimilation, and interest group mobilization and participation via political pluralism.

Finally, there was the watershed Chicano Movement of the 1960s and 1970s, a student-centered political movement founded by the first generation of Mexican Americans to attend college in relatively large numbers (see Muñoz 1989 for an excellent summary and analysis; but also see Navarro 2000). While militancy was the order of the day for the movement, their aims included pluralistic inclusion in the dominant institutions as well as radical efforts to undermine the political economic capitalist system and "cultural nationalist" efforts to develop and maintain separate and equal ethnoracial Chicano communities throughout the Southwest (or *Aztlán* as the area was known to movement activists). These nationalist efforts also spawned La Raza Unida Party, which briefly captured electoral control of city governments in Crystal City, Texas, and Parlier, California. While the movement's political organizational efforts were largely dissipated by the mid-1970s, it continues to have an effect on Mexican Americans through Chicano/Latino studies programs in higher education institutions and through the (mostly pluralist) political activities of these programs' alumni.

Puerto Ricans

The second largest Latino group in the United States, Puerto Ricans also became part of the United States as a consequence of military actions. The so-called Spanish American War, which began in 1898, led to Spain losing its remaining colonial territories in the Western Hemisphere, most importantly Puerto Rico and Cuba. After that, Puerto Ricans were ruled as colonial subjects of the United States until 1917, when they were granted U.S. citizenship under the Jones Act (passed without the consent of the Puerto Rican people). The island then was ruled by appointed governors until 1952, when it gained commonwealth status. As a commonwealth, the island enjoys some of the powers of states in the United States (e.g., election of governors, legislators, and local government officials), but not others (e.g., residents of Puerto Rico have no voting representation in the U.S. Congress, despite being U.S. citizens). Economic and military development of the island remains firmly in the hands of the U.S. federal government.

Since the mid–twentieth century, the primary fault lines in Puerto Rican politics have followed competing visions of the most appropriate relationship between the island and the United States: (1) Puerto Rico as an independent nation; (2) Puerto Rican statehood as the fifty-first U.S. state; or (3) continued commonwealth status, with some measures of independence and some measures of integration into the United States (e.g., Puerto Rican residents of the island are subject to the draft as U.S. citizens, but do not pay U.S. income taxes; and businesses located in Puerto Rico enjoy tax privileges not available to firms located on the mainland). The third position holds sway, but does not have consistent majority support among Puerto Ricans (Barreto 1998).

Puerto Ricans migrating to the mainland are not immigrants but U.S. citizens whose move is akin to that of mainland residents moving from one state to another. Most migration has occurred in the post–World War II period, and by the 2000 census, Puerto Ricans were nearly evenly split between the island and the mainland (with more than 3 million in each group).

The economic development of Puerto Rico via U.S. corporate investments seems to have played an important role in the stimulation of migration from the island to the mainland. "Part of the government's strategy in Puerto Rico was to establish a 'safety valve' for the economic costs of industrializing Puerto Rico" (Jennings 1988, 66–67).

Racialization has been different than that of African Americans and Mexican Americans, and the island and the mainland experiences have differed. However, there are some similarities: for example, Puerto Ricans (both on the island and the mainland) have experienced the dual wage system (in which White persons are paid more for doing the same work in the same jobs) and occupational stratification (in which certain higher job classifications are not filled by people of color).

While segregation has not been a central issue on the island (since Puerto Ricans make up the vast majority of the population), Puerto Ricans on the mainland have experienced discrimination in housing (leading to segregation), in employment, and in access to cultural institutions (see, e.g., Pérez y Gonzáles 2000, chaps. 6, 7; Rodriguez 2005, chap. 1). Moreover, the strong Americanization campaigns in education left their mark through an idealization of White and a concomitant disparagement of Puerto Rican culture and language, which helps promote racialization (Rodriguez 2005, chap. 1).

Color has also played a role in the racialization of Puerto Ricans. Like other Latin American countries, Puerto Ricans had a complex and multifaceted understanding of race, one that combined characteristics of culture, education, wealth, social status, and many gradations of color and phenotype. Rodriguez argues, however, that over time the Puerto Rican understanding of race—both on the island and along the eastern seaboard of the mainland, where most mainland Puerto Ricans reside—has moved toward a more biracial model of race, with light-skinned and highly assimilated Puerto Ricans becoming White and others becoming Black. Thus, the Euro-Indian *mestizaje* that has played such a critical role in a Mexican American racial identity seems to be much less significant for a racialized Puerto Rican identity.

For many mainland Puerto Ricans, racialization has been a "conflation" of race, class, and culture (including language).

> Activities seen as typical of bad citizens (dropping out of school, becoming teenage mothers, taking drugs, committing crimes, going on welfare) are habitually associated with, for example, *Puerto Ricans,* and become "explanations" for their "failure."
> . . . Spanish itself is regarded as a barrier to class mobility because it displaces English. Accents, "broken" English, and "mixing" become signs of illiteracy and laziness. . . . Being "low class" and Puerto Rican or black are . . . typically associated. Like a default setting, this conflation is the normal point of reference . . . (Urciuoli 1996, 26–27)

Such racialization processes create social, economic, and political disadvantage. Though challenging the typical understanding of "Puerto Ricans as victims," Sánchez nevertheless succinctly summarizes some of the consequences of Puerto Rican racialization.

Only 60 percent of U.S. [i.e., mainland] Puerto Ricans have graduated from high school. This rate is not only lower than that of non-Latino whites (85 percent); it is lower than that of non-Latino blacks (at 73 percent). . . . Only about 54 percent of Puerto Ricans participate in the labor force. This compares to about 65 percent for all Latinos, 66 percent for non-Latino whites, and 62 percent for non-Latino blacks. . . . Almost 39 percent of all Puerto Ricans live in poverty, compared to 31 percent for all Latinos, 10 percent for non-Latino whites, and 33 percent for non-Latino blacks. . . . The economic and social picture for Puerto Ricans was actually better in the 1950s than it is now. (2007, 9)

Puerto Ricans have worked to improve their circumstances through both economic and political activities. Puerto Rican cigar makers in New York City, for example, helped to lead a significant and successful strike as early as 1919 (Sánchez 2007, chap. 2). By the 1930s, the Puerto Rican population in New York City had "become too large for politicians to ignore." In 1937 the first Puerto Rican official from New York City was elected, to the New York State Assembly, yet through the 1940s and 1950s there was a "virtual absence of Puerto Ricans from New York City politics" (Falcón 1984). Several explanations have been offered for the relatively low levels of political activity.

One explanation is that machine politics had declined by the time of major Puerto Rican population growth in New York City. The machines were less able to offer patronage in return for electoral support. Another reason is that the Democratic Party was becoming increasingly conservative, and there was a perception that Puerto Ricans "were nonwhite and hence a threat to the city's white population." They were also perceived as a "troublesome" group because they had strongly supported leftist congressional candidates in New York City, and Puerto Rican nationalists had attacked President Truman (in 1950) and congressmen in the U.S. House of Representatives (in 1952). Finally, the Puerto Rican government sought to ensure that Puerto Ricans in New York City would remain in the City and not return, so that New York might remain a safety valve for the island. Toward that end, the Puerto Rican government set up a Migration Division in the city "that took on the functions that ethnic politicians had served for earlier immigrant groups. The presence of the Division slowed the growth of a Puerto Rican leadership cadre in New York City" (Baver 1984, 44–45). Finally, because Puerto Ricans have often *not* seen themselves as permanent residents on the American mainland—due to a sense that they will return to the island—they did not develop the political attachments on the mainland that many immigrant groups have.

Puerto Rican political activism increased in the 1960s, due in part to the funding directed to minority communities through the War on Poverty programs of President Lyndon Johnson's Great Society. These antipoverty agencies provided social and political resources, but these "poverty-crats" could never play the same political role of developing ethnic power as had been the case for other groups in the early 1900s. The bureaucratic regulations and procedures that constrained these programs meant that they could not address the concerns of particular ethnic/racial groups (Jennings 1988, 71).

In the 1960s, Puerto Rican militancy could be seen in groups such as the Young Lords. Characterizing themselves as "socialists and revolutionary nationalists," they used a strategy that "was a mixture of confrontation and community service." Notable among New York's Puerto Rican militants was "their linking of the Puerto Rican struggle for social justice in New York with the struggle for independence of the island. In the political analysis of many militants, Puerto Ricans on the island live in a U.S. colony, while Puerto Ricans in mainland ghettos live under conditions of internal colonialism" (Baver 1984, 47).

The 1960s also saw major electoral activity. Puerto Rican politicians emerged from the reform wing of the City's Democratic Party. Perhaps most important was Herman Badillo, "a moderate . . . working in relatively mainstream context," who later became a U.S. Congressman (Baver 1984, 48). From about the mid-1970s to the present Puerto Rican politics has emphasized expanded participation and a practical orientation. A significant development of this period has been that the local Democratic Party has been more receptive of Puerto Ricans, to the extent that most Puerto Rican politicians now have some link with the party. Another development has been efforts to assure the fair drawing of council districts in the city so that Puerto Ricans can gain a more meaningful political voice.

Cubans

The Spanish American War was launched because of a conflict between Spain and the United States over Cuba, not Puerto Rico. While Cuba was never formally incorporated into the United States as a colony, the United States made it clear to both Cubans and other Latin Americans that it intended to maintain close control over the island's political and economic development. Through the Platt Amendment of 1901 (which was incorporated into Cuba's constitution), the United States placed Cuba under an American "protectorate," which "meant that Cuban politics and the Cuban economy were [to be] dominated by Americans" (Painter 1987, 141). The United States continued to have a dominant role in the island's political and economic affairs until the 1959 revolution.

Cuban immigrants began to arrive in the United States before the Spanish American War, but substantial Cuban migration to the United States did not begin until after Castro ousted the U.S.-backed Batista regime. With assistance from the United States, tens of thousands of anti-Castro Cubans emigrated to the United States (principally to the south Florida area). Post-1959 Cuban immigration came in three waves: the first soon after Castro's victory, and a second in the mid-1960s, following the abortive Bay of Pigs invasion of 1961.

These first two migrations resulted in the transformation of Miami into what some have called "the capital of Latin America." The experience of these Cubans was very different from that of Mexican Americans and Puerto Ricans, as the early Cuban exiles usually had access to greater economic, social, and personal capital. They used these resources to establish an ethnic "enclave" in the Miami area that enabled them to prosper economically and politically (Portes and Bach 1985). Because of Castro's declared communism and his opposition to the United States, and because of the exiles' fierce opposition to Castro and communism, the United States government gave them substantial assistance, including unlimited authorization to immigrate—something not experienced by other Latino groups.

> The Cuban immigrants of the early 1960s . . . included many accomplished professionals who combined personal effort with an "open-armed" immigration policy and substantial federal economic assistance in establishing themselves in Miami. Subsequent groups of Cuban entrants throughout the 1960s brought a large portion of the Cuban middle class as well as an upwardly mobile working class to Miami. . . . Cuban immigration in general has been accompanied by rapid economic incorporation. (Moreno 1997, 213–14)

Despite relatively favorable circumstances, Cuban exiles did experience considerable opposition and ethnic hostility from other groups. Still, most of the Cuban immigrants during the 1960s and 1970s were relatively light-skinned as well as economically and socially connected, and they did not experience the racialization that had such a negative impact on Mexican Americans and Puerto Ricans. Furthermore, they came to the United States at a time when the harshest racialization was in the process of being declared illegal or unconstitutional by Congress and/or the courts. De jure segregation of schools had been rejected in 1954 (in *Brown v. Board of Education*), and laws would soon outlaw racial discrimination in housing and employment. Cuban immigrants of the 1960s would never know the degree of racialization endured by earlier generations of Americans of African, Asian, Puerto Rican, or Mexican ancestry.

The third post-1959 wave was the 1980 Marielitos. Totaling about 120,000, these Cubans were of lower socioeconomic status and darker-skinned, and included some who had been convicted of crimes in Cuba. They had less favorable circumstances than did earlier waves (Portes and Rumbaut 2001, 262–63) and were more likely to experience discrimination and racialization. Furthermore, with the expanded diversity of Latin American immigrants in South Florida in recent years, racialization appears to be more in flux now. Nevertheless, the political status of Cubans in South Florida is quite favorable. The group has been incorporated into the political and economic elite for several decades (e.g., Moreno 1997) and also benefits from other factors that distinguish them from most other Latinos.

One such factor has been a strong foreign policy emphasis in Cuban American politics, with voters and political leaders demanding strong adherence to an anti-Castro and anticommunist line. A second is that a strong majority of Cuban voters (especially in South Florida) has supported the Republican Party since the 1960s (Moreno 1997). In these ways, Cuban Americans differ considerably from their presumed panethnic cohorts with origins in Mexico, Puerto Rico, or other parts of Latin America. On domestic policy issues, however, Cuban Americans do not differ much from other Latino groups: they are strongly supportive of bilingual education, and most adhere to a moderately liberal stance in relation to social and economic policy (see, e.g., de la Garza et al. 1992; de la Garza 2004; Democracy Corps 2005; Pew Hispanic Center/Kaiser Family Foundation 2004; Uhlaner and Garcia 2002; *Washington Post*/Kaiser Family Foundation/Harvard University Survey Project 1999).

Given the highly successful political incorporation of Cuban Americans in the South Florida area, many scholars have suggested that a pluralist/immigrant interpretation is appropriate for this group, rather than the racial hierarchy perspective that seems more appropriate for Mexican or Puerto Rican political experiences (e.g., Hero 1992). Nonetheless, a "tension has been a constant element in nearly two centuries" of relations between Cuba and the United States, due in part to the proximity of the two countries and their intertwined destinies; this tension is bound to be reflected in the orientations and actions of Cuban Americans who retain some political interest in their country of origin (see, e.g., Perez 1990, 364–65).

Other Latinos/Hispanics

These three national-origin groups are the most frequently mentioned Latino groups, but the 1965 immigration reform law triggered major changes in the composition of U.S. Latinos. By 2000, other national-origin groups had grown. The largest of these new groups are from the Dominican Republic and El Salvador, with more than a million having origins in each country, followed by Guatemala and Colombia, each of which has more than 600,000 national-origin coethnics living in the United States (U.S. Census Bureau 2007c, 2). The political effects of this increasing diversification are among the primary foci of this study.

Panethnicity, Racialization, and the "New" Latino/Hispanic Community

How have the growth and diversification of Latino communities across the country—as outlined in chapter 1—changed the ethnoracial context for political incorporation of U.S. Hispanics? Our aim here is not to answer this question in detail but to provide a rough overview that might guide our focus on specific aspects of their political incorporation, to be explored in part 3.

First, there is impressionistic evidence of racialization. For many decades prior to the contemporary period, some Cubans, Central Americans, Puerto Ricans, and Mexican-origin peoples migrated to cities, neighborhoods, and *colonias* that were historically settled by members of other Latino groups, but they were often stigmatized by non-Latino residents without regard to national origin. For example, Puerto Ricans, Cubans, Salvadorans, and Guatemalans (particularly those with darker skin tones and other Indian phenotypical features) living in Southern California have routinely been perceived and treated as Mexicans by non-Latino residents, their demurrals notwithstanding. Similarly, Mexicans, Salvadorans, Cubans, and Guatemalans living in predominantly Puerto

Rican neighborhoods in the Northeast have also been routinely tagged as Puerto Ricans. In this regard, Latino racialization has been similar to that experienced by Asian Americans.

Reinforcing this tendency have been four decades of U.S. Census practices, and those of reporters, academics, and political leaders, all of whom often use a panethnic label to identify Americans with roots in Latin America and the Spanish-speaking Caribbean. A 2006 national survey of U.S. Hispanics found that nearly two-thirds of all Latinos in the United States hold a tripartite group identity: 65 percent identifying as "Americans," 84 percent holding a national-origin self-identity, and 87 percent holding a panethnic "Latino" or "Hispanic" identity (Fraga et al. 2006, slide 6). These findings are held strongly among all the national-origin groups in the survey. This level of panethnic identity is substantially higher than in a similar survey taken in 1989 (de la Garza et al. 1992). It appears that a genuine panethnic identity has grown among Hispanics/Latinos, even as their national-origin identity has persisted.

It is unknown whether the primarily national-origin racialization effects of the past will carry into the future. There is some evidence in the 2006 National Latino Survey that this might be the case, at least for self-identification. More than two-thirds of the survey's respondents identified as members of the Census Bureau's category of "some other race" (i.e., "other" than Black, White, or Asian), and "fully 51% of respondents say Latino/Hispanic is a different race" unto itself. Only 23 percent identified themselves racially as White (Fraga et al. 2006, slide 21). The outlier group is Cuban Americans: about half continue to identify racially as White (Fraga et al. 2006, slide 22). The *meaning* of this racial self-identification remains to be analyzed, so it is yet unknown if it reflects personal experiences of racialization. In any case, it is already clear that the huge increase in immigration from Latin American and Spanish-speaking Caribbean countries has brought dramatic changes in the composition and self-identification of Latino/Hispanic communities all across the country.

Asian Americans and Racialization

As with Latinos, the racialization of Asian Americans highlights the critical role played by the state. Leaders of the anti-Asian forces found it necessary to enlist the coercive powers of government in their quest to marginalize and demonize Asian immigrants.

Asians came to what is now the United States by at least the late eighteenth century, but substantial immigration did not begin until the mid–nineteenth century.[5] The Chinese constituted the first major Asian immigrant stream, followed by growing numbers of Japanese immigrants and smaller numbers of Koreans, Filipinos, and Sikhs (Chan 1991). While Chinese (and Asians more broadly) remained a small portion of the country's population, they quickly established a substantial presence in the California labor force, making up perhaps one-quarter of the available labor force for hire in 1870 (Saxton 1971, chap. 1). Anti-Chinese hostility was muted at first, but racial prejudice and fear of economic competition soon led to efforts to stop Chinese immigration and to make life difficult for the Chinese who had already immigrated.

As early as 1852, the California legislature passed the Foreign Miners License tax. The tax required payments from all miners who did not wish to become citizens, which made Chinese miners an easy target, given that they were widely seen as part of the class of individuals ineligible for citizenship (Parrillo 1982; Chan 1991; Takaki 1998). In 1860, the United States passed a tax of $4 a month on Chinese fishermen, in an effort to discourage them (Tsai 1986, 24). In 1873, the San Francisco Board of Supervisors enacted fees on laundries that charged for each horse used, but placed the heaviest charges on laundries that used no horses—and it was Chinese-owned laundries that usually used no horses (Chan 1991, 46; McClain 1994, 47–50).

The watershed measure, though, was the Chinese Exclusion Act (1882). The first broad immigration restriction law, it gave legal backing to the notion that Chinese were an undesirable and inferior subpopulation. The American political structure had been shaped in fundamental ways by efforts to deny political power to African Americans and American Indians (e.g., Fuchs 1990; Goldfield 1997; Smith 1997), but Asians were not considered when the earliest racial discrimination was built into the American political system. The Chinese Exclusion Act made it clear that domestic systems of racial subordination could be extended to newcomers as well.

The Chinese Exclusion Act suspended the immigration of Chinese laborers for ten years. The Geary Act (1892) extended the ban for another ten years and made it easier to deport Chinese already in the United States (Daniels 1988). By then, however, immigration restrictions had already dramatically reduced Chinese immigration (Hing 1993), and attention turned to a new source of Asian immigrants: Japan. Other Asian immigrants were arriving by the early twentieth century—e.g., Koreans and Asian Indians—but Japanese were more often the target of exclusionists, largely because Japanese were far more numerous (Melendy 1981 [1977], 133–34).

Japanese had been migrating to the United States in small numbers until 1884, when the Japanese government began allowing laborers to emigrate. That same year, the Japanese government and Hawaiian sugar plantation owners signed an agreement allowing the plantation owners to bring in Japanese laborers (Chuman 1976, 10; Daniels 1988, 100). Other Japanese headed to the U.S. West Coast, and the Japanese population grew in the 1880s and 1890s. Prejudice against the Japanese mounted, and in 1906, the San Francisco board of education passed a resolution calling for the Japanese schoolchildren to attend segregated schools with the Chinese (Chuman 1976, chap. 2; Daniels 1988, chap. 4). Like the Chinese before them, Japanese immigrants were being racialized as an inferior and undesirable group.

Government action against the Japanese posed a greater problem than anti-Chinese measures, however. Although restrictions on Japanese immigration seemed inevitable, the growing Japanese military power made it preferable that it be done in a way that did not seem blatantly insulting, and so the Gentlemen's Agreement allowed the Japanese government to save face by administering the immigration restrictions themselves, through refusing to issue passports for travel to the United States (Daniels 1988).[6]

Public policy toward Asian immigrants was influenced by both economic interests and racial prejudice (e.g., Saxton 1971; Modell 1971; Bonacich 1984; Gyory 1998; Gains and Cho 2004). Employers in need of substantial numbers of laborers often favored more immigration. In Hawaii, for instance, the sugar plantations' voracious need for workers led planters to support substantial Asian immigration, striving not for an adequate number of laborers but for a surplus that could help lower wages and combat labor militancy (Takaki 1998, chap. 4; Liu 1984, 202–4). The president was given the power to stop Japanese from migrating from Hawaii to the mainland, allowing Hawaiian plantations to continue recruiting Japanese while preventing those laborers from making a secondary migration to California or other parts of the continental United States.

In California, White miners and others sought to squelch a source of stiff competition, although California also had some who sought more Japanese labor (Kitano 1976; Melendy 1984; Takaki 1998). Contemporary scholars disagree over the extent to which anti-Asian sentiment was driven by economic interests or by racism (e.g., Gyory 1998; Lyman 2000), but there is no question that anti-Asian forces succeeded in passing a number of discriminatory measures.

The most important economic measures were probably the alien land law acts. Japanese immigrants had ended up on farms far more than the Chinese, and the former had enjoyed spectacular success in areas previously considered to be desert. For many Japanese American families, agriculture had the potential for offering a path to substantial economic advancement, at least until state governments moved to shut off that route. California was once again the pioneer, passing the first legislation restricting alien land ownership in 1913 (Chuman 1976, chap. 3; Chan 1991). As with many other discriminatory measures, the law ostensibly singled out no specific group, as it applied to all "aliens ineligible to citizenship." In fact, of course, this meant Asian immigrants; and, in the specific California context, it would have the greatest potential effect on Japanese immigrants, who had been establishing a growing presence in agriculture (Daniels 1988; Chan 1991).[7] Over the next 15 years, several states followed with similar laws (Chan 1991, 47).

In 1917, Congress passed the Barred Zone Act, which sought to ban all immigration from Asia. China, Japan, and the Philippines were not included, however, the first two because they fell under the provisions of earlier legislation or international agreements, and the latter because the Philippines was under the control of the United States. Filipinos were considered to be American nationals, although not American citizens. Seven years later, the Immigration Act of 1924 (also known as the Johnson-Reed Act) provided for even more sweeping immigration restrictions, including banning the remaining Japanese immigration, although Filipinos remained beyond its provisions (Hing 1993).

Filipinos became an increasingly important exception. With immigration greatly restricted from the rest of Asia, employers turned to the Philippines for labor (Melendy 1981, 3–4; Takaki 1998, 318). The Filipino population on the mainland soared from 401 in 1910 to 45,208 by 1930 (Takaki 1998, 315), and by the early 1930s anti-Filipino forces were exerting pressure on Congress to take steps to cut off Filipino immigration. In 1934, Congress passed the Tydings-McDuffie Act, which made the Philippines a commonwealth, with full independence to come in ten years, but with the immediate effect of classifying Filipinos as aliens, ending their status as American nationals and making them subject to the ban on immigration from Asia.

As with African Americans and Latinos, Asian Americans did not simply accept discriminatory treatment. Although they suffered many setbacks, Asian immigrants repeatedly struggled against oppressive treatment (e.g., Chan 1991, chap. 5; McClain and McClain 1991; Lien 2001, chap. 1). For instance, from the latter half of the nineteenth century, Asian workers engaged in periodic strikes to protest working conditions or other grievances (e.g. Takaki 1998, 321–24), while others filed lawsuits seeking to overturn discriminatory laws.

Cases that dealt with questions of naturalization directly addressed the racialization of Asians and helped to highlight the social and political construction of race. While immigration restrictions helped to mark Asians as distinct and unacceptably foreign, they did not deal directly with Asians who had already immigrated to the United States. And, while a strong racial hierarchy was firmly in place (Smith 1997), it had been developed for African Americans and American Indians, leaving the Asian place uncertain in the racial ordering.

Questions about the proper racial classification of Asians arose because racial categories are constructed from a society's particular circumstances. The place of Asians in American racial categories was unclear because those categories were originally constructed for a society that was primarily composed of American Indians, African Americans, and western Europeans. In 1790, Congress had opened naturalization to all "free white persons" without much specification as to who was White (Jacobson 1998, 22). What was clear was that the non-White category encompassed African Americans and American Indians. What could not be determined from the record was whether it also included Asians.

Being declared to be White conveyed obvious advantages, not least of which was the opportunity to naturalize. If Asian immigrants could be prevented from becoming citizens, they would then be vulnerable to a wide range of discriminatory rules—such as laws prohibiting them from owning property.

The first judicial examination of the racial prerequisites for naturalization, *In re Ah Yup* (1878), highlighted one of the central dilemmas facing judges: the lack of literal meaning of the term *white*. The judge accepted Ah Yup's contention that those usually considered to be White are not actually white, but have a wide range of skin tones. However, ruled the judge, both scientific evidence and common knowledge agreed that Chinese were not white (he also concluded that the evidence suggested that Congress did not intend to include Chinese in the "white" category).

To an observer today, it might seem nonsensical that courts would be asked to decide whether Asians were White. However, as Ian Haney López perceptively notes, this reveals much about our biases today.

> That we now view the court's struggle as quaint or absurd should draw attention to our own historical position. Our response betrays that we are the immediate and largely unquestioning inheritors of the pronouncement that Chinese are not White. . . . The lengthy categorical debates . . . seem ridiculous only because we have fully accepted the categories these cases established. (1996, 55)

Most perplexing to the courts were the cases involving individuals from areas to the west of east Asia, such as India, Syria, and Armenia. Some courts ruled that Syrians were White, while others ruled that they were not. Courts also sometimes found Armenians and Asian Indians to be White, and other times found them to be non-White. "During this period, 'white' was a highly unstable legal category, subject to contestation, expansion, and contraction" (Haney López 1996, 68).

The most striking evidence of the racialization of Asians came in the first cases to reach the U.S. Supreme Court. In *Ozawa v. United States* (1922), the Court cited scientific classification to justify its finding that Asians were not White. The plaintiff, Takao Ozawa, argued that the color of his skin and his life history made him indisputably White. The Supreme Court rejected that argument, ruling that popular opinion clearly understood "White" to mean the "Caucasian" race, while scientists found that Japanese were members of the "Mongolian" race (Lyman 1991, 207–8; Haney López 1996, 80–86).

But only three months after *Ozawa*, the Court abandoned its reliance on scientific opinion, revealing how fully race was a social construction. In *Thind v. United States* (1923), Bhagat Singh Thind drew on the supposedly scientific evidence to argue for his right to naturalize. A native of India, Thind noted that he was classified by anthropologists as "Caucasian," not "Mongoloid." The Court, however, refused to accept that Asian Indians and Europeans could be placed in the same racial category. Rejecting the scientific views that it had cited in *Ozawa*, the Court now cited "familiar observation and knowledge" to rule against Thind. In other words, because most people believed that Thind was not White, he was not White (Haney López 1996, 86–91). For the Court, it would seem, the key point was that individuals from Asia were not acceptable members of the American community.

As the United States became increasingly involved in world affairs, however, foreign policy concerns influenced official racialization. Once China became an ally of the United States, many leaders sought to soften discriminatory treatment toward Chinese Americans, although actual change was modest, as Congress seemed more concerned with countering Japanese appeals in Asia than with improving the fortunes of Asian immigrants in America. In 1943, Congress passed a bill that repealed Chinese exclusion and allowed Chinese immigrants to naturalize, but it allowed only 105 Chinese immigrants per year. In 1946, immigration was allowed from India and the Philippines, and immigrants from those countries were also permitted to naturalize (Daniels 1988; Chan 1991; Takaki 1998).

World War II brought modest improvements for many Asians, but conditions worsened dramatically for Japanese Americans. Over 100,000 were sent to "relocation camps," on the grounds of a loosely specified "military necessity" (Petersen 1971, 67–68). However, Hawaii saw no such mass evacuation, although the "military necessity" would presumably be much greater, given its small land mass, greater proximity to Japan, and presence of critical military bases. In fact, military officials were aware that Japan lacked the capability to launch a full-scale attack on North America (Daniels 1988, 201–2). A naval intelligence officer had even organized a break-in at the Japanese consulate in Los Angeles, where they discovered that Japanese officials felt that Japanese Americans "were not to be relied upon for anything important" (Daniels 1988, 212). Even Federal Bureau of Investigation director J. Edgar Hoover, not known for excessive concerns for civil liberties, saw no threat from most Japanese Americans and did not believe that a mass relocation was justified (Takaki 1998, 386). However, the racialized Japanese Americans were easy targets for those who viewed them as unalterably alien. General John L. DeWitt, who oversaw the removal of Japanese Americans from the West Coast, testified before Congress that "A Jap's a Jap. They are a dangerous element, whether loyal or not" (quoted in Melendy 1984, 158).

In the wake of World War II, discriminatory public policy gradually eased. A turnaround in international affairs led to an end to official condemnations of Japanese, as Japan became an ally, while China became an enemy. Most notable was the Immigration and Nationality Act of 1952 (McCarran-Walter Act), which lifted the prohibition against the immigration and naturalization of Asians, although it also made it easier to deport aliens for ideological or moral reasons (Daniels 1988, 305). And, while Asian Americans in general, and Japanese Americans in particular, were seeing statutory discrimination diminishing, Chinese Americans faced growing suspicions and prejudice, as mainland China came to be seen as an enemy of the United States.

But, at the same time, the racialization of Asian Americans was taking a turn that few would have predicted a decade or two earlier. Although still viewed by many as pariahs and fundamentally alien, the most vicious stereotypes were losing some support. In the 1940s and 1950s, public perceptions of Asian Americans were gradually changing (Chan 1991, 141).[8] Although racist views of Asian Americans remained widespread, a new stereotype was beginning to emerge: the model minority.

The symbolic beginnings of the model minority image are usually dated to 1966, when articles lauding Japanese and Chinese Americans appeared in the *New York Times Magazine* and *U.S. News & World Report* (Petersen 1966; "Success Story" 1966). Further laudatory stories emerged in the early 1980s (Osajima 1988), focusing largely on the new Asian immigrants. Although in some ways dramatically different than previous stereotypes, this too racialized Asian Americans, ignoring a vast array of differences and the substantial numbers of poorly educated Asian Americans who lived in poverty. Although the model minority image was a very positive one, many of its proponents seemed as interested in criticizing African Americans as in praising Asians. The *U.S. News* piece emphasized how Chinese Americans had succeeded without government assistance, pointedly noting that other groups were asking for "billions of dollars" in assistance. A few decades later, neoconservatives criticized multicultural education by arguing that earlier Asian immigrants had excelled academically without multiculturalism (e.g., Decter 1991; Glazer 1991). Further evidence of their continued racialization could be found in the continuing perception of Asian Americans as foreign. Even the third-generation Asian Americans—who frequently spoke no language other than English—continued to have Whites ask them what country they were from.

The Development of Asian American Panethnicity

Ironically, increasing assimilation of Asian Americans helped to sharpen the sense of what they shared, and how those shared characteristics distinguished them from White Americans. Although the post-1965 immigration may have weakened the sense of a common identity, research indicates that it survives, although more as a secondary rather than primary identity.

This sense of Asian American panethnicity was not widely held prior to the 1960s. Although there were some notable cases of intergroup alliances, such as interethnic labor coalitions in Hawaii (Takaki 1998), most immigrants identified in terms of their nation of origin, for example, Chinese Americans or Japanese Americans, rather than Asian Americans. Although the term *Orientals* was understood to refer at least to all with roots in east Asia, daily life was organized around ethnic groupings. For example, Japanese Americans might worship in Protestant or Buddhist churches, but primarily with other Japanese Americans, while Chinese Americans established their own congregations. This is hardly surprising, as immigrant groups have usually been most likely to congregate with fellow nationals or, in some cases, with those who come from the same region of their native country.

By the mid-1960s, however, the large number of third-generation Chinese and Japanese Americans were reaching adulthood. Like the third generation of most ethnic groups, they had little contact with their grandparents' native land, and, in many cases, spoke little if any of the grandparents' native language. Growing up, they had discovered that bigots made no ethnic distinctions in their choice of racial slurs: most Japanese Americans had been called *chinks,* and most Chinese Americans had been labeled *japs* at some point in their lives. As the Vietnam War grew, Asian Americans of all ethnicities heard the term *gook* added to the racist vocabulary, a word originally meant as a derogatory term for Vietnamese.

For many young Asian Americans, the lesson seemed clear: the racism they faced bound them together far more strongly than the distinctions that had separated their grandparents in the distant past. For immigrants of the early twentieth century, Japanese and Chinese may have seemed far too different to intermingle, but for those whose entire lives—and whose parents' entire lives—had been spent in the United States, those differences meant little. Far more important was the fact that Asian Americans of all ancestries faced common foes of stereotypes, discrimination, and invisibility.

Inspired by other movements, especially the civil rights efforts of African Americans, young Asian Americans began joining together. Opposition to the Vietnam War was one important bond, as many Asian American activists came to see the war as racially motivated against people who looked like them. The invisibility of Asian Americans in college curricula was another important rallying point and helped galvanize students into what was sometimes called the Asian American Movement and at other times was known as Yellow Power (Ho 2000; Okihiro and Liu 1988; Wei 1993). Spreading the word through Asian American civil society, supporters of a pan-Asian American identity advocated for *Asian American* to replace *Oriental,* and for a panethnic perspective to supplant the ethnic-based ones that had been dominant.

However, just as they were succeeding in establishing a pan-Asian identity, immigration from Asia began to mushroom, bringing newcomers for whom such a panethnic identity was a foreign idea. Acceptance varied, depending on characteristics of each immigrant community (Hein 2006), but the large number of newcomers made it certain that ethnic ties would continue to be important for many Americans of Asian ancestry. For individuals who had grown up overseas, national differences continued to be important.

Pan-Asian American identity continued to persist, however. Ubiquitous race-reporting requirements quickly showed immigrants from Asia that they were classified as "Asian Americans," and children were increasingly likely to hear the term in school. Furthermore, new groups often adopted names that reflected a panethnic orientation—e.g., the National Asian Pacific American Legal Consortium—while older, ethnic-based groups, such as the Organization of Chinese Americans, often joined panethnic coalitions.

Evidence today suggests that a panethnic identity continues to be widely held, although often as a secondary rather than primary identity. One of the most sophisticated investigations of this was done in the Pilot National Asian American Political Survey (PNAAPS), which allowed respondents to reply in their native language, thereby allowing for a much better sample than possible with surveys conducted only in English (Lien, Conway, and Wong 2004). The PNAAPS found that around two-thirds of respondents were most likely to identify in ethnic (e.g., Vietnamese) or "ethnic American" (e.g., Vietnamese American) terms, and only about a fifth identified in panethnic terms (Asian or Asian American). However, among those who identified with ethnic or ethnic American labels, around half said they sometimes identified themselves as Asian Americans, reflecting the multiple ways that people can think about themselves (Lowe 1991). Furthermore, around half of the respondents felt that there were many similarities between Asian American groups, and that what happened to Asian Americans of other ethnicities would affect them as well (Lien, Conway, and Wong 2004, chap. 2). The PNAAPS data suggests that panethnic identification continues to be widespread, although many Asian Americans are likely to identify first with their ethnic group.

Racialization and the New Immigrants

By the late 1960s, then, new immigrants came to a country deeply steeped in a legacy of racialization. Circumstances varied widely, however. The earlier Asian immigrants had faced sweeping discrimination, but their relatively fewer numbers may have helped improve their economic opportunities, as it created less competition for the few niches open to them. African Americans, in contrast, had not only experienced an extensive array of de jure and de facto discrimination but were present in such large numbers as to overwhelm the few sectors open to them. Latino immigrant experiences also varied considerably with the historical circumstances surrounding their migration. The first waves of Cuban immigrants (in the early 1960s), for instance, were fortunate to experience a favorable reception (Portes and Rumbaut 2001, 262); at the other end of the spectrum were Mexican Americans during the Great Depression, who faced intense discriminatory treatment, including illegal deportation to Mexico (Hero 1992, 35).

To assess this more carefully, it is helpful to look at some examples of the concrete legacy of racialization. Perhaps the most significant and obvious case is racial segregation. Segregation has long been seen as an important bulwark of racialization. The very act of racial segregation can help to create the racial stigma that is essential to racialization. Perhaps more important, however, is that tremendous disadvantages often accompany racial segregation. These disadvantages can then be used as justification for further racialization and discrimination. In the next chapter, therefore, we offer an extensive discussion of the degrees to which ethnoracial segregation, as well as ethnoracial economic inequality, remain continuing patterns in this era of large-scale immigration.

4 | The Persistence of Racial Segregation in a Diverse America

As noted in the introduction to part 2, we believe that it is impossible to understand the impacts of recent immigrants on American ethnoracial politics without understanding the historical and social contexts within which these two dynamic political forces are interacting. In the previous chapter we provided some *historical* context for contemporary events by summarizing the impact of racialization on the development of our three primary ethnoracial communities, U.S. Blacks, Latinos, and Asian Americans.

In this chapter, our aim is to illuminate the effects of recent immigration on ethnoracial politics in the United States by exploring several important aspects of the *social context* of these interactions. There is, of course, a wide range of important ways in which social context structures and shapes ethnoracial politics, among which are the amount and nature of social capital available to various population subgroups and communities (see, e.g., Hero 2007); the distribution of economic assets, opportunities, and risks; the distribution of educational resources and opportunities; public attitudes toward various ethnoracial, immigrant, and other groups; the shaping and reshaping of such public attitudes by the media; and too many more to be listed here.

Since here we could only discuss a tiny fraction of the ways in which social contexts are important for understanding the effects of recent immigration on American ethnoracial politics, we have decided to focus on two aspects that we believe are foundationally important influences on racial politics in the United States—residential and educational segregation. In doing so, we take our lead from Massey and Denton, whose *American Apartheid* (1993) presented a bleak portrait of a country that is stubbornly segregated by race, despite years of civil rights legislation aimed at undermining this long-standing reality. Their compelling analysis of the country's apartheid-like situation explained that for White immigrants, residential segregation and ethnic enclaves were temporary, transitional stages in the process of immigrant assimilation, while residential isolation of Blacks, who moved north during the Great Migration, became a permanent part of Black life (Massey and Denton 1993).

Even though there had been some improvement in the overall measures of racial segregation, Massey and Denton's work demonstrated that Blacks remained consistently the most racially isolated group in American society, historically bereft of the resources necessary for socioeconomic mobility. In this chapter, then, we assess the extent to which demographic changes, wrought by the influx of large numbers of immigrants—especially Asians, Latinos, and nonnative Blacks from Africa and the Caribbean—have altered historical patterns of residential segregation as well as school segregation in American society. To supplement this description of ongoing segregation, we also assess the extent of differences in poverty rates and median family incomes between native and immigrant groups. All of these trends will help us to assess the ways in which greater racial and ethnic diversity in the United States seems to have affected the social integration of Americans from different racial and ethnic backgrounds.

In focusing on racial segregation in neighborhoods and schools, we agree with Massey and Denton, as well as scores of other scholars, that racial segregation is not merely a moral dilemma. Instead, it has important implications for the viability of democracy in the United States in several important ways. First, historically, racial segregation in the United States has been marked consistently by a large degree of involuntary social exclusion, and as well has been accompanied by deep-seated social, economic, and political inequality. This is so because segregation systematically blocks opportunities for access to the most crucial mechanisms of socioeconomic mobility, including effective and safe educational resources, viable employment opportunities, and high-quality housing. At the same time, residential segregation means that Blacks (and perhaps other racialized minorities) are unable to translate educational and employment successes into desirable housing choices in ways similar to their non-Black counterparts. As Massey has summarized the point, there is a "close connection between a group's spatial position in society and its socioeconomic well-being" (2000, 44; see also Bobo and Zubrinsky 1996; Farley et al. 1994).

The data presented in this chapter will allow us to update the degree to which Blacks remain segregated relative to other groups, to examine the extent to which immigrant Blacks experience similar levels of racial segregation, and to explore the extent to which Asians and Latinos also experience patterns of segregation similar to that of Blacks. In doing so, our analysis of racial residential segregation will serve as a proxy for measuring the extent to which Blacks, Asians, and Latinos have been socially incorporated over the last four decades, the period of the new immigration.

Toward that end, we investigate how patterns of Black-White segregation have changed over time, and whether Latinos and Asian Americans have experienced levels of segregation that are similar to Blacks. We also discuss the implications of residential segregation for social incorporation in America by focusing specifically on the economic standing of native-born versus foreign-born Whites, Blacks, Latinos, and Asians during the last two decades as a way of discussing the extent to which immigration has affected the socioeconomic outcomes of native groups.

Although analyses of racial segregation raise a host of methodological questions and concerns regarding measurement strategies, we intentionally steer around the question of analyzing statistically the independent effects of the new immigration on racial segregation. Addressing such an analysis would take years and massive amounts of data, most of which are uncollected. Rather, here we focus on addressing the broader question of what changes have occurred in residential segregation within the context of post-1965 immigration, and whether or not Latinos and Asian Americans—groups hugely impacted by immigration—are racially segregated in ways that are similar to or different from their Black counterparts.

By focusing on context, we join the rich tradition of contextual analysis, undergirded by the rationale that place and context structure sociopolitical processes, attitudes, and behaviors in important and relevant ways (Huckfeldt 1986; Alex-Assensoh 1998). The underlying rationale of contextual analysis is that the environments in which individuals live, work, get an education, worship, and network have important political consequences above and beyond the effects of individual behavior. A contextual effect exists when individual, intrinsic explanations alone cannot account for systematic variation in behavior across environments (Huckfeldt and Sprague 1995). This chapter contends, then, that variations in demographic contexts across region, time, and ethnoracial group are important in understanding trends in racial segregation as well as the implications of these trends for social outcomes. We also contend that understanding these contextual factors will better enable us to grasp the ways in which the new immigration is changing ethnoracial politics in the United States.

Exploring Trends in Racial Segregation over the Last Three Decades

The central question to be addressed here is whether the recent decades of high immigration from Latin America and Asia, as well as from Africa and Caribbean countries with high percentages of African-origin peoples, have altered the patterns of the past in relation to residential and school segregation along racial lines. Have the past four decades seemed to continue the pattern of "Black exceptionalism," with high segregation for Black Americans, but not for immigrants, even those from non-European countries such as those in Latin America, the Caribbean, and Asia? Or has the prevalence of large numbers of non-White immigrants in recent decades altered this pattern, generating new segregated ghettoes of a more mixed pattern of peoples of color? What about the experiences of immigrants with origins in Africa, whether from the Caribbean or from Africa itself?

The data and discussions that follow are an attempt to answer these questions. We also take note of the timing and scale of immigrants' arrivals in the United States, since residential patterns of segregation would presumably depend to some degree on the size of immigrant cohorts and the political rhetoric associated with several periods of anti-immigrant outbursts over the past four decades.

In the sections that follow, we examine and assess the trends in racial and ethnic residential segregation from 1970 to 2000. This analysis will provide an opportunity to test alternative answers to our central question about the extent to which racial segregation has changed or remained the same, within the context of post-1965 immigration. The data to test our propositions come largely from the decennial censuses over the last four decades. We focus largely on metropolitan statistical areas, which include both central cities and suburban areas, because unlike earlier nineteenth- and twentieth-century immigration, which included rural and urban areas as primary destinations, the major growth in immigrant populations is occurring in central city and especially suburban communities (Logan 2003a).

Residential Segregation in the Context of Growing Racial and Ethnic Diversity

The United States has become a more racially and ethnically diverse society over the last four decades, as discussed in chapter 1. Population growth among Asians, Latinos, and Blacks, fueled by higher birthrates and post-1965 immigration, has outpaced that of non-Hispanic Whites. Two groups—Asians and Latinos—have experienced remarkable growth within the last four decades, especially since 1980. Moreover, Blacks, Asians, and Latinos are more likely than their White counterparts to live in metropolitan areas, where residential segregation is more prevalent. Therefore, metropolitan areas are the most appropriate contexts in which to examine residential segregation and social incorporation among Blacks, Asians, and Latinos over the last four decades.

We describe trends and patterns of racial segregation in 11 of America's largest metropolitan areas over the last four decades[1] (Iceland, Weinberg, and Steinmetz 2002) against the backdrop of an increasing influx of Asians, Blacks, and Latinos. Even though the immigrant population has grown significantly over the last four decades, the growth is concentrated in particular regions, leaving several areas of the United States virtually untouched until very recently. For example, a quarter of all immigrants live in 13 of America's largest metropolitan areas: Los Angeles–Long Beach, New York, Chicago, Miami, Houston, Orange County, Washington, D.C., Riverside–San Bernardino, San Diego, Dallas, Oakland, San Jose, San Francisco (Logan 2003a). Because of data constraints, we focus on 11 of the 13 metropolitan areas, which provide an assessment of racial housing segregation over the last four decades.

Measuring Residential Segregation: The Dissimilarity Index

Although there are many ways to measure housing segregation, the most widely used method is the dissimilarity index.[2] This index characterizes the levels of segregation between pairs of racial and ethnic groups within a metropolitan area. The values of the dissimilarity index range from 0 to 100. The maximum value indicates that the groups being compared live in completely different neighborhoods, which means that they are completely residentially segregated. In contrast, the minimum value of 0 indicates that the racial and ethnic groups are randomly distributed across neighborhoods, which means that they are residentially integrated. The scores between 0 and 100 reflect the percentage of one group that would have to move to a different neighborhood in order to be residentially distributed in the same way as the other group. In this vein, a White-Black dissimilarity score of 60 percent means that 60 percent of Blacks would have to change neighborhoods to be distributed like Whites.

According to Massey and Denton, European ethnic groups have rarely scored higher than 60 percent on the dissimilarity index, so scores above that range are considered to be high. Scores between 30 and 60 percent are considered as moderate, while a dissimilarity score below 30 percent reflects a low level of residential segregation. Table 4.1 displays the scores for each of the examined ethnoracial groups from the 1970s to 2000.

Black-White Residential Segregation in Metropolitan America

As table 4.1 demonstrates, among Blacks the dissimilarity index reflects the historically high levels of racial segregation in all metropolitan areas, with dissimilarity scores well above the 60 percent mark that few European ethnic groups ever reached. Indeed, high levels of residential segregation among Blacks were common across all cities from the 1970s to 2000, with the lone exception of Riverside, California. There, the level of segregation has remained moderate, ranging from a high of 53 percent in the 1980s to a low of 45 percent in 2000. At the same time, however, there were small declines in racial segregation between 1980 and 1990 and somewhat larger declines between 1990 and 2000. The declines have taken place in the context of long and consistent patterns of Black residential segregation in the United States, coupled with the increased immigration of Blacks from the Caribbean and Africa.

In addition to the high but decreasing levels of residential segregation, the dissimilarity index for African Americans also points to an interesting pattern of regional differences. For example, levels of residential segregation among Blacks in Southern and Western metropolitan areas like Houston, Dallas, Washington, D.C., Riverside, and San Francisco are somewhat lower than those found in Northern and Midwestern metropolitan areas. The dissimilarity indices for metropolitan areas in the South and West tend to cluster around 60 percent compared with the higher ranges of 70 and 90 percent in Northern and Eastern cities. These findings are consistent with previous studies of Black-White segregation, which showed regional differences in Black-White segregation (Frey and Myers 2005; Frey and Farley 1996; Taeuber and Taeuber 1965; Massey and Denton 1987; Iceland 2004; Logan, Stults, and Farley 2004).

The slow but steady decline in residential segregation among Blacks, as measured by the dissimilarity index, can be attributed to a number of factors. For example, the civil rights movement ushered in an array of revolutionary legislation that, when implemented and enforced, led to an increase in the size of the Black middle class as well as a less supportive environment for the practice of racial discrimination in the real estate and

TABLE 4.1. Residential Segregation for Blacks, Hispanics, and Asians: Dissimilarity Indexes for 1970, 1980, 1990, and 2000

Metropolitan Area	Blacks				Hispanics				Asians			
	1970	1980	1990	2000	1970	1980	1990	2000	1970	1980	1990	2000
Chicago, IL	92	88	84	80	58	64	62	61	56	45	44	42
Dallas–Fort Worth, TX	87	77	63	59	43	49	50	54	44	—	—	—
Houston, TX	78	75	66	66	45	50	50	55	43	42	46	48
Los Angeles, CA	91	81	73	69	47	57	61	63	53	47	46	48
Miami, FL	85	79	69	69	50	53	50	44	—	—	—	—
Newark, NJ	81	83	83	80	60	67	67	65	50	31	31	36
New York, NY	81	81	81	81	65	65	66	67	56	49	48	51
Philadelphia, PA	80	78	77	72	54	63	62	60	49	40	43	44
Riverside–San Bernardino, CA	—	53	44	45	37	38	36	43	32	29	33	36
San Francisco–Oakland, CA	80	68	64	60	35	46	50	54	49	51	50	48
Washington, DC	81	69	65	63	32	32	43	48	37	32	26	38

Source: U.S. Census data calculated by the Lewis Mumford Center, http://mumford.albany.edu/census/. The data for 1970 are from Massey 1987.

Note: — = no data.

banking industries. At the same time, the context of post-1965 immigration is also an important explanatory factor because other demographic studies have shown that declines in Black-White segregation have occurred in areas where more than one racial minority group has had a substantial presence (Frey and Farley 1996). Hence, the influx of Latinos, Asians, and even nonnative Blacks appears to have a moderating influence on the racial segregation that Blacks have historically endured. The post-1965 immigration of Asians and Latinos has contributed to the emergence of metropolitan melting pot areas in which racial and ethnic minority groups make up a substantial proportion of the population as compared with a dwindling number of Whites. It is in these racially mixed metropolitan contexts that the Black-White segregation has declined.

The decline in residential segregation among Blacks is also a result of the residential preferences of some West Indian and African Blacks that are shaped by the existing racial hierarchy. In contrast to Asian and Latino immigrants, for whom existing ethnic networks serve as magnets for newer immigrants (Lieberson 1980; Philpott 1978; Zhou 1992), West Indian as well as African Blacks understand the historical stigma attached to being Black in the United States and therefore go to great lengths to differentiate themselves from native-born Blacks in terms of residence, culture, and speech patterns (Waters 1999). Recent studies of West Indian housing preferences have underscored the fact that, unlike their native Black counterparts, many West Indian immigrants have the "ethnic option" of choosing housing accommodations in higher-quality neighborhoods, ones that are racially changing rather than all Black. For example, West Indians in New York are concentrated in a particular set of neighborhoods with a distinctively Caribbean character, such that the reported dissimilarity score between West Indians and Africans as examined during the 1990 census was 43 percent (Crowder 1999). As a consequence, West Indians are not evenly distributed within existing Black communities; rather, there are separate pockets of West Indian neighborhood populations, which are based on ethnic rather than racial affinity.

Latino-White Segregation in Metropolitan America

The dissimilarity scores for Latinos reflect residential segregation among a group whose population has grown rapidly since the 1960s, largely as a result of increased immigration. As a result, Latinos have now replaced Blacks as the largest racial minority group in the country. Although Blacks are more diverse than is often recognized, the Latino population is much more diverse in terms of skin color, ethnicity, and country of origin. More than half of all Latinos are of Mexican origin, but the panethnic group also includes Puerto Ricans, Cubans, and groups from South and Central America, and other islands in the Caribbean (see chaps. 1, 3, this vol.; Guzman 2001; Frey and Myers 2005). Moreover, the Hispanic/Latino population is becoming increasingly diverse in all areas of the country and is becoming a noticeable presence in all parts of the country, with specific national-origin groups less likely to be solely concentrated in specific regions (chap. 1, this vol.). The influx of increasing numbers of Cubans and South Americans over the past 40 years has also helped to diversify the class backgrounds of U.S. Latinos (see, e.g., Logan 2002).

Research on Latino settlement patterns has revealed that until very recently, Latinos initially were more likely to settle in large, port-of-entry metropolitan areas than were other groups. Historically, Puerto Rican migrants were most likely to settle in the Northeast, Mexican immigrants in the Southwest, and Cubans in Florida, but again, these patterns have begun to change rapidly in very recent years, with Latinos now settling in significant numbers in smaller metropolitan areas and in the Midwest and South, as well as the Northwest (see chaps. 1, 3, this vol.; Frey 2001; Frey and Meyers 2005).

Residential segregation among Latinos reflects a picture that contrasts significantly with Blacks. In contrast to Blacks, who have experienced consistently high levels of residential segregation, the dissimilarity index for Latinos reflects a lower level of residential segregation that rarely crosses the 65 percent threshold. There is also more variation across the decades in Latino-White segregation than was evident among Blacks. For example, during the 1970s, residential segregation among Latinos was moderate, ranging between 30 and 60 percent. Since then, many cities have higher levels of Latino-White segregation, ranging from 50 to 65 percent.

Although Latinos differ from Blacks in terms of the intensity of residential segregation, table 4.1 does show a similar, though less marked, pattern of regional difference. Latinos are more likely to be residentially segregated in metropolitan areas located in the Northeast, while there is a somewhat lower level of Latino-White residential segregation in the South and much of the West.

Unlike the situation for Blacks, Latino-White residential segregation has increased consistently since the 1970s. In this sense, Latino-White segregation is distinct from Asian-White as well as Black-White segregation in the consistency and size of residential segregation over the last four decades. Researchers (e.g., Massey 2000) suggest that the increased level of Latino immigration since the late 1960s is an important factor in explaining the increase in Latino residential segregation. Whether continued Latino immigration will continue to increase the degree of this group's residential segregation in the future, or whether Latinos will follow the residential patterns of White ethnics in earlier periods of high immigration by integrating into nonethnic neighborhoods and suburbs, cannot be answered at this time.

Asian-White Residential Segregation in Metropolitan America

Table 4.1 also presents the dissimilarity scores for Asian Americans. As discussed in chapters 1 and 3, Asian Americans, like Latinos, comprise a very diverse group incorporating a wide range of people from different countries, languages, and cultural traditions. In metropolitan areas, the largest Asian groups include the Chinese, Filipinos, and Indians. Koreans, Vietnamese, and Japanese also inhabit metropolitan areas in significant numbers, although in smaller proportions than the aforementioned groups. Equally important is the fact that Asian groups tend to vary in terms of geographic settlement patterns, so residential segregation patterns typically reflect concentrations of different Asian ethnic groups within different metropolitan areas (Frey and Myers 2005).

The data on Asian American segregation in table 4.1 indicate considerable variation—both up and down—over time in many of the metropolitan areas studied, and this varied pattern may reflect a number of factors that we are unable to analyze here. Among these potential influencing factors are variations in immigration rates over time from distinct Asian American groups, and movement of immigrants from one area to another (e.g., some refugee populations from South Asia became more concentrated over time in certain cities after initially being dispersed by U.S. refugee authorities, while other Asian immigrants no doubt initially settled in ethnic enclaves and then later took advantage of other housing opportunities as resources became available).

In any case, overall the levels of residential segregation for Asian Americans are considerably lower than those for Latinos and Blacks. Unlike the case for Blacks and Latinos, there was no marked pattern of regional difference in residential segregation for Asian Americans, though they appeared to be slightly less segregated in the West than in other regions. The lower levels of residential segregation for Asians overall may reflect their smaller numbers (perhaps resulting in a lower perception of threat by White Americans), or it may reflect the somewhat higher educational and economic levels of Asian Americans, or both.

Interracial Residential Segregation: Are Asians, Latinos, and Blacks Segregated from One Another?

In addition to our concern about the extent to which racial segregation has varied over the last four decades, there is an equally important question about the extent to which racial minority groups are residentially segregated from one another. Do Blacks, Asians, and Latinos themselves live in neighborhoods that are diverse in terms of the presence of other racial minorities? Is there evidence of consistent segregation among the groups? Although evidence of interminority group residential segregation is hard to come by, table 4.2 provides us with a picture of residential segregation among Asians, Blacks, and Latinos in 11 of the cities examined previously. Specifically, it compares the levels of racial segregation between Blacks and Latinos, Blacks and Asians, and Asians and Latinos, using the index of dissimilarity described earlier.

Interestingly, the levels of residential segregation between Asians and Blacks are high in almost all of the sampled cities, despite region or the demographic composition of the city. For example, Black-Asian segregation is almost 80 percent in New York (a highly diverse, Northeastern city), as well as in Atlanta (a Southern, Black-majority city), and Miami (a Southern, Latino-majority city). Furthermore, residential segregation between Asians and Blacks hovers around the 70 percent mark in Houston, De-

TABLE 4.2. Interracial Segregation in U.S. Metropolitan Areas, 2000 (in percentages)

Metropolitan Area	Black-Latino	Black-Asian	Latino-Asian
New York, NY	57	79	58
Los Angeles, CA	50	62	48
Jersey City, NJ	48	56	36
Houston, TX	57	67	60
Oakland, CA	35	54	48
Atlanta, GA	63	78	51
Detroit, MI	81	72	67
San Antonio, TX	51	42	57
Miami, FL	81	76	45

Source: Lewis Mumford Center, http://mumford.albany.edu/census/WholePop/WPsort/sort_d1.html.

troit, and Miami. The lowest percentage of residential segregation between Asians and Blacks is in Oakland, California, with a dissimilarity index of 54 percent.

To some extent, the high levels of racial segregation between Asians
and Blacks can be explained by geography and class differences. Among
Blacks, Latinos, and Asians, Blacks are least likely to live in suburban communities, while Asians are most likely to live in the suburbs (Logan 2001).
The data compiled by Logan (2001) indicate that 71 percent of non-Hispanic Whites live in the suburbs, as do nearly 60 percent of Asians, fewer
than half of Latinos, and only 39 percent of Blacks. Given this large disparity between Asians' and Blacks' likelihood to reside in suburban communities, it is not surprising that Asians are less segregated from Whites
and more segregated from Blacks.

In contrast, the residential segregation between Blacks and Latinos is
more moderate, reaching the 80 percent mark only in two of the cities
studied here: Black-majority Detroit in the Midwest and the Cuban-dom-
inated city of Miami in the South. Otherwise, residential segregation between Blacks and Latinos hovers primarily within the 50 to 60 percent
range, with the lowest levels of residential segregation found in Oakland at
approximately 35 percent.

The lowest levels of interminority group residential segregation are
found between Latinos and Asians. Apart from Detroit, where the highest
levels of Asian-Latino segregation almost reach 70 percent, and in Jersey
City, where the nadir of Asian-Latino segregation dipped to about 40 percent, the level of residential segregation between Asians and Latinos is
most accurately characterized as moderate. In the other cities, residential
segregation ranges between 50 and 60 percent, across regions and the demographic composition of cities.

Summary: Residential Segregation among Blacks, Asians, and Latinos since the 1970s

We began our analysis with a central question regarding the extent to
which patterns of residential segregation have changed within the context
of post-1965 immigration. In this era of high-level immigration from
"non-White" regions, has residential segregation continued the biracial
pattern of the past, in which Blacks alone were kept segregated? Or has
that pattern changed in the face of high levels of immigration from Latin
America, the Caribbean, Asia, and Africa?

Although it is tempting to dismiss the first alternative, the findings delineated in table 4.1 actually do provide a modicum of support for the proposition that little has changed in the patterns of residential segregation in America. For example, Black-White residential segregation is still disproportionately high, just as it was prior to the onset of post-1965 immigration. Regional patterns of difference in racial segregation from Whites are still evident. Additionally, the residential segregation of Blacks from Whites remains disproportionately and consistently high. In this sense, the major story line of residential segregation of Blacks has changed little over the last four decades, although the cast has become more varied in terms of characters.

At the same time, significant changes *have* occurred in the patterns of residential segregation, indicating that the traditional pattern is not being simply projected into the future. Indeed, the weight of the evidence leans more in the direction of the second alternative, in the sense that significant changes have occurred in the nature and extent of residential segregation in the United States. First, there is now a pecking order of residential segregation, which extends beyond the Black-White paradigm. Though Blacks remain on the bottom of the pecking order, there is evidence of a steady increase in Latino residential segregation, while Asian groups remain solidly in the middle. The context of post-1965 immigration has also added another layer of regional diversity for Latinos, who, like Blacks, are less likely to experience residential segregation in the metropolitan areas located in the South and West. There is also slight evidence that Asians are less likely to be residentially segregated in the West, where they are most likely to reside. This is a pattern that is opposite from Latinos, who appear to be more segregated in the metropolitan areas where they predominate (Frey and Myers 2005, 12–13). In a nutshell, the census data reveal that residential segregation remains the norm of American life even in the context of a multiracial society. Yet, it is more complex and less Black and White, than it was prior to the recent large increase in numbers of immigrants of color from Asia, Latin America, the Caribbean, and Africa.

Racial School Segregation in America from 1970 to 2000

Another important aspect of racial segregation in America is the extent to which children attend racially separate schools. The U.S. Supreme Court's *Plessy v. Ferguson* (1896) decision established the legal framework for racial segregation of Blacks in public accommodations like schools, restaurants, and hotels. Even though Asians and Latinos challenged the application of the law to them as non-Blacks, they were nevertheless subject to its implications (Haney López 1996; Smith 1997). As a result, Blacks but also Asians and Latinos were sent to schools that were separate from their White counterparts. Like racial segregation in housing, racial school segregation is problematic because separation of the races reflects the existence of different educational opportunity structures for Whites and non-Whites. In some cases, non-Whites were not accorded separate facilities, which meant that Black, Latino, and Asian children sometimes went without an education even though White children's education was funded by taxes collected from all population groups. Most commonly, however, it meant that the schools, resources, and opportunities were vastly unequal. This inequality produced a two-tiered system of education in which Whites received the best resources, teachers, and school buildings, while non-Whites were accorded the remnants. Even though the Supreme Court ruled in the 1954 *Brown v. Board of Education* decision that racially separate schools are inherently unequal and unconstitutional, it was not until the late 1960s that significant headway was made in integrating the country's schools. By the end of the 1970s and throughout the 1980s, however, court challenges to racial school desegregation created an impotent mandate for racial integration, and researchers at Harvard University's Civil Rights Project (recently relocated to UCLA) have contended that many of the country's public schools are more racially segregated today than they were prior to the 1954 *Brown v. Board of Education* decision (Lee 2004; Orfield and Lee 2004, 2005, 2006; but see Logan, Oakley, and Stowell 2006, for a dissenting view).

As with the issue of residential segregation, we believe that it is important to assess the degree of continuing racial school segregation because it has profound implications for the political incorporation of ethnoracial minorities in the United States, as well as for our understanding of equality and racial democracy in American society. That is because the initial conflicts that sparked the 1954 *Brown v. Board of Education* decision were not merely about the opportunity for Whites and Blacks to learn together. More important, *Brown* represented a demand that Black children be given equal access to high-quality education without the stigma and consequences of overt racial exclusion. Similar lawsuits were brought on behalf of Asian and Latino children in state and federal courts.

As Orfield and Lee point out, the context for the political struggle over school segregation, seen in the 1950s and 1960s as primarily a Black-White issue, has changed dramatically in recent decades.

Forty years later, however, the nation's schools have changed almost beyond recognition; the white majority is continuously shrinking, and the segregation has taken on a multiracial character. Unfortunately, though generations of students have been born and graduated, segregation is not gone. In fact, in communities that were desegregated in the Southern and Border regions, segregation is increasing; and in regions that were never substantially desegregated, including many metropolitan areas in the Northeast, Midwest, and West, segregation is growing in degree and complexity as the nation becomes increasingly multiracial. The resegregation of blacks is greatest in the Southern and Border states and appears to be clearly related to the Supreme Court decisions in the 1990s permitting return to segregated neighborhood schools. (2006, 4)

For our purposes, it is important to emphasize that the massive immigration from Latin America and Asia that is the basis for our study appears to have had a major impact on segregation in the public schools. From a Black-White issue, mainly discussed in relation to the Southern states, school segregation is now a national problem, and one that is multiracial in nature. Nationally, White students' proportion of those attending public schools has declined significantly, from more than 80 percent in the 1960s to 58 percent in the 2003–4 school year. And nationally by the 2003–4 school year, Black students made up 17 percent of the nation's public school population, while Latinos had increased to 19 percent, and Asian American students made up 4 percent, with wide variations among the country's regions (Orfield and Lee 2006, 8).

In respect to racial segregation in the schools, perhaps the Civil Rights Project's most telling findings have to do with the degree of racial isolation among students in the country's public schools. Thus, in the 2003–4 school year, the average Black student's classmates were 53 percent Black, despite their making up only 17 percent of the country's students. The average Latino student's classmates, meanwhile, were 55 percent Latino, despite their being 19 percent of the country's public school students. The average Asian American student's classmates were 22 percent Asian, with this group constituting only 4 percent of the country's student population. Most striking of all, 78 percent of the average White student's classmates were White, despite the group's decline in the total population of U.S. public school students to 58 percent (Orfield and Lee 2006, 9). This means that despite the continued segregation of U.S. ethnoracial minority students in the country as a whole, White students are the most racially isolated of all student groups.

Orfield and Lee's analysis of contemporary public school segregation uses three measures of racial segregation: schools are designated as "segregated" if more than 50 percent of the students are minority students (i.e., Black, Latino, and/or Asian American), they are "intensely" segregated if more than 90 percent of the students are minority, and they are "apartheid" schools if minorities make up 99 percent or more of the students. Using these measures, the Civil Rights Project's findings show that, nationally, students from all racial minority groups have become more "segregated" or "intensely segregated" in the period from 1991 to 2003–4, as shown in table 4.3. The only category showing a slight diminution (for Black and Asian students, not Latinos) is that of "apartheid" schools, those with minority student bodies in excess than 99 percent.

It is also illuminating to view the changes in levels of segregation in the data comparing regions. Orfield and Lee divide the United States into five regions.[3] Our discussion examines the changes in levels of public school segregation between 1991–92 and 2003–4 for three primary ethnoracial minority groups, divided into these five regions. Table 4.4 presents this data in a composite form. Overall, the findings here continue the theme of this chapter, indicating that Blacks and Latinos, and to a lesser degree Asian Americans, are highly segregated in contemporary American society, despite the increase in racial diversity.

The data in table 4.4 are noteworthy in several respects. First, school segregation among Black students increased in the 12-year period in every region of the country, and only in the Border region does segregation among Black students drop below 70 percent in 2003–4. In contrast, the patterns for Asian and Latino students vary more across regions than is true of that for Blacks, with Asian school segregation ranging from a high of 66 percent in 2003–4 in the West to a low of 25 percent in the Midwest. Segregation levels for Latinos are highest overall but again show a relatively

TABLE 4.3. Changes in Racial School Segregation, 1991–2004, by Minority Group (in percentages)

Ethnoracial Group	Group in 50–100% Minority Schools		Group in 90–100% Minority Schools		Group in 99–100% Minority Schools	
	1991–92	2003–4	1991–92	2003–4	1991–92	2003–4
Black	66	73	34	38	19	17
Latino	73	77	34	39	10	11
Asian American	53	56	13	15	3	1

Source: Data from Orfield and Lee 2006, tables 3–7, from the Civil Rights Project of Harvard University, http://www.civilrightsproject.harvard.edu.

large degree of variation, from a high of 81 percent in 2003–4 in the West to lows in the middle 50th percentiles in the Border and Midwestern regions.

As Orfield and Lee have also demonstrated, there is a close correlation between the segregation of ethnoracial minority students and the degree to which poverty plays a large role in their lives (2005). Thus, minority students who attend segregated schools are more likely to live in segregated neighborhoods, more likely to come from families with incomes below the poverty line, and more likely to attend schools with the least amount of educational resources (adequate school facilities, experienced and well-paid teaching staffs, up-to-date school equipment and books, etc.). Accordingly, the patterns shown here, of increasing residential and school segregation for students of color, especially for Black and Latino students, is indicative of increasing obstacles for social advancement at a time when the percentage of such students in the overall population has been dramatically increasing. It seems highly likely that immigration has played an important role in the evolution of these patterns, certainly by increasing the ethnoracial diversity of student populations across the country.

Immigration and the Economic Standing of Whites, Blacks, Asians, and Latinos

Given the linkages between residential and school segregation and poverty discussed here, it is important to conclude our examination of the contexts within which immigration is impacting the political incorporation of ethnoracial minorities in the United States with an examination of

TABLE 4.4. Changes in Racial School Segregation, 1991–2003, by Region (in percentages)

Region	Black in 50–100% Minority Schools		Asian in 50–100% Minority Schools		Latino in 50–100% Minority Schools	
	1991–92	2003–4	1991–92	2003–4	1991–92	2003–4
West	70	76	60	66	73	81
Border	59	69	25	35	37	56
Midwest	70	72	19	25	53	57
South	61	71	34	44	77	78
Northeast	76	79	42	50	78	78
Total	66	73	53	56	73	77

Source: Data from Orfield and Lee, tables 3–7, from the Civil Rights Project of Harvard University, http://www.civilrightsproject.harvard.edu.

the changing economic standing of those groups. How do our four primary ethnoracial groups in the United States compare on the question of economic standing, and how might immigration have affected these standings over the past four decades?

Once again space limitations require that we briefly summarize a vast and very complicated amount of information. We do so here by comparing census data from 1990 and 2000 on the median household incomes of native and immigrant ethnoracial groups to see whether immigrants have had a positive or negative impact on the overall standing of these groups.

The data in table 4.5 demonstrate median household incomes for native-born and foreign-born Whites, Blacks, Asians, and Latinos in 1990 and 2000. Among the native-born, the highest incomes are earned by Whites and Asians, followed by Latinos and Blacks. Among the foreign-born, Whites and Asians earn the highest salaries, followed by Blacks and Latinos. The median household income for native-born Whites, Asians, and Latinos is higher than the median household income for their foreign-born counterparts. In contrast, the median household income for foreign-born Blacks is higher than their native-born counterparts in 1990 and 2000. There is a clear native-versus-immigrant advantage among Whites and Asians. The native advantage is also important for Latinos, but the difference in income is much smaller than for Whites and Asians. Among Blacks, however, the expected native advantage is reversed. In 1990, the typical Black immigrant lived in a neighborhood that was about $3,000 wealthier than their native Black counterpart. Though the amount narrowed slightly in the 2000 census, it remained within the $2,000 range.

Table 4.6 depicts the percentages of Blacks, Whites, Latinos, and Asians who fall below the poverty line. Among the native born, Whites and Asians have the lowest percentage of group members in poverty, with Latinos and Blacks basically tying for third place. Among the foreign born, Whites and Asians also have the least percentage of group members in

TABLE 4.5. Median Household Income ($)

Ethnoracial Group	Native Born, 1990	Native Born, 2000	Foreign Born, 1990	Foreign Born, 2000
White	55,000	60,000	54,000	57,000
Black	36,000	40,000	40,000	42,000
Hispanic	37,000	41,000	37,000	39,000
Asian	55,000	59,000	51,000	56,000

Source: Data from Logan 2003a, table 7.

Note: Median household income figures were rounded to the nearest $1,000.

poverty, followed by Blacks and then Latinos. The foreign-born populations of each ethnoracial group tend to be slightly more likely to be impoverished than the native born, with the important exception of Blacks, where the situation is reversed. What is striking to us, nevertheless, is that there is relatively little difference in poverty levels between the native- and foreign-born of each ethnoracial group, despite significant differences between these groups as a whole.

Conclusion

In this chapter, we have explored the patterns of racial segregation in housing and education, as well as income distribution differences between ethnoracial groups, all within the context of post-1965 immigration from Asia, Latin America, the Caribbean, and Africa. Not surprisingly, given the demographic changes we outlined in chapter 1, we have found that issues of ethnoracial segregation are not as "black and white" as they once were perceived. However, the increase in racial diversity has not undermined racial segregation in American society. Instead, racial segregation is now more complicated to the extent that it varies in intensity by ethnoracial group and by region. With the exception of Blacks, racial neighborhood segregation appears to be increasing rather than decreasing or remaining the same. Indeed, Americans of all racial and ethnic groups appear to be racially segregated in neighborhoods, but some groups are more segregated than others. Native-born Blacks, for example, remain the most racially segregated in neighborhoods that are predominantly Black. Even newer Black immigrants tend to congregate in neighborhoods that are ethnically distinct from native-born Blacks.

Racial segregation is also a tenacious fact of American educational life in schools. Blacks have historically been more segregated than any other

TABLE 4.6. Percentage of Racial Group Members below the Poverty Line

Ethnoracial Group	Native Born, 1990	Native Born, 2000	Foreign Born, 1990	Foreign Born, 2000
White	8	8	9	10
Black	21	19	18	17
Hispanic	20	19	21	20
Asian	10	11	12	12

Source: Data from Logan 2003a, table 7.

racial minority, but Latinos are increasingly more segregated especially in the Western, Southern, and Northeastern regions of the country. Although racial school segregation among Asians is increasing, it is less intense than Black or Latino segregation. What appears to be clear, however, is that the smaller numbers of Asians, and probably the group's higher overall economic standing also, has worked well in the group's favor to bring about higher levels of social incorporation, which is revealed by the fact that they are less likely to be segregated from Whites and Latinos in residential and educational venues. It is unclear, nevertheless, what the future holds for Asian social incorporation, as increased immigrants from diverse Asian countries continue to settle in the United States.

In terms of socioeconomic integration, the newer immigrants tend to make less money and live in poorer neighborhoods than their native-born counterparts. The only exception to this pattern is the group of Black immigrants, who tend to make more money and live in less impoverished neighborhoods than native-born Blacks. Unlike the case for White, Asian, and Latino immigrants, who tend to lower the socioeconomic status of their racial groups, Black immigrants tend to raise the socioeconomic status of their counterparts in ways that may facilitate higher levels of social incorporation.

Concluding part 2, then, chapters 3 and 4 have provided important background information regarding the historical and social contexts within which to understand the impacts of recent immigration on American ethnoracial politics. We have found that, despite widely varying experiences in "becoming American" and in treatment by White Americans, each of our three primary ethnoracial minorities has experienced significant racialization in the past, and we believe that these historical realities cannot help but condition the experiences of immigrants from African-origin groups, from Latin America, and from Asia as they too become incorporated into American society. Similarly, we found that the social context of contemporary ethnoracial minority life in the United States is one in which residential and school segregation is greater for minorities than for the White population and appears to be increasing as the society becomes more diverse through continued immigration and its long-term effects. Moreover, we found that poverty levels among all three of our minority groups are significantly higher than is true of the White population and that, again, this is a pattern that seems to have increased in the recent past. Thus, we conclude that the historical patterns of disadvantage experienced by racialized minorities have not magically disappeared in the past 40 years, though they have been reshaped and changed in a period that can be characterized as both the "post–civil rights" and the "new immigration" eras. In part 3, we will move directly toward an assessment of how recent immigration has affected the degree to which these long-standing ethnoracial minority groups have been politically incorporated in the United States.

Part 3 | Political Incorporation in an Era of Immigration

Organizing the Inquiry: Benchmarks of Political Incorporation

We now reach the analytical heart of our book. We began, in part 1, by outlining the dimensions of the new immigration's impacts on the demography of ethnoracial minority groups in the United States, and by outlining four different ways in which ethnoracial politics in the United States may evolve in light of the demographic changes wrought by recent immigration. In part 2, we examined the historical and social contexts within which recent immigrants are interacting with the country's three migration-based, long-standing ethnoracial minority groups. Next we turn to our book's central question: how are recent immigrants changing the efforts and the trajectory of the political incorporation of U.S. Blacks, Latinos, and Asian Americans? Before turning to that question, we need to sketch out how we will organize our inquiry. Our focus, as noted in chapter 1, is on the "political incorporation" of newcomers and outsiders into the U.S. polity. But what do we mean by the phrase *political incorporation*? How do we propose to assess the degree to which Blacks, Latinos, and Asian Americans have been incorporated politically in the United States, as well as the impacts of recent immigrants on those degrees of incorporation?

In part 3 we will focus on four benchmarks of political incorporation that are derived from the political science models of incorporation discussed in chapter 2. These dimensions are: (1) full access to political participation, (2) representation in governmental decision-making offices, (3) substantial power/influence on governmental decisions, leading to (4) adoption of ethnoracially egalitarian public policies.

Each of these dimensions of political incorporation is important, and we believe that all of them need to be realized before it can be said that a given outsider or newcomer group has been fully incorporated into the body politic. Indeed, the basic criterion underlying this focus for our inquiry is the standard of democratic equality. The underlying expectation of this criterion is that *political participation* provides members of the body politic with *voice* to express their views and to help select political leaders, *representation* ensures that individuals find their voices *expressed* in the decision-making arenas of the polity, *power and/or influence* in government demonstrates that their voices are being *heard* effectively, and *public policies* adopted by government reflect the desires and beliefs of the whole membership as well as increase and/or maintain a high level of democratic equality among the members in the polity. With respect to the political incorporation literature in political science, Junn has succinctly summed up the central expectation of that literature.

> More political activity—in this case, expanded expression of voice among individuals—has been advocated as a procedural and substantive solution for distributional inequities in social and political goods. Increasing political activity among those traditionally disadvantaged and politically underrepresented can help create public policies that take their interest into account as well as empower those previously disenfranchised to take political stands in order to develop and forward their interests. (2006, 44)

Thus, with respect to ethnoracial political inequality in the United States, we will conclude that full political incorporation of a given ethnoracial outsider group has not yet been achieved to the degree that it has not reached parity on one or more of these benchmarks in relation to the White or European American ethnoracial group that historically has been the preeminent insider group in the American polity. Further, in assessing the impact of recent immigration on the efforts of outsider groups to become insiders in the political system, we will focus primarily on the ways in which recent immigrants have affected political incorporation in reference to each of these four benchmarks.

By *full access to political participation*, our first benchmark of political incorporation, we mean that unless a person has an equal opportunity to participate in political activities of various kinds—voting, membership in politically active organizations, donating time and/or money to campaigns and efforts to influence public decisions, involvement in political party activities, attending/organizing political demonstrations, running for public office—that person will not be incorporated fully into the body politic. To the extent that the members of some groups have easier access to such forms of participation than do the members of other groups, we should say that the excluded group has not been fully incorporated either. Thus, our primary focus here will be on the degree to which Blacks, Latinos, and Asian Americans participate in political activities, the factors that either facilitate or impede such participation, and the effects of recent immigration on the levels of political participation by members of each group.

Our second benchmark is *political representation in governmental decision-making offices.* The rationale for this dimension is that unless a person's interests are voiced in the governmental venues in which public decisions are made, those interests will likely not find their way into the actions claiming to advance the "common" good. To that degree the political system has operated unequally and unjustly in relation to the excluded person's interests. Further, the assumption is that large numbers of individuals *share* common interests in relation to public decisions and that among these shared interests are those of members of ethnoracial groups. Thus, to the degree that some ethnoracial groups have much more representation in governmental positions than do other groups, the latter groups are not yet fully incorporated into the body politic. There is, of course, a long-term discourse as to what constitutes "representation" of interests (the most widely cited discussion is Pitkin 1967), especially in relation to "descriptive" and "substantive" interest representation in government. Our discussion will focus primarily on the impact of recent immigrants on the degree to which Blacks, Latinos, and Asian Americans are descriptively represented in government, though we will take up the question of substantive representation as well.

The third benchmark is *substantial power and/or influence in governmental decisions.* By this we mean that an outsider or newcomer group's full democratic political incorporation is not reached until that group has the ability to actually influence the decisions made by governmental bodies on behalf of the common good. Here we borrow from Browning, Marshall, and Tabb's (1984) seminal work to articulate the idea that public policy decisions are typically made by dominant "governing coalitions" that in fact operate the political institutions of government. At the local level, particularly in those jurisdictions with formally "nonpartisan" elections, these are often informal coalitions operating in city councils or county commissions. At the state and national levels, the governing coalitions are usually political party organizations, or the dominant factions within the majority political party. The point here is that full democratic political incorporation will not be reached if a significant political group, such as an ethnoracial group, is consistently or usually excluded from active and influential membership in such dominant governing coalitions. So our inquiry in relation to this dimension of political incorporation will focus on the degree to which Blacks, Latinos, and Asian Americans have become members of such dominant political coalitions in U.S. governments, and the ways in which recent immigration has affected their struggles for inclusion in this dimension of political life.

Finally, *adoption of ethnoracially egalitarian public policies* is the fourth benchmark of political incorporation in our framework for inquiry. The rationale for this dimension lies in our perception that at least some of the motivation for political activity is instrumental in nature. We believe one of the primary motivations for people to become involved in politics is that it will have some payoff in the form of public policies that will advance the interests of the player. Further, to the degree that political activists understand representation as involving working toward gaining greater benefits for those whose interests are being represented, in the realm of ethnoracial politics we expect that political activists and representatives are working toward public policies that aim for greater "equality" for outsider and newcomer ethnoracial groups. Since the 1960s a number of public policies and policy proposals have been identified as ethnoracially egalitarian in aim, including the Civil Rights Act, the Voting Rights Act, affirmative action, and bilingual education. Accordingly, our focus here will be on a historical overview of the trajectory of ethnoracially egalitarian public policies since the 1960s, and the ways in which recent immigration has affected that trajectory.

Fuller descriptions of these dimensions of political incorporation will be developed as we pursue our inquiry into these matters. Our aim here is simply to give the reader an overview of our project in the chapters that follow. Before moving into these specific benchmarks of political incorporation, we should also point out the ways in which our inquiry is bounded. There are other ways to define and evaluate political incorporation, and we want to acknowledge here that our focus is quite conventional in several important respects.

Our inquiry, for example, is essentially *integrationist* in its orientation toward political incorporation and the American polity. We assume that the democratic standing of outsiders and newcomers will be improved by their becoming insiders in the political system. We acknowledge that there are many political activists and scholars who believe that this is not the case, but that the U.S. political system is fundamentally elitist and/or antidemocratic in its structure and operation, and that therefore the integration of outsiders and newcomers into that system can mean, in most cases, only manipulation and cooptation and not democratization (for discussions of this issue, see, e.g., Junn 1999, 2006; Walters 2007).

While we recognize the intellectual and political legitimacy of raising the questions generated by this more radical orientation toward U.S. politics, we believe there is nevertheless validity in our assessment of the degree to which the integrationist project of democratic political incorporation is being affected by recent international migrants to the United States. Moreover, we want to note that our framework of four dimensions of political incorporation sets a very high standard of democratization. For example, if we find that U.S. ethnoracial minority groups have been substantially included into the voting and representational dimensions of American politics but continue to be excluded from substantial influence or power over governmental decisions, and that the dominant public policies adopted by governments continue to reinforce ethnoracial inequality rather than promoting greater equality, then we would find substantial failure in the degree to which these groups have been politically incorporated.

Another way in which our approach is quite conventional is its inherently *nationalist* frame of reference. Our focus is on the degrees to which ethnoracial outsiders and newcomers are becoming insiders in a *national* polity, that of the United States. This perspective, we acknowledge, eclipses other perspectives that may contribute much to the questions we take up in this book. Among these alternative perspectives is the *transnational*. That is, as we noted in chapter 2, some scholars have argued that the globalization of daily life has generated a substantial increase in *transnational* orientations toward behaviors in political life, and that traditional notions of single-state citizenship cannot encompass the realities of political life in the twenty-first century. Again, we acknowledge that these perspectives raise important and legitimate intellectual and political questions that need to be addressed. While we explored various ways to incorporate these perspectives into our inquiry, we decided that to do so would hopelessly complicate an already incredibly difficult intellectual challenge. Accordingly, while we do try to take into account the ways in which transnational political identities affect the political incorporation of immigrants in the contemporary United States, we have not incorporated these perspectives into our framework for inquiry. What we offer, rather, is an account of how the political incorporation of immigrant newcomers is affecting the efforts of long-standing ethnoracially identified outsiders to become fully incorporated insiders in the U.S. polity.

5 | Political Participation, Descriptive Representation, and the Quest for Political Power

Political participation is the core foundation for any democratic form of government. It is through participation that members of a political community share in processes of choosing public officials, holding public officials accountable for their actions, deliberate with other members on the most advantageous courses of action for the community, and try to persuade, pressure or otherwise influence public officials' actions on behalf of the community. Sometimes, as well, members participate directly in the adoption or rejection of public policy measures that have been proposed through voter initiatives, or decide through referenda whether policies adopted by public officials should be overturned. In short, if democracy's core meaning is "rule by the people," then political participation is the work through which this rule takes place.

Newcomers or outsiders who seek to become full members—insiders—in a political community, therefore, must work to become included in these processes of participation. For many decades—even centuries, as we have seen—members of racialized groups were excluded from full participation in American politics in various ways. Much of the political energy of African Americans, Latinos, and Asian/Pacific Islander Americans in the past was directed toward gaining access to the right to fully engage in the multiple dimensions of political participation. As noted earlier, the aim of many ethnoracial minority political activists was to become full participants in the democratic process so as to gain representation in government, and to exercise real influence over the decisions made by government in order to gain greater social equality in the United States.

In relation to gaining real political influence, Barker, Jones, and Tate (1999) argued in a seminal study of Black politics that individuals or groups seeking to bring about change through politics need to have the power to either persuade or force other political actors to have a response that is supportive of the desired change. In order to bring about such a response, the group in search of the change should not only have the resources necessary to influence the target group but also the means to convert the resources into actual power by bringing them to bear upon individuals whose behavior must be influenced.

> In democratic societies, such as the United States, economic wealth, favorable population distribution, voting, and holding public office are all potential sources of power. Each of these can be used to political advantage by those who possess them, providing they have the means for converting them into actual power. (Barker, Jones, and Tate 1999, 72)

In line with this analysis, our focus here is on the efforts of Blacks, Latinos, and Asian Americans to develop higher levels of political participation and descriptive representation in public office, with the aim of converting these into sufficient political power to enable these communities to become full insiders as equal members of the political community of the United States.

In developing our analysis here, we explore a number of subjects that go beyond simple voting and running for public office. In addition to those core subjects of political analysis, we explore such topics as the access of ethnoracial minorities to legal rights to political participation and representation, and the efforts of politically active group members to develop collective resources for mobilizing more group members to fully utilize their legal access to conventional politics. In this light, we examine such subjects as socioeconomic status (SES), group consciousness in relation to political life, degrees of group partisanship, and citizenship, all of which are crucial resources in conventional electoral and nonelectoral participation. Full access to participation, however, is a limited resource, especially as real power in electoral politics emanates from the expression of these participatory rights in the form of voter registration, voter turnout, the development of a viable pool of candidates, voter support for these candidates, and substantive policy.

Moving to our second benchmark of political incorporation, we also explore each group's efforts to increase political representation in public offices. This is important because, alone, the right to vote is impotent unless it is linked with the ability to elect candidates who are preferred by ethnoracial minority groups. As part of our analysis of political representation, therefore, we examine the extent to which there is a representational gap between the population of minorities and the percentage of respective elected officials. In this sense, we focus primarily on the issue of descriptive representation, which is the foundational aspect of political representation. As we analyze each group's efforts to obtain full access to political participation and also to achieve effective levels of political representation, we do so against the backdrop of post-1965 immigration. In this respect, we focus on how the influx of non-White immigrants from Asia, Latin America, the Caribbean, and sub-Saharan Africa has affected each group's potential as well as its capacity as related to resources, its potential power as well as actual turnout.

Our analysis demonstrates that each ethnoracial group has gained some ground, but the struggles for full access to participation and political representation are far from over. Indeed, immigration has affected participatory and representational activities in positive as well as challenging ways. In the end, these struggles are ongoing, with different ethnoracial groups at varying stages in a complicated, multidimensional, and nonlinear process.

Movements, Protests, and Organizational Activity

Historically, American civil rights movements, protest activities, and political organizations have been used by outsider groups to seek basic, but long-denied citizenship rights for those denied access to the electoral system. Even though many Americans trace ethnoracial protest and movement activities to the 1960s, protest activity had its genesis long before that time. For example, in the seventeenth and eighteenth centuries, Blacks struggled for personal liberation from slavery and state-sanctioned violence before abolition, while Latinos resisted efforts to strip their citizenship rights granted under the Treaty of Guadalupe Hidalgo, and Asian Americans and Pacific Islanders engaged in fierce labor protests, union organizing, and struggles against exclusionary policies (Harding 1981; Hero 1992; Lien 2001; Takaki 1993).

The Black, Latino, and Asian American/Pacific Islander movements of the 1960s were similar to these earlier movements in that each group used protest as a strategy to facilitate better access to such formal participatory mechanisms as voting, elected office, and party politics. Gaining access to full participation was, in part, synonymous with shedding second-class citizenship status and, in the end, assuming all of the participatory rights entitled to first-class citizens. In its earliest stages, full access to participation simply meant the *right* to participate freely and equally in America's system of governance, a right that had been withheld and denied over centuries of struggle. Yet, from the 1950s to the 1970s, each group utilized different strategies and agendas to bring about higher levels of access to political participation.

Overall, we believe that movement, protest, and organizational work have improved access to political participation in four ways. First, movement, protest, and organizational work affected elite decision making in ways that led to laws and institutional arrangements that were beneficial to ethnoracial minorities, particularly the core civil rights policies adopted in the mid-1960s. At times, Blacks, Latinos, and Asian Americans and Pacific Islanders organized and protested in support of new legislation, while, in other instances, they organized and protested to prevent the adoption of new legislation. Second, ethnoracial minorities used group-based as well as institutional resources, ranging from churches to schools, to participate more effectively in politics. Third, even after the marching and protests of the 1960s and early 1970s diminished in subsequent years, the movements did not end. Rather, post-1965 movement, protest, and organizational activities were transformed into a different manifestation of struggle, in which elected officials served as institutional activists to mobilize the resources of conventional governance in ways that are beneficial to the interests of their groups (Santoro 1999). Fourth, immigration broadened and expanded the scope of each movement in terms of agenda, strategies, and outcomes.

Among all three of the ethnoracial groups in focus here, social movement, protest, and organizational work have continued unabated since the civil rights movement's heyday from the 1950s to 1970s. There is not space to recount such activities in detail here, but the following represents a cross section illustrative of such activities that we believe have supported and enhanced the political participation of peoples of color in the United States.

Blacks and Social Movement Activities

Among Blacks, many of the social movement and organizational activities that have occurred over the past 40 years have been locally based, and these have varied considerably. Among the most important themes in these locally based organizations and activities, however, have been continuing work against both police harassment and police inaction in predominantly Black communities, struggles for better housing conditions and practices, work to improve the quality of public education for Black youth, work to increase Black home ownership and ownership of businesses in Black communities, efforts to improve access for Blacks to health care and to job opportunities and training, efforts to deal more effectively and fairly with substance abuse practices, work to improve the quality of life in Black neighborhoods (e.g., better streets, sidewalks, parks and recreational facilities, more libraries), and work to reduce gangsterism and its related violence. These local organizational efforts often have melded with or worked with political campaigns to increase Black voter turnout and to gain greater Black political representation in local governments.

At the national level, a number of organizational efforts to create broad-based Black social movements and/or political organizations have been mounted over the past four decades. With the passage of major civil rights legislation in the mid-1960s, the Black movement shifted its emphasis from a politics of *rights* to a politics of *resources*. It was not that Blacks had achieved all of their rights, but that it was now time—especially in light of the Voting Rights Act and other civil rights legislation—to focus more energy and resources on the question of securing improvements in the material well-being of American Blacks. With that, the Black civil rights movement launched an electoral strategy that was undergirded by a strong network of race-based organizations like the NAACP, the Urban League, and the Southern Christian Leadership Conference. These organizations focused attention on electoral politics and getting candidates elected to office. These civil rights organizations—joined together with other like-minded groups into an umbrella National Conference on Civil Rights—also functioned as interest groups, mobilizing support for national legislation that would improve the social and economic prospects of Blacks and others.

Beyond these activities by civil rights organizations, Blacks made several other notable efforts to mount national movements. Among these were the Black Reparations movement, launched in 1969 by James Farmer (then director of the Congress of Racial Equality), which would fail to gain purchase until it became a major issue in Black politics in the early twenty-first century (Assensoh and Alex-Assensoh 1998). National Black political conventions were held as well in the 1970s in an effort to gain broad backing for a cohesive political agenda among Black activists. In the late 1990s, Nation of Islam leader Louis Farrakhan drew national attention by organizing the Million Man March in Washington, D.C., to bring about reconciliation between Black men and their families and communities.

In reviewing these highlights of movement activities over four decades, it is notable that immigration and immigrants have played little role in the movement politics of Black communities in the United States. To what degree, for example, has movement activity focused on the interests and opinions of newcomer Black immigrants from the Caribbean and sub-Sahara Africa? In a well-regarded study, Reuel Rogers (2006) has argued that Afro-Caribbean immigrants and native Blacks have a host of mutually intersecting political interests, including anti-Black violence, police brutality, educational inequalities, and inadequate housing. Yet, when it comes to electoral politics, the traditional Black civil rights movement organizations tend to embrace native-born candidates more than interested candidates among naturalized Black immigrants.

In that regard, a Jamaican-born politician from the New York area commented, "I helped to elect almost every African-American in Central Brooklyn, and when my time came to run they were far and few in between that supported me" (Rogers 2006, 124). A similar level of ambivalence was noted in the Black community with regard to the early stages of the presidential campaign of Illinois senator Barack Obama (Obama's father—as is well known—migrated from Kenya to advance his education in the United States). Incidents like these indicate a definite political tension between long-time members of the Black community and recent immigrants. One reason is that immigrants long have been perceived as competing with native Blacks—who have historically been located at the bottom of the socioeconomic ladder—for precious housing, employment, and educational resources, often leaving Blacks behind as they rise on the ladder of success. In fact, there is research demonstrating that urban employers perceive native-born Blacks to be more confrontational and less accommodating than immigrants. As a result, employers are less likely to hire native-born Blacks than immigrants as employees (Neckerman 1991).

This tension between native-born Blacks and immigrants may help explain the absence of immigration and immigrant settlement issues from among the organizational agendas of the U.S. Black civil rights organizations, despite the fact that almost 900,000 African and over 1.6 million Afro-Caribbean immigrants were counted in the 2000 census. While these numbers are large, they still represent a small proportion of the U.S. Black population. In the absence of a visible panethnic Black organization to proactively socialize Black immigrants, these newcomers from the Caribbean nations and sub-Sahara Africa have developed a rich array of sociopolitical networks that not only provide opportunities to socialize immigrants from home but also facilitate transnational activities with their home countries.

At the same time, there is evidence of collaboration between Black civil rights leaders and emerging Black immigrant communities in relation to nonelectoral political issues. Established over two decades ago, for example, the National Coalition for Haitian Rights (NCHR) was organized specifically to fight for Haitian rights in the United States and abroad. NCHR lobbies the president and Congress regarding immigration processes and legislation that is beneficial or favorable to Haitian immigrants and refugees. Reverend Benjamin Hooks, who served as executive director of the NAACP from 1977 to 1992, was a founder of NCHR and helped to organize a Haitian March on Washington in 1981 to protest discrimination against Haitian immigrants. In addition, the Congressional Black Caucus has been helpful to the NCHR in its lobbying efforts on Capitol Hill to get more parity between Haitian and Cuban immigration policy.[1] These collaborative efforts have provided the context for increased participation that might, in turn, foster a greater awareness among Blacks about these issues and more participation in the form of letter writing to elected officials and protest activity to draw attention to these issues.

Immigration has also facilitated additional opportunities for nonelectoral participation across intraracial and interethnic lines. In cities like Los Angeles, for example, native-born Blacks and African immigrants are engaging in panethnic organizing as a way to foster awareness and understanding of Black immigrants in general. One example of this is the Priority Africa Network (PAN), a volunteer organization made up of Africans from Eritrea and other countries, as well as native-born Blacks. The forum's goal is to foster understanding about and among each group's history and to help Black immigrants understand what it means to be Black in America (Ruffin 2006). In this sense, Black immigration from the Caribbean and sub-Sahara Africa is the result of the U.S. civil rights movement and its success at creating the impression that America truly welcomes the "huddled masses yearning to breathe free."

Latino Social Movement and Organizational Activities

Civil rights movement activities among Latinos, which reached their peak from the mid-1960s to the mid-1970s, initially involved protest activities by Puerto Ricans on the East Coast and Mexican Americans in the Southwest. While Cubans came to be a significant ethnic group within the larger Latino community during the 1960s, this group's experience with U.S. politics—particularly among those concentrated in south Florida—was significantly different than the experiences of other Latino groups in the same period, as we saw in chapter 3.

Among Puerto Ricans and Mexican Americans, locally based social movement activities in the post-1970s era have included much the same agenda as that of Blacks. That is, protest and social movement activities among Latinos have centered on efforts to reduce both police harassment and police inaction in Latino communities, struggles for better housing conditions and practices, work to improve the quality of public education and access to higher education for Latino youth, efforts to improve access for Latinos to health care and to job opportunities and training, efforts to deal more effectively and more fairly with substance abuse practices, work for improving the quality of life in Latino neighborhoods (e.g., better streets, sidewalks, parks and recreational facilities, as well as more libraries), and work to engage members of youth gangs in more socially productive pursuits. Hundreds, if not thousands, of community-based organizations devoted to dealing with one or more of these issues have formed throughout the country over the past four decades, some having had more success than others (see, e.g., Rodriguez 2005; Torres and Katsiaficas 1999). A primary issue for such groups is always the question of resources, particularly since the early 1980s when the Reagan administration dramatically cut federal spending on grants for such purposes. Some groups survived by gaining corporate sponsorship, but all such groups have had consistent difficulty in maintaining sufficient resources to do the work for which they were formed (see, e.g., Schmidt 1988).

Taking a broader perspective than the local, there have been many efforts to organize Latinos in the United States for self-help and for political representation, most of which began with a national-origins focus (Mexican American, Puerto Rican, Cuban, etc.). By the 1980s, the group that had emerged with the largest and most geographically widespread membership base was the League of United Latin American Citizens (LULAC). Originally formed in Texas by middle-class Mexican Americans seeking to gain full citizenship rights, by the 1970s LULAC had begun to define itself as a national panethnic group (see, e.g., Marquez 1993). Other Latino groups with a national focus and presence are the Mexican American Legal Defense and Education Fund (MALDEF), the Puerto Rican Legal Defense and Education Fund (PRLDEF), and the National Council of La Raza (NCLR), which was founded with a Mexican American focus but later sought to represent the interests of Latinos panethnically on a national level (see, e.g., Garcia and Sanchez 2008, chap. 7; Geron 2005, chap. 4).

In addition to these prominent organizations, there are a number of other groups seeking to bring people together to work on behalf of Latino social and political interests from a national perspective. Among these are several that focus specifically on increasing the number of Latino voters. Perhaps the most prominent examples of these are the Southwest Voter Registration Education Project (SVREP) and the William C. Velasquez Institute (WCVI), both of which operate large-scale voter registration and get-out-the-vote campaigns in areas with large numbers of Latinos, among other related projects. In similar fashion, the National Association of Latino Elected Officials (NALEO), an organization made up of Latino elected officials from all levels of government, has mounted a number of naturalization campaigns among Latino immigrants, as well as voter registration and get-out-the-vote campaigns in high concentration Latino areas (see, e.g., DeSipio 1996, chap. 6). Since 2006, a yearly Latino National Congreso has been organized by a coalition of Latino civil rights and voting rights organizations to generate a joint public policy agenda on behalf of the interests of Latinos in the United States. These are only a fraction of the organizational efforts being made by, and on behalf of, Latinos in recent decades, but this brief description should provide some insight into the kinds of organizational efforts that have been undertaken.

Immigration has had a major impact on the work of Latino community-based organizations and protest groups. In the Northeast, for example, a large influx of immigrants from the Caribbean and from Central and South America brought many new groups (e.g., Dominicans, Ecuadorans, Colombians), who became part of the larger Hispanic communities of urban areas, bringing much greater diversity, and sometimes tensions, to an urban region in which the concerns of Puerto Ricans had long dominated political interactions between White politicos and Latinos (see, e.g., Jones-Correa 1998). Similarly, in the Southwest, a continuing wave of Mexican immigrants—a significant percentage of whom were unauthorized immigrants—inundated long-standing Chicano neighborhoods and began to expand the Latino population into areas in which they had not previously lived. Those living in the Southwest also witnessed growing numbers of non-Mexican Latin American and Caribbean immigrants, beginning to diversify the politics in urban and rural areas in which Chicano identities and concerns had long held sway. The result was rapid growth of new community-based organizations, some of which were focused on the concerns of newly arrived or newly expanded national-origin Latino groups (e.g., Nicaraguans, Salvadorans, Hondurans), as well as a reorientation of some older community-based groups. Quite notable in both the Northeast and the Southwest were the establishment and/or expansion of community-based organizations dedicated to serving the needs of immigrants—both authorized and unauthorized—from Latin America and the Spanish-speaking Caribbean.

At the national level, too, immigration has generated an expanded and somewhat altered agenda among Latino political organizations. In the 1970s, for example, the legislative agenda of Latino activists rarely included immigration as a major policy issue, or the political incorporation of immigrants as a central political imperative. By the 1980s, however, this had changed, and by the mid-1980s national Latino organizations such as the LULAC, NCLR, MALDEF, and PRLDEF had coalesced behind a strong push to prevent anti-immigration sentiment from being legislated into a punitive reform of the country's immigration policies. This coalition was instrumental, for example, in assuring that the 1986 congressional immigration reform law provided an amnesty program for some undocumented immigrants, and that it enforced the borders through employer sanctions as well as through efforts to apprehend and expel unauthorized migrants (see, e.g., Sierra 1991). Latino political organizations have increasingly focused their efforts on working to ensure that the rights and interests of Latino immigrants—both authorized and unauthorized—are factored into public policies.

Asian American/Pacific Islander Social Movement and Organizational Activities

Among Asian Americans and Pacific Islanders, pre-1960s social movement work was largely characterized by ethnic rather than panethnic activity. This was probably due to several factors, including long-standing animosities between Asian national-origin groups deriving from historical conflicts between Asian nation-states, differing immigration experiences (e.g., peaking at different times in U.S. history, under differing circumstances), and the fact that anti-Asian prejudice and discrimination were usually directed against specific national-origin groups under specific historical circumstances (anti-Chinese sentiment in California in the late nineteenth century, anti-Japanese sentiment during World War II, etc.) (see, e.g., Espiritu 1992).

Panethnic Asian American and Pacific Islander protest began to develop during the late 1960s, led primarily by middle-class college students. Organizational activities initially focused on liberation from racial oppression through panethnic collaboration. In fact, it was in this context that the term *Asian American* was first deployed as a social identity for political mobilization (Espiritu 1992, 33). Out of these student movement activities came the establishment of Asian American studies programs on university and college campuses, and in many ways these programs served as models for the establishment of similar Black studies and Latino studies programs as well. The programs, moreover, led to the initiation of several journals (e.g., *Amerasia Journal, Getting Together, Gidra*) that have helped to develop panethnic consciousness across the country.

Following the students' example, professional and community leaders used the pan-Asian concept to also lobby for health and welfare benefits for people of Asian descent and to establish professional organizations ranging from the Asian American Social Workers to the caucuses for Asians within national professional organizations like the American Public Health Association and the American Libraries Association.

Given the huge influx of immigrants from a large number of Asian and Pacific Island nations during the past four decades, however, it is not surprising that panethnic activists have struggled to develop increasing panethnic consciousness (Espiritu 1992). Most immigrants understandably have identified initially more with their nations of origin than with a U.S.-oriented panethnic identity.

One factor countering this centrifugal force, however, has been a series of anti-Asian hate crimes that have served as major stimuli for panethnic political mobilizations among Asian American/Pacific Islander peoples in the United States. Of particular importance was the 1982 murder of Vincent Chin by two Detroit autoworkers, who mistook Chin (a Chinese American) for a Japanese, and whose outburst of murderous violence was apparently stimulated by animosity for the Japanese auto industry's sales in the United States. Chin's murder led to the initiation of a panethnic organization, American Citizens for Justice (ACJ), whose first members were Chinese Americans in Detroit but that later came to have a panethnic membership base. While Chin's murderers avoided prosecution based on a technicality (Lien 2004), his murder served as a rallying call for the next wave of panethnic identity among Asian Americans and Pacific Islanders that would socialize newer immigrants of Asian descent.

Again and again over the past four decades, it has been external forces of discrimination and violence that have provided the momentum for ethnic as well as panethnic organizing among Asian Americans and Pacific Islanders. In the 1990s, for example, investigations of 1996 campaign finance scandals involving Chinese officials and several Asian Americans and Pacific Islanders led to broad racializing attacks in the media, stimulating new panethnic consciousness among many Asian Americans and

Pacific Islanders (Gotanda 2001). Then came the false accusations of spying for the Chinese government by U.S. government scientist Wen Ho Lee, which led to similar panethnic organizational activities and protests of anti-Asian stigmatization and discrimination.

More broadly, Asian American and Pacific Islander political activists called for an investigation of Secretary of Labor Elaine Chao's refusal (during the early years of the George W. Bush administration) to investigate civil rights abuses against Asian American and Pacific Islander applicants for managerial positions. The complaint was that a glass ceiling exists, keeping otherwise qualified Asian Americans and Pacific Islanders outside of the managerial class, but Chao, an Asian American, was ambivalent about moving ahead on this group's request. In addition to discrimination, some American citizens of Asian ancestry have lost their lives because of recent anti-Asian violence, causing an increase in the numbers of Asian Americans and Pacific Islanders embracing panethnic political organizing.

In fact, the persistence of racial discrimination and attempts to undermine affirmative action, bilingual education, and social welfare for permanent residents have fostered the creation of more recent panethnic political organizations that address issues through legal and electoral means. Included among the growing list of organizations are the Asian American Voters Coalition (Lien 2004), Asian American Institute of Congressional Studies (AAICS), Asian Pacific Islander American Health Forum (API-AHF), and the U.S. Pan-Asian American Chamber of Commerce (US-PAACC). Most of these organizations have headquarters in Washington, D.C. In this sense, the Asian American and Pacific Islander community appears to be organizing in ways that foster strength within ethnic communities as well as strength across communities. At the same time, some researchers suggest that organizing among Asian Americans and Pacific Islanders lacks the community-based focus on power that animates much of the Black and Latino organizations, limiting mobilization opportunities that might lead to lasting and significant change (Kim 2007).

Lien argues that, in retrospect, the 1982 Chin murder ushered in a second phase of the Asian American and Pacific Islander civil rights movement, especially in terms of electoral politics, agenda setting, and organization building. In terms of electoral politics, groups have been organized to cater specifically to ethnicities as well as to the larger Asian American and Pacific Islander community. For example, South Asian American Voting Youth (SAAVY) is a national nonprofit group that aims to increase the involvement of South Asian youth in American civic life (Ahmed 2004). Perhaps the most well-known organization that is focused on voter mobilization is the 80-20 Project, a nonpartisan effort aimed at organizing Asian Americans and Pacific Islanders into a national swing-voting bloc.

In sum, the post-1965 immigration of Asians and Pacific Islanders to the United States has had a mixed effect on social movement organizing among Asian Americans/Pacific Islanders. The increased diversity and relative newness to the country have made panethnic organizing more difficult and more complicated, as we have seen. At the same time, the continuing examples of anti-Asian hate crimes and seemingly discriminatory actions by governments against Asian Americans during recent decades have provided renewed reminders and socialization experiences for both newcomers and long-term Americans of Asian descent that have served as incentives for panethnic identities and movement support.

While Asian Americans and Pacific Islanders, Latinos, and Blacks have protested and organized in response to issues affecting their communities, there have been fewer instances of protest and organizational activity across panethnic groups. One important recent exception to this trend was the phenomenon of the spring 2006 immigration protest marches, described in chapter 1. These marches engaged a rainbow coalition of immigrants from all continents, but led by and numerically dominated by Latinos, who organized and protested in American streets against anti-immigrant legislation that would make illegal immigration to the United States a federal offense (Wood 2006). Whether this kind of cross-group panethnic social movement organizing will become more prevalent in the future no doubt depends, to some extent, on the degree to which anti-immigrant sentiment continues to be mobilized across the country.

Immigration-Inspired Protest and Organizational Activity

Historically, movement and organizational activity in the United States has been geared toward participation and representation issues that primarily affect native-born residents. However, since 1965 that characterization has changed, especially as large percentages of Latinos and Asian Americans/Pacific Islanders are immigrants, and as each group seeks greater ethnoracial access to the political system in the form of participation and representation.

As we saw in chapter 1, the intensity of immigrant frustration with anti-immigrant hostility and proposed congressional legislation was evident in the spring 2006 marches, which were staged in various cities across the country. Organized by a broad coalition of interests, they included Latino rights organizations, the Catholic Church, unions with large numbers of Latino members, the Spanish-language media and immigrant organizations representing African, Caribbean, and Asian ethnic groups. These marches, moreover, were deliberately organized to attract a wide array of immigrants: Pacific Islanders, Southeast Asians, Europeans, Africans, and Pakistanis, as well as Latin Americans.

Specifically, the protesters called for a number of changes, including worker protections, civil/human rights measures, family reunification, and immigration reform that would define a "path to citizenship for current undocumented and future immigrants to the U.S." (Wood 2006). An analysis of the 2006 marches was offered by Hong (from the New York Immigrant Coalition, an umbrella organization for about 150 groups in New York State working with immigrants and refugees), stating, "The fight is about whether or not America will continue to be what it has always been, a nation of immigrants. . . . Immigrants have been feeling like a target for all that is wrong and want to stand up and show how they contribute to the diversity and richness of America" (Wood 2006). In addition to protesting, immigrants and their allies are also building organizations and strategies that will lead to greater access to political participation and eventually political representation. Immigrant rights groups are investing time and energy in strategies that would lead to increases in formal mechanisms of participation. Many immigrant rights groups, as well as ethnic and panethnic political organizations, are working to increase the number of immigrants who are naturalized, and therefore eligible to vote in local, state, and national elections (Watanabe 2008).

Overall, it appears that many of the movements, protests, and organizational activities among Blacks, Latinos, and Asian Americans and Pacific Islanders were initially forged to secure full access to participation. The first target was voting rights, which all groups eventually deemed to be important in bringing about political representation and, eventually, policies that would benefit their respective groups. In the process of protesting and organizing for these rights, each group also gained additional resources. Among Blacks, there was the establishment of a leadership cadre, secular and religious organizations, and a sense of group consciousness that facilitated mobilization as well as strategy that moved from protest to an electoral politics–based strategy of change.

Among Latinos, the earlier movement activities led to the foundation of ethnic-based organizations. Since Mexicans and Puerto Ricans made up the largest shares of the Latino population and had the lengthiest experiences as U.S. population groups, much of the organizational activity initially was inspired by the perceived needs of these groups. In the last several decades, as we have seen, several Latino organizations have developed panethnic identities that include multiple Hispanic ethnic groups. As in the case of Blacks, it is clear that many Latino activists also have made the transition from protest to politics, so that protest activities are often used now to supplement the conventional politics, but not as the primary mechanism of access to the political system.

In relation to social movement activities, Asian Americans and Pacific Islanders are both similar to and different from Blacks and Latinos. That is, most of the focus of this group's panethnic activities is on countering and eliminating racial discrimination and stigmatization. At the same time, the group's overall higher level of socioeconomic status means that Asian American/Pacific Islander political struggles are often perceived as focusing more on facilitating connections with political elites and thwarting white-collar discrimination, including glass ceiling issues in businesses and elite universities, rather than bread-and-butter issues involving social welfare. It should be noted, nevertheless, that there are a number of *ethnic* (as distinct from panethnic) Asian organizations working on behalf of Asian national-origin groups (especially refugees from Southeast Asia) that are not so well-off as to reap the benefits of the so-called model minority status and success (see, e.g., Ong 2003, chap. 10).

As each of our primary ethnoracial groups has employed organizational strategies aimed at bringing about fuller access to political participation, it is difficult to gauge the impact of post-1965 immigration on these efforts. While there appear to be some similarities in the influence of immigration, each immigrant group has a different history of immigration in terms of times and nature of entry, which affected the nature of influence on their native-born compatriots. As for similarities, the influx of immigrants has brought Blacks, Latinos, and Asian Americans and Pacific Islanders full circle again, to the question of access to voting. This time, the question is not about voting rights for citizens but for newcomers, and there is much debate about whether the struggle should focus on permanent residents, on all immigrants (including the unauthorized), or on speeding up the process for naturalization. Unlike the civil rights era, when Blacks, Latinos, and Asian Americans and Pacific Islanders agreed that, as citizens, they were entitled to voting rights, there is not a consensus among ethnoracial minorities that immigrants who are not naturalized have an inalienable right to vote.

In addition, the influx of immigrants has broadened the scope of each group's agenda, especially as it pertains to movement and organizational strategies. That is because immigrants bring with them unique issues and problems that often differ from the priorities of native-born ethnoracial minorities. This diversity creates new pressures, especially for Latinos and Asians, with larger percentages of newcomers, to socialize and mobilize these groups for participation in the political system. While the newcomers provide increased capacity for representation in ways that will be discussed in detail later, their presence also adds fuel to the fires of racial animosity, which increases the costs and burdens associated with participation in electoral politics. Among Latinos as well as Asian Americans and Pacific Islanders, the continuous influx of immigrants perpetuates the image in the larger public of Latinos as "illegal immigrants" and "perpetual foreigners" (see, e.g., Garcia Bedolla 2005), so that even Latino elected officials have reported being asked whether they are citizens (Tucker 2006). Blacks too face similar positives and negatives associated with immigration. As discussed later, Black immigrants tend to raise the socioeconomic profile of the Black community in ways that elevate resources for participation. As Black immigrants become naturalized, however, they too demand political inclusion as well as recognition in ways that complicate the already complex negotiations that Black leaders make regarding the issue of immigration.

In spite of these challenges, Blacks, Latinos, and Asian Americans/Pacific Islanders have secured access to meaningful mechanisms of participation, especially the franchise. Accordingly, we next examine how each group has used its electoral resources to increase participation in the political process. We also turn from outsider activities, associated with movements, protests, and organizations, to an analysis of conventional electoral politics, focusing initially on how ethnoracial minority groups have used various resources to engage electoral politics. Among the resources that we investigate are group consciousness, partisanship, socioeconomic status, campaign activity, and citizenship. All of these resources are important in facilitating registration and turnout in elections. We will also assess the role of the Voting Rights Act in relation to registration and voting among ethnoracial minority groups. Then we will examine actual registration and turnout rates among Blacks, Latinos, and Asians over the last three decades, with an eye toward understanding the role that immigration has played in increasing or dampening turnout rates.

Resources and Political Participation

A consistent finding among scholars of political participation is that re-source-rich individuals and groups are more likely to participate than those with limited resources. Among the resources that political scientists have found to be especially important to electoral politics are partisan-ship, socioeconomic status, and citizenship. Further, research has identi-fied group identity as playing an important role in mobilizing African Americans to participate above and beyond what their socioeconomic sta-tus predicts. Accordingly, we turn now to an analysis of how each group has utilized these important resources toward the goal of full access to-ward participation. We begin first with the resource of group identity, fol-lowed by a discussion of partisanship, campaign activity, socioeconomic status, and citizenship.

Group Consciousness

Scholars of political participation have long noted that group identity, es-pecially ethnic or racial group consciousness, plays an important role in facilitating political behavior. In a convincing analysis of machine politics, for example, Erie discussed the important role that group identity played among nineteenth-century European immigrants in mobilizing their par-ticipation in political activities (Erie 1988; see also Wolfinger 1965; Dahl 1961; Pinderhughes 1987). Over time, these ethnic affiliations waned, and the Irish, along with other White ethnics, began to vote more according to individual rather than group-based motivations.

As a political resource, group consciousness among the Irish was im-portant because it mobilized them to participate and vote in blocs that made their votes more valuable in the electoral process. Over time, never-theless, the ethnic identities among White immigrant descendents became more centered on a common White racial identity than on their ethnic di-visions (Omi and Winant 1986). In the next section, we examine the na-ture and extent of group consciousness among Blacks, Latinos, and Asian Americans/Pacific Islanders. As part of that analysis, we discuss how group identity has furthered mobilization efforts that facilitate fuller par-ticipation in our political system.

Black Group Identity

Group consciousness among the Black electorate has been effective in fa-cilitating a sense of working together for the group. Dawson (1994) argued that this sense derived from a conviction among U.S. Blacks that their own individual well-being depended, to an unusually large degree, on the well-being of the group as a whole. Dawson termed this perception as "linked fate." Moreover, Blacks also tend to believe in a "moral claim to group entitlements based on the view that [centuries] of discrimination and [the] economic structure produce an unfair and unequal distribution of resources that can be addressed most effectively through government policy" (Jaynes and Williams 1989, 214). Both this moral claim and sense of collective action were strong motivations underlying the civil rights movement as well as the long-term effort to elect Blacks to positions at the local, state, and national levels. The notion of a moral claim on the government is an important factor distinguishing Blacks' group identity from that of other groups, especially Whites, who tend to believe that government has been established to "nurture liberty for individual advancement" and that the prevailing economic conditions in society are the result of fair competition rather than racial discrimination and systemic bias (Lane 1986).

Native-born Blacks' notions of group identity have often resulted in highly cohesive support for race-based and antidiscriminatory policy. The fact that group consciousness transcends class cleavages does not mean that there are no important differences in Black public opinion. In fact, Katherine Tate's study of Black voters in American elections specifically demonstrates that middle- and upper-class Blacks have weaker racial identities than those who identify with the poorer or working class (1993, 28). Rather, it means that those differences do not undermine the sense of connectedness or linked fate that Blacks feel based on centuries of opposition and discrimination as Blacks in the United States (Dawson 1994).

Some aspects of this distinctive group identity are manifest in public opinion polls. Thus, Blacks are more likely than any other social identity group to support government involvement in redressing issues of discrimination and inequality. It is also evident in a conservative tendency on some social issues, in that Blacks are more likely than those in other racial groups to support school prayer, certain aspects of feminism, gun control, and the death penalty (Cain and Kiewiet 1986, 31). The common understanding of where Blacks stand on certain issues, therefore, makes it easier for electoral officials who desire their support to align with their interests. At the same time, some have also argued that native-born Blacks' steadfast opinions are a foil to political incorporation because politicians and parties have taken the group's support for granted (Hanks 2000; see also Frymer 1999).

In light of the increased Black immigration from Africa and the

Caribbean, it is important to consider the extent to which the existing distinctiveness and influence of Black group consciousness may be changed or moderated by this phenomenon. This is especially important in that Black immigrants harbor different notions of racial identity, as well as attitudes about politics, than do native-born Blacks (see chap. 3, this vol.). Scholars differ, however, in describing how these changes in Black identity will be politically manifested. An older and more established body of literature suggests that Black immigrants from Africa and the Caribbean initially tend to stress their ethnic identities. Over time, however, they are forced by the reality of racial discrimination to identify with African Americans in a shared sense of racial identity (Waters 1994). More recent scholarship, in contrast, suggests that Caribbean immigrants are different from their native-born Black counterparts because they have a different conception of racial identity, but not because they emphasize ethnic identity more than racial identity (Rogers 2006).

If Black newcomers have different conceptions of racial identity, how is it manifested and what does it portend for Blacks' political participation? Rogers argues that while Afro-Caribbean immigrants acknowledge racial similarities with Blacks, they do not express the deep sense of group consciousness that has motivated Blacks to participate in politics above and beyond what their educational and class status predicts. The difference in group consciousness between native-born Blacks and immigrant Blacks from the Caribbean and Africa may result from differences in social networks, frames of reference, experiences in the United States, and ethnic identities. Thus, Blacks from the Caribbean and Africa have lived in societies that have been managed by Black leaders with varying degrees of effectiveness, while most Blacks in the United States have lived as racial minorities in White-dominated society. As a result, immigrant Blacks may not have the same fascination with symbolic representation as do native-born Blacks in America.

In addition, Blacks of Afro-Caribbean and African descent often compare their status with their counterparts in their home countries, often giving them a sense of progress or higher status. In contrast, native-born Blacks compare their status to Whites, a comparison yielding an often strong sense of deprivation. Black immigrants come from societies where ethnic and class divisions, rather than racial divisions explain disparities in material benefits. Furthermore, unlike native-born Blacks who are closely associated with churches and racial organizations that mobilize on the basis of race, African and Afro-Caribbean immigrants are less closely aligned to these organizations, where crucial socialization occurs.

Instead of being linked with these native-born organizations, Rogers and others have argued that Afro-Caribbean immigrants develop their own ethnic and panethnic organizations, often based on neighborhood social networks that connect them with people from their home countries and elsewhere in the Caribbean. Rogers argues that, as a result of these different histories and social networks, Afro-Caribbean and native-born Blacks perceive themselves differently in American society, even though they are viewed by others as coming from a homogeneous racial group. It is unclear, at this point, whether shared perceptions of racial discrimination ultimately will facilitate a panethnic identity that embraces both immigrant and native-born Blacks to facilitate future cooperation in electoral and organizational politics.

Group Identities among Latinos and Asian Americans/Pacific Islanders

To what extent have panethnic group identities emerged among Latinos and Asian Americans/Pacific Islanders? This issue is more complicated for Latinos and Asian Americans/Pacific Islanders because unlike Blacks, new immigrants make up a much larger percentage of these ethnoracial groups. As a result, Latinos and Asian Americans/Pacific Islanders tend to identify themselves based on national origin rather than on the basis of panethnic or racial identity.

With respect to Latinos, for example, internal diversity in group identities has long been noted by scholars studying such national-origin groups as Mexican Americans and Puerto Ricans, and even more so in respect to studies of panethnic identities such as Latino or Hispanic (see, e.g., Schmidt, Barvosa-Carter, and Torres 2000; Garcia Bedolla 2005; Marquez 2007). Survey research findings have been rather consistent that most Latinos identify politically most strongly in relation to their national-origin ethnicities (de la Garza et al. 1992; but see also Jones-Correa and Leal 1996). This may be changing, however. Preliminary analyses of the most thorough (and the most recent available) national survey of Latinos ever conducted (Latino National Survey 2007) reveal a more complex pattern of group identities than most American media interpretations have articulated. That is, recent survey results indicate that most U.S. Latinos conceive of themselves as having *multiple* political group identities, ranging from their national-origin ethnic group identity (e.g., Cuban, Mexican, Puerto Rican, Nicaraguan), to panethnic Latino or Hispanic identity, to a broader national conception of themselves as American. Racially, as well, the Latino National Survey found a more complex pattern than most Americans seem to accept as regards racial identification categories. Using the U.S. Census categories for "race," that is, most Latinos see themselves as neither "White" nor "Black" nor "Asian" nor "American Indian" but as some "other" race, most likely signifying a more complex understanding of race than the U.S. Census categories are able to capture (Latino National Survey 2007).

The fact that nearly half of U.S. Latinos are immigrants, as well as the complex social identity patterns discussed in the previous paragraph (as well as in chap. 3, this vol.), together mean that it is not clear how—or the degree to which—panethnic group identity functions as a positive political resource for members of the diverse Latino community. Jones-Correa (2007) has suggested that some Latino immigrants may avoid political involvements altogether, seeking to escape the cross-pressure of demands from both their countries of origin (transnational politics) and the United States (ethnic politics).

In any case, there are studies ongoing regarding the degree to which "linked fate" plays a significant political role among U.S. Latinos, but it is too early to suggest a clear pattern in the findings of these studies. It is suggestive, however, that one recent analysis of survey research over several decades found that while U.S. Latinos identify most strongly with their national-origin groups, those with a strong "racial" identity as Latinos (as contrasted with national-origin and panethnic identities) were most likely to vote and to participate in other ways in U.S. politics, especially in support of a "Latino cause." Moreover, this study found that U.S.-born Latinos are significantly more likely to have a racial identity as Latinos than are Latino immigrants, indicating that this form of self-identification may increase in the United States as the current generations of Latino immigrants produce native-born offspring (Masuoka 2008).

With respect to Asian Americans and Pacific Islanders, research has yielded a similarly complex pattern of ethnic identity as primary, with some degree of panethnic identity as well. In a survey of Asian Americans and Pacific Islanders, respondents were given the choice to identify themselves as American, Asian American, Asian, ethnic American (Chinese American, Vietnamese American) or based on national origin alone (Lien, Conway, and Wong 2004). A majority of respondents identified themselves as hyphenated Americans, like Chinese American, followed closely by the ethnic identification alone—e.g., Chinese, Japanese, etc. In fact, only a minority of the respondents identified themselves as Asian Americans (Lien, Conway, and Wong 2004). Nevertheless, researchers have identified variations among Asian American/Pacific Islander groups in terms of their identification as panethnic Asian Americans, with Southeast Asians identifying more as Asian Americans than other groups (Lien, Conway, and Wong 2004). Asian Americans and Pacific Islanders also report identity-switching, sometimes identifying as Asian Americans and sometimes in ethnic terms, depending on the context (Lien, Conway, and Wong 2004).

If Asians do not exhibit high levels of panethnic group consciousness, do they harbor a sense of closeness to one another? Data show that over 90 percent of native-born Blacks feel a sense of closeness with other Blacks. This percentage is almost double the 50 percent of Asian Americans and Pacific Islanders who feel that what happens to other Asian Americans and Pacific Islanders affects them (McClain and Stewart 2006; Lien, Conway, and Wong 2004). To some extent, differences in the degree of closeness reported by Blacks and Asians may come from the fact that, until recently, there was less diversity among Blacks than among Asians. Even above and beyond the issue of diversity, immigrants predominate among Asians and Pacific Islanders, and they have encountered fewer opportunities than Blacks to work with other members of their ethnoracial group, especially as they struggle to adapt to life as newcomers in American society.

If there is no inherent force that catalyzes group consciousness, a long and respected line of research in political science and sociology has shown the potency of external forces like opposition, discrimination, and stigmatization in facilitating group consciousness (McAdam 1982; Tilly 2004; Guinier and Torres 2002; Garcia Bedolla 2005). Perceptions of discrimination have often been linked to higher levels of participation in politics, especially among ethnoracial minorities who participate in order to redress grievances. In studies conducted over multiple decades, almost 70 percent of Blacks as compared with less than half of Mexicans, Puerto Ricans, and Asian Americans/Pacific Islanders report that they have been discriminated against personally based on their racial or ethnic identity (Hero 1992; Garcia Bedolla 2005). While all groups perceive a sense of discrimination, native-born Blacks report substantially higher levels of discrimination, which, in part, explains their higher level of group consciousness. Junn argues that the distinctive nature of Black group consciousness, or what she terms ethnic identity with a "political kick," is characterized by deprivation, blame attribution, and collective action that most exemplifies the native-born African American experience (2006). This does not mean that other groups have not experienced discrimination; rather it means that they have perceived it in ways that differ from Blacks' perceptions. It is in this way, however, that we see clearly the impact of immigration on

Latinos and Asian Americans/Pacific Islanders, for whom perceptions of discrimination are not as politically potent, but rather important from time to time in relation to hate crimes, stereotypes, and discrimination.

Regarding immigrants' influences, researchers have shown that first- and second-generation immigrants are less likely to perceive discrimination than are later generations, but the longer they stay in the United States, the more likely they are to perceive ethnic and racial discrimination against their own group (Mollenkopf et al. 2006). This issue is more important for Latinos and Asian Americans/Pacific Islanders than Blacks because of the continuing influx of immigrants, who are less likely to have experienced the factors that facilitate a sense of group consciousness. Prior to the mass influx of Asian immigrants during the early 1980s, Espiritu notes a definite sense of panethnic identity among Asian Americans and Pacific Islanders, especially during the 1960s and 1970s, which has to be renewed time and again, as newcomers' ethnic identities must be either supplanted by or appended to a panethnic bond with diverse ethnic affiliations (1992).

A similar pattern of closeness was identified among some Latino ethnic groups prior to the massive influx of immigrants during the 1980s. Navarro argues that the 1960s to 1970s civil rights movement provided the space for Chicanos to create organizations and identities that would be helpful to the political incorporation efforts of Latinos in general (2004). As part of that effort, Rodolfo Gonzalez's poem "I Am Joaquin" defined the essence of the Chicano experience and served as inspiration for discussions around the nation about ethnic identity among Chicanos (Navarro 2004). Flowing out of this sense of group consciousness was the establishment of La Raza Unida, the only political party devoted exclusively to the needs of Mexican Americans.

On the other hand, some scholars believe that the anti-immigration politics of the mid-2000s decade, perceived as coming particularly from the Republican Party, has generated a much higher level of panethnic solidarity among Latinos (both immigrants and nonimmigrants alike). Further, the anti-immigration politics may have long-lasting consequences for the group's partisan identification, shifting it toward the Democratic Party even among Cuban Americans (see, e.g., Barreto et al. 2008).

Thus, whether immigration and immigration politics have resulted in lower and/or higher levels of group consciousness among Asian Americans/Pacific Islanders and Latinos cannot yet be sorted out with certainty. What is evident, nevertheless, is that group cohesion via group consciousness both helps and hinders political incorporation in interesting ways. If the example of Blacks is useful, group consciousness has the advantage of facilitating participation above and beyond what is expected based on socioeconomic status, especially in promoting a cohesive and dependable voting bloc. This advantage of participation motivated by group consciousness could be an important factor for lower-income immigrants, for whom socioeconomic and educational resources do little to propel them toward the voting booth. On the other hand, the increasing diversity driven by immigration may increase the likelihood that Latinos and Asian Americans/Pacific Islanders are not taken for granted by political party and campaign leaders seeking more votes.

Partisanship, Race, and Political Participation

Another important factor in electoral politics is partisanship because of its potency in turning voter potential into electoral power. Nearly five decades ago, Campbell convincingly argued that "few factors are of greater importance for our national elections than the lasting attachment of tens of millions of Americans to one of the parties," and studies since then have confirmed that importance (Campbell et al. 1960, 121; also see, e.g., Bartels 2000). As we analyze how ethnoracial minorities have made efforts toward fuller access to political participation, the role of parties and partisanship is important to examine.

In the United States, the Democratic and Republican Parties are central institutions connecting people with government. Historically, American political parties played this role by socializing White immigrant groups and mobilizing them, as needed, to participate in politics. However, for ethnoracial minorities and especially for Blacks, parties did not historically provide easy access to participation. In fact, political parties in the United States played a central role in undermining Black access to the voting booth, through the establishment of "white primaries" as well as through political gerrymandering. In these regards, Blacks and other ethnoracial minorities worked through the judiciary to outlaw these exclusionary and discriminatory practices (Stephenson 2004).

In addition to their institutional role, political parties are also important because of voter attachments toward them. Partisanship is known to affect the rate of participation, candidate selection, and policy preferences. Although some argue that American parties are in decline (Wattenberg 1988) research has consistently shown that people with stronger partisan affiliations are more likely to participate, especially to vote, in American elections (Bartels 2000). For ethnoracial minority groups, parties are also important for the role they play in governance, especially in recruiting individuals to run as candidates in elections, in promoting legislative discipline, and in developing a party line regarding important policy issues. As a result, it is important to understand the relationships between Blacks, Latinos, and Asian Americans/Pacific Islanders and political parties, and the extent to which contemporary immigration has affected those relationships.

Blacks and Partisanship

In terms of party affiliation, native-born Blacks voted heavily for the Republican Party from the time of emancipation from slavery until the Great Depression. The New Deal policies of Franklin D. Roosevelt, however, led to a transition in partisan loyalties, and by 1964 Blacks were solidly in the Democratic Party because they felt that Democrats were more sincere in helping them to transform the United States into a more equitable and racially just society. In terms of quid pro quo politics, it is telling that the 1964 Civil Rights Act was introduced by one Democratic president, and signed into law by another, lending a measure of credence to Blacks' perceptions. Since that time, a high percentage of Blacks have voted loyally at the federal, state, and local levels for Democratic candidates.

This does not mean that Blacks support the Democratic Party in every instance. Indeed, there is evidence that younger Blacks have lower levels of partisan attachment than their older counterparts (Jaynes and Williams 1989). But it does reflect a sense of attachment to the Democratic Party that has, in some respects, helped to elect candidates of their choice to office. As will be discussed more fully in later sections of this chapter, there were approximately 300 Black elected officials in 1964, and at this writing there were over 9,000. A large majority of those Black elected officials have been elected as Democratic candidates. In this sense, Blacks are the most concentrated in their single-party loyalty in comparison with any other ethnoracial group and have been so for some half century. For Democratic Party and Republican Party candidates, the central question regarding Blacks in relation to electoral campaigns is whether the group will vote (mostly Democratic) in large numbers, or whether an unusual percentage will sit out the election because of unpopular candidates or for other reasons.

Latinos and Partisanship

The question of Latino partisanship is more complex than that of Blacks, in large part because of its national-origins diversity and the relatively large proportion of its members who are immigrants. Still, with the exception of Cuban Americans, Latinos have been among the most loyal Democrats for over four decades. The "Cuban exception," which is centered in the Cuban American communities of south Florida, is said to derive from the Kennedy administration's disastrous failed invasion of Cuba in 1962, driving most Floridian Cuban Americans into strong loyalty toward the Republican Party. In any case, while the Republican Party has made sporadic efforts to recruit more Latinos, these efforts have not been successful over the long term. The 2007 Latino National Survey, for example, found only 17.2 percent of Latino registered voters signed up as Republicans, as compared with 49.3 percent Democrats, and 11.5 percent were registered as Independents (Latino National Survey 2007, 22; see also Gimpel 2007). Moreover, press reports indicated that during the 2008 election campaign, the number of Independent new registrants among Latinos exceeded the number registering as Republicans, though most new Latino registrants were signing up as Democrats.

Among non-Cuban Latinos, voting patterns tend to skew heavily toward Democratic candidates in most elections (typically ranging from 65 to 75 percent). Overall, then, while Latinos are not as "captured" by the Democratic Party as is true of African Americans, they are nevertheless among the most Democratic-leaning of all ethnic and racial groups in the United States (again with the exception of Cuban Americans), and that has remained true for many decades. We see no evidence that the large influx of immigrants in recent decades is likely to change this pattern in the near future.

Indeed, it seems likely that the anti-immigration campaigns launched by Republican members of Congress in the first decade of the twenty-first century will drive even more Latinos toward affiliation with the Democratic Party. Clarissa Martinez DeCastro, director of state policy and advocacy for the National Council of La Raza, for example, argues that "the way candidates communicate about immigration is a gauge by which Latinos measure the level of respect or the perspective that a candidate or political party has for the community" (Burns 2007).

In July 2008, the Pew Hispanic Center reported that a national survey of Hispanic likely voters found, "Among Latino registered voters who identify with either political party or who say they lean toward a party, Democrats now hold a 39 percentage point advantage—larger than at any time in the past decade—with 65% of registered voters identifying as or leaning toward the Democrats, and 26% identifying as or leaning toward the Republicans" (Pew Hispanic Center 2008, vi).

*Asian Americans/Pacific Islanders
and Partisanship*

To what extent have Asian Americans/Pacific Islanders been aligned with
the Democrats? Despite the fact that some Asian American/Pacific Islander ethnic groups have been in the United States since the late 1700s,
there has not been a long and sustained relationship between Asian Amer-
icans/Pacific Islanders and the two major American political parties. Both
parties were complicit in the denial of U.S. citizenship to Asian immigrants until well into the twentieth century, and without citizenship, Asian
Americans/Pacific Islanders lacked a critical political resource, since only
citizens are allowed to vote in nearly all U.S. elections. As a result, the two
major parties did not expend resources in socializing and mobilizing
members of this ethnoracial group. In addition, it is evident that Asian
Americans/Pacific Islanders have had relatively low attachments to either
major U.S. political party (see, e.g., Lien, Conway, and Wong 2004; Wong
2006; Kim 2007).

While Asian Americans and Pacific Islanders may be less intensely
affiliated with political parties, they have contributed significantly to political campaigns. In comparison to Blacks, whose major campaign contributions have usually been in the form of working on campaigns, Asian
Americans/Pacific Islanders have participated by making financial donations through campaign contributions. The research suggests that Asian
Americans/Pacific Islanders tend to donate to coethnics first and foremost, but to other Asian American/Pacific Islander candidates, too. At the
same time, some Asian Americans/Pacific Islanders have donated generously to the campaigns of White candidates, though Kim (2007) questions
the degree to which such donations have benefited the members of this
panethnic group.

The largely immigrant makeup of Asian Americans/Pacific Islanders
makes it difficult to predict the future in terms of partisan affiliation and
intensity. It appears that currently Asian Americans and Pacific Islanders
are aligning themselves with political elites in the mainstream, although
they are also developing leadership within their communities. For example, the 80-20 Initiative, a project dedicated to organizing Asian Americans into a national swing voting bloc, is poised to use both parties to
achieve their aims. In contrast to Blacks, for whom the Republican Party's
stances make such alliances unpalatable, the 80-20 Initiative supported
two GOP candidates in the 2006 midterm elections and several Democratic candidates in Texas, Illinois, Washington, and New Jersey. The ef-

fects of these efforts to organize Asian Americans into a swing vote bloc have not yet been systematically analyzed.

Socioeconomic Status as a Political Resource

Numerous studies of political participation find that individuals with higher levels of income, education, and occupational prestige participate in politics at higher rates than those with lower levels (Verba, Schlozman, and Brady 1995; Verba and Nie 1972; Rosenstone and Wolfinger 1980). Considering the lower levels of education, income, and occupational prestige found among Blacks, Latinos, and some Asian Americans/Pacific Islanders, we assess two questions here. First, we examine the general standing of ethnoracial minorities as it relates to one another and to Whites. Second, we examine the influence of newcomers' status on existing ethnoracial minority group members.

Table 5.1 shows that ethnoracial minorities are overrepresented among those with the lowest incomes, education, age, and residential stability. Blacks are more likely than all other racial groups to be in the lowest income quintile, while Latinos are the most disproportionately represented among those with only a high school diploma or less. Latinos, followed by Blacks, are more likely to be among the younger age categories, and younger people are less likely to vote. While all Americans appear to be quite mobile, Latinos followed by Blacks appear to be especially mobile, making it difficult to become embedded in communities and more costly to complete the procedures necessary to vote. Regarding mobility and age, therefore, Latinos and Blacks are at an electoral disadvantage. Asian Americans/Pacific Islanders, on the other hand, have the lowest percent-

TABLE 5.1. Percentage of Race/Ethnicity in Demographic Groups with Limited Political Resources

Ethnoracial Group	Income in Bottom Quintile	Highest Educational Attainment High School or Less	Age Group 18 to 29 Years Old	Residency of Less than 5 Years at Current Address
White	18	42	19	40
Black	39	55	26	52
Asian/PI	14	31	22	49
Latino	28	59	29	53
Other	31	48	31	49

Source: Data from Project Vote, "Representational Bias in the 2006 Electorate," figure 2. Accessed at http://www.projectvote.org.

age of individuals in the low income and low educational attainment categories; they are second only to Whites in having smaller percentage of youth and lower levels of residential mobility. Like Whites, therefore, their electoral participation is less likely to be hampered by disadvantages associated with younger and more mobile populations.

Second, we examine the influence that *immigrants'* socioeconomic standing has exerted on the political incorporation efforts of Blacks, Asian Americans/Pacific Islanders, and Latinos. For example, are immigrants' levels of educational attainment elevating the standing of existing ethnoracial minorities, or lowering it? Are there similar or contrasting patterns across time and ethnoracial groups? These questions are important because socioeconomic status is known to be positively associated with participation in political activities. We use an assortment of data to assess immigrants' impacts in this regard.

Table 5.2 presents demographic and socioeconomic data for Blacks, Latinos, and Asian Americans/Pacific Islanders in 1990 and 2000. Unlike most data available on this subject, this table provides an opportunity to

TABLE 5.2. Social and Economic Characteristics of Major U.S. Racial and Ethnic Groups, 1990 and 2000

Ethnoracial Group	Population	Foreign Born (%)	Years of Education	Median Household Income ($)	Unemployed (%)	Below Poverty (%)
1990						
African American	28,034,275	1.8	11.7	29,251	12.5	32.8
Afro-Caribbean	924,693	72.4	12.1	42,927	9.4	17.8
African	229,488	72.1	14.3	35,041	8.5	24.7
Non-Hispanic White	188,013,404	3.9	12.9	47,481	4.7	11.3
Non-Hispanic Black	29,188,456	4.7	11.7	29,850	12.3	32.3
Hispanic	21,836,851	42.7	10.2	35,041	9.9	27.0
Asian	6,977,477	67.5	13.1	54,508	5.0	15.9
2000						
African American	33,048,095	2.2	12.4	33,790	11.2	30.4
Afro-Caribbean	1,542,895	68.3	12.6	43,650	8.7	18.8
African	612,548	78.5	14.0	42,900	7.3	22.1
Non-Hispanic White	194,433,424	4.2	13.5	53,000	4.0	11.2
Non-Hispanic Black	35,203,538	6.4	12.5	34,300	11.0	29.7
Hispanic	35,241,468	40.9	10.5	38,500	8.8	26.0
Asian	10,050,579	66.5	13.9	62,000	4.6	13.9

Source: Logan 2007.

compare within Black populations. Interestingly, in both 1990 and 2000, African immigrants led all other groups, including Whites, in the years of education. However, these higher levels of educational attainment are not reflected in incomes. As the data show, African immigrants make less money than Afro-Caribbeans, Asian Americans/Pacific Islanders, and Whites. Moreover, Africans are more likely to live below the poverty line than Afro-Caribbeans, Asian Americans/Pacific Islanders, and Whites, despite of their higher levels of education. Yet, when native-born Blacks are compared with Africans and Afro-Caribbeans regarding educational attainment, income, and poverty level, it is clear that these newcomer groups elevate rather than diminish the existing socioeconomic status of Blacks. Thus, newcomer Black immigrants, with more economic power and higher levels of education, might participate at levels consistent with Blacks even though they lack native-born Blacks' sense of racial group consciousness. Moreover, the higher levels of income among newcomer Blacks puts them in a better situation to contribute financially to political causes, ranging from electoral campaigns to political movements, adding to the existing pattern of institutional giving from churches and social organizations that is evident in the Black community.

There is substantial research showing the importance of SES resources (like income and education) for voting (Verba, Schlozman, and Brady 1995). Those voting at the highest percentages have U.S. college or university degrees, while the lowest percentage of voters included those with less than a high school education. It is notable that 30 percent of immigrants with no formal U.S. education participated in 2006 midterm elections, but this statistic can be misleading, as significant numbers of newcomers were already highly educated when they arrived in the United States.

Table 5.3 compares educational attainment data between foreign-born and U.S.-born Latinos to assess whether the influx of Latino immigrants has elevated or diminished Latinos' overall educational standing. Regarding educational attainment, Latino immigrants do little to enhance the overall educational standing of Latinos. This is because almost 60 percent of foreign-born Latinos have less than a high school education, and less than 10 percent have earned a college or professional degree. Among native-born Latinos, who like Blacks have lower levels of educational attainment than Whites and Asian Americans/Pacific Islanders, almost 30 percent have less than a high school diploma, while 13 percent hold college degrees.

The levels of educational attainment are echoed in the employment data, shown in table 5.4. Almost 60 percent of foreign-born Latinos have low-wage jobs, compared to about 40 percent of native-born Latinos. In terms of employment in the professional labor pool, only 16 percent of foreign-born Latinos work in these fields as compared to about 30 percent of native-born Latinos. In general, then, the influx of immigrants has dampened the overall socioeconomic standing of Latinos. This does not necessarily mean, however, that low political participation is inevitable. For example, Blacks, who are like Latinos in having low levels of socioeconomic well-being, participate more than Latinos and, in some instances, out-participate Whites. Scholars have linked their participation to mobilization and group consciousness. In contrast, Asian Americans/Pacific Islanders, who earn more than Latinos and have higher levels of educational attainment, often register and vote at lower levels than their Latino counterparts. In some respects, then, it appears that like native Blacks, the newcomer groups of Asian Americans/Pacific Islanders, Latinos, and Blacks are redefining the relationship between socioeconomic status and partici-

TABLE 5.3. Educational Attainment of Foreign-Born and U.S.-Born Hispanics and Non-Hispanics in the United States, 2000 (in percentages, persons 25 years and older)

Ethnic Identity	Foreign Born, Less than High School	Foreign Born, College Graduate or More	U.S. Born, Less than High School	U.S. Born, College Graduate or More
Non-Hispanic	21.3	36	16	25
Hispanic	58.5	8.8	29.1	13.4
Total	37.4	24	16.6	24

Source: Adapted from Panel on Hispanics in the United States and Committee on Population 2006, table 2-13.

TABLE 5.4. Occupation Status of Foreign-Born and U.S.-Born Hispanics and Non-Hispanics in the United States, 2000 (in percentages, employed persons 16 and older)

Ethnic Identity	Foreign Born, Low-Wage Labor	Foreign Born, Professional, Technical, and Managerial	U.S. Born, Low-Wage Labor	U.S. Born, Professional, Technical, and Managerial
Non-Hispanic	30	45.7	30.2	40.1
Hispanic	61.5	15.9	36.4	28.7
Total	44.6	32	30.5	39.5

Source: Adapted from Panel on Hispanics in the United States and Committee on Population, 2006, table 2-14.

pation in ways that lessen its relative impact, or confine that impact to only particular parts of the population.

Citizenship as a Political Resource

Citizenship can be viewed as the possession of rights, powers, and duties associated with formal membership in a political community. As such it is an important resource for political influence. In the United States, ethnoracial minorities have engaged in various struggles to claim rights as citizens, among them the right to vote and to elect representatives of their own choice. For most native-born Blacks, citizenship was ensured with the passage of the Fifteenth Amendment, but Blacks were largely relegated to a de jure existence of "separate but equal," rife with inequality, violence, and political maneuvering that made a mockery of citizenship.

Among Mexican Americans, U.S. citizenship was granted in the Treaty of Guadalupe Hidalgo (1848) to Mexicans remaining in the territory taken from Mexico following the Mexican American War (1846–48). However, as noted in chapter 3, the fact that access to the exercise of citizenship rights was determined largely by state governments, rather than the national government, meant that most Mexicans in the Southwest were unable to practice their citizenship rights until well into the twentieth century. Full and unfettered citizenship opportunities for Asian Americans/Pacific Islanders did not come until 1952, with the McCarran-Walter Act, which struck down the discriminatory immigration laws that excluded the lion's share of Asian American and Pacific Islander immigrants from becoming citizens. By 1965, therefore, most native-born Blacks, Latinos, and Asian Americans/Pacific Islanders had acquired not only the right of citizenship but, as a result of the passage of the Voting Rights Act (which we analyze later), the exercise of citizenship rights as well.

As we have seen, since 1965 immigrants from Asia and Latin America have swelled the ranks of the Asian American/Pacific Islander and Latino ethnoracial groups. For most nonelectoral activities—such as protest, organizational activity, and communicating with government officials—there is no prerequisite that prevents the political involvement of immigrants. However, if immigrants wish to be involved in electoral politics, they must be naturalized as citizens for nearly all elections in the United States.

It is important to note here that the predominant approach to the political incorporation of immigrants in the United States is one of laissez-faire. That is, there are few institutional supports—governmental or civic—for proactively encouraging immigrant newcomers to become full citizen members of the polity. Indeed, research by many scholars analyzes numerous legal and institutional obstacles faced by individuals contemplating the process of naturalization (see, e.g., Bloemraad 2006; DeSipio 2001; Garcia Bedolla 2005; Lee, Ramakrishnan, and Ramirez 2006; Wong 2006). As a result, the process of naturalization is often long and difficult for many immigrants, taking between 5 and 10 years to complete, posing a significant time barrier in the political incorporation process and dampening the electoral strength of both the Latino and Asian American/Pacific Islander ethnoracial groups.

Though naturalization provides the opportunity for immigrants to participate in electoral politics, research on voting participation has consistently demonstrated a relatively lower propensity to vote among naturalized foreign-born citizens (DeSipio 1996). With the exception of Cubans, researchers have consistently reported that foreign-born Latinos vote at lower levels than native-born Latinos as well as non-Latino Blacks and Whites (Pachon 1991; Mollenkopf, Olson, and Ross 2001; Shaw, de la Garza, and Lee 2000; Cassel 2002).

Exit polls conducted in 2006 by the Asian American Legal Defense and Education Fund found that among Asian American naturalized citizens, the largest percentage of voters were those who had been naturalized citizens for more than 10 years (AALDEF 2007b). Citizens who were naturalized less than two years prior to the election were the least likely among naturalized citizens to vote. These findings lend support to the claim that socialization through partisan attachments, protest, and organizational activities go a long way to provide immigrants with the experiences that they need to turn their electoral rights into electoral power for their groups (Ramakrishnan 2005).

When naturalized immigrants feel under attack from anti-immigration policies, they sometimes participate at equal or higher rates as the native born (Pantoja, Ramirez, and Segura 2001). This suggests that immigrant voter turnout also depends on the context of the larger election. Where immigrants feel threatened (as in campaigns seeking to target or attack immigrants), and where there is low participation among the larger public, foreign-born Latinos may vote at higher rates than previously anticipated (Barreto 2005).

Unlike in the period prior to the 1920s, in contemporary politics non-naturalized immigrants have been authorized to vote only in a handful of municipalities in the United States, where citizens are allowed to vote in school board and city council elections as a result of approval from state legislatures (in Maryland, Illinois, and New York). In Maryland, for example, noncitizens can vote and hold municipal office in Takoma Park, Barnesville, Martin's Addition, Somerset, and Chevy Chase. In addition, noncitizen parents in Chicago can vote in school board elections. In New York, noncitizen parents who have not been convicted of a felony or voting fraud can vote in community and school board elections as well as serve as members of the aforementioned boards (Hayduk 2006; Garcia Bedolla 2006). The number of localities that allow voting among immigrants is exceedingly small, despite the enormous influx of immigrants from Asia, Latin America, the Caribbean, and Africa. Much like their native-born predecessors from ethnoracial minority communities, today's non-U.S. citizen immigrants are also disenfranchised from electoral participation.

Voting Rights and Electoral Participation

One of the most important pieces of legislation to emerge from the 1960s civil rights movements was the passage of the 1965 Voting Rights Act (VRA). In 1870, the Fifteenth Amendment extended the voting franchise to former slaves, freed during the Civil War. However, until the passage of the VRA in 1965, the Fifteenth Amendment remained largely unenforced. Blacks were summarily turned away from polling places and subjected to violence, taxes, gerrymandering, and vote dilution to prevent their voting (Hine, Hine, and Harrold 2006).

Under the 1965 VRA, impediments to voter registration, to casting ballots, and to running for office for ethnoracial minorities were undermined, through permanent and renewable sections of the legislation. Among its permanent provisions are bans on literacy tests and obstacles to registration; and it establishes the authority to challenge elections procedures under Section 2 of the VRA. Specifically, Section 2 enables private and government lawsuits that challenge any election procedure that discriminates against racial or language minority groups. To establish a claim under Section 2 of the VRA, plaintiffs must satisfy three preconditions: (1) sufficiently geographically compact; (2) political cohesiveness; and (3) a White majority that votes sufficiently as a bloc to prevent the election of minority-preferred candidates (Sze 2004).

Certain provisions of the Voting Rights Act must be renewed by Congress and supported by the Supreme Court. These include Sections 5 and 203. Section 5 of the VRA covers entire sections of nine states (including seven states of the former Confederacy), as well as some counties and cities in seven other states. This element of the VRA provides the Justice Department with the authority to prevent Voting Rights violations before they occur, which is done through a "pre-clearance" mandate requiring certain jurisdictions with a history of discrimination to have their plans cleared by federal authorities before implementing them.

The dimension of the VRA that has been most important to post-1965 immigrants from Asia and Latin America, as well as to protected language minorities in the United States, is Section 203. Local jurisdictions have to furnish language assistance at all stages of the voting process, if either 5 percent or 10,000 of their voting-age citizens in a jurisdiction with a single-language minority community speak little or no English.[2] First enacted in 1975, the Section covers four language groups: Spanish, Asian, American Indian, and native Alaskan. Jurisdictionally, 31 of the 50 states must comply, comprising over 500 counties.

The VRA was essential in providing unparalleled access to the voting booth and allowing ethnoracial groups to elect candidates of their choice. The largest impact of the VRA has been with African Americans, whose voting and registration had a meteoric rise in the South following passage of the act. Similar increases were noted among Latinos and Asians in years following the implementation of Section 203. In regard to its impact on Latinos, DeSipio argues that the "1975 extension of the VRA defines the beginning of the era of national recognition of and expectations of Hispanic politics rather than the politics of Mexican Americans, Puerto Ricans or Cuban Americans" (2006, 449). In contrast, the impact of the VRA on the Asian American/Pacific Islander communities is noticeably less because these groups generally have higher levels of educational attainment, making them less likely to need non-English language ballots and election materials. Moreover, in the past these groups were not prevented from voting through taxes and intimidation but rather because they were not allowed to become citizens. This prohibition was not fully corrected until the passage of the 1952 McCarran-Walter Act, which allowed Asian immigrants of all ethnicities to be considered for citizenship and the right to vote.

While the VRA has provided large-scale coverage and helped ethnoracial minority groups to eradicate some major discriminatory procedures, its progress has not fully manifested itself in the composition of the electorate. As shown in table 5.5, Whites predominate among the voting-eligible population and are overrepresented relative to other groups among those who reported registering and voting in the 2006 midterm elections.

Although Whites constitute 74 percent of the voting-eligible population, they comprised 78 percent of those who are registered and 80 percent of those who voted. Among the ethnoracial minorities, none of these groups votes at or exceeds their level of the voting-eligible population. Since voting is one of the most direct ways of affecting influence over the policy-making process, the 2006 data show a relative paucity of ethnoracial minorities in the country's voting booths.

Black Electoral Influence

Among the ethnoracial minorities, up to now Blacks have been the most successful in translating their electoral resources into electoral influence, followed by Latinos and Asian Americans and Pacific Islanders. While Blacks have not maximized electoral resources, and while their influence on public policy is quite diminished (see chap. 6, this vol.), electoral participation has been the cornerstone of Blacks' political incorporation efforts since the late 1960s.

Blacks have turned their resources into electoral power by (1) registering and turning out to vote at levels sometimes approaching or in excess of their percentage of the population and (2) largely voting as a consistent and cohesive bloc, primarily aligned with liberal social spending and economic policies and the Democratic Party. Concerning registration and turnout, the percentage of White and Black registrants are similar. There are few differences in registration and turnout between citizens and total population, illustrating the smaller impact that Black immigrants from Africa and the Caribbean have had on national Black registration and turnout patterns.

TABLE 5.5.   Racial/Ethnic Composition of 2006 Voter Eligible Population (in percentages)

Ethnoracial Group	Voter Eligible Population	Registrations	Voters
White	74	78	80
Black	12	11	10
Asian/PI	4	3	2
Latino	9	7	6
Other	2	2	1

Source: Project Vote, "Representational Bias in the 2006 Electorate," figure 2, accessed at http://www.projectvote.org.

Table 5.6 shows the registration and turnout rates for presidential elections from 1980 to 2004. Approximately two-thirds of Whites and Blacks registered, while about half of Blacks have turned out to vote in presidential elections. A similar pattern could be seen in congressional elections during that period, although registration and voting rates are a little lower. In terms of national voter registration and turnout, Black voters as a percentage of the total voting-age population rose significantly from 1966 to 2006. Moreover, Blacks have historically turned out at rates higher than Whites at similar socioeconomic levels (Danigelis 1978; Kleppner 1982; Verba, Schlozman, and Brady 1995), but at rates that are lower than the general population of Whites. At times, however, specific circumstances of elections have raised registration and voting rates among Blacks higher than those of Whites, especially in local-level elections where Black candidates are running for office (Barker, Jones, and Tate 1999).

Black voter turnout in presidential elections appears to be strategic and somewhat contingent upon mobilization. In 1984, for example, Black voter turnout reached almost 60 percent, as Blacks worked hard, but unsuccessfully, to turn Ronald Reagan out of office. However, just four years later, Black voter turnout dipped to a low of approximately 50 percent, as Blacks stayed home to withhold support from the Democratic Party's nominee, Michael Dukakis (Tate 1993). In other instances, low voter turnout among Blacks reflects a lack of mobilization, whereby Blacks simply stay home on Election Day. With Senator Barack Obama as the Democratic Party's nominee for president, exit polls indicated a very high turnout of Black voters in 2008 (McDonald 2008, 3).

The most dramatic prior evidence of turnout, however, has occurred among Blacks in state and municipal elections in which Blacks were running as candidates. The consistent turnout by Blacks over the last four decades is likely responsible for the substantial increase in the number of elected Black officials from around 300 in 1966 to over 9,000 in 2006. Bobo and Gilliam contend that, in some instances, Black elected officials spur participation among Blacks in municipal elections (Bobo and Gilliam 1990).

Another factor that has been important in translating Black electoral resources into electoral power is the highly cohesive nature of the Black voting bloc. Over the last four decades, research has shown that despite increases in Black socioeconomic status, including income, wealth, and education, Blacks at all levels tend to vote as a bloc at national as well as state and local levels. Here again, the impact of group consciousness comes into play to override any countervailing influences such as socioeconomic sta-

TABLE 5.6. Reported Voting and Registration for Total and Citizen Voting-Age Population: Presidential Elections, 1980–2004 (in percentages, population 18 years and over)

Year		Total		White		White Non-Hispanic		Black		Asian[a]		Hispanic (of any race)	
		Total	Citizen	Total	Citizen	Total	Citizen	Total	Citizen	Total	Citizen	Total	Citizen
2004[b]	Registered	65.9	72.1	67.9	73.6	73.5	75.1	64.4	68.7	34.9	51.8	34.9	64.0
	Voted	58.3	63.8	60.3	65.4	65.8	67.2	56.3	60.0	29.8	44.1	28.0	47.2
2004[c]	Registered	65.9	72.1	67.9	73.5	73.5	75.1	64.3	68.6	36.1	52.5	34.9	64.0
	Voted	58.3	63.8	60.3	65.3	65.7	67.1	56.2	59.9	30.7	44.6	28.0	47.2
2000	Registered	63.9	69.5	65.6	70.4	70.0	71.6	63.6	67.5	30.7	52.4	34.9	57.3
	Voted	54.7	59.5	56.4	60.5	60.4	61.8	53.5	56.8	25.4	43.4	27.5	45.1
1996	Registered	65.9	70.9	67.7	72.0	71.6	73.0	63.5	66.4	32.6	57.2	35.7	58.6
	Voted	54.2	58.4	56.0	59.6	59.6	60.7	50.6	53.0	25.7	45.0	26.8	44.0
1992	Registered	68.2	75.2	70.1	76.3	73.5	77.1	63.9	70.0	31.2	61.3	35.0	62.5
	Voted	61.3	67.7	63.6	69.2	66.9	70.2	54.0	59.8	27.3	53.9	28.9	51.6
1988	Registered	66.6	72.1	67.9	72.8	70.8	73.6	64.5	68.8	N.A.	N.A.	35.5	59.1
	Voted	57.4	62.2	59.1	63.4	61.8	64.2	51.5	55.0	N.A.	N.A.	28.8	48.0
1984	Registered	68.3	73.9	69.6	74.5	71.6	75.1	66.3	72.0	N.A.	N.A.	40.1	61.4
	Voted	59.9	64.9	61.4	65.7	63.3	66.4	55.8	60.6	N.A.	N.A.	32.7	50.0
1980	Registered	66.9	72.3	68.4	73.4	70.3	84.7	60.0	64.1	N.A.	N.A.	36.3	56.0
	Voted	59.3	64.0	60.9	65.4	62.8	66.2	50.5	53.9	N.A.	N.A.	29.9	46.1

Source: U.S. Census Bureau, Current Population Survey, November 2004 and earlier reports, Internet Release date May 26, 2005.

Note: Because of changes in the Current Population Survey race categories beginning in 2003, 2004 data on race are not directly comparable with data from earlier years. N.A. = not available.

[a]Prior to 2004, this category was "Asian and Pacific Islanders"; therefore rates are not comparable with rates for prior years.

[b]Shows the single-race population.

[c]Shows the race alone or in-combination population.

tus. While the Republican Party has, on occasion, courted the Black vote and appointed Blacks to high-level cabinet positions, it has been unsuccessful in wooing large percentages of Black voters. To the extent that diversity in voting choices exists among Blacks, it is likely to come from Black immigrants who are more interested in issues of immigration and foreign policy than their native-born counterparts. Patterns of diversity in Black voting are already evident in cities like New York, with significant concentrations of Afro-Caribbean immigrants, who have worked hard in recent years to elect members of their own to office, often in competition with native-born Blacks (Rogers 2006). These patterns suggest that at the national level a Black voting bloc may cohere, while at the municipal and state levels a diverse set of voting blocs may form based on nativity and ethnicity.

Latino Electoral Power

To date, the overall story of Latino electoral power in the United States is one of unfulfilled expectations, as described succinctly by Garcia and Sanchez.

> Regarding Hispanics or Latinos at the beginning of the twenty-first century, the most accurate generalization that one can make about their rate of electoral participation is that it has been and remains strikingly lower than most other demographic segments of the U.S. population, including being lower than other identifiable ethnic and racial groups. (2008, 121)

The reasons for this assessment are not difficult to pinpoint. As noted in chapter 1, Latinos became the largest ethnoracial minority group in the country as of the 2000 decennial census, and made up nearly 15 percent of the U.S. population by 2006. Yet, as noted in table 5.5, Latinos made up only 9 percent of the voter-eligible population in 2006, only 7 percent of registered voters, and only 6 percent of actual voters. Thus, Latino voter turnout is typically well under half of the group's proportion of the U.S. population.

Table 5.6 looks at similar information from a different angle. Here it is evident that, once again, Latinos do not vote at the level that one might expect, given the group's proportion of the population. In the 2004 presidential election, for example, Latinos had the lowest levels of registrants

(35 percent) and voters (28 percent) of any ethnoracial group in the U.S. population. Table 5.6 shows that this has been a relatively consistent pattern for a number of election cycles over the past several decades.

Most political scientists who have studied this matter cite several key factors as reasons for this underrepresentation by Latinos in the electorate. Perhaps the single most important factor is the high share (nearly 30 percent in 2007) of noncitizens among U.S. Hispanics, which means, as we have seen, that nearly one-third of the Latino population is ineligible to vote in most U.S. elections. As table 5.6 shows, if we look only at the U.S. citizens in the Latino population, the proportions of registrants (64 percent) and voters (47 percent) go up substantially in comparison to the 2004 election figures noted in the previous paragraph.

Another strong factor is the relative youth of the Latino population. People under the age of 18 are not eligible to vote, and as Garcia and Sanchez note, in 2002, 34 percent of Hispanics were under age 18, compared with only 23 percent of the non-Hispanic White population (2007, 65). Even beyond that important eligibility age marker, research has consistently shown that young people are significantly less likely to vote than are their middle-aged and senior fellow citizens (see, e.g., Verba, Schlozman, and Brady 1995). Partly due to immigration (young adults are more likely to migrate than older people), the overall Latino population is strikingly younger than is the general U.S. population. Thus, in the 2004 American Community Survey, the Census Bureau found that U.S. Hispanics had a mean "age of 26.9 years, about 13 years younger than the median age of the non-Hispanic White population, 40.1 years" (U.S. Census Bureau 2007c, 7).

A third important factor is that of socioeconomic status, as discussed previously. With respect to SES, educational attainment seems to play a particularly significant role in motivating voters in most ethnoracial groups. Numerous studies of political participation have found that, for members of most groups, the years of schooling have a direct positive impact on a citizen's likelihood to vote (see, e.g., Rosenstone and Wolfinger 1980; Verba, Schlozman, and Brady 1995). The more years of schooling one has, the more likely one is to vote. Here again, Latinos seem to be significantly affected by immigration (a high percentage of immigrants from Latin America, especially from Mexico and Central America, have less than a high school education) and by the inability of American public schools to effectively reach and teach many Latino youngsters. Thus, the Census Bureau's 2004 American Community Survey found that whereas 16 percent of the total U.S. population had less than a high school education, this was true of more than 40 percent of the Latino population (U.S. Census Bureau 2007c, 15). Other SES factors have been shown to play a role in determining the level of voter mobilization as well, as noted previously; Latinos' generally lower incomes, lower wealth, and greater mobility than most other U.S. population groups are likely to play roles in suppressing Latino voting specifically.

In any case, the relatively low voter turnout among Latinos probably contributes significantly to this group's difficulty in exercising the level of political clout that might be expected from the nation's largest ethnoracial community. Some political scientists have suggested, as a consequence, that Latinos count for little in national elections. One prominent political scientist who has reached this conclusion consistently in studies of a number of national elections over the past several decades is Rodolfo de la Garza, of Columbia University.

> "[The Latino vote] is completely irrelevant," says Rodolfo de la Garza, a political science professor at Columbia University and vice president-research with the Los Angeles–based Tomas Rivera Policy Institute. "The myth was created by Latino leaders who wanted to convince politicians nationally about how important Latinos were. They believed that would make themselves and the Latino more important," he adds. "It was well-intentioned. It was also self-aggrandizing." (Yanez 2008)

While some political scientists assert that de la Garza overstates the situation, there is little disagreement that Latinos have not exercised the degree of political clout that might be expected by simply looking at their proportion of the U.S. population.

At the same time, it is important to note that this relative underrepresentation among U.S. voters, much of which can be attributed to the high percentage of immigrants in the Latino population, is offset by another fact attributable to the immigrant population from Latin America and the Spanish-speaking Caribbean: the rapid increase in the U.S. Latino population and a corresponding rapid increase in the *number* of U.S. Latino voters. Thus, in the 1972 presidential election, it is estimated that there were 2.1 million Hispanic voters. By 2004, the number of Latino voters had increased to 7.6 million (Garcia and Sanchez 2007, 139), and some observers have estimated that the number of Latino voters in the 2008 presidential election will exceed 9 million. Given this trajectory of rapid growth, the degree to which national candidates and parties feel compelled to court Latino voters seems likely to increase in the years ahead, even if the percentage of Latino voters continues to lag behind its proportion of the national population. At state and local levels, of course, Latinos already exercise considerable electoral clout in some areas (e.g., New Mexico, California, Florida, Texas; Los Angeles, Miami, Denver, San Antonio, Albuquerque, Phoenix, Las Vegas, New York City, Santa Ana). In any case, our point here is that immigration has been both a positive and a negative factor when it comes to Latino electoral clout, but the immigration-driven growth trajectory of this ethnoracial group seems to assure that its electoral clout will become increasingly significant in the years ahead, especially if the group continues to vote more cohesively than most other panethnic communities in the country.

Asian American Electoral Power

While once confined to descriptions of Latino electoral behavior, since 2000 the label "sleeping giant" has also been applied to Asian Americans/Pacific Islanders. This appellation comes, however, not because of their numbers but because of their fast-paced growth, concentration in key electoral states, and higher rates of naturalization and political unpredictability. Moreover, Asian Americans/ Pacific Islanders are reputed to be open to courting by candidates because of their so-called unpredictability in terms of voting. To what extent have Asian Americans and Pacific Islanders turned their ostensible electoral potential into actual electoral power?

Over the past several decades, as we have seen, there has been immense population growth in Asian American/Pacific Islander ethnic groups. Much of that growth has taken place among individuals who are part of the voting age population. In the electoral cycle between 2000 and 2004 there was a reported exponential increase in participation among Asian Americans/Pacific Islanders, with one million new voters registered, bringing Asian Americans/Pacific Islanders to 6 percent of the national electorate (Ong 2006).

On the other hand, while Asian Americans/Pacific Islanders are more likely than Latinos to become citizens, there is still a sizable gap between population size and voting-age population. Even more notable is the evidence that, considering their population size, Asian Americans/Pacific Islanders register and vote at lower rates relative to the population at large (table 5.6). In San Francisco, for example, Asian Americans/Pacific Islanders constitute more than one-third of San Francisco's population and a similar percentage of registered voters. In recent elections, however, Asian Americans/Pacific Islanders make up less than one-fourth of the voters. In contrast, Whites make up one-half of the city's population and about two-thirds of those who voted in recent elections (Eslinger 2006).

In some states, including California, where they are the third largest ethnoracial voting bloc, Asian Americans/Pacific Islanders vote more cohesively than national patterns reflect (Ong 2006). In other states, such as Oregon and Nevada, frequently cited as battleground states in presidential elections, Asian Americans/Pacific Islanders constitute a large share of the population that is unaffiliated with any party. Asian Americans/Pacific Islanders are also exercising clout at the municipal levels in small and medium-size towns as well. In a 2001 election in Flushing, New York, for example, Asian Americans/Pacific Islanders worked across ethnic lines to elect their first public official—a city councilman—to office. In most communities, however, Asian American/Pacific Islander communities are too few in number to constitute their own voting bloc (Chang 2005).

Compared to Latinos, Asian Americans/Pacific Islanders have higher rates of citizenship, which makes them eligible to register and participate in elections. In California, for example, 71 percent of Asian Americans/Pacific Islanders are citizens either by birth or naturalization. Some believe these high citizenship rates illustrate a propensity among Asian Americans/Pacific Islanders to be involved and contribute to California politics.

Fully transforming this potential into electoral power, however, has been problematic on two fronts. First, Asian Americans/Pacific Islanders continue to have lower levels of voter turnout, even among the native-born. Second, the diversity of this panethnic community is reflected in a lack of a cohesive or bloc voting. Table 5.6 illustrates that Asian Americans and Pacific Islanders usually register and vote at lower levels than Whites, Blacks, and Latinos. The Asian American Legal Defense and Education Fund contends that Asian Americans/Pacific Islanders are often discriminated against at the polls with rude treatment, requests to show identification, and being directed to the wrong polling site (AALDEF 2006, 2007b), which possibly dampens future participation, especially among newcomers to the electoral process.

Moreover, the Asian American/Pacific Islander electorate is not closely aligned with any particular party, as we have seen. Instead, there appear to be voting blocs among Asian Americans and Pacific Islanders that are influenced by local politics, particular election issues and the appeals of candidates. For example, Asian American New Yorkers are diverse, including Indo-Caribbeans in Richmond Hill, Chinese Americans in Sheepshead Bay, and Korean Americans in Flushing, and their ideological leanings and sociodemographic profiles vary widely (Sengupta 2001). Asian Americans/Pacific Islanders have smaller numbers and are less spatially concentrated than other ethnoracial groups. While their residential patterns provide greater opportunities for social assimilation, they undermine geographic cohesiveness, which is often a precursor to political cohesiveness. At the same time, the lack of residential contiguity and of a cohesive voting bloc may render Asian American and Pacific Islander candidates as optimal cross-over candidates, especially since they are more likely than Latinos or Blacks to be elected in nonminority districts.

Summary of Overall Findings on Political Participation

If examined from the vantage point of 1965, when Blacks, Latinos, and Asian Americans/Pacific Islanders were often locked out of the participatory process in American politics, the strides that each group has made in terms of registration and turnout are striking. Blacks have achieved top leadership positions in the Democratic Party. Latinos and Asian Americans/Pacific Islanders are now being courted as voters and as political candidates because of their groups' potential to serve as important players in U.S. presidential and tightly contested elections. National exit polls on election day 2008 indicated that without Black, Latino, and Asian American votes, Senator Barack Obama would not have won the presidential election.

The analysis has also demonstrated the effect of immigrants on ethnoracial minority groups' efforts to bring about full participation in the political process. In relation to political resources, in general African-origin and Asian American/Pacific Islander immigrants have raised the socioeconomic levels of Black and Asian American panethnic communities, while immigrants have depressed the socioeconomic levels of Latinos as a panethnic group. At the same time, large-scale immigration from Asia, the Pacific, Latin America, and the Caribbean has dramatically increased the overall size, and is increasing the electoral size, of the Black, Latino, and Asian American/Pacific Islander communities, while simultaneously reducing the *percentages* of these groups that actively participate in electoral politics. On balance, there is no doubt that the influx of Latino and Asian American/Pacific Islander immigrants has raised the capacity of each group to influence electoral outcomes. Nevertheless, when ethnoracial minority electoral participation is compared to that of Whites, it still lags behind.

Descriptive Representation

In relation to our organizing framework for understanding political incorporation, the franchise and the exercise of electoral power are but the first steps of a larger process of racial democratization. The franchise needs to lead to the election of minority-preferred candidates. In turn, successful candidates are expected to bring about beneficial public policies for ethnoracial group members (Browning, Marshall, and Tabb 1984). The assumption is that, in general, minority elected officials are more likely to advocate strongly for the interests of ethnoracial minority communities than are White officials.

We now turn our attention to the question of political representation, which is our second core benchmark for democratic political incorporation. Scholars have articulated various meanings of political representation (Pitkin 1967), but the most common in relation to ethnoracial politics is that of *descriptive representation*. Scholars and journalists have asked how many Blacks, Latinos, and Asian Americans/Pacific Islanders have been elected (or appointed) to various executive positions, and to legislative and judicial bodies at the national, state, and local levels in relation to each group's proportion in the general population (see, e.g., Mc-Clain and Stewart 2006, chap. 4; Browning, Marshall, and Tabb 1984). While it is not a sufficient condition of minority political incorporation, descriptive representation of excluded minorities is viewed as a *necessary* condition. Without it, peoples of color are left to a "politics of protest" or to being represented by surrogates from outside the excluded ethnoracial group.

First, we want to know whether Blacks, Latinos, and Asian Americans/Pacific Islanders have been elected to office in percentages that are in proportion to their percentage of the population. Are Black, Latino, and Asian American/Pacific Islander representatives only elected from majority-minority districts, or do they find success in districts where their co-ethnics do not predominate? At what levels of government are Black, Latino, and Asian American/Pacific Islander elected officials most likely to serve? How has the influx of immigrants, over the last few years, affected the levels of descriptive representation?

Second, in the context of immigration, we examine the contemporary factors affecting the election of minority representatives. In this respect, the influence of immigration is clear because the Fourteenth Amendment's equal protection clause, upon which the Voting Rights Act is based, applies to "persons" and not just to "citizens"; even the most recently arrived immigrant is counted in calculations of whether or not protected groups have suffered from vote dilution.[3] In a racially polarized community, the numbers of protected Latinos and/or Asian Americans/Pacific Islanders may thus be much larger than the number of eligible voters from the same ethnoracial communities. Even though they are not yet allowed to vote, then, recent immigrants of color are represented in this way *if* they settle in relatively compact areas with high concentrations of members of "their" ethnoracial groups. To the degree that they have done so, these immigrants may indirectly contribute to an increase in electoral representation of Latinos and Asian Americans/Pacific Islanders in government.

Third, we assess the extent to which apportionment—the drawing of electoral district lines, particularly in the central cities—has been made more complex by the arrival of new immigrants. Especially on the West Coast, but also in the East and more recently in the South and Midwest, urban areas that had been numerically dominated by African Americans for several decades have been affected by the influx of large numbers of new immigrants. This has complicated the politics of redistricting because the criteria for determining and overcoming racially polarized vote dilution under the 1986 *Gingles* Supreme Court decision require that a single minority population is large enough and compact enough to form a majority in a district; that the group is politically cohesive; and, at the same time, that it loses consistently to a cohesive White majority. Section 2 of the Voting Rights Act was created in response to discriminatory practices against African Americans in the South. It does not deal with the unique features of the Latino and Asian and Pacific Island communities that pose challenges to political representation.

Descriptive Representation in the Context of Increased Diversity

We begin by providing an analysis of the extent to which Blacks and Latinos, as well as Asian Americans/Pacific Islanders, have achieved political representation over the last four decades at different levels of government. When the electoral gains are examined in comparison with pre-1965 levels of representation, the gains in electoral representation appear to be very large. As we examine trends in the election of Black, Latino, and Asian

American/Pacific Islander officials over the last four decades, however, we are not only interested in the mere percentage of elected officials but also in their distribution across federal, state, and local governmental units. In the American political system, officials elected nationally often wield more power than their counterparts at lower levels of government, while state and municipal leaders have greater face-to-face representation opportunities than their counterparts at the national levels.

In turn, each level of officeholding has implications for the extent to which elected officials exert power and influence over the decision-making processes, which is an important aspect of political incorporation.

Black Elected Officials since 1965

The tremendous increase in Black elected officials after the passage of the 1965 Voting Rights Act demonstrates the opportunity that the law provided for Blacks to elect members of their own ethnic group to office. Prior to the 1965 Voting Rights Act, about 300 Blacks held elective office; just five years later, however, in 1970, the number had increased about fivefold to 1,469 Black elected officials; and between 1970 and 1985, Blacks had been elected to at least one public office in every state except South Dakota (Jaynes and Williams 1989). Blacks were initially most successful in the South. Table 5.7 shows the number and percentages of Black elected officials from 1970 to 2002 and the level of government in which they served. In the context of post-1965 immigration, the nature of Black descriptive representation has changed in some ways and remained the same in other ways. Similarities in Black descriptive representation over the last four decades are most evident at the city and county level. Over 50 percent of all Black elected officials serve at this level, and the number of Black elected officials in municipal offices increased by almost fivefold between 1970 and 1985. Initially, when Blacks served as mayors it was in small towns. The 1967 mayoral elections in Cleveland and Gary, and the 1973 election of Tom Bradley in Los Angeles, however, were early exceptions to that rule. It was not until the 1980s and 1990s that Blacks were elected more consistently to head America's largest cities, including New York, Chicago, Boston, and Philadelphia.

In contrast to the municipal patterns of representation, Black elected officials are least represented at the national and state levels, with less than 10 percent of Black elected officials serving in Congress or in state legislatures. Though small, the numbers do show an increase over earlier figures. For example, until Carol Mosely-Brown was elected to the Senate from

Illinois in 1992, no Blacks had served in the United States Senate since 1978. After Mosely-Brown lost her reelection bid, there were no Blacks in the Senate until the 2004 election of Senator Barack Obama, also from Illinois. In addition, in 1970 there were just 10 Blacks in the U.S. House of Representatives, but this number more than doubled, to 21 in 1984.

By 2006, there were 43 House representatives at the national level, including one senator and two nonvoting members from the District of Columbia. Most Black representatives were historically elected from urban rather than rural districts, a pattern that continues today. While Blacks have attained a measure of success in gaining representation in Congress, they have been more successful numerically in state legislatures. In 1970, for example, there were 31 Black state senators and 137 state representatives. In the years since then, the numbers of Black state legislators have grown dramatically. By 1985, all of the 11 former Confederate states, whose people had earlier been disenfranchised, had at least 1 state senator and no less than 4 Black representatives (Williams 1987). Still, the numbers and proportions of national and state legislators is small relative to the proportions of Blacks within states and nationally.

Descriptive representation in law enforcement has increased as well. In most Southern local governments, the sheriff was the person responsible for enforcing racially discriminatory policy, which often manifested in violence, destruction of property, and injury or even death. By 1985, 31 of the 37 Black sheriffs and marshals were elected in Southern states, though that number remains quite small compared to the number of these officials in the country as a whole.

TABLE 5.7. Distribution of Black Elected Officials, by Office Type, 1970–2002

Elected Offices	1970–79	1980–89	1990–99	2000–2002[a]
U.S. and state legislatures	8% (2,676)	7% (3,899)	7% (4,977)	7% (1,872)
City and county offices	54% (17,485)	67% (34,849)	60% (43,485)	60% (16,230)
Law enforcement	12% (3,610)	12% (6,444)	11% (8,339)	11% (3,078)
Education	26% (8,314)	20% (14,070)	22% (15,986)	21% (5,778)
Total number of elected officials	100% (32,085)	100% (59,262)	100% (72,787)	100% (26,958)

Source: Percentages were tabulated from U.S. Census Bureau, Statistical Abstract of the United States, 126th ed. (Washington, D.C. 2007), table 403, "Black Elected Officials by Office, 1970–2002, and States, 2001."

Note: Some percentages do not total to 100% because of rounding.

[a]Note that this column covers less than a decade.

Overall, the bottom row of table 5.7 illustrates a significant increase in Black elected officials since 1970. While the data provide no breakdown of ethnicity, it does show that the number of Black elected officials more than doubled, from over 32,000 between 1970 and 1979 to almost 73,000 between 1990 and 1999. Moreover, from 2000 to 2002, over 27,000 Black elected officials were elected as compared with the 32,000 that were elected over the course of the entire decade of the 1970s.

Latino Elected Officials

Historically, very few Latinos were elected to national office before the 1960s, the group having had a total of 7 House members (1 from California, 2 from Louisiana, 4 from New Mexico) and 2 U.S. Senators (both from New Mexico) (Garcia 2003, 134). Table 5.8 shows the number of Latino elected officials during times for which data are available over the last three decades from the 1980s to 2005. By 2005, the National Association of Latino Elected Officials (NALEO) listed 26 Latino members of the U.S. Congress (3 in the Senate; 23 in the House of Representatives), and a total of 5,041 Hispanic elected officials in national, state, and local offices (Garcia and Sanchez 2008, 207–8). Most of these elected officials were in the U.S. Southwest, though a growing number could be found in the East, Midwest, and South (especially Florida) as well. As will be shown, most Latinos served in the House of Representatives, and most were Democrats.

TABLE 5.8. Distribution of Latino Elected Officials, by Office Type, 1984–1994 and 2000–2005

Elected Offices	1984–89	1990–94	2000–2005
State executives and legislatures	4% (796)	3% (726)	5% (1,412)
Municipal and county offices	42% (8,505)	41% (9,814)	42% (11,824)
Judicial and law enforcement	16% (3,259)	13% (3,091)	11% (3,298)
Education and school boards	37% (7,312)	42% (10,098)	42% (11,965)
Total number of elected officials	100% (19,872)	100% (23,829)	100% (28,463)

Source: Percentages were tabulated from U.S. Census Bureau, *Statistical Abstract of the United States* (2007) (Washington, DC), table 404, "Hispanic Public Elected Officials, by Office, 1984 to 2005."

Note: Some percentages do not total to 100% because of rounding.

Latino descriptive representation, like Black electoral representation, is most numerous at the city and municipal level and also in the field of education. In fact, almost 93 percent of all Latinos are elected at the local level, and the states with the largest share of local representation have been California, Illinois, and Texas. Elected officials who serve at the local level gain expertise and experience often useful for pursuing elective office at the state and national levels.

Latino descriptive representation is least visible at the state and national levels, where just 5 percent of Latino elected officials served between 2000 and 2005. At the same time, it is important to point out that the number of representatives elected to serve in Congress has continued to grow. By 1984, new Latino representatives were being sent from Texas and New York, while other Latino Congressmen were added to the California and New Mexico delegations (Cruz 2004). After 2006 there were 23 Latinos in the U.S. House of Representatives, and 3 U.S. Senators. There is also evidence of decline in the judicial and law enforcement arena, where the percentage of Latino elected officials has declined consistently since the 1980s, despite the influx of Latino immigrants (Cruz 2004).

Asian American/Pacific Islander Officeholders

The first Asian American/Pacific Islander in the U. S. Congress was Dalip Singh Saund, whose election from a primarily White constituency foreshadowed the fact that, even today, Asian Americans and Pacific Islanders are more likely than Blacks and Latinos to come from districts in which other ethnoracial groups constitute a majority of the voters, especially White voters (Wong et al. 1998). This trend was repeated in the 2007 gubernatorial election of Bobby Jindal, an American of Asian Indian descent, who won 53 percent of the vote in the Louisiana primary, defeating a Republican, a Democrat, and an Independent. Whites constitute the majority of voting-age eligible voters in Louisiana, which does not have a significant Asian American/Pacific Islander population, although New Orleans is home to the longest-established Asian Americans (with roots dating at least to the eighteenth century).

Table 5.9 shows the number of Asian American and Pacific Islander (AAPI) elected officials since the late 1970s. At first glance, it would appear that Asian Americans/Pacific Islanders have different patterns of representational success than Blacks and Latinos. However, this image is distorted by the situation in Hawaii, where large numbers of state legislators are AAPI and, also where AAPI state legislators are almost twice as numerous as AAPI local elected officials. If Hawaii were removed from the calculations, AAPI local elected officials would be considerably more numerous than AAPI state and national elected officials, and the pattern would look more similar to that of Blacks and Latinos.

Asian Americans/Pacific Islanders have more representation among judges, and less representation among school officials, than do Blacks or Latinos. Since judges are often appointed initially (although they may need to run for reelection), this suggests that AAPIs have relied more on executive appointments to reach office, and that electoral politics has been a less successful avenue for them than for Blacks and Latinos. To the extent that executive appointments are the result of campaign donations and cultivation of ties with political elites, the Asian American and Pacific Islander strategy that focuses on relationships with elites as opposed to community organizing may be effective. For much of their history, the very small numbers of AAPI voters meant that AAPI candidates had little chance of being elected on a strategy that targeted coethnics.

In sum, tables 5.7 to 5.9 portray segmented descriptive representation: Black and Latino elected officials are more likely to hold offices at the county and municipal levels and on school boards than at the national and state levels. Although some research has shown that mayoral and other municipal offices are "hollow prizes" for mayors, other literature indicates that it provides opportunity for increased economic growth

TABLE 5.9. Distribution of Asian Pacific American Elected Officials, by Office Type, 1978–2005 (selected years)

Elected Offices	1978–79	1980–84	1995–98	2000–2005
U.S. and state legislatures	40.2% (130)	31.1% (191)	15.0% (213)	19.5% (357)
City and county offices	34.7% (112)	33.4% (205)	21.6% (306)	20.2% (370)
Judicial and law enforcement	17.3% (56)	21.8% (134)	43.8% (621)	39.6% (724)
Education	7.7% (25)	13.7% (84)	19.7% (278)	20.7% (378)
Total number of elected officials	100.0% (323)	100.0% (614)	100.0% (1,418)	100.0% (1,829)

Source: National Asian Pacific American Political Almanac, 1978, 1979, 1980, 1982, 1984, 1995, 1996, 1998, 2000, 2003, 2005. The 1978, 1979, 1980, and 1982 editions are titled National Asian American Roster. The 1984 edition is titled National Asian Pacific American Roster. The 1995 edition is titled National Asian Pacific American Political Roster and Resource Guide.

Note: Numbers in parentheses show the average number of officials for each category, for the years listed. Some percentages do not total to 100% because of rounding.

among minority businesses and better policies in terms of police and educational arena (Nelson 1987). At the same time, municipal officials can only do so much.

City and county officials are often dependent on the support of state and national officials to provide resources necessary to govern their localities. In environments of budget austerity, such dependence limits officials' ability to use government resources to address the socioeconomic problems that often confront disadvantaged Blacks, Latinos, and Asian Americans/Pacific Islanders (Stone 1989; Browning, Marshall, and Tabb 2003).

Ethnic Succession in Municipalities

Despite the constraints on municipal government powers, ethnic and racial groups have typically aspired to see one of their own heading a municipal government. From the Irish at the turn of the twentieth century to the rise of Blacks at the end of the twentieth century, ethnic succession in the mayoralty has been common in American political life. Given the increase in immigration from Asia, Latin America, Africa, and the Caribbean to American cities, it is important to understand the extent to which ethnic succession has occurred with respect to mayors in America's most diverse cities. To what extent, then, have Asians and Latinos replaced Blacks and Whites as mayors in major American cities? One way to assess this question is to examine diverse cities (as opposed to cities numerically dominated by one ethnoracial group) because they provide ideal contexts for ethnic competition and Latino as well as Asian succession.

An implicit assumption about political incorporation is that Blacks, Asian Americans/Pacific Islanders, and Latinos will gain elective office by displacing previously dominant White officeholders. However, the increase in immigration has brought about a different possibility: As ethnoracial minorities themselves become elected to office, they, in turn, might be replaced by a coethnic or a member of another ethnic group.

Table 5.10 lists the mayors in America's 13 most diverse cities, up to and as of 2007. It provides the name, race, year, and term of the first minority mayor as well as information about the mayor's successors. The data demonstrate the extent to which increased diversity has facilitated ethnic succession. We examine two questions: (1) the extent to which White incumbents are being replaced by the election of Latino, Asian, and Black mayors in America's most diverse cities and/or (2) whether or not minor-

TABLE 5.10. Minority Mayors and Succession in America's Most Diverse Cities

Metropolitan Area	Name of First Minority Mayor	Race of First Minority Mayor	Term of First Minority Mayor	Name/Race of Mayor Who Succeeded First Minority Mayor	Name of Second Minority Mayor	Race/Term of Second Minority Mayor
Chicago, IL	Harold Washington	African American	1983–87	Richard Daley/White	N.A.	N.A.
San Francisco, CA	Willie Brown	African American	1996–2004	Gavin Newsome/White	N.A.	N.A.
Dallas, TX	Ron Kirk	African American	1995–2002	Laura Miller/White	N.A.	N.A.
Houston, TX	Patrick Lee Brown	African American	1998–2004	Bill White/White	N.A.	N.A.
San Jose, CA	Norman Mineta	Asian American	1971–82	Janet Gray Hayes/White	Ron Gonzales	Latino/1999–2006
San Diego, CA	N.A.	N.A.	N.A.	N.A.	N.A.	N.A.
Los Angeles, CA	Tom Bradley	African American	1973–93	Richard Riordan/White	Antonio Villaraigosa	Latino/2005–present
Long Beach, CA	N.A.	N.A.	N.A.	N.A.	N.A.	N.A.
New York, NY	David Dinkins	African American	1990–93	Rudolph Giuliani/White	N.A.	N.A.
Miami, FL	Xavier Suarez	Latino	1985–93	Joe Carollo/Latino	Xavier Suarez	Latino/1997–95
Washington, DC	Walter Washington	African American	1975–79	Marian Berry/African American	Sharon Kelly	African American/1991–95
Oakland, CA	Lionel J. Wilson	African American	1977–91	Jerry Brown/White	Ronald Dellums	African American/2007–present

Source: Compiled from Biography Resource Center at www.galecengage.com/BiographyRC (accessed online on May 12, 2007); http://www.answers.com (accessed online on May 12, 2007); and Joint Center for Political and Economic Studies, Washington, D.C. (accessed at www.jointcenter.org on May 12, 2007).

Note: N.A. = not applicable.

ity mayors are being succeeded by another racial minority or a White mayor.

In 8 of the 13 cities, African American mayors were the first to succeed Whites. In Miami and San Jose, respectively, Cuban and Japanese American mayors were the first racial minority mayors to be elected. No Latino, Asian, or African American has been elected mayor in San Diego, Long Beach, or Orange County, California, despite their noted ethnoracial diversity. In Miami and Washington, D.C., the first minority mayors were succeeded by Cuban and African American coethnics, respectively.

Therefore, ethnic succession has occurred with the replacement of White incumbent mayors with Latino, African American, and Asian mayors. However, in America's most diverse cities, there is little evidence of racial competition among Asians, Latinos, and Blacks over the mayoralty. In most cities, minority mayors were succeeded by Whites rather than by another racial minority. Only two cities witnessed ethnic succession whereby a different racial minority replaced a previous mayor. But the succession in both cases took place over a decade after the previous racial minority mayor left office. For example, over a decade after the first Asian American mayor finished his term, citizens of San Jose elected a Latino mayor. Then, in Los Angeles, the first Latino mayor was elected in 2005, over 12 years after Tom Bradley's five terms as the first African American mayor of Los Angeles.

In terms of mayoral office in America's most diverse cities, there is no evidence to date in support of successful ethnic succession among Latinos, Asians, and Blacks over the last four decades. This does not mean that Blacks, Latinos, and Asian Americans/Pacific Islanders have not contested for mayoral positions. There were contested elections between Latinos and Blacks in Houston, Texas, and in Oakland, California.

Demographic Change and Descriptive Representation of Latinos in Congress: 1960–2000

We next examine how descriptive representation is influenced by immigration, which is affected by the fact that congressional districts are drawn on the basis of the number of people living in them, rather than the number of citizens. We examine the impact of changes in the demographic composition of congressional districts and implications for the number of Latino members of the U.S. House of Representatives. We focus on Latinos because of the unprecedented growth in their population, which provides an optimal opportunity to examine the influences of immigration.

The effects of immigration on descriptive representation are more evident after 1982, when Congress amended Section 2 of the 1965 Voting Rights Act.[4] The amendment protects the rights of minority voters to have equal opportunities to elect their candidates of choice when their numbers and configuration fit certain requirements. In a racially polarized community the numbers of protected Latinos and/or Asian Pacific Americans may thus be much larger than the number of eligible voters from the same ethnoracial communities. As mentioned earlier, even though they are not yet allowed to vote, recent immigrants are represented in this way *if* they settle in relatively compact areas with high concentrations of members of "their" ethnoracial groups. Since Latinos are more likely than Asians to be residentially segregated (see chap. 4, this vol.) the post-1965 immigration has brought increased *capacity* for Latino representation in government. The immediate consequence of the 1982 amendment was that in 1992, there were 10 new majority-Latino congressional districts, just 5 less than the 15 new majority–African American districts (Canon 2006).

In tables 5.11 through 5.14, we present data indicating the influence of concentrated Latino populations in congressional districts, as well as the contributions made by immigrants in those districts in four states with high Latino populations: Texas, California, New York, and Florida. In each table, we provide information for the 1960–2009 period on the name and party of each Latino House member, years served in Congress, the mean percentage of Latinos living in their districts while they served in Congress, and the mean percentage of foreign-born for the same time periods. We believe these data portray a clear pattern regarding the descriptive representation of Latinos in the Congress: most Latinos elected to Congress come from districts with a high concentration of Latino residents, and most of those districts have relatively high percentages of immigrants. In this sense, we believe that the U.S. Supreme Court's *Gingles* decision and the Voting Rights Act Amendments of 1982, as well as immigrants, have had positive impacts on the descriptive representation of Latinos in the U.S. House of Representatives.

Texas. The effects of immigration on increased capacity for Latino descriptive representation can be seen in Texas. According to the 1960 census, there was only 1 congressional district in Texas (out of 22) in which Latinos made up a majority of the population. By the 2000 census there were 6 Latino-majority districts (out of 30), all of which were served by a Latino representative. Much of this change can be accounted for—directly

and indirectly—by the influx of Latino immigrants over the 40-year period. Many of the foreign-born, moreover, tend to reside in congressional
districts already predominated by their coethnics. This concentration provides an ideal context under Section 2 of the Voting Rights Amendment,
as well as under *Gingles,* for the creation of Latino-majority districts. Over
time, descriptive representation increased from 0 in 1960 to 6 in 2000
(table 5.11). Descriptive representation among Latinos in Texas has occurred primarily in districts where Latinos make up more than 65 percent
of the population, but high percentages of Latinos do not necessarily assure descriptive representation for Latinos.

California. Once again, the data show (table 5.12) that opportunities
for descriptive representation among Latinos have increased by virtue of
the influx and concentration of Latino immigrants. In nearly every case of
Latino congressional representation in this state since 1960, there was a
Latino population majority and a relatively high proportion of immigrant
residents in the congressional district. In the 1960 census, there was not a
single congressional district in California (out of 38 total) that had a
Latino majority. By 2000 there were 11 districts (out of 52) with a Latino-
majority population, with 7 of these represented by a Latino. Following
the post-2000 redistricting, California was represented by 9 Latinos in

TABLE 5.11. Latino Congress Members in Texas

Congress Member and Party	Term	District	Latino in District (%)	Foreign Born in District (%)
Henry Gonzales—D	1962–2001	20	59	14
Eligio de la Garza—D	1965–97	15	72	28
Solomon Ortiz—D	1983–2009	27	63	13
Albert Bustamente—D	1985–93	23	55	16
Henry Bonilla—R	1993–2007	23	65	18
Frank Tejeda—D	1993–97	28	60	13
Silvestre Reyes—D	1997–2009	16	74	26
Ciro Rodriquez—D	1997–2009	28 (1997–2005);	63	10
		23 (2007–9)	55	19
Rubin Hinojosa—D	1997–2009	15	73	20
Charles Gonzales—D	1999–2009	20	69	11
Henry Cueller—D	2005–2009	28	65	12

Source: Compiled from Biography Resource Center at www.galecengage.com/BiographyRC; www.an
swers.com; National Association of Latino Elected and Appointed Officials, Washington, D.C.; and National
Roster of Hispanic Elected Officials, annual, accessed at www.naleo.org. Data for Latino in District are from
Michael Barone et al., *The Almanac of American Politics* (Washington, D.C., 1974, 1976, 1978, 1980, 1982,
1984, 1986, 1988, 1990, 1992, 1994, 1996, 1998, 2000, 2002, 2004, 2006.)

Note: Latino in District represents the mean from census data during representatives' terms served. Foreign Born in District represents the mean from diennial census data during representatives' terms served.

Congress, from the 11 districts with Latino majority populations. Again, many of these districts had a high percentage of foreign-born residents, having a net positive impact on Latino representation.

New York.   The data for New York is similar to that reported for Texas and California. During the 1960s and 1970s, there were no congressional districts (out of 23 total) in New York with majority populations of Latinos. By the 2000 census, there were 2 Latino-majority districts in New York (table 5.13). Both have Puerto Rican representatives, unlike California and Texas where most Latino representatives are Mexican Americans. Since Puerto Ricans are not "foreign-born" citizens, however, it is more difficult to gauge the effects of immigrants on Latino representation in this state.

TABLE 5.12.   Latino Congress Members in California

Congress Member and Party	Term	District	Latino in District (%)	Foreign Born in District (%)
Edward Roybal—D	1963–93	30 (1963–75);	50	55
		25 (1975–93)	67	25
Anthony Coehlo—D	1979–89	15	23	17
Matthew Martinez— D/R[a]	1982–2001	30 (1983–93);	55	45
		31 (1993–2001)	53	47
Esteban Torres—D	1983–99	34	51	25
Lucielle Roybal- Allard—D	1993–2009	33 (1993–2003);	84	55
		34 (2003–9)	77	35
Xavier Becerra—D	1993–2009	30 (1993–2003);	60	58
		31 (2003–9)	70	49
Loretta Sanchez—D	1997–2009	46 (1997–2001);	56	47
		47 (2001–9)	65	25
Joe Baca—D	1999–2009	42 (1999–2003);	51	19
		43 (2003–9)	58	18
Grace Napolitano—D	1999–2009	34 (1999–2003);	72	33
		38 (2003–9)	71	25
Hilda Solis—D	2001–9	31 (2001–3);	59	49
		32 (2003–9)	62	33
Linda Sanchez—D	2003–9	39	61	28
Dennis Cardoza—D	2003–9	18	42	20
Devin Nunes—D	2003–9	21	43	13

Source: Compiled from Biography Resource Center at www.galecengage.com/BiographyRC; www.answers.com; National Association of Latino Elected and Appointed Officials, Washington, D.C.; and National Roster of Hispanic Elected Officials, annual, accessed at www.naleo.org. Data for Latino in District are from Michael Barone, et.al., *The Almanac of American Politics* (Washington, D.C., 1974, 1976, 1978, 1980, 1982, 1984, 1986, 1988, 1990, 1992, 1994, 1996, 1998, 2000, 2002, 2004, 2006).

Note: Latino in District represents the mean from census data during representatives' terms served. Foreign Born in District represents the mean from diennial census data during representatives' terms served.

[a]Matthew Martinez switched from the Democratic Party to the Republican Party in 2000.

Florida. This state's story of Latino congressional representation differs in some ways from those of the preceding three states. Descriptive representation of Latinos in Florida's congressional delegation did not begin until 1989, no doubt because the large increase in the state's Latino population did not begin until the early 1960s, following Fidel Castro's overthrow of the Batista regime in 1959 (chap. 3, this vol.). For a period of time following and during the large influx of refugees from Castro's Cuba, most of the state's Latinos were not yet U.S. citizens and could not vote. By 1980, however, Florida had its first Latino-majority congressional district, and by the end of that decade, Florida had its first Latina House member (table 5.14). Following the 2000 census, Florida had three districts with Latino members of Congress, all three coming from Latino-majority dis-

TABLE 5.13. Latino Congress Members in New York

Congress Member and Party	Term	District	Latino in District (%)	Foreign Born in District (%)
Herman Badillo—D	1971–79	21	44	14
Robert Garcia—D	1978–90	21 (1978–83);	79	14
		18 (1983–90)	48	20
Jose Serreno—D	1990–2005	18 (1990–93);	51	14
		16 (1993–2009)	60	21
Nydia Velazquez—D	1993–2009	12	53	42

Source: Compiled from Biography Resource Center at www.galecengage.com/BiographyRC; www .answers.com; National Association of Latino Elected and Appointed Officials, Washington, D.C.; and National Roster of Hispanic Elected Officials, annual, accessed at www.naleo.org. Data for Latino in District are from Michael Barone, et.al., *The Almanac of American Politics* (Washington, D.C., 1974, 1976, 1978, 1980, 1982, 1984, 1986, 1988, 1990, 1992, 1994, 1996, 1998, 2000, 2002, 2004, 2006).

Note: Latino in District represents the mean from census data during representatives' terms served. Foreign Born in District represents the mean from diennial census data during representatives' terms served.

TABLE 5.14. Latino Congress Members in Florida

Congress Member and Party	Term	District	Latino in District (%)	Foreign Born in District (%)
Ileana Ros-Letinen—R	1989–2009	18	63	56
Lincoln Diaz-Balart—R	1993–2009	21	70	58
Mario Diaz-Balart—R	2003–2009	25	62	N.A.

Source: Compiled from Biography Resource Center at www.galecengage.com/BiographyRC; www .answers.com; National Association of Latino Elected and Appointed Officials, Washington, D.C.; and National Roster of Hispanic Elected Officials, annual, accessed at www.naleo.org. Data for Latino in District are from Michael Barone, et. al., *The Almanac of American Politics* (Washington, D.C., 1974, 1976, 1978, 1980, 1982, 1984, 1986, 1988, 1990, 1992, 1994, 1996, 1998, 2000, 2002, 2004, 2006).

Note: Latino in District represents the mean from census data during representatives' terms served. Foreign Born in District represents the mean from diennial census data during representatives' terms served. N.A. = not available.

tricts. Party affiliation, of course, marks another significant difference between Florida's Latino representatives and those of our other three states described in this section, since all three of Florida's House members are Republicans.

To summarize, we believe that the data presented here clearly illustrate, if not definitively describe, the impacts that immigrants have on the descriptive representation of Latinos in the U.S. Congress. Immigration directly and indirectly increased the numbers and percentages of Latinos in the overall population, making it more likely that there will be increasing numbers of congressional districts with Latino majority populations. This last factor, in conjunction with the redistricting criteria supplied by the Supreme Court's *Gingles* decision and the 1982 amendments to the Voting Rights Act, has directly led to increases in the number of Latino members of the U.S. House of Representatives. To put this process into a larger perspective, we turn now to a description of the relationship between the Voting Rights Act and the descriptive representation of U.S. ethnoracial minorities.

The Voting Rights Act and the Election of Black, Latino, and Asian American/Pacific Islander Officials

Having assessed the percentages of Black, Latino, and Asian American/Pacific Islander elected officials as part of a larger focus on political incorporation, we now consider the impact of the Voting Rights Act on political representation. Overall, the data suggest that Latinos, Blacks, and Asian Americans/Pacific Islanders have gained increased percentages of the elected officials since the passage of the 1965 Voting Rights Act. An additional question, though, is whether this is merely a coincidence. Did Blacks' and other groups' efforts to secure passage of this legislation really create opportunity for substantial political representation of Blacks, Latinos, and Asian Americans/Pacific Islanders as elected officials? In what specific ways did the VRA facilitate ethnoracial political representation, and to what extent has the immigration of non-English-speaking immigrants affected the applicability of the VRA to newcomer groups?

We previously provided an overview of the 1965 Voting Rights Act as well as subsequent amendments. In the summer of 2006, Congress renewed Sections 5 and 203 of the Voting Rights for 25 years under the Fannie Lou Hamer, Rosa Parks, and Coretta Scott King Voting Rights Act Reauthorization and Amendments Act of 2006. Section 5 requires jurisdictions covered under the VRA to obtain pre-clearance before they change any of the electoral laws or arrangements, while Section 203 mandates language assistance. Under the renewal legislation, Congress expanded the law's coverage to include jurisdictions with 10,000 or more single-language minorities in the population in light of evidence of continuing violations.

There is considerable evidence that Sections 5 and 203 were very important in eliminating barriers to the election of Blacks, Latinos, and Asian Americans/Pacific Islanders to office. In 2003, the states of Louisiana and Texas attempted to move forward with redistricting plans that would have diminished the political opportunities for Blacks and Latinos, respectively, according to critics (Fredrickson and Vagins 2006). Litigants in Louisiana successfully challenged these efforts under Section 5 of the VRA, and a federal court held that the state must withdraw its plan and restore a district where Blacks had an opportunity to elect a candidate of their choice. Litigants in Texas also used the VRA to strike down a redistricting plan that was allegedly drawn purposely to limit Latino political representation (Fredrickson and Vagins 2006).

Latinos and Asians have also used Section 203 of the Voting Rights Act, which contains language assistance election requirements, to seek to increase their share of elected officials. Prior to the inclusion of Section 203 in the 1975 Renewal of the Voting Rights Act, a large portion of the Latino population did not register to vote because they could not read the election material and could not communicate well with pollsters (Fredrickson and Vagins 2006). Just a year after it was enacted, Latinos cast 2 million ballots in the 1976 presidential election. Prior to its enactment in 1974, there were only 1,200 Latino elected officials compared with a fivefold increase to 6,000 in 2004 (Fredrickson and Vagins 2006). Among Asians, the effect of Section 203 was evident as first-generation Asian Americans/Pacific Islanders went to the polls in 2001 to help elect John Liu as New York's first Asian American/Pacific Islander to the New York City Council. Then, in 2004, the provisions were again relevant as first-generation Asian Americans/Pacific Islanders turned out to elect Jimmy Meng as the first Asian American and Pacific Islander member of the New York State Assembly.

When the Department of Justice intervened to ensure that language assistance would be provided to Vietnamese Americans in Harris County, Texas, they turned out to bring about the election of the first Vietnamese American to the Texas state legislature in 2004 (Fredrickson and Vagins 2006). In a recent study, researchers have shown that the VRA has provided an important context "for the ascension of non-White groups into elected leadership of the nation" (Lien et al. 2007, 489). They offer as evidence in support of this contention the fact that VRA Amendments provided the opportunity for the creation of majority-minority districts. While Asians are often elected from districts that are composed of other ethnic groups, Blacks and Latinos are largely elected from majority-minority districts, in which their groups predominate. The sole exception to this pattern exists for Blacks at the local and county levels, where only a fraction of Black local officials were elected from majority-Black counties. Second, their research shows that in the U.S. House of Representatives most non-White members were elected from districts covered by the VRA, which provided conditions in which the rules for elections and electoral processes could not be changed without prior approval (Lien et al. 2007). Third, these protections increased the actual number of Black, Latino, and Asian American/Pacific Islander elected officials at all levels of government.

At the same time, there remains a large representational gap whereby Whites have received the highest levels of descriptive racial representation and are, in fact, the only group overrepresented, while Blacks followed by Latinos and Asian Americans/Pacific Islanders are underrepresented. As Blacks, Latinos, and Asians attempt to use electoral politics to obtain higher levels of representation in elected office, however, they are encountering two issues.

First, there is a growing number of Supreme Court cases that are undermining the effectiveness of the Voting Rights Act (Johnson 1995). In *Shaw v. Reno* 113 S. Ct. 2816 (1993), the Supreme Court invalidated a reapportionment plan that was designed to remedy voting rights violations. The following year, in *Johnson v. DeGrandy* 114 S.Ct. 2647 (1994), the Supreme Court reversed an earlier decision in favor of Latino litigants that a reapportionment scheme violated the Voting Rights Act. Also in 1994, the Supreme Court, in *Holder v. Hall,* 572 U.S. 874 (1994), decided that the rights of plaintiffs cannot be based on the size of the governing authority.

Second, immigration has created a multiracial context that moves issues beyond the White-Black framework of the VRA. These challenges are especially prominent in the battle for apportionment; when electoral districts are drawn, Whites, Blacks, Latinos, and Asian Americans/Pacific Islanders contend for political representation through the electoral process. Unlike earlier scenarios in which Blacks, Asian Americans/Pacific Islanders, and Latinos could draw from the framework of Sections 5 or 203 of the VRA, this legislation does not provide answers to multiracial contexts affected by post-1965 immigration.

In fact, immigration is revealing the limits of the Voting Rights Act, as it applies to some multiracial jurisdictions. For example, in *Cano v. Davis*, the Mexican American Legal Defense and Education Fund (MALDEF) contended that the California legislature used the state's congressional redistricting process to dilute Latino voting power in violation of the Voting Rights Act (211 F. Supp. 2d 1208 [C.D. Cal. 2002], aff'd 537 U.S. 1100 123 S. Ct. 851 [2003]). Some legal scholars contend that this conflict within the Latino community portends or begs for a future conflict over political representation. There may be disagreements involving Central Americans, who made up almost 9 percent of the Latino population in Los Angeles County and who argue that they are being locked out of the electoral process by politicians of Mexican ancestry, who make up the vast majority of Latino state and local elected offices in California (Johnson 2003).

In San Francisco, Asian Americans and Pacific Islanders, who previously held 3 of the 11 supervisor seats in San Francisco County, lost 2 seats after a change from at-large to district elections in 2000 (Sze 2004). The result was ironic because minorities usually fare better in district rather than at-large elections and also because San Francisco is one of the most Asian American cities. However, Section 2 of the VRA is not really a remedy for this type of situation because, as currently constituted, Asian Americans and Pacific Islanders do not meet the requirements of the three-prong test developed in *Thornburg v. Gingles*: (1) minority group must be sufficiently large and geographically compact to constitute a majority district in a single-member district; (2) be politically cohesive; (3) Whites vote sufficiently as a bloc to defeat minority-preferred candidates (*Thornburg v. Gingles*, 478 U.S. at 47 [1986]).

So far, most Asian American and Pacific Islander communities are heterogeneous in terms of nationality, language, educational attainment, health, economics, and political attitudes, which means that they have little in common with one another. Using traditional measures like partisan affiliation and ideology, they do not behave like a politically cohesive group, either. Moreover, efforts to disaggregate the Asian and Pacific Island community into smaller ethnic constituencies presents problems in meeting the condition of having sufficient numerical size. The current *Gingles* criteria framework does not provide a way for panethnic coalition formation among Asian American and Pacific Islander ethnic groups to meet the VRA requirements (Sze 2004).

Currently, there are only a few districts in the country where an Asian American and Pacific Islander community is sufficiently large, geographically compact and cohesive enough to fulfill the *Gingles* factors. The equipopulation principle, which governs redistricting, requires that all electoral districts must contain approximately the same number of people, but even the largest Asian concentrations in Southern California are insufficient to meet the electoral standards (Yoshino 1999).

Conclusion

Three major themes emerge from our discussion in this chapter. First, Blacks, Latinos, and Asian Americans/Pacific Islanders have achieved significantly more access to participation, and immigrants have both helped and hindered that process in different ways and at different points of time. Second, while important gains have been made, the presence of the newcomers has illuminated the existence of barriers that were heretofore invisible. Third, political representation is a result of groups' success at increasing access to participation, of residential housing patterns, and of ever-changing court decisions about the constitutionality of majority-minority districts. In the wake of post-1965 immigration, majority-minority districts have the added complexity of a multiracial population and the difficulty of deciding what group to advantage, especially since there is now more than one disadvantaged ethnoracial minority group in many districts. In the next chapter we will take up the next two criteria for full political incorporation that we address in this book: the degrees to which Blacks, Latinos, and Asian Americans/Pacific Islanders have realized membership in the dominant governing coalitions of American politics, and the degrees to which they have been able to secure adoption of ethnoracially egalitarian public policies.

6 | Political Incorporation, Governing Coalitions, and Public Policy

Having provided an overview of the ways in which recent immigrants have affected the degree to which U.S. Blacks, Latinos, and Asian Americans (1) are participants in and (2) are represented in the political process, we turn now to an examination of our next two benchmarks of political incorporation: (3) substantial influence or power over governmental decisions through membership in governing coalitions, and (4) the adoption of public policies aimed at realizing greater ethnoracial equality in U.S. society and political life.

Immigrants, Racial Politics, and Governing Coalitions

Beyond political participation and representational parity, the analytical framework we are using in this book suggests that full incorporation of an outsider group requires that the group also has a share in the actual decision-making processes of authoritative governmental institutions. That is, fully incorporated group members will have substantive participation in, and influence on, governmental decisions about public policy and appointments to government offices (judicial appointments, political executive appointments, etc.).

In their foundational study of minority political incorporation in 10 San Francisco Bay Area cities, for example, Browning, Marshall, and Tabb (1984) argued that representation of minority voters is necessary but insufficient for attaining full incorporation. This is so because in a racially polarized polity, being "represented" does not prevent the dominant ethnoracial group from ignoring a minority community's interests when making governmental decisions. The minority group will not be fully incorporated if it loses most of the time on policy issues thought important by the minority community and its leaders. Thus, Browning, Marshall, and Tabb argued, a minority community needs to become part of a governing coalition that can dominate city politics most of the time before it can be considered fully incorporated. They summarized their criteria for incorporation as follows.

> A group that has achieved substantial political incorporation has taken a major step toward political equality. It is in a position to articulate its interests, its demands will be heard, and through the dominant coalition it can ensure that certain interests will be protected, even though it may not win on every issue. The group will have successfully opened the system and gained the kind of ability to make its interests prevail that other groups have already achieved. (1984, 27)

A similar point was made differently by Guinier (1994) in her analysis of Voting Rights Act litigation. Guinier argued that the Voting Rights Act was adopted in hopes of achieving the central aim of the civil rights movement: realizing genuine democratic fairness in the U.S. political system. While gaining *access* to the political process (through overturning various kinds of voting rights denial), and *representation* in the political system (through overturning various forms of voting rights dilution) are necessary steps in that process, they are insufficient for achieving democratic fairness. This is so because in a racially polarized polity, minority voices and minority interests might still be suppressed and/or overridden through tyranny of the majority. Under simple majority rule, for example, minority representatives in legislative bodies might still lose every single vote on issues perceived by them as essential for overturning an antidemocratic racial hierarchy. Guinier argued this violates fundamental democratic fairness, and she called for legalizing the principle of *interest representation* as the necessary next step (a third generation of reform) toward democratization of the U.S. political system. To remedy this problem, Guinier proposed that U.S. governments adopt decision rules[1] that would force a majority population to hear, consider, and sometimes compromise with a minority population in a racialized political context. The arguments of Guinier, and of Browning, Marshall, and Tabb, then, recognize that unless a racialized minority has ways to effectively and substantially influence governmental decisions, it may continue to suffer from majority tyranny, despite having access to the political arena, and despite having been able to achieve some measure of representation.

It should be noted, moreover, that most of the literature in political science on the political incorporation of outsider groups approaches its subject from a pluralist perspective. That is, while many individual voters from among the country's ethnoracial groups may (now or someday) participate in political life as assimilated individuals without conscious attachments to their groups of origin, minority group members who are in public office are routinely viewed by others as descriptive representatives of their ethnoracial groups of origin, and there is strong pressure on them to substantively represent and to otherwise identify with those groups. At the level of public officialdom, then, the central question generating most studies on political incorporation is whether the outsider group has been sufficiently incorporated to be depicted accurately as pluralist, or whether substantial obstacles to full incorporation remain so that either biracial or multiracial hierarchy is a more accurate depiction of the political power relationships in the governmental bodies in question.

This approach to minority political incorporation, in sum, views this subject from the perspective that members of ethnoracial minority groups active in politics (as well as members of other significant political groups) tend to seek political empowerment through cohesive group action, and that gaining membership in the governing or dominant coalitions that exercise the greatest amount of influence over governmental decisions is vital to full incorporation. At the local level, particularly in nonpartisan jurisdictions, this most often means gaining membership in informal dominant coalitions among city council members or county legislators, and (sometimes) elected executives. For most *partisan* governments, however, these dominant coalitions are typically made up of the most powerful leaders of the majority political party. At the national political level, for example, having substantial influence over public policy decisions would require gaining membership in the leadership cohorts of the dominant political party in the U.S. House of Representatives and/or Senate; in the most powerful groups in the party controlling the White House; and/or in the senior levels of the permanent civil service in a particular administrative agency.

From this perspective, the full political incorporation of minority outsider groups involves their becoming full-fledged peers with other members of the dominant coalitions of various governmental bodies—city councils, state legislatures, executive agencies, the U.S. Congress—in the United States. This section of our analysis, therefore, will be addressed to the questions of the degree to which this kind of political incorporation of Blacks, Latinos, and Asian Americans has taken place in the United States over the past four decades, and the effects of large-scale immigration on this aspect of political incorporation.

Since our inquiry is national in scope, and the development and maintenance of governing coalitions are inherently subject to instability and political change even in the absence of high levels of immigration, we cannot hope to provide a thorough description and analysis of the effects of immigration on this rapidly changing and highly complex subject. What we will do is provide a summary of some of the most important studies that have been done attempting to track the influence of immigrants on ethnoracial minority coalition-building politics in key urban areas of the country, and then we will address the question of the impact of immigration on minority efforts to gain greater influence in dominant political coalitions at state and national levels. We believe these summaries will be helpful in gauging the general trajectory of ethnoracial politics in the United States some forty to fifty years into this era of large-scale immigration. Before we turn to this investigation, however, it is necessary to examine in a general way the interplay between *immigrant* incorporation and the efforts of our three ethnoracial minority groups to gain membership in dominant or governing coalitions in government.

Immigrants, Incorporation, and Minority Access to Governing Coalitions

There seems little doubt that attempts to increase membership of ethnoracial minority groups in dominant or governing coalitions have been affected by the influx of new immigrants in recent decades. Research on this specific topic, however, is very sparse. Understanding the impacts of immigrants on minority group membership in governing coalitions requires attention to prior and changing ethnoracial coalitional work and how immigration is altering this work and its accomplishments across the American political landscape. It is important also to understand the types of policy issues at stake in coalitional activity, and the institutional contexts that modulate the interactions between ethnoracial politics and immigrants. To consider these questions and to illustrate central points, we draw upon what existing research we have found that might help us assess the broader implications of the research for our central questions in this work.

Exploring the impact of immigration on governing coalitions, of course, presumes there are identifiable governing coalitions that include minority groups that exist (or once existed) in the first place and that, in turn, that might be affected by immigration issues or immigrants. Systematically examining this supposition exposes some of the immense complexity of our inquiry. Immigration and immigrants may have an impact on existing or previously existing coalitions, and they may also affect the actual or potential formation of coalitions. The impacts may be direct or indirect and may arise from within government and/or from external influences upon government. The discussion that follows summarizes some of the major research on minorities and coalitions, and in the process also considers a number of venues through which immigrants and immigration issues may affect coalition formation and sustenance and how these are manifest at different levels or arenas of the American (federal) political system. Each is illustrated through examples. Despite this complexity, however, the broad contours of the findings reported herein are consistent with the findings reported in other chapters and later in this chapter—namely, that there is continuing evidence of racial hierarchy in American politics, and the new immigration has not (thus far) diminished that pattern, despite the continuing efforts of minority political leaders and activists to break down those hierarchical patterns toward a more pluralistic pattern of political power.

It is well established that both race/ethnicity and immigration have had major impacts on American politics (e.g., Hero 1998; DeSipio and de la Garza 1998); at the same time, politics has an impact on both race/ethnicity and immigration policy. Adding to the complexity of our subject matter, then, is the fact that ethnoracial political patterns and immigration/immigrants, can be either—or both—causes and/or effects politically. "They can be causes in the sense that identities can shape political opinions, policy preferences, and party attachments, of immigrants and others, and they can be effects in the sense that politics and partisanship can alter how people think about race/ethnicity and immigration and immigrants" (Cain 1998). Similarly, such predispositions and perceptions make certain political information and evidence more or less salient and influences interpretations of that information as well. Whether, when, and how groups are seen as contenders, dependents, or deviants are substantially shaped by these cause-and-effect relationships (cf. Ingram and Schneider 1993).

Underscoring this point, and important in its own right, is that along with, yet also apart from, immigrants who have naturalized and become citizens, "U.S. society has created a separate statutory niche for immigrants and then, among immigrants, has distinguished between permanent residents and the undocumented." Permanent residents are "entitled to many but not all of the rights and privileges of U.S. citizens." The undocumented, in turn, "are entitled to basic civil and procedural rights under the Constitution, but they are denied most statutory privileges and face the continual threat of deportation" (DeSipio and de la Garza 1998, 107). But the situations of these various populations—"native" minority groups, naturalized citizens, permanent residents, and the undocumented—typically interconnect in complex ways that affect intraethnoracial group as well as intergroup relationships, and in the process this affects ethnoracial politics in general, including coalitional politics.

Presence and Impact. Immigrants' mere presence has political consequences, and that presence may pose procedural policy questions in itself. As we saw in chapter 5, as "persons" recognized under the Fourteenth Amendment to the U.S. Constitution, immigrants—whether citizens or not, whether authorized permanent residents or not—are counted in the official U.S. Census every decade and therefore automatically play a passive role in decisions involving legislative apportionment and the drawing of district lines every ten years. As a result, electoral legislative boundaries at all levels—congressional, state legislative, city council districts—are drawn and allocated based on the inclusion of populations that may be viewed as distinct, or even problematic, in relation to other segments of American society. Some have argued that such inclusion distorts or even perverts notions of political representation. In a related vein, questions have been raised whether recent immigrants should have access to (any) special, "redistributive" programs, particularly those that are race/group based, such as affirmative action, because those programs were intended to address problems of native minority populations (see, e.g., DeSipio and de la Garza 1998; also, see the discussion of public policy in the next section). These questions are pertinent for relationships both between and within racial/ethnic groups.

Another way in which the sheer presence of immigrants broadly shapes policy coalitions involves the perceptions of language abilities and associated inferences drawn about group patriotism, loyalty, and inclination to assimilate (cf. Citrin, Reingold, and Green 1990; Huntington 2004). Continuing influxes of non-English-speaking individuals create and reinforce a perception that they (usually Latinos or Asians) are resistant to learning to speak English. While the social-scientific evidence on this question clearly points toward rapid linguistic assimilation of immigrant groups, including recent Latino immigrants (see, e.g., Pew Hispanic Center 2006b; Rumbaut, Massey, and Bean 2006), public perceptions to the contrary may very well negatively affect the propensity of existing groups to welcome outsider groups with high percentages of immigrants into coalitional relationships in politics. As Garcia Bedolla's (2005, chap. 3) analysis has indicated, the stigma of foreignness attached to languages other than English has far-reaching political effects not only between, but within, ethnoracial minority groups. Beyond these general institutional and perceptual factors, other dimensions of the impact of immigrants on coalitions will be explored in relation to the local, state, and national arenas of U.S. governments.

Political Incorporation and Urban Politics

By far the largest number of analyses on minority group influence in politics and on minorities in governing coalitions have focused on the city or urban level of government, similar to what has long been the case regarding the understanding and study of ethnoracial politics generally in the United States (cf. Dahl 1961). As noted previously, in their landmark study of "the struggle of blacks and Hispanics for equality in urban politics" Browning, Marshall, and Tabb (1984, 25) measured "the political incorporation of black and Hispanic minorities by assessing the extent to which they were represented in coalitions that dominated city policy making on minority-related issues." Browning, Marshall, and Tabb relied on this measure "rather than on representation alone" because of their studied observation that

> identifiable coalitions typically controlled city policy on issues of central concern to minority groups and that participation in such dominant coalitions produced more important changes in governmental policy than simple representation did. Minority roles in dominant coalitions determined coalition commitment to minority interests. (25)

Thus, in their study of 10 California cities, Browning, Marshall, and Tabb examined cities according to "minority representation on city council and representation in dominant coalitions" (1984, 25–31; also see 272–76). In cities with 1 or 2 minority members as part of a city council's dominant coalition the overall level of incorporation was rated as modest (3 or 4 on a scale of 0 to 9), cities with "several members in the dominant coalition" were rated somewhat higher, and those with "minority control of mayor's office" were rated the highest. Where there was no minority representation or there was little minority presence on the council but not in the dominant coalition, incorporation was rated as low. In 1978, the overall average incorporation score for minorities (Blacks and Hispanics combined) was 2.8, for Blacks alone it was 2.6, and for Hispanics alone it was 0.5. As they hypothesized, those cities with the greatest degree of minority incorporation in dominant coalitions also had the greatest amount of minority-backed appointments to public offices and adoptions of public policies thought to facilitate greater racial equality.

This 1984 book was followed by a series of studies (published primarily in edited volumes) that applied the essentially pluralist analytical framework of Browning, Marshall, and Tabb to a larger group of American cities in addition to the 10 originally studied (see Browning, Marshall, and Tabb 1990, 1997, 2003). That group of cities has included Los Angeles, Philadelphia, New York, Chicago, Atlanta, New Orleans, Baltimore, Miami, and Denver. While the findings of these various studies—regarding numerous cities, and over time—are difficult to summarize, some selected major conclusions from Browning, Marshall, and Tabb's most recent edited volume on the topic can be highlighted here.

First, Browning, Marshall, and Tabb's overall assessment of these studies' depiction of minority political incorporation is mixed: "In the past 40 years, African Americans and, to a lesser extent, Latinos and Asians, have increased their political power in many of the 20 cities [examined in these edited volumes]. However, minority incorporation is uneven and incomplete; its achievement, ongoing" (Browning, Marshall, and Tabb 2003, 357). This general assessment is based on observations such as the fact that when minority electoral and governing coalitions have been defeated at the polls (and there have been numerous instances of such defeats) they have not necessarily been excluded from successor regimes, nor has there necessarily been an end to minority influence in these cities. Minorities have sometimes, but not always, held onto some of the power they achieved. Minority-oriented city governments that had "achieved incorporation" have been responsive to minority concerns "in significant, but limited, areas, but the performance of too many minority oriented regimes is disappointing." Furthermore, over time "minority political power has become more varied and complex, with crosscutting and shifting coalitions," complicated by various factors, with immigration being primary among them (Browning, Marshall, and Tabb 2003, 357).

> The ground on which coalitions are built has been transformed by immigration. In many cities the future of incorporation will be very

different from the enduring biracial coalitions that produced strong incorporation of African Americans in the last decades of the twentieth century. African Americans especially will have to adapt quickly to the new demographic reality if they are to sustain or improve their political positions. Issues that reach across immigrant and racial groups will increasingly structure urban coalitions. (357–58)

Among the factors making their full incorporation difficult for minority groups is their fragmentation. While this may be a general issue affecting all minority coalitions, this point is especially evident in some cities, of which New York is probably the leading example (see Mollenkopf 2003). "Blacks and Latinos in New York are further split within each group by ancestry and nativity—blacks of West Indian birth or origin as well as blacks of southern origin; Latinos of Puerto Rican birth or ancestry but also Dominicans and other immigrant groups—and by place of residence in the boroughs" (Browning, Marshall, and Tabb 2003, 363).

In assessing the development of minority influence in the various cities over time, Browning, Marshall, and Tabb suggest that the levels of incorporation that groups achieve are changeable. The rapid growth of Latino and Asian populations in recent decades—stimulated primarily by immigration—has been a major feature of the new era in minority politics. The absolute and relative size of Latino and Asian populations in many cities has led to corresponding increases in electoral effort and officeholding, as seen in the previous chapter. That growth shifts the ground beneath biracial coalitions that were founded on the premise that the fundamental alliance would be between Blacks and Whites.

The extent of minority group presence and influence in governing coalitions across American cities has varied and continues to vary considerably, but on the whole seems to fall well short of full incorporation. Assuming that the substantial and enduring presence of minorities in dominant governing coalitions is part of what the actual achievement of democratic pluralism would require, the evidence from the various studies of urban politics suggests limited achievement at most. Immigration is making urban politics more fluid and complex in general, as well as more specifically in relations between, and within, minority groups, with broader consequences for overall minority influence in governing coalitions. Several examples underscore these points.

At the level of urban politics, group histories and layers of complexity—whether cross-cutting, reinforcing, or some of both—are the most dense and immediate compared to other levels of the political system and may produce a politics that goes beyond pluralism toward hyperpluralism. This latter pattern, paradoxically, also lends itself to racial hierarchy because group differentiation is extensive and coalition formation is made especially difficult (discussed later). In general, cities are both microcosms of, but also magnify, the racial politics of the new immigration, as the following illustrations make clear.

New York City and Los Angeles, which together accounted for almost one-third of the nation's immigrant population in 2004, provide leading examples of the impacts of immigration on ethnoracial politics, as detailed in an analysis by Mollenkopf (2005). The large number of new immigrants to these cities, 70 percent of whom are Asian or Hispanic, are entering an urban society where they "do not easily fit, or see themselves as fitting, into a black-white dichotomy or continuum" (Mollenkopf 2005, 2). Data indicate how very different the racial and ethnic profiles are in these two and in other American cities, and also suggest that cities have attracted distinctive mixes of immigrants, reflecting their position in the global network. For example, in New York City, Dominican immigrants have become most numerous; in Los Angeles, Mexicans are the dominant immigrant group; and in Miami, Haitians predominate among recent immigrants. Additional complexity exists, however, because approximately 30 percent of immigrants are White or Black, and immigration can thus abet but also cut across older racial categories; further, the degree to which national-origin background cuts across racial categories varies across cities (see Mollenkopf 2005, esp. tables, pp. 3–4).

This immigration has led to conditions posing what Mollenkopf refers to as a "new civil rights challenge" of increased political inequality linked to the lack of naturalization, the age profile, and the "racial/ethnic composition of the citizenry and elected officials of these cities" that has "increasingly diverged from that of their resident populations [who are typically immigrant and noncitizens]" (Mollenkopf 2005, 4–5). The 1940s to 1980s was a period during which the extension of "basic political rights" to (native) "minority" populations was at issue, and "an entrenched white political establishment was the main obstacle to minority political progress" (15). One consequence of the earlier civil rights movement was that it helped some number of Latinos and African Americans gain elective office and to some degree become part of the political establishment; many of these minority officeholders are the very ones who currently represent districts with substantial and growing immigrant populations. But White voting-age citizens continue to have a considerably larger share of the electorate than do voting-age citizens among Latinos and Asians. Blacks also have a political edge over the immigrant groups, although not as much as do Whites. Demographic trends, including the future pace of immigration, birth and death rates, and naturalization rates among others, will surely affect social configurations and politics (Mollenkopf 2005; see also Rogers 2004).

Not only are new immigrants likely to be younger and less likely to register, join a party, or vote, but established political actors, including incumbent officeholders, political parties, and native voters, may be resistant to supporting new immigrant candidates and causes. Furthermore, polarization among and within the Black, Latino, and Asian electorates sometimes weakens support for new immigrant candidates from other groups (Mollenkopf 2005, 10).

Blacks in Los Angeles and New York have typically been in a weaker political position than have Whites, but stronger than the position of Latinos (at least until about 2005). Mollenkopf's interpretation is that for most of the 1990s Blacks were not part of the governing coalition in either city, though they had significant political influence at times prior to that. A legacy of the earlier periods is that in recent years Blacks have been slightly overrepresented among both eligible voters and officeholders relative to their share of the overall population. The histories and later developments thus add another layer of complexity to the Black, and broader racial, conditions in these cities. New York's Black population is larger than that of Los Angeles and is also more diverse; growth in West Indian immigration is compensating for the decline in New York's Black population but is also complicating intra- and interracial politics considerably (see our discussion of Rogers's findings).

On the other hand, a relatively small Black population in Los Angeles was part of a governing coalition with liberal Whites during Black mayor Tom Bradley's five terms in office, ending in 1993; Black influence has been subsequently more tenuous (see Sonenshein 2003a). Sonenshein suggests that immigration was in part responsible for the decline and fall of the biracial coalition that had existed in Los Angeles from the early 1970s to early 1990s, during the Tom Bradley era in that city.

> In the diverse global city, there were increasingly cross-cutting conflicts at the street level. . . . Citywide issues of black and white were replaced by localized conflicts between blacks and immigrant Latinos for construction jobs and between blacks and Korean-American storeowners. Less visibly, but crucially, the immigration

issue was related to a wide concern among whites—and many blacks—that the city was changing in an unpredictable and uncomfortable direction. (2003a, 61–62)

Similarly, Vaca recounts differences between Latinos and Blacks over counting of populations for purposes of calculating parity in employment in Los Angeles County in the 1980s, that is, whether percentage in workforce or percentage in general population should be used and how this would affect the implementation and evaluation of (redistributive) policies and programs (Vaca 2004, chap. 2). In Mollenkopf's view, Blacks face "an ambiguous position" in both cities, "outside the circle of powerful whites, yet enough of a political establishment to worry about challenges from newer, faster-growing immigrant minority groups" (2005). Ultimately, in both Los Angeles and New York, Blacks are in tenuous, in-between circumstances regarding other groups; Latinos and Asians (both natives and immigrants) are also in uncertain, unsettled political predicaments. The election of Antonio Villaraigosa as mayor of Los Angeles in 2005 does not really change that situation, as his influence on the City Council has not yet approached the level enjoyed by Tom Bradley during the latter's reign as an "incorporated" Black mayor.

On the one hand, Latinos and Asian Americans/Pacific Islanders, like Blacks, have a sense of being racialized minority groups in the American ethnoracial order. At the same time, because such large proportions of both the former two groups are recent immigrants, they also tend to have a lesser position in politics than do Blacks, and they face a variety of other obstacles to gaining political power deriving from their immigrant status—language issues, noncitizenship, stigmatization as foreigners as well as non-Whites, etc. To further complicate matters, in Los Angeles and New York (as well as other cities, such as Miami) there are other instances of potential intragroup ethnic interactions and conflicts. Mollenkopf remarks that "a large Latino population with a long history . . . is witnessing the rapid growth of newer Latino groups who may contend for [their] political offices." Specifically, he notes, in New York the "Puerto Rican population is declining relative to the Dominican and other Latino populations, and in Los Angeles second and third generation Mexican-American population is declining vis-à-vis more recent Mexican immigrants and the rapidly growing Salvadoran population." The larger, longer-present Latino groups have not yet developed a common bond with newer groups from Latin America (Mollenkopf 2005, 14).

In addition to all this, other immigrant minority groups have backgrounds that situate them more uncertainly in urban (and, more generally, American) racial settings. Some, such as South American, Chinese, Indian, Korean, and Pakistani—immigrants with higher socioeconomic resources—as well as the significant numbers of recent immigrants from Muslim countries in the Middle East, may follow what might be seen as a more pluralist path through ethnic group organization and political involvements along ethnic identity lines. Others from the same groups may experience their situations as something other than that of racialized minorities. Individual assimilation, sometimes facilitated by intragroup support, could well be the preferred approach for members of these groups.

The most likely institutions to mobilize immigrant groups from a pluralist perspective, such as labor unions and political parties, are not always inclined to do so because they are themselves implicated in the prevailing status quo. A labor (SEIU)/Latino alliance (see Milkman 2005, and our following discussion) in Los Angeles seems an exception, one that is not replicated in New York or in other cities and states. On the whole, it appears that such mediating institutions contribute to limited, incremental change, and often signal to new immigrant groups to "wait their turn" (Mollenkopf 2005, 12).

While discussed here in broad terms (chap. 1, this vol.), Rogers's extensive examination of Blacks/West Indian relations in New York City (2006) provides lessons relevant for other intragroup situations in cities. Rogers observes that "friction" has been common between Afro-Caribbean immigrants and African Americans over the past two decades in New York. He and others (e.g., Sonenshein 2003b) have argued that certain factors are necessary for racial/ethnic coalitions—strong leadership, common interests, and shared ideology. While race might ostensibly be an obvious focal point for collaboration between these groups, through some blending of interests and ideology, it actually has serious constraints as a basis for a coalition among non-Whites. In fact, it may actually increase perceived difference between racial minority and immigrant groups by stressing some interests over others. Color is not necessarily an interest, although race and color sometimes very much correlate with interests and ideology (Rogers 2006).

The discord, according to Rogers, has been primarily at the elite level, between group leaders. Most often the discord has centered on arguments between African American and Afro-Caribbean leaders over efforts of the latter group to seek political influence—through attaining descriptive representation—for what are asserted to be distinct Caribbean constituency interests. Some African Americans claim that the mobilization on behalf of (alleged) unique Afro-Caribbean concerns is divisive, and it undermines race as a basis for group political cohesion and, by extension, inhibits broader Black influence. Afro-Caribbeans see the opposition from African American leaders as narrow and unfair because they see the immigrant community as worthy of its own representatives due to its large size and distinctive issues that should not be subsumed within or overridden by allusions to Black racial solidarity. In any case, Rogers notes that racial solidarity in politics does not in and of itself prescribe or legitimate particular policies, issue positions, or specific candidates (Rogers 2004).

Notably, Rogers indicates these conflicts have not extended to rank-and-file Afro-Caribbean and African American constituents, and they have not included matters of "competing economic interests, substantive policy differences, or ideological disagreements." Yet appeals to racial solidarity often implicitly privilege one set of interests over others without any open debate. Biases may be obscured by reference to "natural" or "collective" racial interests said to benefit the entire Black population but actually benefit disproportionately those who already have more influence due to their size, history, or other factors. Racial group unity can be used to discourage mobilization by particular interests. New groups may imply political displacement as well as economic backsliding. Hence, Rogers's findings imply that coalitions among ostensible coethnics—native-born minorities and their immigrant counterparts—are hardly assured, and to the extent they occur they may not function or have the impacts commonly assumed.

Rogers, as well as others, claims that institutional factors, such as at-large versus district elections, are important in understanding minority/immigrant group interactions and outcomes. For example, he suggests that Black and Afro-Caribbean relations have been better and more cohesive in Hartford, Connecticut, than in New York City because at-large elections in the former induce cooperation while New York's district election system does not encourage intergroup collaboration. On the other hand, it has been claimed (Mollenkopf 2005) that physical separation and segregation of racial groups means that one group will hold sway in a given neighborhood, while other groups will be prominent in others. As a result, "inter-racial conflict would seem more likely at the city-wide level than neighborhoods" (Mollenkopf 2005, 11). These sets of comments suggest that spatial as well as institutional factors are yet another set of factors to consider in seeking to understand conditions affecting inter- and intra-group coalition activities.

Vaca (2004) documents Latino and Black conflicts in Compton (California), Houston, and Miami (as well as in Los Angeles and New York City) in his broader study of Latino/Black political relations. Miami has been profoundly influenced by successive waves of Cuban immigrants dating back to the 1960s. To begin, as noted in chapter 3, Cuban exiles have been granted special status permitting them to enter the United States without restrictions that apply to other immigrant groups, including their Mexican, Central American, or South American counterparts. In addition, the Cuban Adjustment Act (1966) gave automatic legal residency to any Cuban after only a year and a day in the United States, no matter how the person entered the country. Many Nicaraguans fleeing the Sandinista regime also came to Miami in the late 1980s. This expansion and diversification of the Latino population of Miami led Blacks to fear they would lose jobs to these newcomers and that public resources and services would be diverted to the new immigrant group. Latino/Cuban immigration in the Miami areas has also been a source of tension in other ways.

> The African American community was also angry with the treatment that Haitians were being accorded. While Latino groups were being welcomed with open arms, Haitians were met at sea and returned to Haiti. Nor were they (Haitians) being granted political asylum in the same numbers as Nicaraguans even though they were fleeing a dictatorship every bit as repressive and cruel as that alleged to be found in Nicaragua. (Vaca 2004, 119)

In sum, there are reasons to believe that for the foreseeable future, ethnoracial minority efforts to gain parity membership in the dominant governing coalitions of city politics in the United States are both helped and hindered by the influx of new immigrants in recent decades. These efforts have been "helped" insofar as the increased numbers of peoples of color have provided foundations for increased minority representation in the ranks of public officials at the city level, making it more likely that minority representatives will be included among those in urban governing coalitions. At the same time, there is no automatic translation of increased numbers of peoples of color into membership in dominant political coalitions. Many obstacles to such membership remain, including low levels of citizenship among immigrants and relatively low levels of voter participation.

State Politics, Immigrants, and Minority Incorporation

Studies of minority groups' impacts in state politics have, as with studies of urban politics, indicated ambiguous and/or limited levels of influence. However, the extent to which immigration is (re)shaping minority influence in state government has been the subject of very few systematic studies. Two analyses—one on Blacks, the other on Latinos—in state legislatures can be noted. A third study, one that more directly engages immigration issues, will also be discussed briefly.

The first analysis to be summarized here (Preuhs 2006), a study of Black influence in state legislatures, suggests that the notion of "incorporation" should be clarified as to its breadth. Most generally, and in relation to the basic notion of "simple incorporation," Preuhs suggests that at the state legislature level Black representation only affects policy if it occurs in a liberal governing coalition. This is so because the vast majority of Black representatives in state legislatures are liberal Democrats, and it follows that Black influence in Republican-dominated legislatures is severely limited. Accordingly, Preuhs calculates the degree of Black influence through an interaction term between Black presence (percentage in the state legislature) and unified Democratic government (Preuhs 2006, 590). "Liberal coalition" and "unified Democratic government" are used by Preuhs as essentially synonymous; however, this closely parallels Browning, Marshall, and Tabb's notion of "liberal" coalitions in city politics. In urban settings, elections are much more commonly nonpartisan, and Browning, Marshall, and Tabb thus characterize coalitions in ideological rather than political party terms, per se. Preuhs further differentiates the concept of incorporation between "specific" and "broad 'institutional incorporation.'"

Specific institutional incorporation means that when minority representatives hold institutional positions germane to specific policy areas, such as chair of a legislative committee with jurisdiction over social welfare programs, minority influence over that specific policy area increases. On the other hand, *broad* institutional incorporation suggests that minority control over formal leadership positions, "regardless of policy area, is positively associated with minority group influence" in the representative governmental body as a whole (Preuhs 2006, 594).

Another way in which minorities may be part of a dominant governing coalition is when political "parties that share the policy goals of minority representatives hold power"; in this case, the party is the direct source of "substantive representation," and the impact of minority presence and/or their holding of institutional positions has little additional independent impact, but, again, policy influence compatible with Black preferences is achieved through liberal (Democratic) party dominance. On the other hand, if a political context is "highly racialized," minority legislators' impact may be constrained. A minority group (Black) "institutional [legislative] incorporation score" that takes into account both the percentage of Black state legislators *and* their presence in major, formal legislative positions is created. Incorporation as conceptualized and measured here is analogous to minority legislators' role in governing coalitions and is examined by Preuhs relative to the level of welfare benefits (the dependent variable).

The study finds that representation, "institutional incorporation" (both specific and broad), and "party as a substantive representative" all have some impact on welfare benefit levels, but those are conditioned by racial context, that is, the findings differ in the South versus non-South. In the Southern context, the impacts of representation, incorporation, and party are diminished considerably and occasionally reversed. Thus, this analysis of Blacks in state politics suggests that various forms of incorporation, of being part of a governing coalition, sometimes does matter, which is broadly consistent with a pluralist interpretation. "Minority [Black] representation, formal institutional positions held by minority lawmakers, and coalition membership all operate as mechanisms for influence, yet these mechanisms are conditioned by the racialization of political context" (Preuhs 2006, 598). But (1) the influence is somewhat modest, and (2) how racialized the context is matters substantially as well; because the level of minority influence is so limited and qualified, we believe the overall pattern suggests an inconsistency with pluralist interpretations and may actually provide some support to racial hierarchy interpretations of the situation in state legislatures. Descriptive data from this study of Blacks in state legislatures is in table 6.1.

TABLE 6.1. Black Representation and Incorporation in 1993

State	Legislature That Is Black (%)	Population That Is Black (%)	Committee and Leadership Position (%)	Incorporation Score
Alabama	15.71429	25.23492	13.93939	1.301578
Alaska	1.666667	4.035455	0	−0.75003
Arizona	4.444445	3.003056	1.984127	−0.39975
Arkansas	9.62963	15.8849	8.791209	0.47675
California	7.5	7.378409	9.521964	0.36974
Colorado	4	3.983698	2.475248	−0.39779
Connecticut	6.417112	8.32233	10.90909	0.388179

TABLE 6.1.—*Continued*

State	Legislature That Is Black (%)	Population That Is Black (%)	Committee and Leadership Position (%)	Incorporation Score
Delaware	4.83871	16.83558	1.675978	−0.39233
Florida	11.875	13.61208	7.709359	0.567237
Georgia	16.94915	26.9355	15.95395	1.538541
Hawaii	0	2.40695	0	−0.8748
Idaho	0	0.362761	0	−0.8748
Illinois	11.29943	14.83206	11.18643	0.773581
Indiana	7.333333	7.751118	4.891304	0.025077
Iowa	0.666667	1.7018	0	−0.8249
Kansas	3.636364	5.728693	0	−0.60257
Kentucky	2.898551	7.111452	0	−0.65781
Louisiana	21.52778	30.77398	16.94915	1.952704
Maine	0	0.435749	0	−0.8748
Maryland	15.95745	24.86781	20.13889	1.764511
Massachusetts	4	4.936935	4.736842	−0.23555
Michigan	9.459459	13.8678	5.803571	0.249688
Minnesota	0.497512	2.166811	0	−0.83756
Mississippi	24.13793	35.59495	5.25798	1.309427
Missouri	8.121827	10.68693	22.37968	1.338657
Montana	0	0.256195	0	−0.8748
Nebraska		3.620279	0	
Nevada	4.761905	6.514975	6.930693	−0.02113
New Hampshire	0.471698	0.645176	0	−0.83949
New Jersey	10	13.39439	0	−0.12617
New Mexico	0	1.968185	0	−0.8748
New York	12.32228	15.89217	5.078125	0.411967
North Carolina	14.70588	21.95414	21.59021	1.774928
North Dakota	0	0.550704	0	−0.8748
Ohio	11.36364	10.6688	9.59596	0.664293
Oklahoma	3.355705	7.3822	6.339522	−0.16881
Oregon	3.333333	1.598276	2.5	−0.44592
Pennsylvania	6.719368	9.139244	11.17353	0.429777
Rhode Island	5.333333	3.787238	4.347826	−0.16364
South Carolina	14.70588	29.82535	5.752294	0.638773
South Dakota	0.952381	0.450144	0	−0.80351
Tennessee	11.36364	15.93277	14.58895	1.022471
Texas	8.839779	11.87378	7.894737	0.353309
Utah	0	0.643006	0	−0.8748
Vermont	1.111111	0.389698	0	−0.79162
Virginia	8.571428	18.79858	0	−0.23312
Washington	1.360544	3.02782	1.935484	−0.63411
West Virginia	0.746269	3.089682	0	−0.81894
Wisconsin	6.060606	4.99397	2.970297	−0.20801
Wyoming	0	0.72467	0	−0.8748

Source: The data in this table were most generously provided by Robert R. Preuhs.

A parallel study of the impact of Latinos' incorporation in state legislatures (Preuhs 2007) also deserves discussion. Measuring Latinos' incorporation in roughly the same way as in the study on Blacks just noted (Preuhs 2006), it was found that Latinos' holding positions on important committees in state legislatures did, in fact, have policy impacts. The incorporation of Latinos was positively associated with welfare expenditure effort, welfare generosity, and welfare benefits in the states. However, that positive effect does not take hold until the Latino population reaches 10 percent, which means that the negative impact of Latino population (by itself) is "not overcome in the majority of state contexts" (Preuhs 2007, 287). There is also evidence (Preuhs 2005) that a primary impact of Latino representatives in state legislatures is in *blocking legislation* they deem objectionable; for example, by stopping "Official English" legislation in the state legislatures. Descriptive data from this study of Latinos in state legislatures is in table 6.2.

TABLE 6.2. Latino Representation and Incorporation in 2002

State	Legislature That Is Latino (%)	Population That Is Latino (%)	Committee and Leadership Position (%)	Incorporation Score
Alabama	0	1.917075	0	−0.27607
Alaska	0	4.378882	0	−0.27607
Arizona	13.33333	27.06913	0	0.795121
Arkansas	0	3.579336	0	−0.27607
California	21.66667	33.99305	18	2.598109
Colorado	10	18.15822	0	0.527323
Connecticut	2.673797	9.981216	0	−0.06126
Delaware	1.612903	5.115184	0	−0.14649
Florida	9.375	18.06558	6	0.854942
Georgia	0	6.033667	0	−0.27607
Hawaii	1.315789	7.309824	0	−0.17036
Idaho	0	8.493029	0	−0.27607
Illinois	3.389831	13.34381	0	−0.00373
Indiana	0.666667	3.838285	0	−0.22251
Iowa	0	3.05094	0	−0.27607
Kansas	1.212121	7.610737	0	−0.17869
Kentucky	0	1.68096	0	−0.27607
Louisiana	0.694444	2.556552	0	−0.22028
Maine	0	0.795674	0	−0.27607
Maryland	0	4.699438	0	−0.27607
Massachusetts	1.5	7.269984	0	−0.15556
Michigan	1.351351	3.473459	0	−0.1675
Minnesota	0.497512	3.161543	0	−0.2361
Mississippi	0	1.493837	0	−0.27607

TABLE 6.2.—*Continued*

State	Legislature That Is Latino (%)	Population That Is Latino (%)	Committee and Leadership Position (%)	Incorporation Score
Missouri	0	2.244121	0	−0.27607
Montana	0	2.100055	0	−0.27607
Nebraska		5.991556	0	
Nevada	1.587302	21.28825	0	−0.14855
New Hampshire	0.235849	1.764567	0	−0.25712
New Jersey	4.166667	14.21021	0	0.058676
New Mexico	38.39286	42.91952	70	7.216418
New York	5.687204	16.0428	0	0.180835
North Carolina	0.588235	5.342484	0	−0.22881
North Dakota	0	1.293171	0	−0.27607
Ohio	0	2.005026	0	−0.27607
Oklahoma	0	5.518505	0	−0.27607
Oregon	1.111111	8.87122	0	−0.18681
Pennsylvania	0.395257	3.370058	0	−0.24432
Rhode Island	1.333333	9.245584	0	−0.16895
South Carolina	0	2.66118	0	−0.27607
South Dakota	0	1.510971	0	−0.27607
Tennessee	0.757576	2.413192	0	−0.21521
Texas	19.33702	33.5828	9	1.8442
Utah	0.961538	9.683547	0	−0.19882
Vermont	0	0.940642	0	−0.27607
Virginia	0	5.184068	0	−0.27607
Washington	2.040816	8.080542	1	−0.04914
West Virginia	0	0.693712	0	−0.27607
Wisconsin	0.757576	3.842902	0	−0.21521
Wyoming	1.111111	6.697413	0	−0.18681

Note: The data in this table were most generously provided by Robert R. Preuhs.

A number of studies find that the size of minority populations (Black and/or Latino) within political jurisdictions, taken alone, is associated with negative legislative outcomes for minorities. Only if and when minority population size leads to substantial levels of representation and/or incorporation in state legislatures do larger minority populations generate "policy responsiveness" (Preuhs 2007; Hero and Preuhs 2007). Short of substantial representation/incorporation in state institutions, the size of the minority population and the impact of interest groups associated with minority concerns have little or no (positive) impacts. However, no studies (to our knowledge) have directly or systematically examined the impact of immigration on minority groups and their role in governing coalitions in state politics. However, one study that indirectly speaks to such questions can be noted.

Following the 1996 welfare reform legislation by the U.S. Congress, state governments were granted significantly increased discretion to determine eligibility for welfare. Prior to this reform, the national government had substantial influence on such decisions. As part of their new discretion, states could now decide whether to make immigrants eligible for welfare. This policy change raises the question of whether specified characteristics of states might be associated with the degree to which immigrants were included. States' racial/ethnic composition (percentage Latino, as well as percentage Black) is an obvious factor to investigate, and minority institutional incorporation would also be useful to consider. A study that examined this issue (Hero and Preuhs 2007) found that the percentage of Latino population in states was not significantly related one way or another to the states' decisions to include immigrants for (or exclude them from) welfare eligibility (nor was the Black percentage of the states' populations). (Note that in this study minority "institutional incorporation" was not assessed as a factor influencing welfare eligibility.) On the other hand, percentage Latino and percentage Black in the states' populations were both significantly *negatively* related to *lower* welfare cash benefits; further, the size of the noncitizen immigrant population was also significantly negatively related to decisions to include or exclude immigrants for welfare eligibility.

Though this analysis (Hero and Preuhs 2007) did not evaluate minority incorporation in governing coalitions per se, the (1) nonfinding regarding the impact of the size of minority populations on immigrant in/exclusion for welfare, (2) the negative impact of the size of minority population, and (3) the negative effect of the interaction of noncitizen population with welfare eligibility in/exclusion on benefit levels are nonetheless germane to our larger assessment of racial/ethnic group influence. This seems particularly notable because it concerns state policies regarding immigrants and public policy. While not easy to characterize simply, these findings do not seem to offer support for standard pluralist interpretations of political incorporation. To underscore this point, finally, consistently low perceptions of political influence have been found in studies rating the impacts of formally organized interest groups acting on behalf of minority groups (Blacks and/or Latinos) by trying to influence state government policy from outside government (see, e.g., Thomas and Hrebenar 2004, 119–20).

State Electoral Coalition Issues. Apart from these scant formal social-scientific studies, several narratives exist focused on the impacts of recent immigration on politics in a number of U.S. states. While key immigrant receiving states such as California, Florida, New York, Texas, and Arizona have received widespread attention, other states have also been substantially affected both directly and indirectly. A brief discussion of some of the more apparent political consequences of immigration for governing coalitions in states is presented later.

California. Probably the clearest manifestation of the tensions wrought by immigration has been in the state of California, and certainly this state has received the greatest amount of journalistic and scholarly attention in relation to immigration's impacts on politics. Not only is California home to the largest number and highest percentage of immigrants of any U.S. state's population, but the state is important for other reasons as well. Its overall population makes it by far the most populous state in the country, and its economy is so huge that it is commonly characterized by journalists and public officials as ranking alone as the seventh or eighth largest economy in the world. Moreover, California's politics is characterized by extensive use of the initiative process, which greatly complicates the nature of governing coalition politics in the state. Indeed, decisions made through initiatives resulting from ad hoc electoral coalitions might be seen accurately as de facto governing coalitions with respect to the particular policies dealt with through specific ballot measures.

Governing coalition politics in California is characterized by a key mismatch between the demographic characteristics of the state and the politics of its voting citizens. In a demographic shift driven largely by post-1965 immigration, California became the first mainland state in the United States (excluding Hawaii) to have a non-White majority of the population, a fact that became reality before 2000. This steady increase in the ethnoracial minority population over the past four decades (in which—as noted earlier—all residents, not just citizens, are counted for purposes of drawing district lines for state legislative and congressional seats), combined with the impacts of the Voting Rights Act provisions requiring "majority-minority" districts under certain circumstances present in California, meant that the number and percentage of minority (particularly Latino) representatives in the state's legislature increased dramatically over that period. Indeed, three of the five Speakers of the California state Assembly since the early 1990s have been Latino Democrats (and a fourth was a Black Democrat). Thus, minority representation in the governing coalition of California legislature politics has been substantial since the early 1990s.

At the same time, however, this apparent level of minority political incorporation has been offset by other important aspects of California politics. Significant among these is the fact that California's Constitution requires a two-thirds approval vote by the legislature for adoption of any state budget and/or any tax increase, thus effectively giving conservative Republicans (a highly cohesive minority of the state's legislators for most of the past two decades) a veto power over the state's fiscal policies. But even more important has been the fact that statewide, California voters remain overwhelmingly White. As table 6.3 indicates, while California's White population had dropped to 43 percent by 2006, this group made up two-thirds (67 percent) of the state's voters in the 2006 state elections, a pattern of overrepresentation that has been consistently replicated in other California elections over the past several decades.

Politically, this means that in statewide elections (e.g., for governor and for other elected executive positions, as well as for voter initiative campaigns), the White population has continued to have commanding influence over the state's public policy. This fact may have something to do with the increased use of initiative campaigns by conservative groups in recent decades. In any case, it is a fact that many of the state's most important public policies having to do with the ethnoracial diversity of California have been adopted by voter initiative, not by the legislature (which is somewhat more representative of the state's ethnoracial demography than is the statewide electorate), and virtually all of the policies adopted on this subject have been opposed by a majority of the state's Black, Latino, and Asian American/Pacific Islander voters.

To illustrate, since the 1960s the following ethnoracially focused public policies have been adopted in California through voter initiatives in which clear majorities of Black, Latino, and Asian/Pacific Islander voters *opposed* each of the measures: (1) Proposition 14 (1964)—rescinded the Rumford

TABLE 6.3. California Political Demography, Voting and Representation (2006)

Ethnoracial Group	California Population %	California Voters, 2006 %	California Legislators (%)
White	43	67	52
Black	6	6	7
Latino	36	17	22
APIA[a]	12	9	5

Source: U.S. Census Bureau, Current Population Survey; U.S. Census Bureau 2007; California State Legislative Caucuses.

[a]APIA includes both Asian Americans and Native Hawaiian and Other Pacific Islanders.

Fair Housing Act, which forbade racial discrimination in the sale and rental of housing; (2) Proposition 21 (1972)—overturned California judicial rulings requiring racial integration of public schools in cases of de facto segregation; (3) Proposition 38 (1984)—expressed California's opposition to U.S. Voting Rights Act provisions requiring ballots and election materials in languages other than English; (4) Proposition 63 (1986)—made English the sole official language of California; (5) Proposition 187 (1994)—sought to eliminate public services (e.g., health care, education) to undocumented immigrants in California; (6) Proposition 209 (1996)—eliminated California's affirmative action policies; (7) Proposition 227 (1998)—eliminated bilingual education in California's public schools. Moreover, a variety of additional measures supported by minority legislators have been vetoed by Republican governors elected with primary support from the continuing White majority in the California electorate (including bills that would have extended California's sun-setting bilingual education law prior to the 1998 elimination of bilingual education by the state's voters and granted access to drivers' licenses by undocumented immigrants).

Underlying these voting patterns are clear differences in public opinion along both ethnoracial and partisan lines, differences that must have an impact on the development and maintenance of multiracial coalitions in California politics. Immigration has apparently played a strong role in recent decades in reinforcing these divisions. Baldassare's (2000) analysis of a Public Policy Institute of California survey, for example, found that Mexican immigration is perceived by Californians (accurately, in fact) as the largest component of immigrants in the state. How do Californians feel about Mexican immigrants, specifically? Baldassare indicates that a majority of Californians (52 percent) say they consider Mexican immigrants a "benefit" because of their "hard work and job skills"; yet a third (36 percent) describe Mexican immigrants as a "burden" because they use public services and schools. These aggregate opinions mask large differences of opinion across racial/ethnic lines, however: Latinos (70 percent) are much more likely than Blacks (55 percent) and Asians (52 percent) to describe Mexicans as beneficial. Among Whites, 45 percent say Mexican immigrants are a benefit, and 42 percent perceive these immigrants as a burden.

The data also suggest how political partisan orientations contribute to and/or are reinforced by immigration issues. Among Republicans, 35 percent see immigration in positive terms, while 57 percent of Democrats respond positively (Baldassare 2000). There are also racial/ethic and partisan differences in the extent to which *illegal* immigration has been viewed as a big problem. Whites (53 percent) are more likely to say this than Latinos, Asians, and Blacks (42 percent, in the latter case).

In sum, then, minority efforts to gain greater influence in California's political system seem to have been impacted by immigration in complex ways. On the one hand, the immigration-driven shift in the state's ethnoracial demography over the past four decades has brought a dramatic increase in minority representation in the state legislature (thanks to requirements of the Voting Rights Act), placing minorities in legislative leadership positions unprecedented in the state's history. On the other hand, the dramatic increase in immigrants in the state, combined with the exclusion of noncitizens from all voting in California, has helped to increase the political gap between the state's electorate and its overall population in ways that seem to have contributed to the adoption of a series of ethnoracially focused public policies opposed by the state's minority populations. In this way, immigration seems to have contributed indirectly to the continuation of a demographically unrepresentative governing coalition in the electorate that has important public policy consequences for the state's Black, Latino, and Asian American populations.

Florida.[2]   Immigration from Mexico, particularly to the Southwestern United States, has captured much of the public and scholarly attention. Also notable, however, has been the immigration and political change regarding Hispanics/Latinos in Florida, including the influence of Cubans in the Miami–Dade County area, but also beyond, and how this has altered state politics and presidential elections in Florida. But the situation has been more complex than that of Cuban immigrants. Hispanic immigration and other developments, such as a large non-Latino influx from other parts of the United States to Florida, accelerated the state's shift toward Republican Party dominance and has also altered the political influence of Blacks in state politics. In addition, the number of Cubans has been surpassed in recent years by other Latino immigrants, many of whom are not reliably Republican voters.

Along with Latino immigration, new migration from the Caribbean has also affected the national-origin configuration of the state's Black population. This influx grew substantially during the 1980s and 1990s "with large migrations from Haiti and the English speaking Caribbean, most notably Jamaica" (Hill and Moreno 2008). The unique composition of the Black population in South Florida likely foreshadows a different kind of African American politics. For one thing, the Black population of north Florida is native born and is thus different than the Black population that is becoming increasingly influential in the southern part of the state. Moreover, intra-Black political competition has been evident in south Florida since at least 2002 when an African American, a Jamaican American, and a Haitian American all sought the same state legislative seat in central Broward County, and in subsequent elections for local and state legislative positions. Given that the African American population has remained stable while the Caribbean population of Florida has grown, these types of political battles will probably occur more often in the future (Hill and Moreno 2008).

Another outgrowth of immigration and the evolution of party politics in Florida is that African Americans have become an increasingly influential part of a weakened Democratic Party. "The flight of whites from the Democratic Party, coupled with successful Republican partisan redistricting in 2002, has created a situation where a disproportionate percentage of Democrats elected to state and federal offices are black" (Hill and Moreno 2008, 92). At the same time, greater national-origin diversity of Hispanic legislators led the Cuban-American Caucus to change its name to the Hispanic Caucus in 2002. Moreover, the legislature's Hispanic Caucus, though heavily Republican (12 of its 14 members), was, unlike most Republicans, supportive of state legislation permitting local "living wage" ordinances. These living wage measures have strong support among Hispanics (perhaps surprising to some), as well as among Blacks in south Florida (Hill and Moreno 2008).

More generally across the country the saliency of immigration issues has increased substantially in recent years, even in places that historically have had small Latino populations, as well as in states with longer histories of substantial presence of Latinos and Asian Americans. This development has injected new policy, political coalition, and governance challenges in many U.S. states. Among these issues are whether drivers' licenses should be issued to the undocumented, the costs associated with educating immigrant populations, how immigrants should be categorized for purposes of higher education and college tuition, and whether, how, and who should pay for health insurance and health care costs associated with hospitals and emergency care used by immigrants. Immigrant workers are especially prominent in the poultry, construction, and service industries and hence raise questions about state regulatory and economic policies, among others. In Georgia, for example, the question of whether to designate Latinos as a minority for purposes of set-aside policies has been controversial; the proposal to include Latinos for such purposes encountered substantial Black opposition (Vaca 2004). To summarize, then, it seems evident that the struggle of Blacks, Latinos, and Asian Americans to increase their political clout in state-level politics through membership in these states' governing coalitions is still an ongoing challenge, and the impact of immigration on these efforts is an important complicating factor that remains understudied by political scientists.

National Politics, Immigrants, and Minority Incorporation

When it comes to assessing the political clout of minorities and their place in governing coalitions at the national level, the primary research focus has been political parties. This is because both the Democratic and Republican Parties are essentially political coalitions seeking to capture control of "the government," so that coalition members can dominate the institutions responsible for allocating political appointments and making and implementing public policies in line with the preferences of their constituencies.

The complication in the U.S. government, of course, is that this government's authority is divided and parceled out among a wide variety of institutions with some measure of political independence, not only between states and the national government (the federal principle) but also between core institutions designed according to Madison's famous principle of "checks and balances." Racial minority group political activists seeking to increase their presence and power in national politics, therefore, have had to be concerned with gaining greater influence in a wide variety of political arenas in the national political system. Among these arenas are (1) the politics of presidential elections (see, e.g., Henderson 1987), which can lead (in the event of victory) to important presidential appointments to judicial and executive offices, as well as to gaining an advantageous place on the president's policy agenda; (2) the politics surrounding the development and implementation of public policy in the career executive agencies of national government; and (3) the politics surrounding the federal judiciary (both judicial appointments and litigation).

However, much of the political science literature on minority political incorporation at the national level has been focused on minority representation and involvement in the U.S. Congress. As we saw in the previous chapter, descriptive representation of ethnoracial minorities has been a primary concern of scholars for some time. While minority members of Congress may be more disposed to focus on and to support those policies most important to minority constituents, the number of minority members of Congress is quite small (in the 2007–9 Congress, 68 out of a total of 535 members of Congress: 42 Blacks, 21 Latinos, 5 Asians), so that even assuming unanimous agreement, their ability to assure passage of preferred legislation—or to defeat objectionable legislation—is quite limited.

Again, political parties are the most important institutional vehicles for the development of governing coalitions in national politics, and this is true in Congress as well as throughout the national government more generally. The surest path to political influence in Congress is to be a prominent member of the dominant (majority) political party. Since the vast majority of the racial/ethnic minority members of Congress are Democrats, it follows that minority members have some possibility of being part of that institution's governing coalition only if the Democrats control the Congress. During the past several decades, of course, Democrats lost control of Congress from 1995 to 2007, thereby severely limiting racial minority political influence during that time. Of course, this influence was further limited by Republican control of the White House and executive branch following the 2000 election.

Given the importance of political parties for racial minority political incorporation and, in turn, parties' important role within the formal decision-making institutions of American national government, attention to some additional claims is appropriate here. For our purposes, perhaps the most important claim in recent years is that of Frymer (1999, 2005), who has contended that many basic aspects of the American political system are structured to dissipate and avoid fundamental conflicts over race. Specifically, Frymer contends that the majoritarian electoral system in the United States operates to systematically stifle and deflect the claims of Black voters for more political responsiveness from the Democratic Party, even when that party is victorious in elections due to very high levels of Black support. This is so because in closely contested elections, the median voter is particularly and consistently important in the quest for electoral victory. *Median voters* are those who lie nearest the center of the American political spectrum (left vs. right) and are most likely to switch their votes from one party to another. These voters, Frymer demonstrates, are least likely to be favorably disposed toward African American political issues, while African American voters have been "captured" by the Democratic Party (cf. Hochschild 1995). As a result, the Democratic Party leadership (the party to which most minority members of Congress belong) has little incentive to take on policy issues aimed at increasing racial equality because doing so might alienate the very voters most likely at play in national elections, and thereby fracture the Democrats' electoral and, by extension, government coalitions. Similar claims have been made by other scholars in relation to the Democratic Party's responsiveness to Asian American concerns (Kim 2007) and to Latino concerns (Fraga and Leal 2004).

Given the critical role of party as the potential centerpiece of governing coalitions in Congress (and elsewhere), Frymer's thesis is telling for present purposes. Consistent with Frymer's assertion, it has been argued that when the Democrats control legislative bodies, such as the U.S. House, there may be a muffling of Black and other minorities' concerns that is not always apparent. Party leaders do not want to show a split in the party and, as a consequence, the (only) votes that come to the floor are ones on which White and Black Democrats usually agree: controversial racial issues are censored before they reach the stage of a House vote. According to arguments and evidence such as this, then, issue legacies rooted in race were and continue to be manifested in party behavior in the governing process (Minta 2007, 5).

How has the influx of immigrants in the post-1965 period affected the efforts of Blacks, Latinos, and Asian Americans to gain greater effective power in national politics? This, again, is a large question that cannot be answered sufficiently here. But if Frymer's analysis (and Kim's, as well as Fraga and Leal's) is correct, there are political structural factors at play that may be more important in deflecting minority efforts to become core players in the nation's governing coalitions than is immigration. We have seen that immigration has played a role in increasing the number of Latino and Asian American elected officials at the national level (as well as at state and local levels), but beyond that there have been few studies of these questions in relation to immigration's effects on ethnoracial minority political power in national government institutions. Some have argued that the demographic transformations wrought by immigration in the United States over the last several decades have served to undermine and/or deflect the national commitment to ethnoracial equality that seemed to become dominant in the 1960s and early 1970s. Consideration of that question will be taken up later, but first we examine briefly how the large increase in immigration has affected several aspects of national politics outside of government institutions.

Immigrants, Nonelectoral Politics, and Coalitions

Apart from trying to increase their presence and power in national government institutions per se, ethnoracial minorities have also attempted to exercise influence on those institutions through external political organizations such as interest groups. How have immigrants affected these efforts? Probably the leading example of immigrants themselves influencing politics through nonelectoral channels is that of labor union activity. Noncitizens are permitted to exercise free speech, to engage in religious activity, and to join organizations. As described extensively in Milkman's research (2005), for example, Latino immigrants in California became very politically mobilized through labor unions during the 1990s and have become the centerpiece of labor union activism "laying the groundwork for a burgeoning labor-Latino alliance that came to be the most potent force in Los Angeles and statewide politics" (Milkman 2005, 2). Particularly important have been the Service Employees International Union (SEIU) and a variety of community-based organizations (CBOs). Alongside the unions' efforts to recruit immigrants, CBOs in California with "a focus on economic justice issues" were influential through their "advocacy for low-wage workers—which in practice meant mainly the foreign-born, who dominate the lower reaches of the labor market" (Milkman 2005, 3). Latino immigrants have been consistently at the forefront of a number of union efforts and were also involved in grassroots political activism. (Milkman is careful to emphasize that the impact of Latino immigrants should not be overstated, but she still claims that the impacts have not been given their due in previous assessments.)

Milkman provides other notable insights. In Los Angeles and in California "*inequality by both class and nativity* is . . . stark" and immigrants are "overwhelmingly" affected (Milkman 2005, 2, emphasis added; cf. Sonenshein 2003a). Furthermore, immigrants are seldom employed in the public sector; this is important for analyzing the questions of "political incorporation" and may be particularly so to the present discussion because numerous studies of racial/ethnic groups have stressed *public* employment as an indicator of minority group political influence, incorporation, and policy responsiveness (cf. Browning, Marshall, and Tabb's [1984] standards for incorporation). Linking the issues of inequality to the tremendous growth of SEIU's national membership, which tripled from the 1980s to about 2003 (to about 1.8 million workers), Milkman says that Mexican and Central American immigrants (in Los Angeles and California) have been unusually well-disposed toward unionism. The presumed reasons for that receptiveness seem relevant for understanding immigrants' potential impact on American racial/ethnic politics.

More specifically, Milkman (2005, 12–15) suggests three factors facilitating immigrant union organizing. One is networks: "working class immigrants tend to have much stronger social networks than natives," and this in turn encouraged the development of association and informal and formal organizations. A second factor is the immigrants' (and especially Latino immigrants') "world-views." They may "find class-based collective organizations like unions or CBOs more compatible with their past lived experience, world-views, and sense of identity than do most native-born workers." Finally, Milkman claims "the shared experience of stigmatization among immigrants, both during the migration process itself and even after many years of settlement, may foster a sense of unity." Such feelings were forcefully fostered by several ballot propositions of the 1990s in California: 187, eliminating services to undocumented immigrants (1994); 209, "anti–affirmative action" (1996); and 227, restricting bilingual education (1998). "In reaching out to the immigrant community in opposing these, the labor movement—both unions and CBOs—found itself greeted with open arms; . . . the labor movement skillfully channeled the outrage of immigrants and others regarding these measures into progressive electoral politics" (Milkman 2005, 18; see also DeSipio and Sonenshein 2004). Labor unions have also been found important for immigrant groups in New York city (see Mollenkopf 2005).

The same year, 1994, that Proposition 187 was passed by California voters, the L.A. County Federation of Labor expanded its activities in grassroots-based field mobilization, "devot[ing] resources to helping immigrants eligible for nationalization become citizens (and thus potential voters), which many were eager to do" in the aftermath of 187. In the process, a "new cadre of Latino labor leaders emerged and began to edge out the old guard Mexican-American political leadership" (Milkman 2005, 17). There are several examples of Latino public officials with union backgrounds. Antonio Villaraigosa, for instance, was involved with successful labor efforts to defeat a ballot proposition that would have constrained the use of union dues for political purposes; Latinos voted against this measure by a 3 to 1 margin. Villaraigosa was later elected to a state Assembly seat from northeast LA and subsequently became speaker of the California State Assembly. In 2001 he was the runner-up in the Los Angeles mayoral race and in 2005 was elected to that position. In 1998 another Latino with union links, Cruz Bustamante, was elected lieutenant governor, the first to win statewide office in the twentieth century; he had previously been Speaker of the State Assembly. Other Latinos who also went on to win prominent public offices emerged from union activities.

Finally, Milkman adds "that immigrants had become a key political constituency for organized labor in California also had *national* repercussions" (2005, 19, emphasis added). Union leaders from California led the effort to change labor's immigration policy in the late 1990s, winning support for an AFL-CIO Executive Council resolution that officially reversed previous support for employer sanctions "and calling for a new immigrant legalization program" (19). Unions, she argues, have become leading advocates for immigrant rights rather than being major supporters of restricting immigration, as had been the case through much of U.S. history (20).

Summing up, the implications of immigration for the formation and sustenance of governing coalitions are surely great, but not easy to identify, quantify, or categorize, and in any case the phenomena have not been studied extensively or systematically. In part the research is sparse because coalition formation is continually unfolding, fluid and often nebulous. Another factor stems from the fact that some of the players, particularly the undocumented or illegal, are on the periphery of political activity, though their presence is often pivotal to the issues. The limited research findings available that are directly pertinent to assessing the importance of immigration for coalitions indicate that immigration has both helped and hurt ethnoracial minority efforts to fully incorporate through increasing minority memberships in governing coalitions. At a more general level, we have presented some evidence that there has been an increase in minority presence in dominant governing coalitions in some circumstances, but these increases have not been sufficiently stable over time or unidirectional enough to enable us to say that full democratic political incorporation has taken place at any level of government in the United States.

Immigrants and the Public Policy Agenda
for Ethnoracial Equality

Our focus to this point has been on the ways immigrants have affected the efforts of ethnoracial minority political activists and political leaders to increase the participation and representation of Blacks, Latinos, and Asian Americans in U.S. politics, as well as to increase these groups' influence on governmental decision making. We now turn to the last benchmark of political incorporation in our study, which is the adoption of ethnoracially egalitarian public policies. This section will ask the degree to which the increased immigration in the past four decades, and the presence of millions of new immigrants in the U.S. population, have affected the efforts of Black, Latino, and Asian American political activists and leaders who have sought to see such ethnoracially egalitarian policies adopted and implemented by governments at all levels in the American political system.

In framing our inquiry in this way, we make the assumption that the "minority empowerment" aspirations of Black, Latino, and Asian American political activists include the adoption of public policies that will aim at "racial equality" in the United States. That is, we are not aware of any ethnoracial minority activists and leaders who have claimed to be working on behalf of public policies that would make the United States more *unequal* in respect to race and ethnicity. Indeed, in the wake of the successes of the civil rights movement in the 1960s and 1970s, the rhetoric of virtually *all* policymakers and activists in the United States asserts that racial equality is the appropriate standard for the public interest in this country. In that sense, Tocqueville's description of democracy's trajectory in the modern world seems to have run its full rhetorical course in the United States, even with respect to race: "The gradual unfurling of equality . . . is, therefore, a providential fact which reflects its principal characteristics; it is universal, it is lasting, and it constantly eludes human interference; its development is served equally by every event and every human being" (Tocqueville 2003 [1835], 15).

Despite the nearly universally avowed political aim for racial equality as a principle of public policy, however, the meaning of this aspiration remains highly controversial. To some degree this is true even among the ethnoracial minority communities, activists, and political leaders in focus in this book. Based on previous research and analysis (Schmidt 2002), we believe that there are several core disagreements among those who are politically engaged in the relationship between public policy and racial equality. More specifically, we think there are two core conflicts in U.S. politics regarding the relationship between ethnoracial equality and public policy.

1. To what degree should governments work proactively to reduce the systematic inequalities that have existed between ethnoracial groups throughout the history of the United States?
2. In aiming for greater racial equality in the United States, should public policies recognize and reinforce existing ethnoracial and cultural differences, or should the country's public policies aim at being color-blind and monocultural so that all Americans are treated alike?

These two questions have generated political disagreements not only among members of the country's White majority but also among political activists and political leaders within U.S. ethnoracial minority groups.

With respect to the first core conflict, there has been a clear division between liberals and conservatives in American politics throughout the post-1965 period. Liberals or progressives have argued that individuals cannot legitimately be held accountable for the circumstances of their lives over which they have had no control, and therefore are not responsible for the inequalities in life chances they face as they struggle to gain more of the "goods" that living in the United States offers (educational attainment, access to health care, access to good jobs and housing in good neighborhoods, etc.). As a result, "fair" equality of opportunity requires that government takes steps (through structural change policies to alter the environments in which individuals live their lives, or through investing in the "human capital" development of those who are handicapped by poverty, racial discrimination, sexual discrimination, etc.). In relation to ethnoracial inequality, this view was perhaps best summarized by former president Lyndon Johnson's famous defense of affirmative action policy in a speech at Howard University in 1965.

> You do not take a person who for years has been hobbled by chains and liberate him, bring him to the starting line of a race and then say: "You are free to compete with all the others." . . . Legal equity is not enough. We seek not just equality as a right . . . but equality as a fact and as a result. (Johnson 1965)

Conservatives, of course, have disagreed consistently with this position, arguing that there is no fair or effective way for government to try to ensure "equality of result" in the competitions between individuals and groups. Conservatives believe, further, that government interventions aiming to advance social equality not only stifle individual initiative and responsibility but generate unhealthy dependence on government as well as vast bureaucratic inefficiencies and waste. Equality of opportunity is best realized, in the conservative view, by ensuring formal equality before the law—making sure that no individual is discriminated against by other individuals on such arbitrary grounds as race, sex, religion, or national origin—but beyond this government has no legitimate role in seeking to ensure equality between individuals from diverse backgrounds.[3]

The second core conflict divides those holding vastly different views on the very nature of American nationhood. On the one hand are those—we call them *monoculturalists*—who argue that equality will never exist in the United States until its people share one common culture and for whom ethnoracial communities have no legitimate place in American public life.

Those who take this view of American nationhood may uphold the freedom of individuals and families to retain ethnic connections and loyalties in their private lives—much as we insist on the private exercise of religious belief and practice—but they typically seek to remove all traces of ethnocultural difference or diversity from the country's public institutions and public policies. For adherents of this view, it seems obvious that the only possible path toward equality for both newcomer immigrants and outsider minorities is through individual assimilation—through individual effort—into the national cultural and political community. In addition, they believe, government certainly should not take any steps that perpetuate ethnocultural differences.

On the other side of this conflict are the *multiculturalists*, who believe that the United States has been constituted historically—by way, not only of voluntary immigration but also through the slave trade, through conquest and annexation, and through the purchase of vast territories and their diverse peoples—as a nation of multiple ethnocultural communities. On the grounds that individuals have a right to membership in U.S. cultural communities made part of the country through means over which these individuals had no control, multiculturalists insist that equality is not achieved through coerced assimilation. Moreover, they argue, long-standing racial inequalities—many of which were forged through processes of coercive inclusion into the American population—cannot be erased by simply pretending that "race doesn't matter" and that formal equality will ensure fairness in respect to equal opportunity in the allocation of opportunities for good schooling, good jobs, homes in good neighborhoods, and so on. For adherents to this view, public policies aiming at greater ethnoracial equality must attempt to level the playing field in ways that take account of the realities of existing multiple cultural communities and existing social forces that perpetuate racial inequality.

Four Decades of Policy Development: An Overview

We think, then, that the political struggles of the past four decades over public policies aimed at generating greater ethnoracial equality in the United States can be framed usefully in relation to the two core disputes outlined previously: (1) To what degree, and in what ways, should governments work to reduce the systematic inequalities that have existed between ethnoracial groups throughout the history of the United States? (2) In aiming for greater equality in the United States, should public policies recognize and reinforce existing ethnoracial and cultural differences, or should the country's public policies aim at being color-blind and mono-cultural so that all Americans are treated alike? These two questions have generated political disagreements not only among members of the country's White majority but to some degree among political activists and political leaders within U.S. ethnoracial minority groups as well. In general, however, ethnoracial minority political leaders and public opinion among Blacks, Latinos, and Asian Americans/Pacific Islanders have been more supportive of the liberal, proactive position on question 1, and more supportive of the multicultural position on question 2, than has been true of White political leaders or members of the White public.

Within the context of these controversies over public policy, our aim here is to describe briefly the trajectory of American public policy over the past four decades in relation to the goal of U.S. ethnoracial equality, and then to assess the degree to which recent immigration has altered or affected this trajectory. In doing so, space limitations prevent us from offering an in-depth account of any single policy issue or event. What we will do is describe a basic overview of the country's policy trajectory on these matters, and then explore two examples of public policy in some depth in order to assess the impact of recent immigration on these examples. Our central theme here is that political conflict over the kinds of public policies needed for the full realization of ethnoracial equality in the United States evolved over time, with certain core policies of the Second Reconstruction becoming a kind of foundation on which policy controversy has evolved over the past four decades.

The 1960s: A New Baseline for Public Policy and Ethnoracial Equality?

As is widely recognized, the 1960s brought a significant change in U.S. public policy in relation to ethnoracial equality. Sometimes termed the Second Reconstruction, the adoption of these policies seemed to establish a new political consensus—at a minimum—in favor of formal equality of opportunity in relation to racial difference. That is, while a coalition of Southern and laissez-faire conservatives fought bitterly against the adoption of these policies in the 1950s and 1960s, their enactment and later approval by the U.S. Supreme Court seemed to establish a fundamental change in the baseline consensus about race relations among both most public officials and the general public in the United States. The central laws in this Second Reconstruction were the Civil Rights Act of 1964, the Voting Rights Act of 1965, and the Housing Act of 1968. Some would include, as well, the Immigration Reform Act of 1965, which eliminated the racially biased national-origins quota system that had governed the allocation of immigration opportunities to the United States since the 1920s. Taken collectively, the implementation of these laws by the federal government meant that most employers, commercial shops and restaurants, public accommodations, school districts, college admissions officers, public transportation companies, home sellers, landlords, election officials, and so on, could no longer use race, national origin, religion, or sex as a criterion for deciding whom to serve, to hire, to assign to a school, to whom to rent or sell a house, or whom to allow to vote.

By the early 1970s, public opinion, as well as public officials in most parts of the country, seemed to have accepted these laws as a minimum foundation for race relations in the United States. Public opinion surveys, for example, demonstrated a major shift in the White public's view of the appropriate relationships between Blacks and Whites in American society after the 1960s, as summarized by Bobo.

> Whereas a solid majority, 68 percent, of white Americans in 1942 favored racially segregated schools, only 7 percent took such a position as early as 1985. Similarly, 55 percent of whites surveyed in 1944 believed whites should receive preference over blacks in access to jobs, as compared with only 3 percent who offered such an opinion as early as 1972. Indeed, so few people are willing to endorse a discriminatory response to either question that both have been dropped from ongoing social surveys. On both of these issues, once-pivotal features of the Jim Crow racist ideology—majority endorsements of the principles of segregation and discrimination—have given way to overwhelming support for the principles of integration and equal treatment. (1997, 36)

By the mid-1970s it was difficult to find any elected official or candidate for public office who was willing to argue publicly and explicitly on behalf of the principles of racial segregation or discrimination in employment or in other aspects of public life. Thus, by the time that immigration policy reemerged as a major political issue in the United States in the 1980s, it appears that a national consensus had developed on the principles of formal equality of opportunity between the races. Nevertheless, controversy and political conflict over the appropriate relationships between public policy and ethnoracial equality have continued in U.S. politics at all levels of government.

Proactive Policies for Social and Ethnoracial Equality

Controversy erupted by the mid-1960s in relation to both of the core policy questions outlined here. Leading up to the adoption of the central policies of the Second Reconstruction, virtually all supporters of the cause of racial equality were united in backing their adoption. Virtually all those working on behalf of racial equality, from Malcolm X to Martin Luther King Jr. to White supporters of the civil rights movement, agreed that government's rules should ensure that no one is discriminated against or excluded on the basis of race, national origin, religion, or sex, in the public spaces of civil society and the marketplace. As we have seen, even conservatives came to publicly support the same principles within a decade or two after the legislation's adoption.

Many liberals and social democrats who had worked on behalf of racial equality, however, believed that these core laws promoting the principles of formal equality of opportunity were but the beginning steps in relation to what was necessary to achieve genuine racial equality in the United States. Much more change in the basic institutions of American society was necessary before the playing field would be level for members of all ethnoracial groups. Here a wide range of policy alternatives was proposed by political advocates of ethnoracial equality.

Many of these proposals in the 1960s and 1970s called for expansion and elaboration of the Great Society programs that were initiated by President Lyndon Johnson's administration. Many were measures intended to provide foundations for greater educational and economic equality among all Americans, regardless of race (i.e., they were race-neutral in conception). The Elementary and Secondary Education Act of 1965, for example, provided federal funds to local school districts, and Title I of that act allocated additional money for districts with large concentrations of poor children. The Economic Opportunity Act of 1964 created a nationwide War on Poverty, establishing local community action agencies across the country to help the poor organize themselves and engage in a variety of methods to gain greater economic opportunity (Head Start programs for preschool children, adult basic education for high school dropouts, job training programs for unemployed youths and adults, etc.). The Model Cities Act of 1966 provided federal funds, mainly for the central cities, to enable local communities to develop and implement plans for the revitalization and renewal of decaying and demoralized areas of the city. The adoption of the Medicare and Medicaid programs in 1965, meanwhile, established a foundation for health care provision to both the aged and the poor.

Some momentum for the expansion of social services programs continued during the early years of the Nixon administration (1969–73), as President Nixon asked Congress in 1969 to adopt a "guaranteed minimum income" law to replace and expand some aspects of the federal welfare program Aid to Families with Dependent Children. Though that initiative was not adopted by Congress, a "welfare rights movement"—partly organized by workers in the federally funded War on Poverty—continued to press for more generous benefits, economic stability, and educational opportunities for welfare recipients. Moreover, President Nixon's Comprehensive Employment and Training Act of 1973 (CETA), later expanded during Jimmy Carter's presidency (1977–81), provided federal funds to thousands of public agencies throughout the country for giving temporary employment and job training to tens of thousands of unemployed Americans.

Most of these policies, proposed or adopted in the 1960s and early 1970s, were aimed at providing support for those who were disadvantaged in relation to the opportunities, resources, and social networks routinely available to the middle and upper classes of American society. How are these policies connected to the struggle for greater ethnoracial equality in the United States? Many political activists and public officials believed that a dramatic expansion of policies such as these was necessary to achieve greater racial equality precisely because a disproportionate percentage of those who were poor and economically disadvantaged were also people of color. Fair equality of opportunity required that the poor be given a "hand up" through a wide variety of social services programs, and the cause of racial equality would be advanced because many of those benefiting from these programs would be members of racialized minorities.

Other political leaders and activists argued in the 1960s and 1970s that in order to achieve genuine social equality in the United States, *structural changes* in the economy would be necessary for the country to build upon these human capital development programs. That is, they argued that the United States would need to change the rules under which capital is accumulated and concentrated because existing policies systematically favored those who already had much, disadvantaged those who had little, and paid little heed to the common good of the whole society. Among the proposals made at the time were those for more public accountability and control of corporations to force them to operate more in the public interest by, for example, requiring more public scrutiny and control of corporate mergers and buyouts; greater corporate responsibility for the effects of their operations on their own workers' well-being (e.g., OSHA), and on public health and safety (e.g., the Product Safety Commission); and greater protection against the pollution of water, air, and land (e.g., the Environmental Protection Act). Other structural reform measures called for a more graduated income tax, as well as higher taxes on corporate profits, and on profits from securities and other forms of nonproductive wealth, and greater public investment in institutions that produce social or common goods (e.g., public parks and other spaces, public transportation, and other infrastructure).

Most of the policies and policy proposals described in the previous four paragraphs fall into the category of race-neutral or culturally monistic. That is, they are conceived in relation to categories of eligibility or funding that are not referenced to racial or cultural group membership, or they are designed as public goods available to all. Other policy proposals aimed more directly at *ethnoracial pluralism,* seeking to provide benefits or services to specific race-based group members or to minority cultural communities in the United States. The classic example of this approach is affirmative action policy in employment and access to institutions of higher education, begun during the Johnson administration in the 1960s, and significantly expanded by President Richard Nixon's application of the Philadelphia Plan for overcoming institutional bias in employment practices to federal agencies, contractors, and grantees (see, e.g., Kotlowski 2001, chap. 4; Anderson 2004).

At the local government level, the classic study of minority political incorporation in 10 San Francisco Bay area cities by Browning, Marshall, and Tabb (1984) identified a cluster of policy changes that were often sought by Black public officials, and their allies, in those cities: minority hiring programs in city governments, particularly in police and fire departments, as well as in administrative positions; increased spending on infrastructure improvements (e.g., streets, gutters, streetlights, public transit) in minority neighborhoods; improved and expanded public facilities, such as libraries, parks, playgrounds, and recreation centers, in minority neighborhoods; the creation of "police review boards" with powers to influence police behavior in minority neighborhoods; and minority appointments to city boards and commissions. (Browning, Marshall, and Tabb 1984, chaps. 4–5). These were racially focused, specific benefits provided by governments for the betterment of neighborhoods and groups that were believed to have been overlooked, neglected, or discriminated against in the past under city governments without significant minority representation.

Other examples of policies and programs that similarly sought to generate greater social equality for ethnoracial minority groups included measures for community control of neighborhood schools; bilingual education programs; the requirements for ballots and election materials in non-English languages; multicultural education programs aimed at teaching students a range of cultural traditions and accomplishments from a variety of American ethnocultural groups; multicultural public library programs; the creation of ethnic studies programs in colleges and universities; and the expansion of radio and television broadcasting licenses for media outlets operating in languages other than English.

At every level of government, Black, Latino, and Asian American political leaders and public officials were among the most consistent supporters of the whole range of proactive, "fair equality of opportunity" public policies discussed earlier. For example, the Black Caucus in Congress and, later, the Hispanic Caucus as well could be counted on to be among the strongest and most consistent voting blocs of support for the whole range of public policies developed to invest more public funds in human capital development programs for the poor and disadvantaged, to invest in the infrastructures of central cities and other low-income communities, as well as the programs—such as affirmative action and bilingual education—that were more targeted toward specific minority groups. Most Black, Latino, and Asian American political leaders, in short, favored more governmental action to help level the playing fields of American society, whether in the form of economic structural change, human resource development, or race-based or culturally pluralistic programs.

The Conservative Backlash to the Second Reconstruction

At the same time that programs such as these were taking off in the late 1960s and 1970s, however, an intensified oppositional movement was beginning to develop as well. By the mid-1980s (during the administration of President Ronald Reagan) most of these proactive policies aimed at generating greater ethnoracial equality had been severely cut back or were completely eliminated. The War on Poverty, for example, was effectively dead by the end of the Nixon administration, as was the model cities program, and discussions of federal welfare policy turned from talk of guaranteed minimum incomes to "tough love" measures that would provide strong incentives to recipients to get into the workforce and become self-sufficient by tightening the rules and shortening the time-span of eligibility. Not coincidentally, the Reagan administration mounted a concerted effort to diminish the influence of unions in the public sector, the fastest growing segment of the union movement.

Public spending on education increased, but classroom sizes increased even more, and many proactive programs aiming at leveling the playing field for minorities and the poor were replaced by new programs aimed at standardized test-score measures of educational achievement, with built-in material disincentives for failure. Bilingual education programs were eliminated in some states (e.g., California, Massachusetts) and were replaced in most school districts by short-term English immersion programs. Public funds for community-based organizations operating ethnoculturally pluralistic social services and training programs became increasingly scarce, and by the mid-1980s, if not sooner, most such programs either died or languished in marginal corners of minority neighborhoods. Others transformed their missions and modes of operation in order to find corporate sponsors.

By 1996, a Democratic president, Bill Clinton, presided over a major change in federal welfare law, reducing income and social services for the poor from an entitlement program (required by the federal government for all impoverished people who met certain eligibility criteria) to a new policy (Temporary Assistance to Needy Families) giving state governments considerable flexibility in allocating funds and establishing new eligibility requirements for temporary assistance. As a consequence, there was less and less economic security in the country's safety net for those poor families in dire need. Finally, arguments for egalitarian structural economic changes became increasingly far-fetched in the new political climate and were soon confined to isolated discussions among academics.

In short, while there appeared—in the mid-1960s—to be realistic political prospects for a variety of more proactive policies aiming at fair equality of opportunity and greater social equality among U.S. ethnoracial groups, within a decade those prospects were largely displaced from the American public policy agenda. Apart from a brief, vaguely defined, and inconsequential race initiative at the outset of the second Clinton administration, the issue of racial equality has not been a priority concern in American political life—at either the national, state, or local levels of government—for more than two decades. Other issues, other concerns have taken priority.

In the decades since the 1960s, the core policies of the Second Reconstruction—the Civil Rights Act of 1964, the Voting Rights Act of 1965, the Fair Housing Act of 1968—have remained intact and appear to be politically sacrosanct even during periods of conservative political monopoly. However, more expansive and proactive policies for social equality—whether race-neutral or ethnoracially pluralistic—have remained highly controversial, and most have been cut back or eliminated altogether from American public policy.

Explanations for the "Great Reversal" on Public Policy and Racial Equality

How is this great reversal in the public policy agenda for ethnoracial equality to be explained? And what role, if any, have the increased numbers of immigrants played in that reversal? This is a highly complex question that we cannot hope to resolve here. A variety of explanations has been offered to account for the stall and reversal in public policy priorities. Among the most prominent explanations are the following.

- Conservatives have argued since soon after the policies were adopted that the core policies creating formal equality of opportunity were the appropriate end point for reform of race relations in the United States, and that any proactive policy moves beyond that were illegitimate and deserved to be reversed. Indeed, conservatives continue to campaign—in the courts, in the executive branch, and in legislative bodies—against those few prominent egalitarian policies still in existence (affirmative action policy in both employment and higher education, the expansion of Voting Rights Act coverage to include vote dilution as well as vote denial, the extension of Voting Rights Act coverage to include language minorities, etc.). In each of these cases, conservatives continue to argue that these policies were adopted without good cause, that they distort and undermine the legitimate role of government, and that in many cases they violate the individualist precepts of the U.S. Constitution. In addition, of course, for the same reasons, conservatives have fought to eliminate, or to prevent adoption of, virtually the entire panoply of policy proposals discussed in the previous section. So to the degree that political conservatives have exercised power in the federal government, and in state and local governments, their opposition to the proactive public policy agenda for social and ethnoracial equality supported by most ethnoracial minority political activists may provide a measure of explanation. From the conservative point of view, the expansive policies and proposals of the 1960s were a mistake and an aberration from long-standing American political values.

- Closely related to this principled line of argument by conservatives was that made by a group of public intellectuals who became quite influential in the 1970s and remained so thereafter, a group known as the *neoconservatives*. Most of them former liberal Democrats or even social democrats, this group (which included individuals such as Daniel Moynihan, Nathan Glazer, Irving Kristol, James Q. Wilson, Norman Podhoretz, Arthur Schlesinger Jr., and others associated with the journals *Commentary* and *The Public Interest*) developed a highly influential line of argument claiming that President Johnson's most ambitious initiatives for social equality—especially the War on Poverty and affirmative action—were poorly conceived in that they were based on false assumptions about the abilities and the appropriate role of government in society, and that these programs were therefore colossal wastes of societal energy and resources. In particular, neoconservatives argued that the misconceived Great Society programs of the Johnson administration demonstrated that social equality is not an appropriate role for government action, and that no government can effectively and fairly work toward any egalitarian goal beyond formal equality of opportunity. Further, they argued forcefully that race-based and culturally pluralistic programs were contrary to the individualistic values and understandings that made America strong and revered in the world (for a good overview, see Steinfels 1979).

The collective onslaught of this group's attacks forced those pushing for expansion of an egalitarian public policy agenda into not only responding to the laissez-faire arguments of traditional U.S. conservatives, but also the arguments of these formerly liberal allies. This development helped to reverse the momentum that had been building in favor of such a public policy agenda and gave further fuel to long-standing political critics of that agenda. Indeed, it was a melding of the arguments of traditional conservatives and those of the 1970s neoconservatives that helped create a new conservatism supportive of a color-blind and formal approach to public policy in the name of equality of opportunity. By the 1980s, in the words of one social democratic historian, the country's frame of reference for social policy had shifted "from the war on poverty to the war on welfare" (Katz 1989).

• Another line of explanation for the reversal of fortunes for an expansive egalitarian public policy agenda focuses on important changes in viewpoint regarding the *appropriate relationship between government and the economy*. Until the 1970s, there had seemed to be a growing consensus among political elites in the United States in favor of a Keynesian approach to fiscal and monetary policy, such that government could be used proactively to support continued prosperity and expansion via an inclusive expansion of consumerism. The early formulations of this approach assumed that a more egalitarian society—one in which workers would enjoy secure employment, health care benefits, a secure pension for retirement, and steady increases in wages—would keep the economy expanding, generating stable and expansive prosperity for all social classes.

Even before the end of Lyndon Johnson's presidency in 1969, however, critics were arguing that Johnson's "guns and butter" strategy of pursuing egalitarian social policies at home as well as a costly war in Vietnam was undermining the strength and vitality of the American economy. By the 1970s, in the face of new forms of global economic competition, corporate leaders and political conservatives had begun to develop a concerted and frontal attack on an egalitarian version of Keynesianism, and many centrist Democrats endorsed the new economic strategy that emerged in its stead (for analyses of this shift, see, e.g., Ferguson and Rogers 1986; Harrison and Bluestone 1988). The stagflation and oil crisis of the mid-1970s seemed to seal the fate of egalitarian fiscal and monetary policy, leading to a form of monetarism that emphasized raising corporate profits over strengthening the economic position and buying power of workers.

By the time of Ronald Reagan's presidency in the 1980s, supply side economics had come to dominate conservative political thought in the Republican Party. In the course of this transition to a new economic reality, Reagan—the "great communicator," as his supporters called him—appeared to succeed in shifting a majority of the public's view of expectations from government. The dominant tune in the country's economic policy choir had become that of laissez-faire, and "the market" became the default arbiter of economic development, at least in ideological terms. Not coincidentally, the Reagan years witnessed a series of deep cuts in social spending by governments, as well as huge increases in public debt occasioned by increased defense spending and tax cuts. By the time of George W. Bush's presidency two decades later, the idea that government policy should be used to ensure greater social equality in the United States seemed to many a quixotic and foolhardy dream of the past (see, e.g., Hacker 2006). In this sort of ideological and political climate, it is unsurprising that a proactive public policy agenda for greater ethnoracial equality has been largely absent from view, not even on the back burner for most public officials.

- Another prominent explanation for the reversal of fortunes for an expansive public policy agenda on racial equality is the phenomenon known as *White backlash*. As several historians have documented, the push for racial egalitarianism through public policy had alienated many White working- and middle-class voters outside the South long before the fact became recognized by elite observers (see, e.g., Gerstle 1995; Hirsch 1995; Sugrue 1995). Politicians, particularly former Georgia governor George Wallace, tapped into this racial resentment and began to demonstrate its electoral potential in the North and Midwest—even among registered Democrats—in the 1968 presidential primaries. Richard Nixon, too, developed a Southern strategy in the 1968 election designed to win alienated White voters leaving the Democratic Party in the wake of the Voting Rights Act of 1965, as well as disaffected White Democrats in other parts of the country.

Ironically, perhaps, while President Nixon was a prime moving force behind the expansion of affirmative action policy, the development of minority set-asides for federal contracts, and proposals for an expansive approach to federal welfare policy in his first two years in office, by the end of his first term he was one of their foremost public critics (see, e.g., Horton 2005, chap. 8). Moreover, Nixon became one of the most effective political leaders in reversing the momentum for the use of busing to integrate public schools, and for enforcing and enhancing open housing policy. Thus, by the end of Nixon's first term in 1973, an increasingly conservative Republican Party had become clearly identified in the public mind with opposition to the use of federal policy to achieve racial equality, apart from the most minimal forms of formal equality of opportunity. Since the 1970s, according to Thomas and Mary Edsell, "the pitting of whites and blacks at the low end of the income distribution against each other has intensified the view among many whites that the condition of life for the disadvantaged—particularly for disadvantaged blacks—is the responsibility of those afflicted, and not the responsibility of the larger society" (Edsell 1992, 4).

Throughout the more than three decades since Richard Nixon left the White House in disgrace, the race card has played an important, if usually implicit, role in numerous electoral campaigns in American politics (see, e.g., Mendelberg 2001), and this fact has had important public policy consequences (see, e.g., Hancock 2004). Responding to and reinforcing White beliefs and resentments about perceived special treatment and minority preferences in government policy, electoral politicians and the media have kept up a steady stream of reinforcements that has consistently undermined efforts to restart public policy initiatives for greater social equality generally, or ethnoracial equality specifically. Horton concludes, "The fortunes of left-of-center liberalism have remained essentially moribund since the implosion of social liberalism in the late 1960s. This is particularly true with regard to issues of socioeconomic equity, with regard to both race and the population more broadly" (2005, 223–24).

Accordingly, a recent analysis of the relationship between "inequality and public policy" found that, on balance, U.S. public policies help to reinforce, rather than undermine, economic and political inequalities, and ethnoracial minorities—disproportionately represented among the least well off—are impacted negatively by these policies more than are those in the White majority (Hacker, Mettler, and Pinderhughes 2005). Given the analyses of the trajectory of public policy in the years since the 1960s by Horton and others, it is perhaps ironic that the racial resentments of the U.S. White population have played a major role in this ongoing public policy reality.

The Role of Immigrants in the "Great Reversal"

Until the mid-1990s, scholars and political activists writing about the collapse of the liberal agenda on behalf of greater social equality in general, and of ethnoracial equality in particular, paid little attention to the role of immigrants in keeping egalitarian proposals off the public policy agenda. Since 1994, however, when California voters passed Proposition 187 by a wide margin, immigrants have come to occupy center stage in the great American debate over racial equality. As it happens, Proposition 187 was overturned by the courts and was never implemented by California's government. If it had been implemented in accord with the voters' wishes, however, it would have banned undocumented immigrants from attending public schools in California, or from receiving any of a variety of specified social policy benefits, and it would have required public employees (including school teachers, nurses, doctors, as well as police officers) to verify the documentation status of immigrants with whom they came into contact in the course of their work and to report any unauthorized migrants to federal immigration officials. The approval of this initiative proposal by California voters signaled the beginning of a new nationwide public policy confrontation over immigrants throughout the country, a confrontation that continues to the present.

There is some indication that in the period since the mid-1990s, the continued increase in foreign-born residents—particularly unauthorized immigration by non-White, mostly Mexican migrants—has added fuel to the fire of White resentments toward both general egalitarian social policies and programs, and to programs designed specifically for ethnoracial minorities. The approval of Proposition 187 by California voters in 1994 was said to have influenced President Clinton's reelection strategy for the 1996 election, as signaled by his directive to the border patrol to more aggressively police the border with Mexico in California. Moreover, when House Republicans insisted on excluding all immigrants (both authorized and unauthorized) from access to federal welfare funds as an amendment to the Clinton-led 1996 reform of federal welfare policy, the president acquiesced. It seems likely, then, that the changes in federal welfare law overall, thought by many observers to have a disproportionate impact on members of ethnoracial minorities (see, e.g., Neubeck and Cazenave 2001; Hancock 2004), were abetted by concerns about immigrants' impacts on taxpayers and government budgets.

Indeed, since at least the mid-1990s, a common response among political conservatives to calls by political leaders for increased public expenditures on public schools, public health care programs, and a variety of other social programs and public sector facilities has been that it is only America's "uncontrolled" borders and overgenerous immigration policies that generate such a "need," and therefore such increased spending must be resisted until the borders are secured. The mantra of many conservative commentators is that providing social service benefits, including public education, to immigrants—both legal and "illegal"—only encourages more immigration, particularly from countries with relatively less prosperous economies and less developed educational systems. According to this line of thinking, any improvements in public sector social programs or infrastructure must be resisted, lest they become an added incentive for immigrants to migrate to the United States.

This position has been reiterated repeatedly at national, state, and local government levels in respect to proposals for reducing public school class sizes through building more classrooms and hiring more teachers, for expanding medical care programs for the poor and low-income workers, for expanding and improving public recreational facilities, and so forth. In short, any expansion or improvement of public sector facilities or services falls under the suspicion that it will serve as a magnet for more immigration, especially unauthorized immigration. In this political environment, the public policy momentum has certainly not been in the direction of developing a concerted effort for greater social and ethnoracial equality.

The Federation for American Immigration Reform (FAIR), for example, has posted a number of studies on its Web sites purporting to demonstrate the inordinate costs of immigration to U.S. governments for programs such as public education, health care, welfare, housing services, criminal justice and incarceration, and so forth (see, e.g., Huddle 1997; Stewart 2002; Martin 2007). Similarly, a 2004 study by a researcher at the Center for Immigration Studies argued that the "cheap labor" of illegal immigrants "imposed more than $26.3 billion in costs on the federal government in 2002 and paid only $16 billion in taxes, creating a net fiscal deficit of almost $10.4 billion, or $2,700 per illegal household" (Camerota 2004, 5).

Following this drumbeat of policy-related analyses by conservative think tanks and advocacy groups, leaders of the U.S. House of Representatives held a number of hearings on immigration policy reform in the spring and summer of 2006, seemingly aimed at convincing voters to return a Republican majority to Congress in the November 2006 elections. Figuring prominently in these hearings was the thesis that immigrants are a net drain on the fiscal standing of governments at the local, state, and national levels. Prominent among the titles of the hearings were the following: *Porous Borders and Downstream Costs: The Cost of Illegal Immigration on State, County, and Local Governments* (U.S. House of Representatives, Committee on Government Reform 2006) and *How Does Illegal Immigration Impact American Taxpayers and Will the Reid-Kennedy Amnesty Worsen the Blow?* (U.S. House of Representatives, Committee on the Judiciary 2006). The point here is not to question the appropriateness of these hearings but to demonstrate once again the political climate in which they were held. In a climate focused on the costs and dangers of illegal immigration (and secondarily, of immigration more generally), there is little time or attention given to the question of whether governments should be making more efforts to create or expand policies designed to increase ethnoracial equality in the United States.

By the early years of the first decade of the twenty-first century, some scholars had begun to argue that the increase in immigrants over the period since the 1960s had directly undermined some measures created to foster greater ethnoracial equality. No public policy has received more scrutiny in this context than has affirmative action.[4] Two primary sticking points are at issue here. One raises questions about the appropriateness of including voluntary immigrants only recently arrived in this country in a program whose most common rationale is that historical injustices (involuntary segregation, discrimination, etc.) perpetrated against the protected groups—typically Blacks, Latinos, Asian Americans, Native Americans, and women—have generated unearned disadvantages in relation to their acquisition of both human capital (e.g., academic skills, educational credentials, business know-how, social interaction skills desired by employers) and social capital (e.g., employment and socially advantageous connections) that cause them to be at an unfair disadvantage in relation to these realms of opportunity for social mobility. That is, many critics have suggested that people who have voluntarily moved to the United States to seek improvements in their lives cannot fairly be said to have suffered *historical* injustices as members of U.S. racial minority groups. Including immigrants as eligible in such a program is an insult to those who have been historically victimized, as well as unfair to others competing for similar jobs, contracts, or access to higher education. Scholars such as Graham (2001, 2002) have argued that this "strange convergence" between two policies (the Civil Rights Act of 1964 and the Immigration Reform Act of 1965) adopted for the purpose of supporting greater racial equality has operated to undermine the public credibility of both. That is, affirmative action policy is discredited by the "unfair" eligibility of voluntary immigrants who happen to be "non-White" and/or women, and immigration policy's public support is undermined in that immigrant participation in affirmative action is seen as one more example of immigrants "taking advantage" of American generosity and gullibility.

A second sticking point in relation to affirmative action policy and immigrants is that, even if the inclusion of some immigrants may be justified on other grounds (e.g., they are *currently*—not historically—discriminated against because of their race, national origin, or gender), the vagueness and sweeping character of eligibility categories generates additional injustices, especially in the case of some immigrants. Commonly expressed examples are those of relatively well-educated and prosperous immigrants—from, for example, India, China, Nigeria, or Cuba—taking advantage of opportunities for jobs, government contracts, or admission to highly selective universities because they are Asian Americans, African Americans, or Latinos, and therefore presumably disadvantaged (see, e.g., La Noue and Sullivan 2001). These examples, in turn, generate horror stories in the media about the "obvious injustice" of affirmative action programs in general.

A similar—and even more powerful—kind of "strange convergence" has arisen in respect to the relationship in the public mind between immigration policy and language policy in the United States. Bilingual education was initiated as a federal policy, for example, because former Senator Ralph Yarborough (D-Tex.) was convinced that Mexican American students—who typically spoke Spanish at home and who typically attended public schools that had poor facilities, few current textbooks and learning materials, and among the lowest-paid teachers—were disadvantaged by these facts through no fault of their own. Being taught in a language they did not speak at home, Yarborough thought, was in part responsible for the comparatively high dropout rates of Mexican American students. Yarborough was further convinced that students could be helped by being taught initially in a language they already understood, while learning English as well (Schmidt 2000, chap. 1). Senator Yarborough's proposed 1968 Bilingual Education Act Amendment (Title VII) to President Johnson's Elementary and Secondary Education Act of 1965 was supported by most Democrats in Congress, and by the then-powerful umbrella lobbying group the National Conference for Civil Rights, because Mexican Americans were recognized by them as a long-standing U.S. minority group that had been discriminated against both racially and culturally. Further, Mexican Americans were also recognized as a long-standing language minority whose members had typically spoken Spanish since being incorporated into the United States by forceful annexation after the Mexican American War ending in 1848 (see chap. 3, this vol.). Thus, in its inception and development, bilingual education was not understood—by Congress, by its interest group supporters, or by educators implementing it—as a program for immigrants. Rather, it was a program designed to seek greater educational success, and thereby greater social equality, for a disadvantaged ethnoracial minority group.

A similar line of thinking led to the inclusion of "language minorities" as a protected group under the Voting Rights Act of 1965. Based on several studies conducted by the U.S. Commission on Civil Rights, and on testimony from Mexican American political activists from Texas, Congress amended the VRA in 1975 to include protection for "language minorities." Congress's rationale for this amendment (which requires U.S. elections jurisdictions with large concentrations of people who are speakers of Spanish, Asian languages, or Native American languages to provide election materials and ballots in those languages) is worth quoting at length in this context.

> The Congress finds that voting discrimination against citizens of language minorities is pervasive and national in scope. Such minority citizens are from environments in which the dominant language is other than English. In addition they have been denied equal educational opportunities by State and local governments, resulting in severe disabilities and continuing illiteracy in the English language. The Congress further finds that, where State and local officials conduct elections only in English, language minority citizens are excluded from participating in the electoral process. In many areas of the country, this exclusion is aggravated by acts of physical, economic, and political intimidation. The Congress declares that, in order to enforce the guarantees of the fourteenth and fifteenth amendments to the United States Constitution, it is necessary to eliminate such discrimination by prohibiting English-only elections, and by prescribing other remedial devices. (U.S. Commission on Civil Rights 1981, 120)

Again, the entirety of Congress's rationale for this law is focused on the "voting discrimination" suffered by "language minorities" who are U.S. citizens, and there is not a hint that this program might be directed at helping immigrants. The presumption in the rationale is that languages other than English are the native languages of important groups of U.S. citizens and not "foreign" intrusions into America's monistic and English-only culture.

Despite these perspectives and findings, critics of bilingualism in the schools and in the voting booths quickly seized upon the idea that these programs were directed mainly at immigrants, and that they were preventing immigrants from becoming properly "Americanized." And in truth, it is likely that by the early 1980s a clear majority of the students in bilingual education classes and perhaps even citizens taking advantage of non-English ballots were either first- or second-generation immigrants. By the end of the 1980s, bilingual education was in evident decline, and while the language minority provisions of the Voting Rights Act were not eliminated in the law's most recent renewal (in 2006), there is no doubt that the whole question of bilingualism in American public life has been transformed in most people's minds from a question of ethnoracial equality for long-standing U.S. minority communities to one of how best to settle immigrant foreigners in the United States. In the process of this transition, the understanding that the United States has always been a multilingual country—with communities of people speaking languages other than English extant throughout its history—has been lost under the vast numbers of immigrants who have come speaking some of those same languages, though speaking many other languages as well.

To summarize, then, it seems likely to us that immigrants *have* affected the political standing of the expansive and proactive public policy agenda for greater ethnoracial equality that was pieced together in the 1960s and early 1970s. It seems clear that the vast numbers of immigrants—and probably most especially the large number of unauthorized immigrants—have had a dampening effect on efforts to revive and expand policies fought for by political activists and public officials committed to a conception of fair equality of opportunity. At the same time, we believe it is wrong to say that immigration has been the major factor in this ongoing story of the triumph of formal equality of opportunity and a laissez-faire approach to ethnoracial equality in the United States. For, as outlined here, much of that expansive and proactive public policy agenda was already in steep political decline before immigrants became a major factor in political debate or in public policy conflict in the 1980s and, especially, in the 1990s. It seems more likely that in the 1990s immigrants became a handy new fuel to throw onto a fire that had already virtually destroyed the proactive and expansive push for public policies aimed at leveling the playing field between peoples of color and White Americans. But that is another analysis that may bear fruit in the final and concluding chapter of our book.

Part 4 | Conclusions

7 | Immigrants and the Future of American Ethnoracial Politics

This book has aimed at bringing better understanding of the impacts of recent immigration on the political efforts of three U.S. ethnoracial minority groups—Blacks, Latinos, and Asian Americans/Pacific Islanders—to gain fuller democratic inclusion into American society and politics. We have identified and explained the ways in which immigrant newcomers to the United States are affecting the efforts of the country's long-standing ethnoracial outsiders to become fully incorporated insiders in the American polity. What conclusions do we draw from this inquiry? We address this broad question here in our summary and associated conclusions.

We have affirmed that the era of large-scale immigration of the past four decades has dramatically and decisively changed the face of U.S. ethnoracial politics in significant ways. That Latinos replaced Blacks as the country's largest ethnoracial minority group around the time of the 2000 census is directly traceable to the scale of migration from Latin America and the Spanish-speaking Caribbean over the past four decades. As we saw in chapter 1, the percentage of Blacks in the U.S. population has increased slightly over the past four decades, from just over 10 percent in 1970 to 12 percent in 2005, while the percentage of U.S. Hispanics/Latinos increased over the same time period from 4.5 percent to more than 14 percent of the U.S. population. Further, the fact that Latinos are migrating increasingly to areas outside their long-standing geographic concentrations (especially the Southwest, Northeast, and south Florida) into virtually every state in the union, and that Asian Americans and Pacific Islanders are dramatically expanding their numbers in multiple states, means that the binary Black/White paradigm through which U.S. ethnoracial politics has been interpreted by many observers no longer fits the lived experience of most Americans. It is increasingly clear to most that the United States is a multiracial—not a biracial—country.

We have presented an array of evidence that immigrants during the recent era have also wrought significant changes *within* each of the primary ethnoracial groups we considered. Immigrants from Africa and from the African diaspora in the Caribbean, with relatively higher levels of income and education but lower levels of residential segregation, have brought change and added complexity to Black politics in various parts of the country, just as the large-scale influx of immigrants from Central and South America, as well as from the Caribbean, has brought new complexity to Hispanic or Latino politics. But extensive as it is, the increased internal diversity of these groups is exceeded by that resulting from the expansion of multiple national-origin groups that have been lumped into the U.S. Census category of "Asian Americans and Pacific Islanders." How, then, have these demographic changes affected ethnoracial politics in the United States?

In chapter 2 we outlined four plausible scenarios for making sense of these changes. First, we suggested that precisely because immigrants are newcomers and thus less affected by historical racial fault lines in the United States, it is possible that so-called non-White immigrants might bypass the ghettoization of ethnoracial isolation and/or inequality, and we suggested that it might be possible for optimistic, hard-working, energetic, and ambitious people of color to *assimilate as individuals* into the post-1965 ostensibly color-blind possibilities of American life. These immigrants, we said, might follow the American Dream of economic, social, and political success through individual assimilation. Their political behavior, as a result, would not be determined by the confinements of ethnoracial group politics but by their own interests and aspirations as fully incorporated individual Americans. Further, we suggested, the self-evident success of these upwardly mobile immigrants and their children could inspire other people of color by their example, leading to a gradual individual assimilation of all those who follow the immigrants' examples through their own forward-looking hard work and ambition. Politically, this trajectory into the future would be marked by an increasing inability of scholars and political actors to identify or predict the political loyalties and behaviors of individual Americans—of all skin hues or cultural backgrounds—by taking note of their ethnoracial group origins.

The second scenario outlined was *political pluralism,* in which members of ethnoracial minority groups perceive and act upon common political interests as members of these groups and act together to enhance their political, social, and economic well-being in a polity that rewards cohesive group-based political action. This scenario anticipates that increasing numbers of immigrants from Latin America and Asia, but also Africa, are and will continue to be socialized by American life into recognizing some common ethnoracial interests with other Americans of long standing whose origins lie in Africa, Asia, or Latin America. Immigrants, accordingly, are seen as swelling the ranks of the ethnoracial groups we commonly label Latino, Asian/Pacific Islander American, and Black, and this increase in numbers should be accompanied by an increase in the political involvement and clout of these groups in American political life. Moreover, because few racial barriers to equality remain in U.S. society, and the U.S. political system is relatively open to the efforts of groups with increasing resources and an interest in using them for political ends, city councils, state legislatures, political party leaders, and federal government officials should be paying increasing attention to the opinions and political desires of America's ethnoracial minority groups. In short, this scenario predicts that the steadily increasing numbers of non-White Americans, a direct result of immigration in the past four decades, should be generating increasing political power and political benefits for the country's ethnoracial minority communities as political interest groups.

The third scenario is one of *biracial hierarchy*. This scenario predicts that the Black-White division that has dominated social and political consciousness in much of the United States throughout most of its history will reassert itself politically by facilitating the incorporation of immigrants—even those from Asia, the Pacific, Latin America, and the Caribbean—into *either* of the White or Black/Minority "races." Moreover, those marked as Black would be the primary exceptions to an upwardly mobile path open to those accepted as White. Thus, while most Asians and light-skinned Latinos would likely be assimilated into a deracialized path of upward mobility and inclusion as insiders, most Blacks would continue to find themselves excluded from upward social and economic mobility and marginalized from meaningful political power, despite the fact that the ranks of the Black population are increasing through immigration from Africa and the Caribbean, and by dark-skinned immigrants from Latin America.

This scenario, in short, foresees something like the pattern in twentieth-century Chicago, when Irish, Polish, and Italian immigrants were incorporated into the White population—both as individuals and as politically engaged ethnic groups—while Black migrants from the South found themselves racialized and excluded from the centers of political power despite their growing numbers in the city's population (Pinderhughes 1987). Thus, most Latinos and Asian Americans—like most European-origin Americans—would be increasingly assimilated or integrated into the patterns of political participation, representation, power, and policy success prevalent among long-standing insider ethnic groups. Black Americans, however, including those immigrants and their offspring incorporated into this group, would continue to find themselves excluded from meaningful political power and policy success.

The final scenario regarding the future of American ethnoracial politics is one in which the pattern of *multiracial hierarchy*—most prevalent in the western part of the United States since at least the mid–nineteenth century—will become dominant throughout the country, as non-White immigrants from continents other than Europe continue to transform the nation's demographic composition. In this understanding of race, members of ethnoracial minority groups can be racialized in multiple ways—for example, inferior versus superior, perpetual foreigner/outsider versus prototypical American insider—all of which foster a continuing privileged position for the historically dominant White group. In this case, moreover, the institutions and practices of the American polity—economic, social, and political—work to systematically disadvantage peoples of color while continuing to confer comparative advantages to the European-origin White population. This scenario predicts a much more complex series of possibilities than do the other scenarios—racial minority rainbow coalitions, political competition and conflict *between* ethnoracial minority groups, both ethnic and panethnic political organizations, and so forth. However, the dominant overriding pattern throughout these varied possibilities would be one in which U.S. institutions operate to continue the relative exclusion and disadvantage of multiple peoples of color in comparison with the White population regarding political power and the adoption of public policies sought by minority activists and public officials. This scenario, in short, sees the changed ethnoracial composition of immigrants to the United States in the last four decades as bringing about a much more complex, yet still essentially hierarchical, ethnoracial politics throughout the country.

Where, then, does the evidence point in relation to these varying scenarios for America's ethnoracial future? In organizing and presenting our information, we looked at four benchmarks of democratic political incorporation: (1) participation in political activities, (2) political representation in governmental offices, (3) membership in dominant governing coalitions within public decision-making institutions, and (4) successful adoption of public policies thought by minority group leaders to facilitate greater ethnoracial equality in American society. How has immigration over the past four decades affected the efforts of long-standing U.S. ethnoracial minority groups to gain full democratic inclusion in relation to these four dimensions? Where does our evidence point?

We believe the evidence does not point unequivocally toward one of these various scenarios, nor to the dismissal of the others. In the end, the evidence requires interpretation, and different individuals may reasonably find competing and differing interpretations to be persuasive. Further, the American population has continued to grow and change, as new immigrants have continued to stream into all parts of the country even as we have been gathering our evidence and writing, and new U.S. citizens continue to be born to immigrant parents as well, so that the subject under our scholarly lens has continued to evolve even as we try to gain purchase on it for understanding and articulation. In short, we believe it is possible to find evidence in support of any one—and all—of the four scenarios we sketched out as alternative futures for U.S. ethnoracial politics, depending on the dimension under examination. At the same time, we believe that the preponderance of the evidence points toward one scenario as being more likely than the others.

Optimistic Scenarios: Individual Assimilation and Political Pluralism; Or, the Glass Is Half Full

It is possible to read the evidence as supportive of an *individual assimilationist* interpretation of the effects of recent immigration on the country's politics. Those inclined to see politics primarily in individualistic terms—as an individual pursuit of self-interest and/or public interest, through democratic institutions such as voting—will find much to be sanguine about in the materials presented here. The context for this optimism is that all legal barriers to political participation by American citizens—of whatever skin hue or racial group background—have been formally removed from American political life for more than 40 years. Further, not only have ethnoracial barriers to *immigration* been gone for more than two generations, but increasing numbers of Latin American, African, Caribbean, Asian, and Pacific Islander immigrants have naturalized and begun to participate in American politics as U.S. citizens. Moreover, despite occasional highly publicized hate crimes against racial minorities, organized patterns of social intimidation aiming to dissuade racial minority voting or political participation seem to be largely absent from American political life, particularly in comparison with times past. In other words, it is possible to look at the operation of American political and electoral institutions and largely see Welcome signs for individual newcomers and outsiders seeking to become part of the American polity.

African Americans have voted and campaigned for public office in rough proportion to White Americans for at least three decades. In this context, it is not surprising that increasing numbers of Latinos and Asian Americans/Pacific Islanders have become voters and candidates for elective and appointive office in American political life as well. Nor is it surprising to see Latinos, Asian Americans, and Pacific Islanders affiliating themselves as individuals between the political parties and organized interest groups in the American polity, and doing so according to their individual political interests and beliefs. While Latinos and Asian Americans do not yet vote in numbers that match their relative proportions of the U.S. population, this is to be expected when large percentages of them are immigrants still finding their way. The important thing to keep in mind from this interpretation is that the opportunities are there for them to advance on the road to success in American life. Beyond that, it will take time and individual initiative for these newcomers and their offspring to find their way according to their talents, aspirations, and hard work.

Most advocates and supporters of an assimilationist position do not expect that other criteria (such as those articulated later) should exist for determining the degree to which *successful* political incorporation has taken place. Individuals take advantage of their opportunities as they see fit, and the extent to which they participate in voting and other political activities is up to that individual. So long as elections are free and open, and there are no formal or legal barriers to political participation, whatever levels of participation or political success that result from the efforts (or lack thereof) of individuals are the fair and appropriate outcomes of a democratic political system as understood and evaluated from the assimilationist view.

It is also possible to find evidence for the second scenario, *political pluralism*. Pluralists look for group involvement, organization, participation, and representation of shared interests in a political system that is relatively open to new claimants for power. Chapters 5 and 6 offered a good deal of evidence indicating that immigrants have increased the political presence of American ethnoracial minority groups in U.S. politics. Immigrants have swollen the voting numbers of Latinos and Asian Americans/Pacific Islanders in recent decades, and they have modestly increased the numbers of Black voters as well. Moreover, evidence of expanding interest group activity aiming to organize and represent a variety of national-origin, ethnic, and panethnic communities—both new and old—is not hard to find. Long-standing interest group organizations—labor unions, for example—have been infused with, and in some cases dramatically revitalized by new members from immigrant and ethnoracial minority communities. Naturalization drives and get-out-the-vote (GOTV) campaigns by ethnoracial minority group organizations have increased dramatically in recent decades, a move directed toward tapping the political potential of the increasing numbers of immigrant coethnic Latinos, Asian Americans, and Blacks for group advancement toward greater political clout. In conjunction with the Voting Rights Act and the burgeoning numbers of immigrants—particularly Latino immigrants—there has been a dramatic increase in the proportion of elected officials from among ethnoracial minority groups at the local, state, and national levels of government (chap. 5, this vol.). Further, Black immigrants from Africa and the Caribbean, as we showed, have increased the levels of educational achievement and economic standing of the U.S. Black population overall, and these resources can be seen as having helped increase the political standing and power of that population as well. Immigrants from Africa and the African diaspora have forged new political alliances among Blacks as well as across racial groups.

All of this is evidence of the vitality and growth of ethnoracial minority group involvement in the American political system, and while their numbers and political clout do not yet match their proportions of the U.S. population, this is to be expected among groups that are still composed of large percentages of foreign-born, especially for Latinos and Asian Americans/Pacific Islanders. Moreover, while we can expect to see conflicts over the spoils of political representation and power between and among the Black, Latino, and Asian American/Pacific Islander populations in the United States, this too is a sign of the growing political presence and incorporation of what are, after all, very diverse population groups.

The key point is that Blacks, Latinos, and Asian Americans/Pacific Islanders are gradually becoming increasingly important political constituencies for elected officials at all levels of American government, and their political influence can only be expected to grow—perhaps even grow dramatically—in the years to come. This expectation is based not only on the symbolic and material incentives for political participation that exist for all population groups but also on the fact that there are no substantial obstacles to minority political participation in the laws or other formal structures in the United States. The system *is* relatively open and accessible to new groups, and there is every indication that both newcomer and previously outsider ethnoracial minority groups are being incorporated—as insiders—into all levels in the U.S. political system. This incorporation is perhaps not proceeding at the pace that the most politically active members of those groups would hope, but that is true of all aspiring political groups during periods of political change.

In short, by looking at the large processes of political change that have taken place in relation to ethnoracial politics in the United States, those who expect to see genuine progress in relation to the political incorporation of newcomers from Latin America, Asia, Africa, the Caribbean, and the Pacific can find numerous signs of positive transformations. These are being wrought in part by the demographic changes generated by the large-scale immigration of the past four decades. There are bumps in the road, to be sure. But the overall trajectory can be seen as very favorable in relation to the political incorporation of U.S. peoples of color, particularly in comparison with both the U.S. past and with many other countries in the world where recent increased immigration has brought (or rekindled) bitter conflicts, violent confrontations, and/or the resurgence to political power of White hypernationalist and anti-immigrant political parties.

While these relatively optimistic scenarios—individual assimilationist and political pluralist—regarding the successful political incorporation of both immigrant newcomers and minority outsiders can be seen as persuasive interpretations of the data available to us, we believe that it is equally important to consider the information presented in previous chapters through the somewhat more pessimistic lens of racial hierarchy. For taking the rosy, optimistic view of these matters requires the studied neglect of certain troublesome and continuing realities of American political life. Despite the clear changes in American ethnoracial political life brought about through the core policies of the Second Reconstruction in the 1960s, holding the United States to more rigorous standards of democratic inclusion than those considered sufficient by assimilationists and pluralists yields the perception that much remains to be done before the country can be considered an ethnoracial democracy. Viewing the impacts of immigrants on the basic criteria of these more rigorous standards of democratic inclusion yields a picture less optimistic than those sketched here.

Pessimistic Scenarios: Immigrants and the Continuation
of Racial Hierarchy in the United States;
Or, the Glass Is Half Empty

A racial hierarchy interpretation of American democracy suggests that unless ethnoracial minority communities can go beyond descriptive representation to *membership in the governing coalitions* of American political institutions at all levels of the federal system, and unless those governing coalitions adopt *ethnoracially egalitarian public policies,* then two core criteria for racial democracy have not been met, and the United States cannot be characterized fairly as a racially egalitarian democracy. These criteria do not appear in analyses of political incorporation if there is no comparative and critical analysis of the *political interests* of differing political groups.

For example, the individual assimilationist view does not consider what is at stake in politics for the various individuals that make up the membership of the political community. From an assimilationist perspective, so long as individuals are not formally blocked from participation, it is up to those individuals to articulate their own interests and engage politically as they see fit, and *procedural* democratic fairness might require only that all elections and policy decisions be decided on the basis of majority rule. Similarly, traditional political pluralists are not challenged with a critical analysis of conflicting political interests; rather, they conceive all political groups as fundamentally the same since, by definition, each political group is formed from within by individuals who perceive themselves as sharing certain politically important interests, and the members voluntarily come together to advance those shared interests within the competitive arenas of the polity. As with assimilationists, so long as pluralists see no formal or legal obstacles (such as the Jim Crow laws and practices of segregation so common in the Southern states prior to the mid-1960s) to voluntary group formation or to the engagement of those groups in the competitive arenas of politics, then the conditions requisite for fair democratic inclusion obtain. Failure to gain substantial power under these conditions of fair competition can only be attributed to the weakness of the interests that lose, but this cannot be attributed to an unjust system of politics, according to pluralist tenets.

In contrast, a racial hierarchy perspective argues that *structural inequalities* in American public life stack the deck of the political game in ways that are fundamentally unfair and undemocratic. As Charles Lindblom has noted concerning the operation of the market system, there are substantially important "prior determinations" (inherited wealth or lack thereof, socially constructed advantages and disadvantages in the distribution of connections, wide variations in opportunities for intellectual and skill development, etc.) that help to determine market outcomes, though they are not normally taken into account by free market economists in assessing market efficiencies (Lindblom 2001, chap. 12).

We believe these same factors commonly operate to allocate inequalities of opportunity in political life, even in the absence of formal, legal barriers. Among the most prevalent and important of these structural inequalities are barriers to equal opportunity and empowerment maintained by the effects of historical (as sketched out in chap. 3, this vol.), as well as ongoing and contemporary, practices of racialization. These racial barriers to equal opportunity, combined with important economic and gender barriers, create important stumbling blocks inhibiting the country's ability to realize its greater or fuller democratization. As shown in chapter 4, moreover, persistent inequalities are evident in the school and neighborhood segregation among Blacks, Latinos, and, to a lesser extent, Asians that continues to exist in the midst of increasing racial and ethnic diversity.

From this perspective, genuine democracy cannot be said to exist in the United States so long as the political voices of significant ethnoracial groups are substantially underrepresented in the dominant political coalitions that govern American political institutions and that develop and implement governmental policy. In particular, the racial hierarchy perspective asks whether there remain significant obstacles to equality of power and political outcomes between the White majority and one or more of the minority groups that have experienced the most severe and long-lasting racialization in U.S. political development. In the analytical framework used in this book, racial hierarchy can be said to exist if—despite relatively open channels of participation and some measure of descriptive representation—peoples of color remain for the most part outsiders in relation to the dominant governing coalitions of American political decision making and in their inability to secure adoption of important ethnoracially egalitarian public policies.

After more than 40 years of high levels of non-White immigration, how does the data presented in the foregoing chapters look through this lens of racial hierarchy? Further, to the degree that racial hierarchy remains a significant factor in American political life, is that hierarchy best understood as fundamentally *bi*-racial or as *multi*-racial? To address these questions, we provide an overview of our evidence in relation to Black Americans, and then we take up the question of whether Latinos and Asian Americans/Pacific Islanders also suffer the exclusionary effects of racial hierarchy in American political life. Throughout we will attempt to factor in the influence of recent immigrants on the trajectory of racial hierarchy in U.S. politics.

Racial Hierarchy and Black Americans

The 1960s marked the removal of the most onerous formal and legal road-blocks to Black participation in American public and political life. Especially after passage of the Voting Rights Act of 1965, the country witnessed a substantial increase in Black voter participation and election and/or appointment to public offices at all levels of government, as documented in chapter 5. Still, there is reason to believe that Black Americans remain political outsiders when it comes to their membership in the dominant coalitions of American government, and in relation to the adoption of public policies perceived as important to the realization of ethnoracial equality in American society.

Black representatives have gained membership in dominant governing coalitions in some urban areas and in some state governments during the past four decades, but their coalitional roles have not achieved a level of stability or strength sufficient to consistently ensure the adoption and implementation of the kinds of public policies thought necessary by most Black Americans to realize ethnoracial equality (chap. 6, this vol.). Rather, as we have seen, even when significant influence has been achieved by Black representatives in such dominant coalitions, the coalitions themselves typically have lost power before much of their policy agenda could be realized.

At the national level, moreover, Black political influence has remained weak since soon after adoption of the core civil rights policies of the mid-1960s. Presidents from both political parties have not been reluctant to appoint Blacks to high-level cabinet posts, and the Congressional Black Caucus has sometimes had the ear of congressional leaders and/or the White House. But the logic of political party competition, as we have seen, leads Democratic Party leaders to aim for the persuadable, median voters in closely contested elections, ignoring the interests of electorally captive groups such as Blacks (Frymer 1999). As a consequence, the opinions and interests of the substantial majority of the U.S. Black population remain off the agendas of both presidents and Congress, even when the Democratic Party controls both branches of the national government. Policies strongly supported by a substantial majority of the Black population (Dawson 1994, 2001), policies aiming to confront and alleviate the substantial remaining inequalities between Blacks and Whites in income, wealth, educational achievement, health, housing quality, and so on, remain too controversial for priority consideration by Democratic Party leaders (see, e.g., Jacobs and Skocpol 2005, chaps. 3, 4). National Republican leaders, meanwhile, show little interest in or support for addressing ethnoracial inequalities through public policy.

In short, while the Black population of the United States votes in rough proportion to its share of the population, and while substantial numbers of Black Americans hold elective and appointive office at local, state, and national levels of government, there is strong evidence in support of understanding the operation of American politics in terms of a racial hierarchy model. As a group, Blacks remain considerably disadvantaged relative to the White population in relation to most criteria used to determine relative social standing and well-being in American life, and the arenas of governance (both public and private) in the country remain substantially unresponsive to the interests of most Black Americans when it comes to the adoption of the kinds of policies that most Blacks believe are necessary to ensure a more fair distribution of opportunities and well-being. Thus, there is little reason to believe that individual assimilation will be the actual or preferred route among most of the Black population to becoming insiders in the American political system. Blacks continue to expend considerable resources organizing and mobilizing for pluralistic pressure-group activity both inside and outside the governance institutions of American political and civic life. However, despite such efforts, the evidence we presented does not indicate that the national political alignment against an egalitarian public policy agenda on ethnoracial issues shows signs of breaking loose soon. Nor does it appear that the increased presence of substantial numbers of immigrants from non-White regions of the world has increased the efficacy of those efforts. In this sense, the evidence for continuing racial hierarchy in relation to the U.S. Black population appears persuasive, even though many African immigrants have higher incomes and education levels, and lower levels of residential segregation, than do native-born Black Americans. The achievement of ethnoracial democracy remains an unfinished project for the Black population, and the immigration-generated changing skin tones of the American people have not altered that reality.

Racial Hierarchy and U.S. Latinos

To what extent is the U.S. Latino population also subject to the effects of a racial hierarchy in American public life? This is a very complicated and highly disputed question. As we have shown, the U.S. Latino population is highly diverse and is becoming more so quite rapidly in relation to national origins (chaps. 1, 3, this vol.). Further, Latinos have a varied and complex history in relation to U.S. domestic politics and even its international relations. Nevertheless, we believe the information we have presented can be read as supporting the view that a significant number of Latinos continue to experience a substantial degree of racial hierarchy in U.S. political life.

In terms of social integration and social standing, in some ways Latinos are as disadvantaged in American public life as are Black Americans. That is, in the aggregate Latinos have lower incomes and wealth, and lower levels of educational achievement, and they also have similar levels of residential and educational segregation as do members of the Black population in the United States. Moreover, as is true of Black Americans, substantial numbers of Latinos believe that most Americans are prejudiced against their group, and that many Latinos suffer from discrimination because of their ethnoracial identities. The reasons cited for these feelings of prejudice and discrimination range from Latinos' use of the Spanish language, to skin color and phenotype, to cultural dissimilarities and economic competition. Whatever the reasons, many Latinos continue to believe that their group suffers from social stigmatization and political exclusion (see, e.g., Garcia Bedolla 2005).

Regarding political participation and involvement, Latinos lag far behind both White and Black Americans. Many Latinos are prevented from voting or running for office because they are not U.S. citizens; and even when taking only citizens into account, Latinos continue to lag behind both Whites and Blacks in political involvement and participation. Thus, despite significant advances in recent decades, their voices are relatively unheard in the halls of government. Moreover, little interest is being shown by American political leaders, whether governmental or party leaders, in initiating steps toward increasing the levels of naturalization and/or political participation of the Latino population. Indeed, the political and social climate toward Latinos seems to have become increasingly chilly in recent years, especially as an identification between Latinos and the immigrant population continues to be made by a large number of Americans. Hence, with the exception of close electoral races, efforts to politically incorporate Latinos in the United States are almost exclusively being made by Latino community and political groups, and not by political party or governmental leaders. While Latinos have shown a willingness to engage in social movement activities such as marches and demonstrations, and have devoted considerable resources to the organization and deployment of pluralist political pressure groups as well, there is little evidence to indicate that these efforts have met with substantial success in relation to the groups' goals for public policy.

If we go further and apply the more rigorous standards for political incorporation of *membership in dominant governing coalitions* and *adoption of ethnoracially egalitarian public policies* favored by most group members, the situation for many Latinos continues to appear relatively bleak. That is, there are few local and state governments in which Latinos have become full-fledged and equal members of stable governing coalitions. At the national level, the Congressional Hispanic Caucus, like the Congressional Black Caucus, saw its power and influence in Congress severely diminished after the Republican Party takeover following the 1994 elections, and the restoration of Democratic Party control after the 2006 elections has not resulted in significant new empowerment, especially concerning the party leadership's stance on ethnoracially egalitarian public policies. Indeed, the logic of the "median voter" strategy on Democratic Party leaders seems to weaken the impact of Latino empowerment and policy preferences about as much as it does those of the Black population (Fraga and Leal 2004). In both cases, Democratic Party efforts to attract the median swing voters mean that party leaders believe they can ill afford to adopt legislation that would firmly bring Congress into line with Latino public policy preferences. Thus, the desire of most Latinos for active egalitarian-oriented government programs in education, economic development and job creation, housing assistance, and health care, as well as affirmative action and bilingual education programs, fails to generate strong support among congressional leaders even when the Democratic Party controls Congress. The same can be said of Latino preferences regarding border enforcement and comprehensive immigration reform.

In short, when it comes to membership in the governing coalitions in the central institutions of American government, and even more to the adoption of ethnoracially egalitarian public policies, it appears that Latinos experience conditions of racial hierarchy. Moreover, the large surge of immigration over the past 40 years from Latin America and the Spanish-speaking Caribbean has reinforced these conditions among Latinos for a variety of reasons (discussed in chaps. 5, 6). Absent a strong federal government commitment to more focused and assertive policies of ethnoracial inclusion and equality, the continued settlement of Latino immigrants in low-income central cities throughout the country, as well as in rural areas of the Midwest and South, leads us to believe that there will likely be large numbers of Latinos facing a continuation of these conditions of racial hierarchy for many decades into the future.

Racial Hierarchy and Asian Americans

Among the three ethnoracial groups in focus in this book, most Americans would almost certainly aim their highest degree of skepticism at the proposition that Asian Americans/Pacific Islanders suffer from the effects of racial hierarchy in American public life. After all, Asian Americans are widely perceived as the model minority, proof positive of the country's success in providing equal opportunities for realizing the American Dream. During the past four decades, millions of Asian-origin immigrants have made their way to the United States—some as refugees, some as family-unification immigrants, and many as highly prized skilled worker immigrants. In the aggregate, Asian Americans have been very successful in achieving unusually high levels of educational and economic achievement in the United States, as we have seen.

As we assess the possibility that Asian Americans continue to experience racial hierarchy in American public life, it is necessary, further, to keep in mind once again the high degree of internal diversity among those categorized as members of this ethnoracial group, making generalizations about this population very hazardous. Nevertheless, there are ways in which the racial hierarchy model seems to fit the experience of many Asian Americans in contemporary U.S. political life. We have shown extensive public opinion data indicating that many Americans continue to view Asian Americans as forever foreign, no matter how many generations their families may have lived in, and been citizens of, the United States. Further, data presented in chapter 5 make it clear that while Asian American immigrants naturalize as U.S. citizens at a faster rate than do immigrants from Latin America, this does not necessarily translate into higher levels of political incorporation. Asian Americans vote at lower rates than do other ethnoracial groups, despite the fact that their relatively high levels of educational achievement are associated with much higher levels of voting in other ethnoracial groups. Moreover, Asian Americans are the ethnoracial groups with the lowest affiliation rates with U.S. political parties, with relatively large percentages seeming to find no partisan home or attachment in American politics. This degree of detachment and, perhaps, alienation from the party system may indicate continued feelings of exclusion from U.S. politics, or at the least, the sense that neither major party speaks compellingly to the interests of many members of this population group. Asian Americans are still significantly underrepresented in elective and appointive public offices.

Another factor in the continuing relative nonengagement of many

Asian Americans with U.S. politics may derive from their high degree of geographic dispersal in the states in which they are concentrated. That is, relative economic success has made it possible for many Asian Americans to physically integrate into middle- and upper-middle-class neighborhoods and suburbs, but when combined with the continuation of being marked as foreign, the combination may translate into greater levels of political distancing since there are relatively few places where members of this highly diverse group can be strongly influential in politics.

However that may be, Asian Americans are not well represented among the inner circles of the dominant governing coalitions in virtually all levels and arenas of American politics. As Kim (2007) has shown, the logic of competition for the median voter leads party leaders in the United States to avoid including the interests of Asian Americans in their strategic calculations for electoral success. Further, though the group is generally more internally diverse with respect to public policy preferences than are other ethnoracial minority groups, Asian Americans are significantly more supportive of proactive egalitarian policy proposals than are White Americans. Thus, this group, too, is relatively disempowered in relation to all four dimensions of our criteria for the political incorporation of ethnoracial groups.

As with Latinos, the presence of high percentages of immigrants among Asian Americans contributes to these relatively low levels of political incorporation. Accordingly, the question of the political incorporation of Asian Americans over the long term will largely depend on the ways in which contemporary Asian American immigrants and their offspring are integrated into American society. If there is a continuation of the relative economic success of most Asian Americans over a substantial period, and if this leads other Americans to drop their perception of Asian Americans as forever foreign, these developments could lead to a more successful political incorporation of this group through individual assimilation and/or political pluralism. However, if there is little effort on the part of government and political parties to proactively seek to include the interests of Asian Americans in U.S. politics, and if significant numbers of Asian Americans are integrated into U.S. society through processes of segmented assimilation, then it is quite conceivable that the pattern of racial hierarchy will be further solidified as an accurate description of the relationship between many Asian Americans and the American political order.

To conclude, while it is possible to argue that the ways that recent immigration is affecting the political incorporation of America's ethnoracial minority groups supports assimilationist and/or political pluralist interpretations, there is, at the same time, ample evidence that recent immigration will not eliminate the pattern of racial hierarchy that has long existed in the United States. Indeed, there is reason to believe that racial hierarchy might very well be elaborated and extended in more complex and multiracial ways as a result of the large-scale immigration of the past four decades. Whatever potential scenarios, or combination of scenarios, in fact occur, it is important to acknowledge and understand that the effective and democratic incorporation of both newcomers and long-standing outsider groups is not an automatic result of a smoothly functioning, integrative melting pot. The ways in which immigrants and ethnoracial minorities are (more or less) incorporated into American political life are the result of human behavior, attitudes, and social constructions as these are played out in the practices of Americans' lives and their governmental institutions and political processes. There is no doubt that the changed demography of American society means that no place or group in U.S. society is any longer unaffected by issues of ethnoracial exclusion and/or incorporation. It is our hope that this book has clarified the dimensions of these issues and can serve as a systematic guide for assessing the extent and nature of democratic and racially egalitarian politics of inclusion.

Postscript on Barack Obama and the 2008
Presidential Election

We were completing the writing of this book just as the remarkable 2008 presidential election was racing toward a conclusion. Discussions of our project raised the question of the implications of Barack Obama's election as president of the United States for the analysis we have made.

In some respects, Barack Obama's personal history lies at the heart of our inquiry. His individual story as the child of a Kenyan immigrant father, his subsequent marriage to a Black American woman who grew up on the South Side of Chicago, and his election as a state senator from a largely Black district on Chicago's South Side, is one (very prominent) aspect of the larger story that this book set out to understand. Obama's transition from immigrant-family biracial presidential candidate—initially met with considerable skepticism by Black political activists inclined to support the candidacy of a prominent ally of the Black community, Hillary Rodham Clinton (wife of the man often dubbed the "first Black President of the United States")—to a Black candidate winning the enthusiastic support of the highest percentage of Blacks voting in a presidential campaign in the nation's history, also speaks to the central narrative of this book: immigrant-family newcomer becomes most successful racial minority outsider candidate to become the world's most powerful political insider.

From this angle, Obama's story is surely best understood as the ultimate triumph of the *individual assimilation* scenario of American ethnoracial politics, but one made possible by the evident reality of democratic pluralism: ethnically mobilized Black, Latino, and Asian American voters, alongside millions of White voters, achieved the election of the country's first Black president. Is this the central meaning of Obama's election as president of the United States in relation to our book's inquiry?

We believe that this interpretation of the Obama candidacy and victory holds much truth. That is, this election does provide a powerful demonstration that—despite a considerable undertow of confusion, prejudice, and direct opposition based on ethnoracial factors during the 2008 presidential election—the United States has come a great distance from the not-so-long-ago days when such an outcome would have been unimaginable. In that sense, this election symbolizes a validation of equal membership in the American polity more powerful than any other event in the country's history. As such, this event is a hugely important step for Blacks and other persons of color, and for all Americans, that will reverberate in many ways, not only in this country but throughout the world. This aspect of the election's meaning may be encapsulated best in a phrase that crisscrossed its way through the internet during the fall 2008 election campaign: "Rosa sat so that Martin could walk so that Barack could run so that our children could fly."

While all of this is true, and important, and we do not want to discount it in any way, at the same time we do *not* believe that this overcoming of ethnoracial exclusion means that Obama's nomination and election as president signals the demise of ethnoracial hierarchy in American political life. Why not? On one level it comes down to whether one believes that the election of Barack Obama as the country's first Black president means that racial democracy has been achieved, or whether this election means that the campaign for racial democracy—a quest that has been on hold on the national political and policy agenda for nearly four decades—may now begin again. We hold the latter view, for if our preceding analysis in this book is correct, then Obama's election cannot mean—in itself—that racial democracy has been achieved, since the racial hierarchy we described and analyzed here is not changed as a result of one person's electoral success. For us, then, the question is whether Obama's election means that the campaign for racial democracy will now begin again in earnest.

Our position is best understood in relation to the four benchmarks for ethnoracial democracy that formed the heart of our analysis in this book. Obama's nomination and election were dependent on high levels of minority political participation, and his successful campaign resulted in his becoming the highest-level example of descriptive representation in the country's history. As president, further, Obama is assured of being the central player of the dominant governing coalition in the most powerful governing institutions in the United States. Still, we believe it is doubtful that Obama will use his political capital to mount a concerted campaign to enact a racially egalitarian public policy agenda that might substantially remove ethnoracial hierarchy in this country.

We have two main reasons for reaching this conclusion. First, we have made much use of the median voter hypothesis in American elections in this book (see our use of the analyses of Frymer 1999, Fraga and Leal 2004, and Kim 2007 in this chapter and in chapter 6), and we believe it will work very powerfully to keep President Obama from making ethnoracial equality a central part of his public policy agenda. Simply put, Obama's election depended on the votes of millions of White Americans, just as it required those of millions of ethnoracial minority Americans. Based upon what we know about ethnoracial voting patterns in this country, it seems very likely that a substantial proportion of those White voters would not have cast their votes for Obama had he focused his campaign on the need to overcome racial hierarchy in the United States. Thus, assuming that President Obama will be seeking a second term in the White House, we believe there are too many White swing voters who will need to be kept from believing that Obama wants to use his considerable power as president to help "them" (Blacks and other minorities) at the expense of "us" (the White population) for him to make the achievement of ethnoracial equality in the United States a centerpiece of his presidential rhetoric and program.

Our second reason for doubting that President Obama will make the elimination of ethnoracial hierarchy a central feature of his public policy agenda is that enacting this goal would require strong political support from Congress, from state and local political leaders, and ultimately, from the American people as a whole. Even if he were inclined to mount such a public policy campaign, President Obama is not likely to have enough support from the congressional leadership, even in a time when the Democratic Party has increased its majority in both houses of the Congress, to be successful in getting such a campaign adopted in Congress. This is because most White Americans are convinced that racial democracy already exists in this country, and any public policy moves toward realizing greater ethnoracial equality will come at their expense. Ironically, and contrapuntally, Obama's electoral victory in 2008 will likely be perceived widely as strong evidence that racial democracy already does exist in the United States. Until more White Americans believe that their own fates—and the fates of their children—are linked with the fates of Blacks, Latinos, and Asian Americans/Pacific Islanders, and that those fates require a concerted public policy effort to ensure greater ethnoracial equality, it is unlikely that the dominant governing coalitions in Congress, and in state legislatures across the country, will support such a public policy agenda.

It is on this last point, however, that we believe Barack Obama's election as president could yield a more egalitarian policy result, beginning to undermine the continuing reality of racial hierarchy in the United States. Obama's oratory throughout his long campaign for the presidency has stressed the interdependency of American lives. He has used the metaphor of "all-in-the-same-boat" in relation to numerous issues facing the country, from the effects of global warming to the financial crisis that exploded in the midst of the fall 2008 campaign. If Obama uses his considerable oratorical and political skills to build a congressional coalition, and public support, in favor of policies that substantially reduce *economic* inequality in the United States, even without focusing on the ethnoracial inequalities that lie embedded within U.S. economic inequality,[1] such a public policy agenda could make progress toward reducing the size and impacts of ethnoracial hierarchy as such. For example, if Obama mounts a successful FDR-like campaign of economic recovery in 2009, centered around public works, alternative energy, and human capital investments—only this time without the racially discriminatory barriers that were embedded in much of FDR's New Deal legislation (see, e.g., Katznelson 2005)—such a campaign could do much to reduce unequal access to jobs, to transportation, and to valuable human capital resources, and these changes would likely have a positive effect on further reducing racial hierarchy across the country. That prospect, however, would require not only Obama's oratorical and political skills but the energy and skills of a broad coalition of long-standing political insiders, as well as recently incorporated newcomers and former outsiders who have become political players in a more racially democratic country.

Notes

INTRODUCTION

1. Following Hollinger (1995), we use the term *ethnoracial* to signify that the groups in focus in this book—Black Americans, Latino (or Hispanic) Americans, and Asian (and Pacific Island) Americans—are often perceived as racial groups, but they have important ethnic characteristics as well. These are "racial" population groupings insofar as physical appearance is used widely in U.S. political discourse to color-code identity group memberships in the United States. Thus, the country's population is routinely described as composed of the following color categories: White (typically European-origin Americans), Black (African-origin), Red (Native or indigenous peoples), Brown (Latinos or Hispanics), and Yellow (Asian Pacific Americans). However, the groups are also ethnic insofar as they are routinely described—by both group insiders and outsiders—as cultural communities as well. Following convention (see, e.g., McClain and Stewart 2006), we begin from the assumption that the non-White groups listed here are those included in discussions of U.S. political "minorities."

We do not include American Indians (or "Native Americans") in our book's focus or analysis, however, for two reasons. First, we believe that American Indian politics is fundamentally dissimilar from the politics of other U.S. ethnoracial minority groups in virtue of the continuing treaty relationship between many tribal nations and the U.S. government. That relationship raises political and legal issues of American Indian sovereignty that simply do not exist in the politics of other U.S. communities of color (with the partial exception of Puerto Rico's relationship to the United States). Our second reason for excluding American Indian politics from our analysis is that the recent influx of immigrants to the United States has not had a direct impact on American Indian politics in the way that it has on Blacks, Latinos, and Asian Americans. Accordingly, we have chosen to limit our already complex task of description and analysis to the three groups noted.

2. These benchmarks, too, were initially developed by previous scholars. In particular, see Browning, Marshall, and Tabb 1984.

CHAPTER 1

1. U.S. Department of Homeland Security, *Yearbook of Immigration Statistics: 2007, Immigrants.* These numbers, of course, should be used with caution, as they do not

reflect the following: (1) undocumented immigrants are not included; (2) emigration is not recorded; (3) some migrants (e.g., parolees, refugees) reside permanently in the United States without ever being recorded as immigrants, because they are not required to adjust their status to permanent resident; and (4) there are some "missing values" each year. For example, around 3 million refugees and asylees were reported to have arrived between 1980 and 2007. It is interesting to note that INS data for the previous four-decade peak period of immigration, from 1881–1920, lists 23,465,374 documented immigrants, while that of the contemporary period, 1961–2001, lists 24,248,470.

2. The census data reported herein come from the March 2007 *American Community Survey* (U.S. Census Bureau 2007d) and from the 1970 U.S. Census, unless otherwise noted. Prior to 2000, the Census Bureau did not give respondents the option to choose more than one race, so figures prior to 2000 are not strictly comparable to figures from 2000 and later years. When comparing different ethnoracial groups, we use the "race alone" numbers (figures for those who only selected one race). This produces slightly smaller numbers than if we used the totals for all those who chose a particular ethnoracial category, but we feel that it allows for better comparisons of the relative size of ethnoracial groups.

3. The first peak period, in the mid–nineteenth century, was numerically dominated by migrants from northern Europe and the British Isles, including Ireland, while the second (in the late nineteenth and early twentieth centuries) was numerically dominated by those from southern and eastern Europe (see Dinnerstein, Nichols, and Reimers 2003, for a good overview).

4. This figure is for those who chose one race only and includes only Asian Americans (i.e., it does not include Native Hawaiians and Other Pacific Islanders).

5. There is evidence that recent immigrants from sub-Saharan Africa are much more likely to desire to make the United States their home and to participate in U.S. politics than was true of African immigrants in the 1960s or earlier, who were more likely to desire to return home after gaining a higher education in the United States. See, e.g., Assensoh 2000; Takougang 2004.

6. The Pew Hispanic Center's analysis is based on the birthrate of "immigrants and their off-spring," which includes the immigrant generation, their children, and grandchildren.

7. When discussing only figures for Census 2000 and later, we use totals for those who reported one race only. Prior to Census 2000, respondents did not have the option to report more than one race, so data from Census 2000 and later is not strictly comparable to previous Census Bureau data. In table 1.8, we use figures for those who reported one race and also those who reported more than one race ("one race or in combination with one or more other races"). We believe that this figure gives the best comparison with data collected prior to Census 2000.

8. Census 2000 placed Native Hawaiians and Other Pacific Islander Americans (NHPI) in their own racial category, but, prior to that, the census grouped them with Asian Americans. Together, the two subpopulations make up the Asian and Pacific Islander American (APIA) racial category. When discussing immigration, Asian immigrants make up the vast majority of the APIA category, so we will often refer only to Asian Americans or Asian immigrants, although pre-2000 figures usually include a very small number of Pacific Islanders as well. In addition, the NHPI category is dominated by native Hawaiians, an indigenous population that has not been greatly influenced by

immigration. However, for table 1.8, we combine the Asian American and NHPI data. We do that because this allows us the best comparability with years prior to 2000, when the Asian American and NHPI populations were not tabulated separately.

CHAPTER 2

1. This research tradition began with the so-called Chicago school of sociologists led by Robert Park in the 1920s, but in political science it might best be represented by studies of individual voter attitudes and behavior, beginning, e.g., with *The American Voter* (Campbell, Converse, Miller, and Stokes 1960).

2. See Polsby 1963 for a theoretical elaboration of the early model and its claims.

3. It should be noted, however, that later iterations of Browning, Marshall, and Tabb's thesis (see, e.g., their edited volume, *Racial Politics in American Cities,* 2003) articulated a less optimistic, more structurally constrained, understanding of the possibilities for egalitarian racial inclusion in American politics.

4. De la Garza notes, however, that the continuation of this pluralistic pattern depends upon the successful political incorporation of Latino immigrants, something that he believes cannot be taken for granted (de la Garza 2004, 116).

CHAPTER 3

1. As noted in the Introduction, we use the concept of "ethnoracial" group to refer to the five color-coded demographic categories commonly used in U.S. political discourse: White (European-origin Americans), Black (African-origin Americans), Brown (Hispanic or Latino Americans), Red (Native Americans), and Yellow (Asian/Pacific Americans). It is our premise, as we emphasized earlier, that, like all ethnic and racial identities, these groups are socially constructed and have no basis in biological difference as such, but they do rely on varying, dynamic, and contested combinations of both "racial" and "ethnic" characteristics. Our analysis does not include Native Americans, however, since this is an indigenous category and not impacted in a similar way by immigration.

2. There continues to be disagreement within the medical profession over the utility of the concept of race. For some time, geneticists have understood that there is a connection between common location and shared genetic traits. Genetic traits, therefore, tend to be geographically concentrated. Medical researchers have long known that certain ailments tend to be concentrated in subpopulations from certain regions of the world. Some researchers have argued that inhabitants of these regions correspond to racial groups, and that race is therefore a convenient way of identifying people who might have certain genetically based vulnerabilities. Many medical researchers disagree. What is clear, however, is that the specific racial definitions used in the United States and other countries often do not correspond well to geographic population distributions: e.g., by the standard of genetic variation, South Asians are probably closer to Europeans than to East Asians. Furthermore, racial definitions often change in a relatively short time, which clearly cannot be based on genetic change. Again, racial categories as they are usually used are socially and politically constructed.

3. Geneticists continue to debate whether the concept of race is a useful one (e.g., Wade 2004). What is clear, however, is that "race," as it has been used in the United States, cannot be based on genetics, given that racial categories have changed frequently, sometimes in as little as a decade. No geneticist claims that a new race could appear in ten years.

4. Antimiscegenation laws sought to stop marriages between Whites and non-Whites. Members of different non-White races were usually not prevented from marrying each other (Lee and Edmonston 2005).

5. Around 1565, Filipino sailors forced into service aboard Spanish galleons appear to have jumped ship when the galleons stopped in the vicinity of the Yucatan Peninsula. Some made their way northward, and Filipinos (presumably their descendants) were reported to be in the New Orleans area by the late eighteenth century (Espina 1988). There are also reports of a few Asians living in colonial America (Tsai 1986, 1–2).

6. The Japanese succeeded in negotiating a critical concession, however: Japanese men already in the United States could bring wives from Japan, which led to a doubling of the Japanese American population in less than 20 years (Kitano 1976; Daniels 1988; Hing 1993).

7. The 1913 law forbade "aliens ineligible for citizenship" from owning land, limited land leases to three years, and prohibited land-owning corporations themselves from having over 50 percent of their stock owned by aliens ineligible for citizenship (Daniels 1988). This obviously allowed for various methods of evading the law: placing 51 percent of a corporation's stock in the hands of American citizens, buying land in the name of American-born children of Asian immigrants, or simply signing leases that did not exceed three years.

8. In late 1965 and early 1966, two articles appeared, both advancing the notion that Japanese or Chinese Americans had achieved remarkable success in the face of overwhelming obstacles (Petersen 1966; "Success Story" 1966). These two articles are usually considered to mark the beginning of the model minority concept.

CHAPTER 4

1. We selected metropolitan statistical areas where at least 3 percent of each minority group was represented. Non-Hispanic Whites are the reference group in each of the metropolitan areas.

2. In general, measures of residential segregation reflect the distribution of different racial and ethnic groups across spatial boundaries. Although residential segregation can occur at a variety of geographical levels, this study will focus on metropolitan areas, because the metropolitan context provides the best opportunity to examine, in a comparative fashion, patterns and trends of residential segregation. Moreover, governmental processes and political activities are more discernible in metropolitan contexts.

3. The Civil Rights Project's definition of the regions is as follows: *South:* Alabama, Arkansas, Florida, Georgia, Louisiana, Mississippi, North Carolina, South Carolina, Tennessee, Texas, and Virginia; *Border:* Delaware, Kentucky, Maryland, Missouri, Oklahoma, and West Virginia; *Northeast:* Connecticut, Maine, Massachusetts, New Hampshire, New Jersey, New York, Pennsylvania, Rhode Island, and Vermont; *Midwest:* Illi-

nois, Indiana, Iowa, Kansas, Michigan, Minnesota, Nebraska, North Dakota, Ohio, South Dakota, and Wisconsin; *West:* Arizona, California, Colorado, Montana, Nevada, New Mexico, Oregon, Utah, Washington, and Wyoming. Hawaii and Alaska, which have very distinctive populations, are treated separately, and the District of Columbia is treated as a city rather than a state. See Orfield and Lee 2006, footnote 13.

CHAPTER 5

1. The United States has a "dry foot/wet foot" policy with Cuban immigrants. That is, if a Cuban national is caught in the water (wet foot) by U.S. authorities, he is sent back to Cuba. If he is caught on American soil (dry foot), he is deemed to be a refugee. In contrast, Haitian immigrants are usually either returned to Haiti or detained.

2. The 1975 provision only included a 5 percent threshold, which was too high for smaller Asian communities. After aggressive lobbying by Asian ethnic and panethnic groups as well as other civil rights organizations, Section 203 of the VRA was amended in 1992 to include large communities that either met the 5 percent test or had at least 10,000 voting age citizens.

3. See, e.g., *Garza v. County of Los Angeles* (1990).

4. Congress amended the VRA in 1982 with a "results test," which aimed at ensuring that minority voters have an equal opportunity to elect representatives of their choice, whether or not this results in proportionate descriptive representation (Grofman and Davidson 1992, 319). This "results test," upheld and interpreted in *Thornburg v. Gingles* (1986), led to a substantial increase (particularly following the post-1990 census redistricting) in the number of minority elected officials at all levels of government in the United States (see, e.g., McClain and Stewart 2006, chap. 4).

The demographic basis that is utilized for determining the VRA "results test" has important implications for post-1965 immigration, especially in areas that have witnessed large increases in the arrival of Latino (and, to a lesser degree, Asian Pacific American and African-origin) immigrants.

CHAPTER 6

1. Guinier explored, e.g., proportional representation voting arrangements, and cumulative voting and supermajority requirements in legislative bodies.

2. The information in this section is from Kevin Hill and Dario Moreno, in J. Edwin Benton, editor, *Government and Politics in Florida* (2008).

3. Not all claiming the conservative identity agree, however. See D'Souza 1995, 543–46, for a spirited defense of the employer's right to discriminate in the choice of employees for reasons of race, religion, national origin, and sex.

4. By *affirmative action* we mean programs that aim to correct unaccountable and/or unjustifiable disparities in results that disadvantage ethnoracial minority groups and women in decisions regarding employment, the allocation of government contracts, and admissions to selective institutions of higher education.

CHAPTER 7

1. This strategic approach to gaining public support for ethnoracial equality, attempting to bypass the strong racial divisions within traditional Democratic Party constituent groups, has been strongly articulated by sociologist William Julius Wilson (2001). While we do not think that such an approach would reduce all aspects of ethnoracial hierarchy in the U.S. polity, we do agree that it would be a good beginning step.

References

AALDEF (Asian American Legal Defense and Education Fund). 2006. "Asian Americans and The Voting Rights Act: The Case for Reauthorization: A Report of the AALDEF." May. Accessed online at www.aaldef.org, on February 6, 2007.

AALDEF (Asian American Legal Defense and Education Fund). 2007a. "Asian American Election Protection 2000." November 5. Accessed online at www.aaldef.org, on January 3, 2008.

AALDEF (Asian American Legal Defense and Education Fund). 2007b. "The Asian American Vote in the 2006 Midterm Elections." Accessed online at http://www.aaldef.org/docs/AALDEF2006ExitPollReportMay2007.pdf, on January 3, 2008.

Acuña, Rodolfo. 2006. *Occupied America: A History of Chicanos.* 6th ed. New York: Longman.

Ahmed, Tanzila. 2004. "SAAVY for Mobilizing South Asian Youth Vote." February 27. Accessed online at http://www.thesouthasian.org, on June 12, 2006.

Alba, Richard. 1990. *Ethnic Identity: The Transformation of White America.* New Haven: Yale University Press.

Alba, Richard, and Victor Nee. 2003. *Remaking the American Mainstream: Assimilation and Contemporary Immigration.* Cambridge: Harvard University Press.

Alex-Assensoh, Yvette M. 1998. *Neighborhoods, Family, and Political Behavior in Urban America.* New York: Garland Publishing Co.

Anderson, Margo J. 1988. *The American Census: A Social History.* New Haven: Yale University Press.

Anderson, Terry. 2004. *The Pursuit of Fairness: A History of Affirmative Action.* New York: Oxford University Press.

Appiah, Anthony, and Amy Gutmann. 1996. *Color Conscious.* Princeton: Princeton University Press.

Archdeacon, Thomas J. 1983. *Becoming American: An Ethnic History.* New York: Free Press.

Assensoh, Akwasi B. 2000. "Conflict or Cooperation? Africans and African Americans in Multiracial America." In Yvette M. Alex-Assensoh and Lawrence Hanks, eds., *Black and Multiracial Politics in America,* 113–30. New York: New York University Press.

Assensoh, Akwasi B., and Yvette M. Alex-Assensoh. 1998. "The Leadership of the American Civil Rights Movement and African Liberation Movements: Their Connection and Similarities." *Proteus* 15 (1): 23–28.

Bailey, Benjamin. 2001. "Dominican-American Ethnic/Racial Identities and United States Social Categories." *International Migration Review* 35 (3): 677–708.

Baldassare, Mark. 2000. *California in the New Millennium: The Changing Social and Political Landscape.* Berkeley: University of California Press.

Banfield, Edward C., and James Q. Wilson. 1963. *City Politics.* New York: Vintage Books.

Barkan, Elazar. 1992. *The Retreat of Scientific Racism: Changing Concepts of Race in Britain and the United States Between the World Wars.* Cambridge: Cambridge University Press.

Barker, Lucius J., Mack H. Jones, and Katherine Tate. 1999. *African Americans and the American Political System.* 4th ed. Englewood Cliffs, N.J.: Prentice-Hall.

Barlett, Donald L. 2004. *America: Who Really Pays the Taxes?* New York: Simon and Schuster.

Barrera, Mario. 1979. *Race and Class in the Southwest: A Theory of Racial Inequality.* Notre Dame: University of Notre Dame Press.

Barrera, Mario. 1985. "The Historical Evolution of Chicano Ethnic Goals: A Bibliographic Essay." *Sage Race Relations Abstracts* 10 (1): 1–48.

Barrera, Mario. 1988. *Beyond Aztlan: Ethnic Autonomy in Comparative Perspective.* New York: Praeger.

Barreto, Amilcar A. 1998. *Language, Elites, and the State: Nationalism in Puerto Rico and Quebec.* New York: Greenwood.

Barreto, Matt A. 2005. "Latino Immigrants at the Polls: Foreign Born Voter Turnout in the 2002 Elections." *Political Research Quarterly* 58 (1): 79–86.

Barreto, Matt A., Luis R. Fraga, Sylvia Manzano, Valerie Martinez-Ebers, and Gary M. Segura. 2008. " 'Should They Dance with the One Who Brung 'Em?' Latinos and the 2008 Presidential Election." *PS: Political Science and Politics* 41 (4): 753–60.

Bartels, Larry. 2000. "Partisanship and Voting Behavior, 1952–1996." *American Journal of Political Science* 44:35–50.

Barth, Frederik. 1969. "Introduction." In Frederik Barth, ed., *Ethnic Groups and Boundaries,* 9–38. Boston: Little, Brown.

Baver, Sherrie. 1984. "Puerto Rican Politics in New York City: The Post–World War II Period." In James Jennings and Monte Rivera, eds., *Puerto Rican Politics in Urban America,* 43–60. New York: Greenwood.

Bell, Derrick. 2005. *Silent Covenants: Brown v. Board of Education and the Unfulfilled Hopes for Racial Reform.* New York: Oxford University Press.

Bloemraad, Irene. 2006. *Becoming a Citizen: Incorporating Immigrants and Refugees in the United States and Canada.* Berkeley: University of California Press.

Bobo, Lawrence D. 1997. "The Color Line, the Dilemma, and the Dream: Race Relations in America at the Close of the Twentieth Century." In John Higham, ed., *Civil Rights and Social Wrongs,* 31–55. University Park: Pennsylvania State University Press.

Bobo, Lawrence, and Franklin D. Gilliam Jr. 1990. "Race, Sociopolitical Participation, and Black Empowerment." *American Political Science Review* 84:377–93.

Bobo, Lawrence D., and Devon Johnson. 2000. "Racial Attitudes in a Prismatic Metropolis: Mapping Identity Stereotypes, Competition, and Views on Affirmative Action." In Lawrence D. Bobo, Melvin L. Oliver, James H. Johnson Jr., and Abel Valenzuela Jr., eds., *Prismatic Metropolis: Inequality in Los Angeles,* 81–163. New York: Russell Sage Foundation.

Bobo, Lawrence, and Camille Zubrinsky. 1996. "Attitudes toward Residential Integration: Perceived Status Differences, Mere In-Group Preferences, or Racial Prejudice?" *Social Forces* 74 (3): 883–909.

Bonacich, Edna. 1984. "Some Basic Facts: Patterns of Asian Immigration and Exclusion." In Lucie Cheng and Edna Bonacich, eds., *Labor Immigration under Capitalism: Asian Workers in the United States before World War II*, 60–77. Berkeley: University of California Press.

Bonilla-Silva, Eduardo. 2004. "From Bi-racial to Tri-racial: Towards a New System of Racial Stratification in the United States." *Ethnic and Racial Studies* 27 (6) (November): 931–50.

Brodkin, Karen. 1998. *How Jews Became White Folks and What That Says about Race in America*. New Brunswick, N.J.: Rutgers University Press.

Brown, Michael K., Martin Carnoy, Elliott Currie, Troy Duster, David B. Oppenheimer, Marjorie M. Shultz, and David Wellman. 2005. *Whitewashing Race: The Myth of a Color-Blind Society*. Berkeley: University of California Press.

Browning, Rufus P., Dale Rogers Marshall, and David H. Tabb. 1984. *Protest Is Not Enough: The Struggle of Blacks and Hispanics for Equality in Urban Politics*. Berkeley: University of California Press.

Browning, Rufus P., Dale Rogers Marshall, and David H. Tabb, eds. 1990. *Racial Politics in American Cities*. New York: Longman.

Browning, Rufus P., Dale Rogers Marshall, and David H. Tabb, eds. 1997. *Racial Politics in American Cities*. 2d ed. New York: Longman.

Browning, Rufus P., Dale Rogers Marshall, and David H. Tabb, eds. 2003. *Racial Politics in American Cities*. 3d ed. New York: Longman.

Bryce-Laporte, R. S. 1972. "Black Immigrants: The Experience of Invisibility and Inequality." *Journal of Black Studies* 41 (1): 29–56.

Burns, Jane. 2007. *Conscience: The News Journal of Catholic Opinion* (Summer). Accessed online at www.catholicsforchoice.com, on February 22, 2008.

Cain, Bruce E. 1998. "The Politicization of Race and Ethnicity in the Nineties." In Michael B. Preston, Bruce E. Cain, and Sandra Bass, eds., *Racial and Ethnic Politics in California*, 457–68. Berkeley: Institute for Governmental Studies Press.

Cain, Bruce E., and D. Roderick Kiewiet. 1986. *Minorities in California*. Pasadena: California Institute of Technology.

Camarillo, Albert. 1984. *Chicanos in California: A History of Mexican Americans in California*. San Francisco: Boyd and Fraser.

Camerota, Steven A. 2004. *The High Cost of Cheap Labor: Illegal Immigration and the Federal Budget*. Washington, D.C.: Center for Immigration Studies. Accessed online at http://www.cis.org/articles/2004/fiscal.pdf, on February 12, 2007.

Campbell, Angus, Phillip Converse, Warren E. Miller, and Donald E. Stokes. 1960. *The American Voter*. Chicago: University of Chicago Press.

Cano v. Davis, 191 F. Supp. 2d 1135 (2001).

Canon, David. 2006. "U.S. Senate Committee on the Judiciary Testimony on the Voting Rights Act." July 21.

Carmines, Edward G., and James A. Stimson. 1989. *Issue Evolution: Race and the Transformation of American Politics*. Princeton: Princeton University Press.

Cassel, Carol A. 2002. "Hispanic Turnout: Estimates From Validated Voting Data." *Political Research Quarterly* 55 (2): 391–408.

Chan, Sucheng. 1991. *Asian Americans: An Interpretive History*. London: Twayne.

Chang, Cindy. 2005. "Asian American Influence Growing at Polls." *AsianAmericanLife* .*net*. Accessed online at http://asianamericanlife.net.

Chavez, Linda. 1991. *Out of the Barrio: Toward a New Politics of Hispanic Assimilation.* New York: Basic Books.

Chuman, Frank F. 1976. *The Bamboo People: The Law and Japanese-Americans.* Del Mar, Calif.: Publisher's Inc.

Citrin, Jack, Beth Reingold, and Donald Green. 1990. "American Identity and the Politics of Ethnic Change." *Journal of Politics* 52 (4): 1124–54.

Committee of 100. 2001. *American Attitudes toward Chinese Americans and Asian Americans.* New York: Committee of 100. Accessed online at http://www.committee100 .org/publications/survey/C100survey.pdf, on June 17, 2003.

Crowder, Kyle. 1999. "Residential Segregation of West Indians in the New York/New Jersey Metropolitan Area: The Roles of Race and Ethnicity." *International Migration Review* 33 (1): 79–113.

Cruz, Jose. 2004. "Latinos in Office." In Sharon Ann Navarro, ed., *Latino Americans and Political Participation: A Reference Handbook,* 173–226. Santa Barbara: ABC-CLIO.

Dahl, Robert A. 1961. *Who Governs? Democracy and Power in an American City.* New Haven: Yale University Press.

Daniels, Roger. 1988. *Asian America: Chinese and Japanese in the United States since 1850.* Seattle: University of Washington Press.

Danigelis, Nicholas L. 1978. "Black Political Participation in the United States: Some Recent Evidence. *American Sociological Review* 43 (October): 756–71.

Dawson, Michael C. 1994. *Behind the Mule: Race, Class, and African American Politics.* Princeton: Princeton University Press.

Dawson, Michael C. 2001. *Black Visions: The Roots of Contemporary African-American Political Ideologies.* Chicago: University of Chicago Press.

Decter, Midge. 1991. "E Pluribus Nihil: Multiculturalism and Black Children." *Commentary* 92, no. 3 (September): 19–25.

de la Garza, Rodolfo O. 2004. "Latino Politics." *Annual Review of Political Science* 7:91–173.

de la Garza, Rodolfo, Louis DeSipio, F. Chris Garcia, John Garcia, and Angelo Falcón. 1992. *Latino Voices: Mexican, Puerto Rican, and Cuban Perspectives on American Politics.* Boulder: Westview.

Democracy Corps. 2005. "Hispanic Survey Frequency Questionnaire." June 5–16. Accessed online at www.democracycorps.com, on June 12, 2006.

DeSipio, Louis. 1996. *Counting on the Latino Vote: Latinos as a New Electorate.* Charlottesville: University of Virginia Press.

DeSipio, Louis. 2001. "Building America, One Person at a Time: Naturalization and Political Behavior of the Naturalized in Contemporary Politics." In Gary Gerstle and John Mollenkopf, eds., *E Pluribus Unum? Contemporary and Historical Perspectives on Immigrant Political Incorporation,* 67–106. New York: Russell Sage.

DeSipio, Louis. 2006. "Latino Civic and Political Participation." In Marta Tienda and Faith Mitchell, eds., *Hispanics and the Future of America,* 447–79. Washington, D.C.: National Academies Press.

DeSipio, Louis, and Rodolfo de la Garza. 1998. *Making Americans, Remaking America.* New York: Westview.

Dhingra, Pawan H. 2003. "Being American between Black and White: Second-Generation Asian American Professionals' Racial Identities." *Journal of Asian American Studies* 6 (2) (June): 117–47.

Dinnerstein, Leonard, Roger L. Nichols, and David M. Reimers. 2003. *Natives and Strangers: A Multicultural History of Americans*. New York: Oxford University Press.

D'Souza, Dinesh. 1995. *The End of Racism*. New York: Free Press.

Edsell, Thomas, with Mary Edsell. 1992. *Chain Reaction: The Impact of Race, Rights, and Taxes on American Politics*. New York: W. W. Norton.

Erie, Steven. 1988. *Rainbow's End: Irish Americans and the Dilemmas of Urban Machine Politics, 1840–1985*. Berkeley: University of California Press.

Eslinger, Bonnie. 2006. "Asian-American Politicians Try To Rally Voting Bloc." October 16. *Examiner.com*. Accessed online at www.examiner.com, on October 17, 2006.

Espina, Marina E. 1988. *Filipinos in Louisiana*. New Orleans: A. F. Laborde and Sons.

Espiritu, Yen Le. 1992. *Asian American Panethnicity: Bridging Institutions and Identities*. Philadelpha: Temple University Press.

Espiritu, Yen Le, and Michael Omi. 2000. "Who Are You Calling Asian? Shifting Identity Claims, Racial Classifications, and the Census." In Paul M. Ong, ed., *The State of Asian Pacific America: Transforming Race Relations*, 43–101. Los Angeles: LEAP Asian Pacific American Public Policy Institute and UCLA Asian American Studies Center.

Falcón, Angelo. 1984. "Puerto Rican Politics in New York City, 1860s to 1945." In James Jennings and Monte Rivera, eds., *Puerto Rican Politics in Urban America*, 15–42. New York: Greenwood.

Farley, Reynolds, Charlotte Steeh, Maria Krysan, Tara Jackson, and Keith Reeves. 1994. "Stereotypes and Segregation: Neighborhoods in the Detroit Area." *American Journal of Sociology* 100 (3):750–80.

Ferguson, Thomas, and Joel Rogers. 1986. *Right Turn: The Decline of the Democrats and the Future of American Politics*. New York: Hill and Wang.

Flores-Gonzalez, Nilda. 1994. "The Racialization of Latinos: The Meaning of Latino Identity for the Second Generation." *Latino Studies Journal* 10 (3) (Fall): 3–31.

Foner, Nancy. 1987. "The Jamaicans: Race and Ethnicity among Migrants in New York City." In Nancy Foner, ed., *New Immigrants in New York*, 195–217. New York: Columbia University Press.

Foner, Nancy, and George M. Fredrickson. 2004. "Immigration, Race, and Ethnicity in the United States: Social Constructions and Social Relations in Historical and Contemporary Perspective." In Nancy Foner and George M. Fredrickson, eds., *Not Just Black and White: Historical and Contemporary Perspectives on Immigration, Race, and Ethnicity in the United States*, 1–19. New York: Russell Sage.

Fraga, Luis, John Garcia, Rodney Hero, Michael Jones-Correa, Valerie Martinez, and Gary Segura. 2003. Unpublished working paper for the Latino National Survey; used by permission of the authors.

Fraga, Luis, John Garcia, Rodney Hero, Michael Jones-Correa, Valerie Martinez-Ebers, and Gary M. Segura. 2006. "Redefining America: Key Findings from the 2006 Latino National Survey." Presentation at the Woodrow Wilson International Center for Scholars, Washington, D.C., December 6. Accessed online at http://depts.washington.edu/uwiser/documents/WWC_Rollout_FINAL_06.12.07a.ppt, on October 14, 2007.

Fraga, Luis Ricardo, and David L. Leal. 2004. "Playing the 'Latino Card': Race, Ethnicity, and National Party Politics." *Du Bois Review* 1 (2) (2004): 297–319.

Franklin, John Hope, and Alfred A. Moss. 1998. *From Slavery to Freedom: A History of African Americans*. New York: McGraw-Hill.

Fredrickson, Caroline, and Deborah J. Vagins. 2006. "Promises to Keep: The Impact of the Voting Rights Act in 2006." *ACLU Washington Legislative Office*. March. Accessed online at www.aclu.org on October 25, 2007.

Fredrickson, George M. 2002. *Racism: A Short History*. Princeton: Princeton University Press.

Frey, William H. 2001. "Melting Pot Suburbs: A Census 2000 Study of Suburban Diversity." *Census 2000 Series*. Washington, D.C.: Center on Urban and Metropolitan Policy, Brookings Institution.

Frey, William H. 2006. *Diversity Spreads Out: Metropolitan Shifts in Hispanic, Asian, and Black Populations since 2000*. Washington, D.C.: Brookings Institution, Metropolitan Policy Program.

Frey, William H., and Reynolds Farley. 1996. "Latino, Asian and Black Segregation in U.S. Metropolitan Areas: Are Multi-Ethnic Metros Different?" *Demography* 33 (1): 35–50.

Frey, William H., and Dowell Myers. 2005. "Racial Segregation in US Metropolitan Areas and Cities, 1990–2000: Patterns, Trends, and Explanations." *Population Studies Center Research Report* 05-573. April.

Frymer, Paul. 1999. *Uneasy Alliances: Race and Party Competition in America*. Princeton: Princeton University Press.

Frymer, Paul. 2005. "Race, Parties, and Democratic Inclusion." In Christina Wolbrecht and Rodney E. Hero, with Peri Arnold and Alvin Tillery, eds., *The Politics of Democratic Inclusion*, 122–42. Philadelphia: Temple University Press.

Fuchs, Lawrence H. 1990. *The American Kaleidoscope: Race, Ethnicity, and the Civic Culture*. Hanover: University Press of New England.

Gaines, Brian J., and Wendy K. Tam Cho. 2004. "On California's 1920 Alien Land Law: The Psychology and Economics of Racial Discrimination." *State Politics and Policy Quarterly* 4 (3) (Fall): 271–93.

Gans, Herbert. 1979. "Symbolic Ethnicity: The Future of Ethnic Groups and Cultures in America." *Ethnic and Racial Studies* 2:1–20.

Garcia, F. Chris, and Rodolfo de la Garza. 1977. *The Chicano Political Experience: Three Perspectives*. North Scituate, Mass.: Duxbury.

Garcia, F. Chris, and Gabriel R. Sanchez. 2008. *Hispanics and the U.S. Political System: Moving into the Mainstream*. Upper Saddle River, N.J.: Pearson Prentice-Hall.

Garcia, John A. 2003. *Latino Politics in America: Community, Culture, and Interests*. Lanham, Md.: Rowman and Littlefield.

Garcia Bedolla, Lisa. 2005. *Fluid Borders: Latino Power, Identity, and Politics in Los Angeles*. Berkeley: University of California Press.

Garcia Bedolla, Lisa. 2006. "Rethinking Citizenship: Noncitizen Voting and Immigrant Political Engagement in the United States." In Taeku Lee, S. Karthick Ramakrishnan, and Ricardo Ramirez, eds., *Transforming Politics, Transforming America: The Political and Civic Incorporation of Immigrants in the United States*, 51–70. Charlottesville: University of Virginia Press.

Garza v. County of Los Angeles, 918 F.2d 763 (9th Cir. 1990)

Geron, Kim. 2005. *Latino Political Power*. Boulder: Lynne Reinner.

Gerstle, Gary. 1995. "Race and the Myth of the Liberal Consensus." *Journal of American History* 82 (2) (September): 579–86.

Gimpel, James G. 2007. "Latino Voting in the 2006 Election: Realignment to the GOP Remains Distant." *Center for Immigration Studies*. March. Accessed online at www.cis.org, on November 12, 2007.

Glazer, Nathan, ed. 1985. *Clamor at the Gates: The New American Immigration*. San Francisco: Institute for Contemporary Studies Press.

Glazer, Nathan. 1991. "In Defense of Multiculturalism." *New Republic* (September 21): 18–22.

Goldberg, David Theo. 1993. *Racist Culture: Philosophy and the Politics of Meaning*. Cambridge: Blackwell.

Goldfield, Michael. 1997. *The Color of Politics: Race and the Mainsprings of American Politics*. New York: New Press.

Gotanda, Neil T. 2001. *Asian Americans and Politics: Perspectives, Experiences, and People*. Gordan H. Chang, ed. Washington, D.C.: Woodrow Wilson Center Press.

Graham, Hugh Davis. 2001. "Affirmative Action for Immigrants? The Unintended Consequences of Reform." In John David Skrentny, ed., *Color Lines: Affirmative Action, Immigration, and Civil Rights Options for America*, 53–70. Chicago: University of Chicago Press.

Graham, Hugh Davis. 2002. *Collision Course: The Strange Convergence of Affirmative Action and Immigration Policy in America*. New York: Oxford University Press.

Graves, Joseph L., Jr. 2004. *The Race Myth: Why We Pretend Race Exists in America*. New York: Dutton.

Guarnizo, Luis Eduardo. 2001. "On the Political Participation of Transnational Migrants: Old Practices and New Trends." In Gary Gerstle and John Mollenkopf, eds., *E Pluribus Unum? Contemporary and Historical Perspectives on Immigrant Political Incorporation*, 213–63. New York: Russell Sage Foundation.

Guglielmo, Jennifer, and Salvatore Salerno, eds. 2003. *Are Italians White? How Race Is Made in America*. New York: Routledge.

Guinier, Lani. 1994. *The Tyranny of the Majority: Fundamental Fairness and Representative Democracy*. New York: Free Press.

Guinier, Lani, and Gerrald Torres. 2002. *The Miner's Canary: Enlisting Race, Resisting Power, Transforming Democracy*. Cambridge: Harvard University Press.

Guterl, Matthew Pratt. 2001. *The Color of Race in America, 1900–1940*. Cambridge: Harvard University Press.

Guzman, Betsy. 2001. "The Hispanic Population." *Census 2000 Brief* (May): 1–8.

Gyory, Andrew. 1998. *Closing the Gates: Race, Politics, and the Chinese Exclusion Act*. Chapel Hill: University of North Carolina Press.

Hacker, Jacob S. 2006. *The Great Risk Shift: The Assault on American Jobs, Families, Health Care, and Retirement, and How You Can Fight Back*. New York: Oxford University Press.

Hacker, Jacob S., Suzanne Mettler, and Dianne Pinderhughes. 2005. "Inequality and Public Policy." In Lawrence R. Jacobs and Theda Skocpol, eds., *Inequality and American Democracy: What We Know and What We Need to Learn*, 156–213. New York: Russell Sage Foundation.

Hancock, Ange-Marie. 2004. *The Politics of Disgust: The Public Identity of the Welfare Queen*. New York: New York University Press.

Haney López, Ian F. 1996. *White by Law: The Legal Construction of Race*. New York: New York University Press.

Hanks, Lawrence J. 1994. *Black Political Empowerment*. Knoxville: University of Tennessee Press.

Hanks, Lawrence. 2000. "Pride and Pragmatism: Two Arguments for the Diversification of Party Interests." *Black and Multiracial Politics in America*. New York: New York University Press.

Harding, Vincent. 1983. *There Is a River: The Black Struggle for Freedom in America*. New York: Vintage Books.

Harrison, Bennett, and Barry Bluestone. 1988. *The Great U-Turn: Corporate Restructuring and the Polarizing of America*. New York: Basic Books.

Hayduk, Ron. 2006. *Democracy for All: Restoring Immigrant Voting Rights in the United States*. New York: Routledge.

Hein, Jeremy. 2006. *Ethnic Origins: The Adaptation of Cambodian and Hmong Refugees in Four American Cities*. New York: Russell Sage.

Henderson, Lenneal, Jr. 1987. "Black Politics and American Presidential Elections." In Michael Preston, Lenneal Henderson Jr., and Paul Puryear, eds., *The New Black Politics*, 3–28. 2d ed. New York: Longman.

Herberg, Will. 1960. *Protestant-Catholic-Jew: An Essay in Religious Sociology*. Rev. ed. Garden City, N.Y.: Anchor Books.

Hero, Rodney E. 1992. *Latinos and the U.S. Political System: Two-Tiered Pluralism*. Philadelphia: Temple University Press.

Hero, Rodney E. 1998. *Faces of Inequality: Social Diversity in American Politics*. New York: Oxford University Press.

Hero, Rodney E. 2007. *Racial Diversity and Social Capital: Equality and Community in America*. New York: Cambridge University Press.

Hero, Rodney E., and Robert R. Preuhs. 2007. "Immigration and the Evolving American Welfare State: Examining Policies in the U.S. States." *American Journal of Political Science* 51 (3) (July): 498–517.

Herrnstein, Richard, and Charles Murray. 1996. *Bell Curve: Intelligence and Class Structure in American Life*. New York: Free Press.

Higham, John. 1984. *Send These to Me: Immigrants in Urban America*. Rev. ed. Baltimore: Johns Hopkins University Press.

Hill, Kevin, and Dario Moreno. 2008. "Politics and Ethnic Change in Florida." In J. Edwin Benton, ed., *Government and Politics in Florida*, 80–101. Gainesville: University Press of Florida.

Hine, Darlene Clark, William C. Hine, and Stanley Harrold. 2006. *The African-American Odyssey*. Englewood Cliffs, N.J.: Prentice-Hall.

Hing, Bill Ong. 1993. *Making and Remaking Asian America through Immigration Policy, 1850–1990*. Stanford: Stanford University Press.

Hirsch, Arnold R. 1995. "Massive Resistance in the Urban North: Trumbell Park, Chicago, 1953–1966." *Journal of American History* 82 (2) (September): 522–50.

Ho, Fred, ed. 2000. *Legacy to Liberation: Politics and Culture of Revolutionary Asian Pacific America*. San Francisco: Big Red Media and AK Press.

Hochschild, Jennifer L. 1995. *Facing Up to the American Dream*. Princeton: Princeton University Press.

Hochschild, Jennifer, and Reuel Rogers. 2000. "Race Relations in a Diversifying Nation." In James Jackson, ed., *New Directions: African Americans in a Diversifying Nation*, 45–85. Washington, D.C.: National Policy Association.

Holder v. Hall, 512 U.S. 874 (1994).

Hollinger, David. 1995. *Post-Ethnic America: Beyond Multiculturalism.* New York: Basic Books.

Horsman, Reginald. 1981. *Race and Manifest Destiny: The Origins of American Racial Anglo-Saxonism.* Cambridge: Harvard University Press.

Horton, Carol A. 2005. *Race and the Making of American Liberalism.* New York: Oxford University Press.

Howe, Irving. 1976. *World of Our Fathers: The Journey of the East European Jews to America and the Life They Found and Made.* New York: Simon and Schuster.

Huckfeldt, Robert. 1986. *Politics in Context: Assimilation and Conflict in Urban Neighborhoods.* New York: Agathan.

Huckfeldt, Robert, and John Sprague. 1995. *Citizens, Politics, and Social Communication: Information and Influence in an Election Campaign.* New York: Cambridge University Press.

Huddle, Donald. 1997. "The Net National Costs of Immigration: Fiscal Effects of Welfare Restorations to Legal Immigrants." Posted by Federation for American Immigration Reform, accessed online at www.fairus.org, on May 2, 2002.

Huggins, Nathan Irvin. 1977. *Black Odyssey: The Afro-American Ordeal in Slavery.* New York: Pantheon Books.

Huntington, Samuel P. 2004. *Who Are We: The Challenges to America's National Identity.* New York: Simon and Schuster.

Iceland, John. 2004. "Beyond Black and White: Metropolitan Residential Segregation in Multi-ethnic America." *Social Science Research* 33 (2): 248–71.

Iceland, John, Daniel H. Weinberg, and Erika Steinmetz. 2002. "Racial and Ethnic Residential Segregation in the United States, 1980–2000." Washington, D.C.: U.S. Census Bureau, Series CENSR-3, U.S. Government Printing Office.

Ignatiev, Noel. 1995. *How the Irish Became White.* New York: Routledge.

In re Ah Yup. 1878. 1 F. Cas. 223 (C.C.D. Cal.).

Ingram, Helen, and Anne Schneider. 1993. "Social Construction of Target Populations: Implications for Politics and Policy." *American Political Science Review* 87 (2): 33–47.

Itzigsohn, José. 2004. "The Formation of Latino and Latina Panethnic Identities." In Nancy Foner and George M. Frederickson, eds., *Not Just Black and White: Historical and Contemporary Perspectives on Immigration, Race, and Ethnicity in the United States,* 197–216. New York: Russell Sage.

Jacobs, Lawrence R., and Theda Skocpol, eds. 2005. *Inequality and American Democracy: What We Know and What We Need to Learn.* New York: Russell Sage Foundation.

Jacobson, Matthew Frye. 1998. *Whiteness of a Different Color: European Immigrants and the Alchemy of Race.* Cambridge: Harvard University Press.

Jaynes, Gerald David, and Robin M. Williams Jr. 1989. *A Common Destiny: Blacks and American Society.* Washington, D.C.: National Academy Press.

Jennings, James. 1988. "The Puerto Rican Community: Its Political Background." In F. Chris Garcia, ed., *Latinos and the Political System,* 65–80. Notre Dame: University of Notre Dame Press.

Johnson v. DeGrandy 114 S. Ct. 2647 (1994).

Johnson, Lyndon Baines. 1965. "Howard University Commencement Address." June 4. *Public Papers of the Presidents: Johnson, 1965* 1:635–36.

Jones-Correa, Michael. 1998. *Between Two Nations: The Political Predicament of Latinos in New York City.* Ithaca: Cornell University Press.

Jones-Correa, Michael. 2007. "Fuzzy Distinctions and Blurred Boundaries: Transnational, Ethnic, and Immigrant Politics." In Rodolfo Espino, David L. Leal, and Kenneth J. Meier, eds., *Latino Politics: Identity, Mobilization, and Representation,* 44–60. Charlottesville: University of Virginia Press.

Jones-Correa, Michael, and David L. Leal. 1996. "Becoming Hispanic: Secondary Panethnic Identification among Latin American-Origin Populations in the United States." *Hispanic Journal of Behavioral Sciences* 18:214–53.

Junn, Jane. 1999. "Participation in Liberal Democracy: The Political Assimilation of Immigrants and Ethnic Minorities in the United States." *American Behavioral Scientist* 42 (9) (June): 1417–38.

Junn, Jane. 2006. "Mobilizing Group Consciousness: When Does Ethnicity Have Political Consequences?" In Taeku Lee, S. Karthick Ramakrishnan, and Ricardo Ramirez, eds., *Transforming Politics, Transforming America: The Political and Civic Incorporation of Immigrants in the United States,* 32–47. Charlottesville: University of Virginia Press.

Kasinitz, Paul. 1992. *Caribbean New York: Black Immigrants and the Politics of Race.* Ithaca: Cornell University Press.

Katz, Michael B. 1989. *The Undeserving Poor: From the War on Poverty to the War on Welfare.* New York: Pantheon Books.

Katznelson, Ira. 2005. *When Affirmative Action Was White: An Untold History of Racial Inequality in Twentieth Century America.* New York: W. W. Norton.

Kennedy, Ruby Jo Reeves. 1944. "Single or Triple Melting Pot? Intermarriage Trends in New Haven, 1870–1940." *American Journal of Sociology* 49 (4) (January): 331–39.

Kim, Claire Jean. 1999. "The Racial Triangulation of Asian Americans." *Politics and Society* 27 (1) (March): 105–38.

Kim, Claire Jean. 2000. *Bitter Fruit: The Politics of Black-Korean Conflict in New York City.* New Haven: Yale University Press.

Kim, Thomas P. 2007. *The Racial Logic of Politics: Asian Americans and Party Competition.* Philadelphia: Temple University Press.

Kinder, Donald R., and Lynn M. Sanders. 1996. *Divided by Color: Racial Politics and Democratic Ideals.* Chicago: University of Chicago Press.

King, Martin Luther, Jr. 1986. *A Testament of Hope: The Essential Writings and Speeches of Martin Luther King, Jr.* Ed. James M. Washington. New York: HarperCollins.

Kitano, Harry H. L. 1976. *Japanese Americans: The Evolution of a Subculture.* 2d ed. Englewood Cliffs, N.J.: Prentice-Hall.

Kleppner, Paul. 1982. *Who Voted? The Dynamics of Electoral Turnout, 1870–1980.* New York: Praeger.

Kloss, Heinz. 1977. *The American Bilingual Tradition.* Rowley, Mass.: Newbury House.

Kotlowski, Dean J. 2001. *Nixon's Civil Rights: Politics, Principle, and Policy.* Cambridge: Harvard University Press.

La Noue, George R., and John C. Sullivan. 2001. "Deconstructing Affirmative Action Categories." In John David Skrentny, ed., *Color Lines: Affirmative Action, Immigration, and Civil Rights Options for America,* 71–86. Chicago: University of Chicago Press.

Lane, Robert E. 1986. "Market Justice, Political Justice." *American Political Science Review* 80 (June): 383–402.

Latino National Survey. 2007. "Latino National Survey Toplines." Dated April 16, 2007. Accessed online at http://depts.washington.edu/uwiser/LNS.shtml on October 29, 2008.

Lee, Chungmei. 2004. *Is Resegregation Real?* Cambridge: Civil Rights Project at Harvard University. Accessed online at http://www.civilrightsproject.ucla.edu/research/re sego3/mumford_response.php, on September 12, 2008.

Lee, Sharon M., and Barry Edmonston. 2005. "New Marriages, New Families: U.S. Racial and Hispanic Intermarriage." *Population Bulletin* 60:2. Washington, D.C.: Population Reference Bureau.

Lee, Taeku, S. Karthick Ramakrishnan, and Ricardo Ramirez, eds. 2006. *Transforming Politics, Transforming America: The Political and Civic Incorporation of Immigrants in the United States.* Charlottesville: University of Virginia Press.

Lieberson, Stanley. 1980. *A Piece of the Pie: Black and White Immigrants since 1880.* Berkeley: University of California Press.

Lien, Pei-te. 2001. *The Making of Asian America through Political Participation.* Philadelphia: Temple University Press.

Lien, Pei-te. 2004. "Asian Americans and Voting Participation: Comparing Racial and Ethnic Differences in Recent U.S. Elections." *International Migration Review* 38 (2) (Summer): 493–517.

Lien, Pei-te, M. Margaret Conway, and Janelle Wong. 2004. *The Politics of Asian Americans: Diversity and Community.* New York: Routledge.

Lien, Pei-te, Dianne M. Pinderhughes, Carol Hardy-Fanta, and Christine Sierra. 2007. "The Voting Rights Act and the Election of Nonwhite Officials." *PS: Political Science and Politics* 40 (3): 489–94.

Lindblom, Charles. 2001. *The Market System: What It Is, How It Works, and What to Make of It.* New Haven: Yale University Press.

Lipsitz, George. 1998. *The Possessive Investment in Whiteness: How White People Profit from Identity Politics.* Philadelphia: Temple University Press.

Lissak, Rivka Shpak. 1989. *Pluralism and Progressives: Hull House and the New Immigrants, 1890–1919.* Chicago: University of Chicago Press.

Liu, Eric. 1999. *The Accidental Asian: Notes of a Native Speaker.* New York: Vintage.

Liu, John M. 1984. "Race, Ethnicity, and the Sugar Plantation System: Asian Labor in Hawaii, 1850 to 1900." In Lucie Cheng and Edna Bonacich, eds., *Labor Immigration under Capitalism: Asian Workers in the United States before World War II,* 186–210. Berkeley: University of California Press.

Logan, John R. 2001. "The New Ethnic Enclaves in America's Suburbs." Lewis Mumford Center for Comparative Urban and Regional Research. July 9.

Logan, John R. 2002. "Hispanic Populations and Their Residential Patterns in the Metropolis." Lewis Mumford Center for Comparative Urban and Regional Research. May 8.

Logan, John R. 2003a. "America's Newcomers." Lewis Mumford Center for Comparative Urban and Regional Research. June 18.

Logan, John R. 2003b. *How Race Counts for Hispanic Americans.* Albany, NY: Lewis Mumford Center, University at Albany.

Logan, John R. 2007. "Who Are the Other African Americans? Contemporary African and Caribbean Immigrants in the United States." In Yoku Shaw-Taylor and Steven Tuch, *The Other African Americans: Contemporary African and Caribbean Immigrants in the United States,* 27–55. Lanham, Md.: Rowman and Littlefield.

Logan, John R., and Glenn Deane. 2003. "Black Diversity in Metropolitan America." Lewis Mumford Center. Accessed online at http://mumford1.dyndns.org/cen2000/report.html, on March 5, 2005.

Logan, John, Deirdre Oakley, and Jacob Stowell. 2006. "Resegregation in U.S. Public Schools or White Decline? A Closer Look at Trends in the 1990s." *Children, Youth, and Environments* 16 (1): 49–68. Accessed online at http://www.colorado.edu/jour nals/cye/16_1/16_1_03_SchoolResegregation.pdf

Logan, John R., Brian J. Stults, and Reynolds Farley. 2004. "Segregation of Minorities in the Metropolis: Two Decades of Change." *Demography* 41 (1) (February): 1–22.

Lowe, Lisa. 1991. "Heterogeneity, Hybridity, Multiplicity: Marking Asian American Differences." *Diaspora* 1 (1): 24–44.

Lyman, Stanford M. 1991. "The Race Question and Liberalism: Casuistries in American Constitutional Law." *International Journal of Politics, Culture, and Society* 5 (2): 183–247.

Lyman, Stanford M. 2000. "The 'Chinese Questions' and American Labor Historians." *New Politics* 28:113–48.

Madison, James. 1787. "Federalist #10." In *The Federalist Papers.* Washington, D.C.: Library of Congress, *Thomas.* Accessed online at http://thomas.loc.gov/home/hist dox/fed_10.html, on March 30, 2008.

Madison, James H. 2003: *Lynching in the Heartland: Race and Memory in America.* New York: Palgrave.

Marquez, Benjamin. 1993. *LULAC: The Evolution of a Mexican American Political Organization.* Austin: University of Texas Press.

Marquez, Benjamin. 2007. "Latino Identity Politics Research: Problems and Opportunities." In Rodolfo Espino, David L. Leal, and Kenneth J. Meier, eds., *Latino Politics: Identity, Mobilization, and Representation,* 17–26. Charlottesville: University of Virginia Press.

Martin, Jack. 2007. "Limited English Proficiency Enrollment and Rapidly Rising Costs." Report of the Federation for Immigration Reform. Accessed online at http://www.fairus.org/site/DocServer/LEP_Special_Report.pdf?docID=1581, on April 3, 2008.

Massey, Douglas S. 1987. "Trends in Residential Segregation of Blacks, Hispanics, and Asians." *American Sociological Review* 52:802–25.

Massey, Douglas S. 2000. "Residential Segregation of Blacks, Hispanics, and Asians, 1970–1990." In Gerald D. Jaynes, ed., *Immigration and Race: New Challenges for American Democracy,* 44–73. New Haven: Yale University Press.

Massey, Douglas S. 2001. "Residential Segregation and Neighborhood Conditions in U.S. Metropolitan Areas." In Neil J. Smelser, William Julius Wilson, and Faith Mitchell, eds., *America Becoming: Racial Trends and Their Consequences,* vol. 1, 391–434. Washington, D.C.: National Academy Press.

Massey, Douglas S., and Nancy A. Denton. 1987. "Trends in Residential Segregation of Blacks, Hispanics, and Asians." *American Sociological Review* 52:802–25.

Massey, Douglas S., and Nancy A. Denton. 1993. *American Apartheid: Segregation and the Making of the Underclass.* Cambridge: Harvard University Press.

Masuoka, Natalie. 2008. "Defining the Group: Latino Identity and Political Participation." *American Politics Research* 36 (1) (January): 33–61.

McAdam, Doug. 1982. *Political Process and Development of Black Insurgency, 1930–1970.* Chicago: University of Chicago Press.

McClain, Charles J. 1994. *In Search of Equality: The Chinese Struggle against Discrimination in Nineteenth-Century America.* Berkeley: University of California Press.

McClain, Charles J., and Laurene Wu McClain. 1991. "The Chinese Contribution to the Development of American Law." In Sucheng Chan, ed., *Entry Denied: Exclusion and the Chinese Community in America, 1882–1943,* 3–24. Philadelphia: Temple University Press.

McClain, Paula D., and Joseph Stewart Jr. 2006. *"Can We All Get Along?" Racial and Ethnic Minorities in American Politics.* 4th ed. Boulder: Westview.

McColley, Robert. 1986. "Slavery in Virginia, 1619–1660: A Reexamination." In Robert H. Abzug and Stephen E. Maizlish, eds., *New Perspectives on Race and Slavery in America: Essays in Honor of Kenneth M. Stampp,* 11–24. Lexington: University Press of Kentucky.

McDonald, Michael P. 2008. "The Return of the Voter: Voter Turnout in the 2008 Presidential Election." *The Forum* (6, no. 4, article 4): 1–10. Berkeley Electronic Press. Accessed online at http://www.bepress.com/forum/vol6/iss4/art4, on March 2, 2009.

Melendy, H. Brett. 1981 [1977]. *Asians in America: Filipinos, Koreans, and East Indians.* New York: Hippocrene Books.

Melendy, H. Brett. 1984. *Chinese and Japanese Americans.* Rev. ed. New York: Hippocrene Books.

Menchaca, Martha. 2001. *Recovering History, Constructing Race: The Indian, Black, and White Roots of Mexican Americans.* Austin: University of Texas Press.

Mendelberg, Tali. 2001. *The Race Card: Campaign Strategy, Implicit Messages, and the Norm of Equality.* Princeton: Princeton University Press.

Milkman, Ruth. 2005. "Latino Immigrant Mobilization and Organized Labor: California's Transformation in the 1990s." Presented at Immigrant Political Incorporation Conference, Radcliffe Institute, Harvard University, April 22–23.

Milkman, Ruth. 2006. *L.A. Story: Immigrant Workers and the Future of the U.S. Labor Movement.* New York: Russell Sage Foundation.

Minta, Michael D. 2007. "Legislative Oversight and the Substantive Representation of Black and Latino Interests in Congress." Unpublished paper sent to coauthor (Hero); used by permission.

Mollenkopf, John. 2003. "New York: Still the Great Anomaly." In Rufus P. Browning, Dale Rogers Marshall, and David H. Tabb, eds., *Racial Politics in American Cities,* 115–42. 3d ed. New York: Longman.

Mollenkopf, John. 2005. "Immigration and the Changing Dynamic of Racial Politics in New York and Los Angeles." Presented at "Immigrant Political Incorporation" conference, Radcliffe Institute, Harvard University, April 22–23.

Mollenkopf, John, Jennifer Holdaway, Philip Kasinitz, and Mary Waters. 2006. "Politics among Young Adults in New York: The Immigrant Second Generation." *Transforming Politics, Transforming America.* Charlottesville: University of Virginia Press.

Mollenkopf, John, David Olson, and Tim Ross. 2001. "Immigrant Political Incorporation in New York and Los Angeles." In Michael Jones-Correa, ed., *Governing American Cities: Interethnic Coalitions, Competition, and Conflict,* 17–70. New York: Sage.

Montejano, David. 1987. *Anglos and Mexicans in the Making of Texas, 1836–1986.* Austin: University of Texas Press.

Moore, Joan, and Harry Pachon. 1985. *Hispanics in the United States.* Englewood Cliffs, N.J.: Prentice-Hall.

Moran, Rachel F. 2001. *Interracial Intimacy: The Regulation of Race and Romance.* Chicago: University of Chicago Press.

Moreno, Dario. 1997. "The Cuban Model: Political Empowerment in Miami." In F. Chris Garcia, ed., *Pursuing Power: Latinos and the Political System,* 208–26. Notre Dame: University of Notre Dame Press.

Muñoz, Carlos, Jr. 1989. *Youth, Identity, Power: The Chicano Movement.* New York: Verso Press.

Muñoz, Victor M. 1988. "The Role of the Labor Movement in the Empowerment of Mexican Americans." In Roberto E. Villareal and Norma G. Hernandez, eds., *Latinos and Political Coalitions: Political Empowerment for the 1990s,* 99–113. Boulder: Greenwood.

Navarro, Armando. 2000. *Raza Unida Party: A Chicano Challenge to the U.S. Two-Party Dictatorship.* Philadelphia: Temple University Press.

Navarro, Armando. 2004. *Mexicano Political Experience in Occupied Aztlan: Struggles and Change.* Lanham, Md.: AltaMira Press.

Neckerman, Kathleen. 1991. "We'd Love to Hire You But . . ." In Christopher Jencks and Paul Peterson, eds., *The Urban Underclass,* 203–32. Washington, D.C.: Brookings Institution.

Nelson, William E. 1987. "Cleveland: The Evolution of Black Political Power." In Michael Preston, Lenneal J. Henderson Jr., and Paul L. Puryear, eds., *The New Black Politics: The Search for Political Power,* 172–99. 2d ed. New York: Longman.

Neubeck, Kenneth J., and Noel A. Cazenave. 2001. *Welfare Racism: Playing the Race Card Against America's Poor.* New York: Routledge.

Nobles, Melissa. 2000. *Shades of Citizenship: Race and the Census in Modern Politics.* Palo Alto: Stanford University Press.

Okihiro, Gary Y. 1994. *Margins and Mainstreams: Asians in American History and Culture.* Seattle: University of Washington Press.

Okihiro, Gary Y., and John M. Liu, eds. 1988. *Reflections on Shattered Windows: Promises and Prospects for Asian American Studies.* Pullman: Washington State University Press.

Oliver, Melvin, and Thomas Shapiro. 1997. *Black Wealth / White Wealth: A New Perspective on Racial Inequality.* New York: Routledge.

Omi, Michael, and Howard Winant. 1986. *Racial Formation in the United States: From the 1960s to the 1980s.* New York: Routledge and Kegan Paul.

Omi, Michael, and Howard Winant. 1994. *Racial Formation in the United States: From the 1960s to the 1990s.* 2d ed. New York: Routledge.

Ong, Aihwa. 2003. *Buddha Is Hiding: Refugees, Citizens, and the New America.* Berkeley: University of California Press.

Ong, Elena. 2006. "GenerASIAN Next! The Power of 1 Million New Asian American Voters." *American Chronicle.* October 5. Accessed online at www.americanchronicle.com, on September 11, 2007.

Orfield, Gary, and Chungmei Lee. 2004. Brown *at 50: King's Dream or* Plessy's *Nightmare?* Cambridge: Civil Rights Project at Harvard University. Accessed online at http://www.civilrightsproject.ucla.edu/research/reseg04/brown50.pdf, on September 22, 2008.

Orfield, Gary, and Chungmei Lee. 2005. *Why Segregation Matters: Poverty and Educational Inequality.* Cambridge: Civil Rights Project at Harvard University. Accessed online at http://www.civilrightsproject.ucla.edu/research/deseg/Why_Segreg_Matters.pdf, on September 22, 2008.

Orfield, Gary, and Chungmei Lee. 2006. *Racial Transformation and the Changing Nature of Segregation.* Cambridge: Civil Rights Project at Harvard University. Accessed online at http://www.civilrightsproject.ucla.edu/research/deseg/Racial_Transformation.pdf, on September 22, 2008.

Osajima, Keith. 1988. "Asian Americans as the Model Minority: An Analysis of the Popular Press Image in the 1960s and 1980s." In Gary Y. Okihiro, Shirley Hune, Arthur A. Hansen, and John M. Liu, eds., *Reflections on Shattered Windows: Promises and Prospects for Asian American Studies,* 165–74. Pullman: Washington State University Press.

Ozawa v. United States. 1922. 260 U.S. 178.

Pachon, Harry. 1991. "U.S. Citizenship and Latino Participation in California." In Byran Jackson and Michael B. Preston, eds., *Racial and Ethnic Politics in California,* 71–88. Berkeley, Calif.: Institute of Governmental Studies.

Padilla, Felix. 1985. *Latino Ethnic Consciousness: The Case of Mexican Americans and Puerto Ricans in Chicago.* Notre Dame: University of Notre Dame Press.

Page, Clarence. 2007. "Black Immigrants Collect Most Degrees, but Affirmative Action Is Losing Direction." *Chicago Tribune,* March 18.

Painter, Nell Irvin. 1987. *Standing at Armageddon: The United States, 1877–1919.* New York: W. W. Norton.

Panel on Hispanics in the United States and Committee on Population, Division of Behavioral and Social Sciences and Education. 2006. *Hispanics and the Future of America,* edited by Marta Tienda and Faith Mitchell. Washington, D.C.: National Academies Press.

Pantoja, Adrian D., Ricardo Ramirez, and Gary M. Segura. 2001. "Citizens by Choice, Voters by Necessity: Patterns in Political Mobilization by Naturalized Latinos." *Political Research Quarterly* 54 (4): 729–50.

Parent, Anthony S., Jr. 2003. *Foul Means: The Formation of a Slave Society in Virginia, 1660–1740.* Chapel Hill: University of North Carolina Press.

Parrillo, Vincent N. 1982. "Asian Americans in American Politics." In Joseph Roucek and Bernard Eisenberg, eds., *America's Ethnic Politics,* 89–111. Westport, Conn.: Greenwood.

Passel, Jeffrey S. 2006. *The Size and Characteristics of the Unauthorized Migrant Population in the U.S.: Estimates Based on the March 2005 Current Population Survey.* Washington, D.C.: Pew Hispanic Center.

Passel, Jeffrey S., and Roberto Suro. 2005. *Rise, Peak, and Decline: Trends in U.S. Immigration, 1992–2004.* September 27. Washington, D.C.: Pew Hispanic Center.

Perez, Louis A., Jr. 1990. Book Review in *American Political Science Review* 84 (1) (March): 364–66.

Pérez y Gonzáles, Maria E. 2000. *Puerto Ricans in the United States.* Westport, Conn.: Greenwood.

Petersen, William. 1966. "Success Story, Japanese-American Style." *New York Times Magazine.* January 9: 20–21, 33, 36, 38, 40–41, 43.

Petersen, William. 1971. *Japanese Americans: Oppression and Success.* New York: Random House.

Petersen, William. 1987. "Politics and the Measurement of Ethnicity." In William Alonso and Paul Starr, eds., *The Politics of Numbers,* 187–233. New York: Russell Sage.

Pew Hispanic Center. 2005. *The New Latino South: The Context and Consequences of Rapid Population Growth.* Washington, D.C.: Pew Hispanic Center.

Pew Hispanic Center. 2006a. *Fact Sheet—From 200 Million to 300 Million: The Numbers behind Population Growth.* Washington, D.C.: Pew Hispanic Center.

Pew Hispanic Center. 2006b. "The Foreign Born at Mid-Decade, Table 19: English Ability by Age and Region of Birth." Accessed online at http://pewhispanic.org/files/other/foreignborn/Table-19.pdf, on April 16, 2007.

Pew Hispanic Center. 2008. *Report: 2008 National Survey of Latino Voters.* Washington, D.C.: Pew Hispanic Center. July 28. Accessed online at http://pewhispanic.org, on August 2, 2008.

Pew Hispanic Center/Kaiser Family Foundation. 2002. "National Survey of Latinos." Accessed online at http://pewhispanic.org/reports/surveys/, on December 12, 2006.

Pew Hispanic Center/Kaiser Family Foundation. 2004. "The 2004 National Survey of Latinos: Politics and Civic Participation." Washington, D.C.: Pew Hispanic Center, on December 12, 2006.

Pew Hispanic Center/Kaiser Family Foundation National Survey of Latinos. 2002. "The Latino Electorate." October 3. Accessed online at www.pewhispanic.org, on April 6, 2008.

Philpott, T. L. 1978. *The Slum and the Ghetto: Neighborhood Deterioration and Middle-Class Reform, Chicago, 1880–1930.* New York: Oxford University Press.

Pinderhughes, Dianne. 1987. *Race and Ethnicity in Chicago Politics: A Reexamination of Pluralist Theory.* Chicago: University of Illinois Press.

Pitkin, Hanna F. 1967. *The Concept of Representation.* Berkeley: University of California Press.

Polsby, Nelson. 1963. *Community Power and Political Theory.* New Haven: Yale University Press.

Portes, Alejandro, and Robert L. Bach. 1985. *Latin Journey: Cuban and Mexican Immigrants in the United States.* Berkeley: University of California Press.

Portes, Alejandro, and Rubén G. Rumbaut. 2001. *Legacies: The Story of the Immigrant Second Generation.* Berkeley: University of California Press.

Portes, Alejandro, and Min Zhou. 1993. "The New Second Generation: Segmented Assimilation and Its Variants." *Annals of the American Academy of Political and Social Sciences* 530:74–96.

Preuhs, Robert R. 2005. "Descriptive Representation, Legislative Leadership, and Direct Democracy: Latino Influence on English Only Laws in the States, 1984–2002." *State Politics and Policy Quarterly* 5 (Fall): 203–24.

Preuhs, Robert R. 2006. "The Conditional Effects of Minority Descriptive Representation: Black Legislators and Policy Influence in the American States." *Journal of Politics* 63 (3) (August): 585–99.

Preuhs, Robert R. 2007. "Descriptive Representations as a Mechanism to Mitigate Policy Backlash." *Political Research Quarterly* 60 (2): 277–92.

Ramakrishnan, S. Karthick. 2005. *Democracy in Immigrant America: Changing Demographics and Political Participation.* Stanford: Stanford University Press.

Renshon, Stanley. 2005. *The 50% American: Immigration and Identity in an Age of Terror.* Washington, D.C.: Georgetown University Press.

Rodriguez, Gregory. 2004. "Mexican-Americans and the Mestizo Melting Pot." In Tamar Jacoby, ed., *Reinventing the Melting Pot: The New Immigrants and What It Means to Be American,* 125–38. New York: Basic Books.

Rodriguez, Richard. 1982. *Hunger of Memory: The Education of Richard Rodriguez.* Boston: David R. Godine.

Rodriguez, Richard. 2002. *Brown: The Last Discovery of America.* New York: Viking.

Rodriguez, Victor M. 2005. *Latino Politics in the United States: Race, Ethnicity, Class, and Gender in the Mexican American and Puerto Rican Experience.* Dubuque: Kendall/Hunt.

Rogers, Reuel. 2000. "Afro-Caribbean Immigrants, African Americans, and the Politics of Group Identity." In Yvette M. Alex-Assensoh and Lawrence Hanks, eds., *Black and Multiracial Politics in America,* 15–59. New York: New York University Press.

Rogers, Reuel R. 2004. "Race-Based Coalitions among Minority Groups: Afro-Caribbean Immigrants and African-Americans in New York City." *Urban Affairs Review* 39 (3): 283–317.

Rogers, Reuel R. 2006. *Afro-Caribbean Immigrants and the Politics of Incorporation: Ethnicity, Exception, or Exit.* New York: Cambridge University Press.

Rosenstone, Steven J., and Raymond Wolfinger. 1980. *Who Votes?* New Haven: Yale University Press.

Ruffin, David C. 2006. "Immigration: Five Black Leaders Lend Their Voices to the Debate." *Crisis Magazine* 113 (4) (July/August): 20–25.

Rumbaut, Rubén G., Douglas S. Massey, and Frank D. Bean. 2006. "Linguistic Life Expectancies: Immigrant Language Retention in Southern California." *Population and Development Review* 32 (3) (December): 1–14.

Sánchez, José Ramón. 2007. *Boricua Power: A Political History of Puerto Ricans in the United States.* New York: New York University Press.

Santa Ana, Otto. 2002. *Brown Tide Rising: Metaphors of Latinos in Contemporary Political Discourse.* Austin: University of Texas Press.

Santoro, Wayne. 1999. "Conventional Politics Takes Center Stage: The Latino Struggle Against English-Only Laws." *Social Forces* 77 (March): 887–909.

Saxton, Alexander. 1971. *The Indispensable Enemy: Labor and the Anti-Chinese Movement in California.* Berkeley: University of California Press.

Schmidt, Ronald. 1988. "Cultural Pluralism and Public Administration: The Role of Community-Based Organizations." *American Review of Public Administration* 18 (2) (June): 189–202.

Schmidt, Ronald Sr. 2000. *Language Policy and Identity Politics in the United States.* Philadelphia: Temple University Press.

Schmidt, Ronald, Sr. 2002. "The Quest for Racial Equality: A Public Policy Framework." Paper presented at the Annual Meeting of the Midwest Political Science Association, Chicago, April 25–28.

Schmidt, Ronald, Edwina Barvosa-Carter, and Rodolfo D. Torres. 2000. "Latina/o Identities: Social Diversity and U.S. Politics." *PS: Political Science and Politics* 33 (3): 563–67.

Sears, David O. 1988. "Symbolic Racism." In Phyllis A. Katz and Dalmas A. Taylor, eds.,

Eliminating Racism: Profiles in Controversy, 53–84. New York and London: Plenum Press.

Sears, David O., Carl P. Hensler, and Leslie K. Speer. 1979. "Whites' Opposition to "Busing": Self-Interest or Symbolic Politics?" *American Political Science Review* 73 (2): 369–84.

Sengupta, Somini. 2001. "New Political Math in the City Raises Power of the Asian Vote." *New York Times.* August 25. Accessed online at http://query.nytimes.com, on September 13, 2007.

Shaw v. Reno, 113 S. Ct. 2816 (1993).

Shaw, Daron, Rodolfo O. de la Garza, and Jongho Lee. 2000. "Examining Latino Turnout in 1996: A Three-State, Validated Survey Approach (California, Florida, Texas)." *American Journal of Political Science* 44 (2): 338–46.

Sickels, Robert J. 1972. *Race, Marriage, and the Law.* Albuquerque: University of New Mexico Press.

Sierra, Christine. 1991. "Latino Organizational Strategies on Immigration Reform: Success and Limits of Public Policy-Making." In R. Villareal and N. Hernandez, eds., *Latinos and Political Coalitions: Political Empowerment for the 1990s,* 61–80. New York: Greenwood.

Skerry, Peter. 1993. *Mexican Americans: The Ambivalent Minority.* New York: Free Press.

Smith, Rogers. 1997. *Civic Ideals: Conflicting Visions of Citizenship in U.S. History.* New Haven: Yale University Press.

Solomos, John, and Les Back. 1995. *Race, Politics, and Social Change.* New York: Routledge.

Sonenshein, Raphael. 1993. *Politics in Black and White: Race and Power in Los Angeles.* Princeton: Princeton University Press.

Sonenshein, Raphael J. 2003a. "Post-incorporation Politics in Los Angeles." In Rufus P. Browning, Dale Rogers Marshall, and David H. Tabb, eds., *Racial Politics in American Cities,* 51–76. 3d ed. New York: Longman.

Sonenshein, Raphael J. 2003b. "The Prospects for Multicultural Coalitions: Lessons from America's Three Largest Cities." In Rufus P. Browning, Dale Rogers Marshall, and David H. Tabb, eds., *Racial Politics in American Cities,* 333–56. 3d ed. New York: Longman.

Sowell, Thomas. 1978. *Essays and Data on American Ethnic Groups.* Washington, D.C.: The Urban Institute.

Sowell, Thomas. 1981. *Ethnic America: A History.* New York: Basic Books.

Spickard, Paul R. 1989. *Mixed Blood: Intermarriage and Ethnic Identity in Twentieth-Century America.* Madison: University of Wisconsin Press.

Stampp, Kenneth M. 1956. *The Peculiar Institution: Slavery in the Ante-Bellum South.* New York: Knopf.

Steele, Shelby. 1990. *The Content of Our Character: A New Vision of Race in America.* New York: HarperCollins.

Steinfels, Peter. 1979. *The Neoconservatives: The Men Who Are Changing America's Politics.* New York: Simon and Schuster.

Stephenson, Donald Grier, Jr. 2004. *The Right to Vote: Rights and Liberties under the Law.* Santa Barbara: ABC CLIO.

Sterne, Evelyn Savidge. 2001. "Beyond the Boss: Immigration and American Political Culture from 1880 to 1940." In Gary Gerstle and John Mollenkopf, eds., *E Pluribus*

Unum? Contemporary and Historical Perspectives on Immigrant Political Incorpora-tion, 33–66. New York: Russell Sage Foundation.

Stewart, David W. 2002. "Immigration and School Overcrowding." Federation for Immigration Reform. Accessed online at http://www.fairus.org, on February 11, 2007.

Stone, Clarence. 1989. *Regime Politics.* Lawrence: University Press of Kansas.

"Success Story of One Minority Group in U.S." 1966. *U.S. News & World Report.* December 26: 73–76.

Sugrue, Thomas J. 1995. "Crabgrass-Roots Politics: Race, Rights, and the Reaction against Liberalism in the Urban North, 1940–1964." *Journal of American History* 82 (2): 551–78.

Swarnes, Rachel L. 2004. "African-American Becomes a Term for Debate." *New York Times.* August 29.

Sze, Felicia. 2004. "Failing Predictions in Pursuit of Proportional Representation: Assuring Asian American Voter Strength in San Francisco through Litigation." *Asian Law Journal* 11:97–116.

Taeuber, Karl D., and Alma F. Taeuber. 1965. *Negroes in Cities.* Chicago: Aldine.

Takaki, Ronald. 1998. *Strangers from a Different Shore: A History of Asian Americans.* Boston: Little, Brown.

Takaki, Ronald. 1993. *A Different Mirror: A History of Multicultural America.* Boston: Little, Brown.

Takougang, Joseph. 2004. "Contemporary African Immigrants to the United States." *Ikinkerindo: A Journal of African Migration,* 1–13.

Tate, Katherine. 1993. *From Protest to Politics: The New Black Voters in American Elections.* New York: Russell Sage Foundation.

Thernstrom, Stephan, and Abigail Thernstrom. 1997. *America in Black and White: One Nation, Indivisible.* New York: Simon and Schuster.

Thind v. United States. 1923. 261 U.S. 204.

Thomas, Clive S., and Ronald J. Hrebenar 2004. "Interest Groups in the States." In Virginia Gray and Russell Hanson, eds., *Politics in the American States,* 100–128. Washington, D.C.: Congressional Quarterly Press.

Thornburg v. Gingles, 478 U.S. (1986).

Tichenor, Daniel J. 2002. *Dividing Lines: The Politics of Immigration Control in America.* Princeton: Princeton University Press.

Tilly, Charles. 2004. *Social Movements, 1768–2004.* Boulder: Paradigm.

Tocqueville, Alexis de. 2003 [1835]. *Democracy in America.* New York: Penguin Books.

Torres, Rodolfo D., and George Katsiaficas, eds. 1999. *Latino Social Movements: Historical and Theoretical Perspectives.* New York: Routledge.

Tsai, Shih-Shan Henry. 1986. *The Chinese Experience in America.* Bloomington: Indiana University Press.

Tuan, Mia. 1998. *Forever Foreigners or Honorary Whites? The Asian Ethnic Experience Today.* New Brunswick: Rutgers University Press.

Tucker, James Thomas. 2006. "'I Was Asked If I Was a Citizen': Latino Elected Officials Speak Out on the Voting Rights Act." National Association of Latino Elected and Appointed Officials (NALEO) Education Fund, September. Accessed on October 27, 2007, at http://www.naleo.org.

Uhlaner, Carole J. 2000. "Political Activity and Preferences of African Americans, Latinos, and Asian Americans." In Gerald D. Jaynes, ed., *Immigration and Race: New Challenges for American Democracy*, 217–54. New Haven: Yale University Press.

Uhlaner, Carole, and F. Chris Garcia. 2002. "Latino Public Opinion." In Barbara Norrander and Clyde Wilcox, eds., *Understanding Public Opinion*, 77–101. Washington, D.C.: Congressional Quarterly Press.

Urciuoli, Bonnie. 1996. *Exposing Prejudice: Puerto Rican Experiences of Language, Race, and Class*. Boulder: Westview.

U.S. Census Bureau. 2006. "Census Bureau Data Show Key Population Changes across Nation," *U.S. Census Bureau News*. Released 12:01 EST, August 15, 2006. Accessed online at http://www.census.gov, on August 15.

U.S. Census Bureau. 2007a. *The American Community—Asians: 2004*. Washington, D.C.: Department of Commerce, U.S. Census Bureau.

U.S. Census Bureau. 2007b. *The American Community—Blacks: 2004*. Washington, D.C.: Department of Commerce, U.S. Census Bureau.

U.S. Census Bureau. 2007c. *The American Community—Hispanics: 2004*. Washington, D.C.: Department of Commerce, U.S. Census Bureau.

U.S. Census Bureau. 2007d. *2007 American Community Survey*. Washington, D.C.: Department of Commerce.

U.S. Census Bureau. 2007e. *National Population Projections I. Summary Files*. Washington, D.C.: Department of Commerce, U.S. Census Bureau, Population Projection Program.

U.S. Commission on Civil Rights. 1981. *The Voting Rights Act: Unfulfilled Goals*. Washington, D.C.: U.S. Government Printing Office.

U.S. Department of Homeland Security. 2008. *2007 Yearbook of Immigration Statistics*. Washington, D.C.: Office of Immigration Statistics.

U.S. House of Representatives, Committee on Government Reform. 2006. *Porous Borders and Downstream Costs: The Cost of Illegal Immigration on State, County, and Local Governments*, Serial No. 109-188. Accessed online at http://www.gpoaccess.gov/congress/index.html, on January 21, 2007.

U.S. House of Representatives, Committee on the Judiciary. 2006. *How Does Illegal Immigration Impact American Taxpayers and Will the Reid-Kennedy Amnesty Worsen the Blow?* Serial No. 109-135. Accessed online at http://judiciary.house.gov, on January 21, 2007.

Vaca, Nicolás C. 2004. *The Presumed Alliance: The Unspoken Conflict between Latinos and Blacks and What It Means for America*. New York: HarperCollins.

Van Sertima, Ivan. 1976. *They Came before Columbus*. New York: Random House.

Vélez-Ibáñez, Carlos G., and Anna Sampaio, eds. 2002. *Transnational Latino Communities: Politics, Processes, and Cultures*. Lanham, Md.: Rowman and Littlefield.

Verba, Sidney, and Norman Nie. 1972. *Political Participation in America: Political Democracy and Social Equality*. New York: Harper and Row.

Verba, Sidney, Kay Lehman Schlozman, and Henry E. Brady. 1995. *Voice and Equality: Civic Voluntarism in American Politics*. Cambridge: Harvard University Press.

Vickerman, Milton. 1999. *Crosscurrents: West Indian Immigrants and Race*. New York: Oxford University Press.

Wade, Nicholas. 2004. "Article Highlights Different Views on Genetic Basis of Race." *New York Times*. October 27. Accessed online at www.nytimes.com on June 9, 2005.

Walters, Dan. 1992. *The New California: Facing the Twenty-first Century*. 2d ed. Sacramento: California Journal Press.

Walters, Ronald. 2007. *Freedom Is Not Enough: Black Voters, Black Candidates, and American Presidential Elections.* New ed. New York: Rowman and Littlefield.

Washington Post/Kaiser Family Foundation/Harvard University Survey Project. 1999. "National Survey on Latinos in America." Menlo Park, Calif.: Kaiser Family Foundation. Accessed online at http://www.kff.org, on June 23, 2004.

Watanabe, Teresa. 2008. "Number of California Potential Immigrant Voters to Swell." *Los Angeles Times.* April 28. Accessed online at http://latimes.com, on April 28, 2008.

Waters, Mary C. 1990. *Ethnic Options: Choosing Identities in America.* Berkeley: University of California Press.

Waters, Mary C. 1994. "Ethnic and Racial Identities of Second Generation Black Immigrants in New York City." *International Migration Review* 20:795–820.

Waters, Mary C. 1999. *Black Identities: West Indian Immigrant Dreams and American Realities.* Cambridge: Harvard University Press.

Wattenberg, Martin. 1988. *The Decline of American Political Parties, 1952–1996.* Cambridge: Harvard University Press.

Wei, William. 1993. *The Asian American Movement.* Philadelphia: Temple University Press.

Williams, Eric E. 1994. *Capitalism and Slavery.* Chapel Hill: University of North Carolina Press.

Wilson, William Julius. 2001. *The Bridge Over the Racial Divide: Rising Inequality and Coalition Politics.* Berkeley: University of California Press.

Woldemikael, Tekle. 1989. "Becoming Black American: Haitian and American Institutions in Evanston, Illinois." New York: AMS Press.

Wolfinger, Raymond E. 1965. "The Development and Persistence of Ethnic Voting." *American Political Science Review* 59:896–908.

Wong, Janelle S. 2006. *Democracy's Promise: Immigrants and American Civic Institutions.* Ann Arbor: University of Michigan Press.

Wong, Paul, Chienping Faith Lai, Richard Nagasawa, and Tieming Lin. 1998. *Sociological Perspectives* 41 (1): 95–118.

Wood, Daniel B. 2006. *Christian Science Monitor,* April 10. Accessed online at http://www.csmonitor.com/200/0410/p01s01-ussc.html, on April 10, 2006.

Woodrow Wilson International Center for Scholars. 2007. Data Base on "Immigrant Rights Marches, Spring 2006." Accessed online at http://www.wilsoncenter.org/index.cfm?topic_id=5949&categoryid=357BE4DA-65BF-E7DC-470FC03539EBF9CB&fuseaction=topics.news_item_topics&news_id=150685, on July 31, 2007.

Wright, Lawrence. 1994. "One Drop of Blood." *New Yorker* (July 25): 46–55.

Yanez, Alonzo. 2008. "Myth of the Latino Vote." Hispanic Link News Service. October 29. Accessed online at http://www.scrippsnews.com/node/37533, on October 29, 2008.

Yanow, Dvora. 2003. *Constructing "Race" and "Ethnicity" in America: Category-Making in Public Policy and Administration.* Armonk, N.Y.: M. E. Sharpe.

Yoshino, Troy. 1999. "Still Keeping the Faith? Asian Pacific Americans, Ballot Initiatives, and the Lessons of Negotiated Rulemaking." *Asian Law Journal* 6:1–66.

Zhou, Min. 1992. *Chinatown: The Socioeconomic Potential of an Urban Enclave.* Philadelphia: Temple University Press.

Zhou, Min. 1997. "Segmented Assimilation: Issues, Controversies, and Recent Research on the New Second Generation." *International Migration Review* 31 (4): 825–58.

Index

Note: Page numbers in italic indicate tables.

AAICS (Asian American Institute of Congressional Studies), 142
AALDEF (Asian American Legal Defense and Education Fund), 163, 173
ACJ (American Citizens for Justice), 141
activism, movements, protests, and organizational activity, 133–34
   of Asian and Pacific Island Americans, 80, 101, 133–34, 140–43, 226
   of Black Americans, 12, 80, 133–37, 226
   elected officials as institutional activists, 134
   immigration and immigrant settlement issues, 136–37, 143–46
   impact of recent immigrants on, 135–36
   of Latino and Hispanic Americans, 80, 133–34, 137–40, 143–46, 226
   marches and demonstrations, 9–11, 143–44
   of Mexican Americans, 12, 84, 85, 137–38, 139, 145
   of Native Americans, 80
   political inequality issues, 203–4
   political participation and, 132, 133–34, 144–46
   public policies supported by, 11–12, 128
   of Puerto Rican Americans, 12, 89, 137–38, 139, 145
   of slaves, 80
affirmative action, 233, 273n4 (chap. 6)

access to, 199
defense of, 227
for immigrants, 243–44
opposition to, 237
racial equality movements and, 12
AFL-CIO, 225
African-origin Americans. *See also* Black Americans; Black exceptionalism
   biracial hierarchy and, 51, 251–52
   characteristics of, 269n1
   citizenship for, 69
   contemporary immigrants, 72–73, 77–78
   diversity of early immigrants, 73–74
   geographic concentrations, 21
   group consciousness, 148–50
   housing patterns, 111
   immigration of, 20–21, 136
   increase in population of, 18
   individual assimilation, 253–54
   pluralism, 250–51, 255–56
   and politics, 22–23, 52, 59–60, 270n5
   racial and ethnic identity of, 149–50
   socioeconomic status of, 159–60, *159*
   status comparison to home countries, 149
   tension between ethnic groups, 136, 206–8
   transnationalism and, 136, 149–50
Aid to Families with Dependent Children, 232

Alabama, 18, 26, *210, 212*
Alaska, 165, *210, 212*, 272–73n3, 273n2
    (chap. 5)
alien land law acts, 96, 272n7
American Apartheid (Massey and Denton), 104–5
American Citizens for Justice (ACJ), 141
American G.I. Forum, 85
antimiscegenation laws, 69–70, 272n4
APIAHF (Asian Pacific Islander American Health Forum), 142
apportionment, 176, 191–92
Arab Americans, 70. *See also* Middle Eastern–origin Americans
Arizona
    African-origin Americans in, *22*
    Black Americans in, *210*
    immigrant population in, 17, 18
    Latino and Hispanic Americans in, 27, *212*
    Mexican Americans in, 83
Arkansas, 18, *210, 212*
Armenian Americans, 98
Asian American Institute of Congressional Studies (AAICS), 142
Asian American Legal Defense and Education Fund (AALDEF), 163, 173
Asian American Voters Coalition, 142
Asian and Pacific Island Americans. *See also* Asian Indian Americans; Chinese Americans; Filipino Americans; Japanese Americans; Korean Americans; Vietnamese Americans
    activism of, 80, 101, 133–34, 140–43, 226
    alien land law acts, 96, 272n7
    assimilation of, 2–3
    biracial hierarchy and, 2–3, 5, 51–52, 251–52
    birthrates, 24, 29
    in California, 215–18, *217*
    campaign contributions by, 157
    census data, racial categories in, 72
    characteristics of, 269n1
    citizenship for, 58, 69, 96, 157, 162, 172, 173
    current status of, 13, 14–15

Democratic Party, responsiveness of, 221
descriptive representation, 176–77, 180–82, *181*, 185, 189–93, *216*, 220–21
discrimination against, 70, 94, 96–97, 98–99, 141–42, 143, 152–53, 173
distinctions between Blacks and, 79–80
diversification and national-origins composition, 30–32, *31*, 113, 151–52, 270–71n8
divisions between national groups, 32
educational opportunities and school segregation, 95, 117–20, *119, 120*, 122–23
geographic concentrations, 32, 113, 264
governing coalitions, 33, 102, 201, 202, 205–6, 220, 264
group consciousness, 150–54
historical racialization experiences, 93–100, 102–3
household incomes, *121*
housing opportunities and segregation, *110*, 113–14, 115–16, 122–23
immigration, *16*, 19, 20, 29–33, 94–95, 96, 101–2, 111, 146, 270n4, 272n5, 272n6
increase in population of, *16*, 18, 29–30, *30*, 108, 202, 249
individual assimilation, 1–2, 37–38, 40, 253–54
interracial housing segregation, 114–15, *114*
judicial and law enforcement, 181
language abilities and linguistic assimilation, 199–200
marriage to, 69
mayoral elections, *181*, 182–84, *183*
McCarran-Walter Act (Immigration and Nationality Act), 99, 162, 165
as model minority, 13, 57, 99–100, 272n8
multiracial hierarchy and, 3, 55–56, 57–58
obstacles to political power, 203–4, 205
panethnicity, 100–102
partisanship, 157–58, 173–74, 263
pluralism, 37–38, 250–51, 254–56

and politics, 2–3, 4, 5, 13, 31–33, 52, 54,
59–60, 126–27, 131–32, 144–46, 172–77,
215–18, 250–58, 263–64
poverty and, 121–22, *122*
prejudice against, 94
public policies toward, 94–96, 234, 264
racial and ethnic identity of, 39–40,
97–98, 100–102, 151–52
racial hierarchy, 263–64
racial inequalities, government involvement to correct, 229, 234
racial isolation of, 118
racial slurs and ethnic distinctions, 101
segregation of, 106
self-identity of, 100–102
sense of closeness to other Asian
Americans, 152, 153
socioeconomic status of, 33, 57, 120–22,
121, 122, 123, 158–62, *158, 159*
triangulated racial order, 57–58
violence against, 141, 142
as voters, 142–43, 157–58, 163, 165, *166,*
168, 172–73, 189–93, 244–45, 273n2
(chap. 5)
Asian Indian Americans
descriptive representation, 180
diversification of Asian American population, 31, *31,* 113
governing coalitions, 206
immigration, 19, 99
racial and ethnic identity of, 98
Asian Pacific Islander American Health
Forum (APIAHF), 142
assimilation. *See also* individual assimilation
biracial hierarchy and, 2–3
foreigner versus insider, 57–58
language abilities and linguistic assimilation, 199–200, 212
segmented assimilation, 56, 59, 78
Atlanta, *26,* 54, *114*

Baca, Joe, *187*
Badillo, Herman, 89, *188*
Barred Zone Act, 96
barriers, racial. *See* racial hierarchy
Becerra, Xavier, *187*

Behind the Mule (Dawson), 53
Berry, Marian, *183*
bilingual education, 217, 234, 235, 244, 245
Bilingual Education Act Amendment, 244
bilingualism in America, 245–46
biracial hierarchy, 2–3, 5, 50–51, 251
African-origin Americans and, 51, 251
Asian and Pacific Island Americans
and, 2–3, 5, 51–52, 251
Black Americans and, 2–3, 5, 51–52,
251–52
Black exceptionalism, 51–52, 53, 107
Caribbean-origin Americans and,
251–52
Latino and Hispanic Americans and,
2–3, 5, 51–52, 251
Middle Eastern–origin Americans and,
51
political incorporation and, 52–54,
251–52
social and political structures and, 38
biracial model, 42, 249
birthrates
Asian and Pacific Island Americans, 24,
29
Black Americans, 24
Latino and Hispanic Americans, 23–24,
270n6
White population, 24
Black Americans. *See also* African-origin
Americans; Black exceptionalism;
Caribbean-origin Americans; civil
rights movement
activism of, 12, 80, 133–37, 226
biracial hierarchy and, 2–3, 5, 51–52,
251–52
birthrates, 24
Black, definition as, 74–75
Black versus White racial politics,
41–42, 239–40
in California, 215–18, *217*
campaign contributions by, 157
census data, racial categories in, 72
characteristics of, 269n1
citizenship for, 162
competition between newcomers and,
80

Black Americans (*continued*)
  Congressional Black Caucus, 137, 234, 259
  contemporary immigrants and racial expectations, 72–73, 77–80
  current status of, 13, 14–15
  Democratic Party, responsiveness of, 221–22
  descriptive representation, 176–79, *178*, 181–82, 189–91, 206–8, *216*, 220–21
  discrimination against, 76, 152–53, 164, 176
  distinctions between Blacks and other immigrant groups, 79–80
  educational opportunities and school segregation, 77, 80, 116–20, *119, 120*, 122–23
  ethnic distinctions, 74
  in Florida, 218–19
  fragmentation of groups, 202
  generational prejudices, 79
  geographic concentrations, 21, *22*
  governing coalitions in politics, 200–211, *210–11*, 213–14, 215–19, 220
  group consciousness, 147–50
  historical racialization experiences, 72–81, 103
  household incomes, *121*
  housing opportunities and segregation, 52, 76, 105, 109–11, *110*, 115–16, 122–23
  immigration, *16*, 19, 20–23, 33, 108, 111, 136, 146, 250
  increase in population of, 249
  individual assimilation, 1–2, 37–38, 41–42, 53, 253–54, 260
  institutional incorporation, 209–10
  interracial housing segregation, 114–15, *114*
  interracial sex and marriage, 69–70, 80, 272n4
  Jim Crow system and, 11, 41
  law enforcement, 178, *178*
  linked fate, 72–73, 148
  March on Washington, 9, 10
  mayoral elections, 48, 53, 177, *178*, 182–84, *183*

  moral claim to group entitlements, 148
  multiracial hierarchy and, 55–56
  native versus immigrant groups, 21–22, 136
  obstacles to political power, 203–4
  one-drop rule for Blackness, 74–75
  partisanship, 22–23, 53, 155, 166, 167, 169, 219, 259–60
  pluralism, 37–38, 48, 250–51, 254–56, 271n3
  and politics, 2–3, 4, 5, 11, 12, 13, 14, 22–23, 48, 52–54, 59–60, 126–27, 131–32, 144–46, 154, 166–69, 174–75, 209–11, *210–11*, 213–14, 215–18, 250–60, 270n5, 271n3
  poverty and, 121–22, *122*
  public policies for equality of opportunities, 233–34
  racial and ethnic identity of, 147–50
  racial hierarchy, 259–60
  racial inequalities, government involvement to correct, 229, 234
  racial isolation of, 105, 118
  racialization of public policy and, 69–70
  segregation of, 105–6
  sense of closeness to other Black Americans, 152
  socioeconomic status of, 80–81, 105, 120–22, *121, 122*, 123, 158–62, *158, 159*
  status comparison to White population, 149
  tax codes and, 76–77
  tension between ethnic groups, 21–22, 136, 206–8
  transnationalism and, 136
  triangulated racial order, 57–58
  violence against, 75–76
  as voters, 11, 154, 164, 165, 166–69, *166, 168*, 188–91
Black exceptionalism, 51–52, 53, 107
Black Reparations movement, 135
Black Utility Heuristic, 53
Bonilla, Henry, *186*
Border region of United States, 272–73n3
  border control and patrols, 241
  school segregation in, 118, 119–20, *120*

Boston, 12, 177
Boynton Beach, Florida, 17
Bradley, Tom, 48, 177, *183*, 184, 204–5
Brown, Jerry, *183*
Brown, Patrick Lee, *183*
Brown, Willie, *183*
Browning, Rufus P., 48, 194–95, 200–202, 233, 271n3
Brown v. Board of Education of Topeka, 11, 77, 91, 117
Bush, George W., 239
Bustamente, Albert, *186*
Bustamente, Cruz, 224

Cable Act (1922), 69
California
  alien land law acts, 96, 272n7
  Asian and Pacific Island Americans, 32, 94, 173, 192–93, 215–18, *216*, *217*
  Asian migration to, 95–96
  Black Americans, 20, *210*, 215–18, *216*, *217*
  border control and patrols, 241
  city politics, governing coalitions in, 200–201
  congressional elections, 185, 186–87, *187*, 192
  Foreign Miners License tax, 94
  immigration, 17, 18, 215, 217–18, 240–41
  initiative process, 215, 216–17
  labor union activity, 206, 223–25
  Latino and Hispanic Americans, 20, 27, 81–82, 179, 180, 186–87, *187*, 192, *212*, 215–18, *216*, *217*
  Mexican Americans, 82–83, 217
  Proposition 187, 240–41
  state politics, governing coalitions in, 215–18, *216*
Cambodian Americans, *31*
Cano v. Davis, 192
Cardoza, Dennis, *187*
Caribbean-origin Americans
  biracial hierarchy and, 251–52
  contemporary immigrants, 72–73, 77–78
  governing coalitions, 218–19
  group consciousness, 148–50

housing patterns, 111
immigration statistics, 19, 136
increase in population of, 18, 249
individual assimilation, 253–54
pluralism, 255–56
and politics, 22–23, 52
racial and ethnic identity of, 149–50
racial hierarchy and, 62
socioeconomic status of, 159–60, *159*
status comparison to home countries, 149
tension between ethnic groups, 21–22, 136, 206–8, 250
transnationalism and, 136, 149–50
Carollo, Joe, *183*
census. *See* United States Census Bureau
Center for Immigration Studies, 242
Central America–origin Americans, 19, 24–25, *25*, 250
CETA (Comprehensive Employment and Training Act), 232
Chao, Elaine, 142
Chavez, Cesar, 85
Chicago
  Black American descriptive representation, 177
  housing segregation dissimilarity index, *110*
  immigrant population in, 108
  Latino American population in, 25
  mayoral elections, *183*
  noncitizen voters, 164
  political system in, 52–53
  racial equality movements, 12
Chicano Movement, 12, 84, 85
Chicanos. *See* Mexican Americans
Chin, Vincent, 141, 142
Chinese Americans. *See also* Asian and Pacific Island Americans
  discrimination against, 94, 98–99
  diversification of Asian American population, 30, *31*, 113
  education for, 95
  governing coalitions, 206
  immigration, 19, 33, 94
  partisanship, 174
  prejudice against, 94

Chinese Americans (*continued*)
  racial and ethnic identity of, 97–98
  racial equality movement, 12
  racial slurs and ethnic distinctions, 101
  restrictions on immigration of, 94, 96,
    99
  self-identity of, 100–101
Chinese Exclusion Act, 94
cities and metropolitan areas
  apportionment, 176, 191–92
  Black American descriptive representa-
    tion, 176, 177, *178*
  complexity of politics in, 202–3
  housing opportunities and segrega-
    tion, 108–14, *110*, 116, 272n1
  interracial housing segregation, 114–15,
    114
  Latino and Hispanic American de-
    scriptive representation, *179*, 180
  mayoral elections, 48, 53, 177, *178, 179,*
    181–84, *181, 183*
  political incorporation and, 200–208
  racial balance in, 19
citizenship
  for African-origin Americans, 69
  for Asian and Pacific Island Americans,
    58, 69, 96, 157, 162, 172, 173
  for Black Americans, 162
  dual nationalities or citizenships, 61
  encouragement of and support for,
    162–63
  for Latino and Hispanic Americans,
    162, 170
  for Mexican Americans, 82–83, 162
  noncitizen voters, 163–64
  political participation and, 162–64
  privileges and status of immigrants,
    198–99
  process of naturalization, 163
  for Puerto Rican Americans, 86
Civil Rights Act, 11, 128
  affirmative action and, 243
  continuation of benefits of, 235–36
  Democratic Party's role in, 155
  equality of opportunities and race rela-
    tions, 229–30
civil rights movement, 135. *See also* activism, movements, protests, and or-
    ganizational activity
  Black Americans as focus of, 10, 80
  legal system and, 11
  legislative processes and, 11
  marches and demonstrations, 9, 10–11
  national expansion of, 12–13
  public opinion changes through, 11, 134
  public policies and, 11
Civil Rights Project, 117–19, 272–73n3
Cleveland, 177
Clinton, Bill, 235, 241
Clinton, Hillary Rodham, 265
coalitions. *See* governing coalitions
Coehlo, Anthony, *187*
colonial labor system, 83, 86–87
Colorado
  African-origin Americans, 22
  Black Americans, *210*
  immigrant population in, 18
  Latino and Hispanic Americans, 27, *212*
community-based organizations (CBOs),
    223, 224
Community Service Organization (CSO),
    85
Comprehensive Employment and Train-
    ing Act (CETA), 232
Compton, California, 208
Congressional Black Caucus, 137, 234,
    259
Congressional Hispanic Caucus, 234,
    262
Connecticut
  African-origin Americans, 21, 22
  Black Americans, *210*
  Latino and Hispanic Americans, 27, *212*
conservative and neoconservative poli-
    tics. *See also* Republican Party
  economic policy, 238–39
  race importance, diminishment of, 40
  racial equality policies, opposition to,
    236–37, 239
  racial inequalities, government in-
    volvement to correct, 227, 273n3
    (chap. 6)
  social programs, encouragement of
    immigration through, 241–42

crime and violence
   against Asian and Pacific Island Americans, 141, 142
   against Black Americans, 75–76
   current status of minority populations, 14
   against Mexican Americans, 84
CSO (Community Service Organization), 85
Cuban Adjustment Act, 208
Cuban Americans
   activism of, 137
   diversification of Latino American population, 24–25, 25, 112
   in Florida, 90, 91, 137, 156, 218–19
   geographic concentrations, 92, 112, 137, 156
   governing coalitions, 91–92, 208, 218, 219
   historical racialization experiences, 90–92, 103
   immigration, 19, 90, 137, 273n1 (chap. 5)
   Marielitos, 91
   mayoral elections, 184
   migration to United States by, 90
   partisanship, 91, 153, 156, 218, 219
   tension between ethnic groups, 208
   transnationalism and, 92
   voter turnout, 163
Cueller, Henry, 186

Dahl, Robert, 47–48
Daley, Richard, 53, 183
Dallas, 108, 109, 110, 183
Dawson, Michael, 53
DeCastro, Clarissa Martinez, 156
de la Garza, Eligio, 186
de la Garza, Rodolfo, 48–49, 171, 271n4
Delaware, 18, 211, 212
Dellums, Ronald, 183
Democratic Party
   Asian and Pacific Island American voters and, 157–58, 222
   Black American voters and, 22–23, 53, 155, 219, 259–60
   Civil Rights Act, role in, 155
   in Florida, 219

   immigration issues, opinions about, 217
   Latino American voters and, 153, 155–56, 262
   national politics and governing coalitions, 220–22
   Puerto Rican American voters and, 89
   responsiveness to minority voter concerns, 221–22
   White backlash, 239
demonstrations and marches. See activism, movements, protests, and organizational activity
Denton, Nancy A., 104–5
descriptive representation, 133, 175–82. See also political representation
   apportionment, 176, 191–92
   Asian and Pacific Island Americans, 175–77, 180–82, 181, 185, 189–93, 216
   Black Americans, 175, 176–79, 178, 181–82, 189–91, 206–8, 209–11, 210–11, 213–14, 216
   congressional elections, 184–89, 186, 187, 188
   Latino and Hispanic Americans, 175–77, 179–80, 179, 181–82, 184–89, 186, 187, 188, 189–92, 212–14, 212–13, 216
   mayoral elections, 48, 53, 177, 178, 179, 181–84, 181, 183
   Voting Rights Act and, 176, 185, 186, 189–93, 273n4 (chap. 5)
Detroit, 12, 17, 114–15, 114
DeWitt, John L., 99
Diaz-Balart, Lincoln, 188
Diaz-Balart, Mario, 188
Dinkins, David, 183
discrimination
   against Asian and Pacific Island Americans, 94, 96–97, 98–99, 141–42, 143, 152–53
   against Black Americans, 152–53, 164, 176
   against Chinese Americans, 94, 98–99
   Civil Rights Act and, 11
   current status of minority populations, 14

discrimination (*continued*)
distinctions between Blacks and other
immigrant groups, 79–80
government involvement to correct,
148, 152
immigration law and quota system, 15
individual assimilation and, 2
against Latino and Hispanic Americans, 152–53, 261
laws against, 11, 12, 91
perception of, participation in politics
and, 152–53
public policies and, 69–70, 229–31
racial equality movements and, 12
supposed inferiority of races and,
70–71, 76
voting rights and, 164–65, 173, 176,
244–45
White privilege, 70
dissimilarity index, 108–14, *110*
Dominican Republic Americans
contemporary immigrants and racial
expectations, 78–79
diversification of Latino American
population, 24–25, *25*
geographic concentrations, 203
immigration statistics, 19, 92
tension between ethnic groups, 205
dual wage system, 83, 86
Dukakis, Michael, 167

Eastern United States, 51
East Orange, New Jersey, 17
economic equality and policies, 231–33,
235, 238–39, 268, 274n1
Economic Opportunity Act, 231
educational opportunities and school
segregation
for Asian and Pacific Island Americans,
95, 117–20, *119*, *120*, 122–23
bilingual education, 217, 234, 235, 244,
245
for Black Americans, 77, 80, 116–20, *119*,
120, 122–23
Brown v. Board of Education of Topeka,
11, 77, 91, 117
busing to integrate schools, 239

for Chinese Americans, 95
current status of minority populations,
13, 14
for Japanese Americans, 95
for Latino and Hispanic Americans,
117–20, *119*, *120*, 122–23, 160–61, *161*,
170–71
for Mexican Americans, 85
Plessy v. Ferguson, 80, 116–17
political struggle over, 117–18
poverty and, 120
public policies and, 233
for Puerto Rican Americans, 87, 88
racial equality movements and, 12
racial isolation in schools, 118
regional differences, 119–20, *120*, 123
socioeconomic status and, 120
80-20 Initiative, 143, 157
Elementary and Secondary Education
Act, 231
El Salvador Americans, 92
employment training and opportunities
affirmative action, 12, 199, 227, 233, 237,
243–44, 273n4 (chap. 6)
colonial labor system, 83, 86–87
current status of minority populations,
13, 14
discrimination in, laws against, 91
equality of opportunities, 227, 273n3
(chap. 6)
labor union activity, 84–85, 206,
223–25, 235, 255
for Latino and Hispanic Americans,
161, *161*
minimum wage law, 232
population statistics and employment
programs, 205
public employment, political incorporation and, 223
public policies for, 232
for Puerto Rican Americans, 86–87, 88
racial equality movements and, 12
ethnic identity. *See* racial and ethnic
identity
ethnoracial democracy
benchmarks of, 3–5, 125–29, 252–58
governing coalitions and, 257–58

median voter and, 221–22, 259, 262, 264, 267

Obama election and, 265–68

obstacles to, 36, 257–58

optimism about, 5, 253–56

pessimism about, 5–6, 256–58

requirements for, 5–6

ethnoracial groups

boundaries of, 68, 71

categories of, 55, 67–68, 70–71, 269n1, 271–72nn1–3

characteristics of, 269n1

class differences in, 60

fragmentation of, 202

genetic traits, 271–72nn2–3

impact of immigrants on other ethnoracial groups, 20, 27–29, 33, 55–56, 59–60, 62, 67, 111, 146, 249–50

interracial sex and marriage, 69–70, 80, 272n4

majority population group, 18, 19, 20, 249

obstacles to political power, 205

statistics on, 15–20, 16, 249, 269–70nn1–2

supposed inferiority of races, 70–71, 76

tension between ethnic groups, 21–22, 136, 205, 206–8, 250

terminology use, 269n1

triangulated racial order, 57–58

ethnoracial pentagon, 55–56

ethnoracial pluralism, 233

ethnoracial politics. See also biracial hierarchy; individual assimilation; multiracial hierarchy; pluralism, political

barriers to political empowerment, 58–59

deracialization of, 46–47

effect of growing Latino population on, 27–29

futures for, 1–3, 37–39, 250–53

historical context of, 65

immigration and, 14–15, 33–34

individual assimilation and, 42–44, 250, 271n1 (chap. 2)

racial hierarchy and, 65

racial politics compared to, 53

transformation of, 14–15

transnationalism and, 38, 60–62, 129

European-origin Americans. See also White population

characteristics of, 269n1

dissimilarity index, 108–9

individual assimilation of, 39–40, 51

peak period of immigrants from, 18, 270n3

political incorporation, 47–48, 52–53, 251

supposed inferiority of races and discrimination, 39–40, 51, 70

Evanston, Illinois, 78

FAIR (Federation for American Immigration Reform), 242

Fair Housing Act, 229–30, 235–36

Farmer, James, 135

Farrakhan, Louis, 135

Federal Housing Administration (FHA), 76

Federalist Paper No. 10, 45–46

Federation for American Immigration Reform (FAIR), 242

Filipino Americans. See also Asian and Pacific Island Americans

diversification of Asian American population, 30, 31, 113

immigration, 19, 94, 99, 272n5

restrictions on immigration of, 96

Florida

African-origin American population, 21, 22

Asian American population in, 32

Black Americans in, 211, 218–19

congressional elections, 185, 188–89, 188

Cuban Americans in, 90, 91, 137, 156, 218–19

immigrant population in, 17

Latino and Hispanic Americans in, 25, 26, 26, 27, 81–82, 112, 180, 188–89, 188, 212, 218–19

state politics, governing coalitions in, 218–19

Flushing, New York, 173

foreigners
    foreigner status and citizenship, 58, 69,
        96, 157
    insider versus, 57–58
    marriage to, 69
Foreign Miners License tax, 94
foreign policy, transnationalism and, 62

Garcia, Robert, *188*
Gary, Indiana, 177
Geary Act, 94
genetic traits, 271–72nn2–3
Gentlemen's Agreement, 95
Georgia
    Black Americans in, *211*
    immigrant population in, 18
    Latino and Hispanic Americans in, *26,
        212*
    state politics and immigrant issue, 219
Gingles, Thornburg v., 176, 185, 186, 189,
    192, 273n4 (chap. 5)
Gonzales, Charles, *186*
Gonzales, Henry, *186*
Gonzales, Ron, *183*
governing coalitions
    Asian and Pacific Island Americans, 33,
        102, 220, 264
    as benchmark of incorporation, 3, 4,
        125–26, 127–28, 194–97, 252
    Black Americans in state politics,
        209–11, *210–11*, 213–14, 218–19, 220
    in California, 200–201, 215–18, *216*
    Caribbean-origin Americans, 218–19
    cities and metropolitan areas, 200–208
    Cuban Americans, 91–92, 218, 219
    ethnoracial democracy and, 5–6,
        257–58
    in Florida, 218–19
    formation of new, 49–50
    identification of, 197–98
    impact of immigrants on, 197–200
    importance of, 3, 49, 225
    incorporation of immigrants into,
        49–50, 225
    influence of, 3, 49, 125–26, 128
    Latino and Hispanic Americans, 20, 29,
        212–14, *212–13,* 220

    legislative outcomes, minority groups'
        influence on, 212, 213–14
    membership in, 4
    Mexican Americans, 85, 153
    national politics, 222–25
    obstacles to political power, 203–4, 205,
        257–58
    Puerto Rican Americans, 88–89
    racial identity and, 39, 45–47
    recruitment of immigrants into, 49
Great Migration, 105
Great Society programs, 89, 231
group consciousness, 132, 147–54
Guatemalan Americans, 92
Guiliani, Rudolph, *183*

Haitian Americans
    contemporary immigrants and racial
        expectations, 78–79
    geographic concentrations, 203
    governing coalitions in state politics,
        218–19
    immigration policy, 137, 273n1 (chap. 5)
    March on Washington by, 137
    National Coalition for Haitian Rights
        (NCHR), 137
Hammond, James, 75
Hartford, Connecticut, 207
Hawaii
    Asian and Pacific Island Americans in,
        32, 95, 180–81
    Black Americans in, *211*
    Civil Rights Project, 272–73n3
    immigrant population in, 17, 215
    Japanese Americans in, treatment dur-
        ing World War II, 99
    Latino and Hispanic Americans in,
        212
Hayes, Janet Gray, *183*
Hinojosa, Rubin, *186*
Hispanic Americans. *See* Latino and His-
    panic Americans
Hmong Americans, *31*
Holder v. Hall, 191
Hooks, Benjamin, 137
Hoover, J. Edgar, 99
household incomes, *121*

housing opportunities and segregation
analysis of differences between immigrant groups, 106
for Asian and Pacific Island Americans,
110, 113–14, 115–16, 122–23
for Black Americans, 52, 76, 105, 109–11,
110, 115–16, 122–23
in cities and metropolitan areas, 108,
116, 272n1
civil rights movement and, 80
current status of minority populations,
13, 14, 115–16, 122–23
discrimination in, laws against, 91
dissimilarity index, 108–14, *110*
interracial segregation, 114–15, *114*
for Latino and Hispanic Americans,
110, 111–13, 115–16, 122–23
measurement of, 108–9, 272n2
for Mexican Americans, 84
native versus immigrant groups, 106
for Puerto Rican Americans, 87
racial equality movements and, 12
trends in, context for understanding,
107
for White population, 104–5
Houston
housing segregation dissimilarity index, 109, *110*
immigrant population in, 108, 208
interracial housing segregation, *114*
mayoral elections, *183*
tension between ethnic groups, 208

Idaho, 18, *211, 212*
illegal immigrants, 24, 143–44, 146, 240–41
Illinois. *See also* Chicago
Asian and Pacific Island Americans in,
32, 157
Black Americans in, 177–78, *211*
contemporary immigrants and racial
expectations, 78
immigrant population in, 17
Latino and Hispanic Americans in, 27,
180, *212*
lynchings in, 75
noncitizen voters, 164
immigrant newcomers. *See* newcomers

immigrant rights march (2006), 10,
143–44
immigration
costs of to U.S. government programs,
242
demographic changes through, 15–20,
16, 107–8, 269–70nn1–2
ethnoracial politics and, 14–15, 33–34
illegal and unauthorized immigrants,
24, 143–44, 146, 240–41
law to regulate, changes in, 15, 140,
143–44
origin of current immigrants, *16*, 18
policies, anti-immigration, 140
policies, parity between, 137, 273n1
(chap. 5)
policies and transnationalism, 62
as political issue, 13
privileges and status of immigrants,
198–99
protests and organizational activity, 10,
136–37, 143–46
quota system for, 15, 230
social programs as encouragement for,
241–42
statistics on, 15–20, *16*, 269–70nn1–2
Immigration Act (Johnson-Reed Act), 96
Immigration and Nationality Act (Mc-
Carran-Walter Act), 99, 162, 165
Immigration Reform Act, 15, 230, 243
income, household, *121*
incorporation. *See* political incorporation
indentured servants, 73
Indiana
Black Americans in, 177, *211*
immigrant population in, 18
Latino and Hispanic Americans in, 26,
212
lynchings in, 75
Indianapolis, 17, *26*
indigenous people, 269n1, 270–71n8. *See
also* Native Americans
individual assimilation
African-origin Americans, 253–54
applicability of, 43
Asian and Pacific Island Americans,
1–2, 37–38, 40, 253–54

individual assimilation (*continued*)
Black Americans, 1–2, 37–38, 41–42, 53, 253–54, 260
Caribbean-origin Americans, 253–54
concept of, 1–2, 3, 39, 250
discrimination and, 2
ethnoracial politics and, 42–44, 250, 257, 271n1 (chap. 2)
European-origin Americans, 39–40, 51
increase in, 5, 253–54
Latino and Hispanic Americans, 1–2, 37–38, 40–41, 253–54
Obama and, 265–66
optimism about, 253–54, 256
racial hierarchy and, 37–38, 42
racial identity and, 39–42
social and political structures and, 38
socioeconomic status and, 206, 250
White population, 58–59
insider, foreigner versus, 57–58
institutional incorporation, 209–10
interest representation, 195
interracial housing segregation, 114–15, *114*
interracial sex and marriage, 69–70, 80, 272n4
Iowa, 18, *211, 212*
Irish Americans
distinctions between Blacks and, 79
group consciousness, 147
peak period of immigrants from, 270n3
political incorporation and, 251
supposed inferiority of races and discrimination, 39–40, 51, 70
Israel, 62
Italian Americans, 39–40, 51, 251

Jackson, Jesse, 12
Jamaican Americans, 78, 218–19
Japanese Americans. *See also* Asian and Pacific Island Americans
activism of, 12
diversification of Asian American population, 30, *31*, 113
education for, 95
immigration, 19, 94–95
mayoral elections, 184
racial slurs and ethnic distinctions, 101
restrictions on immigration of, 94–95, 96, 272n6
segregation of, 95
self-identity of, 100–101
treatment of during World War II, 99
Jersey City, *114*, 115
Jewish Americans, 39–40, 51, 62, 70
Jim Crow system, 11, 41
Jindal, Bobby, 180
jobs. *See* employment training and opportunities
Johnson, Lyndon, 89, 227, 231, 233, 237, 238
Johnson-Reed Act, 96
Johnson v. DeGrandy, 191
Jones Act, 86

Kansas, 18, 82, *211, 212*
Kelly, Sharon, *183*
Kentucky, 18, *211, 212*
Kim, Claire Jean, 57–58
King, Martin Luther, Jr., 9, 12, 231
King, Rodney, 13
Kirk, Ron, *183*
Korean Americans
diversification of Asian American population, 31, *31*, 113
governing coalitions, 206
immigration, 19, 94
partisanship, 174
political empowerment, barriers to, 59–60

labor repression, 83
labor union activity, 84–85, 206, 223–25, 235, 255
land ownership by immigrants, 96, 272n7
language policy
bilingual education, 217, 234, 235, 244, 245
bilingualism in America, 245–46
language abilities and linguistic assimilation, 199–200, 212
language assistance for voting process, 165, 190, 244–45, 273n2 (chap. 5)
Laotian Americans, *31*

Latino and Hispanic Americans. *See also* Cuban Americans; Mexican Americans; Puerto Rican Americans
activism of, 80, 133–34, 137–40, 143–46, 226
assimilation of, 2–3
biracial hierarchy and, 2–3, 5, 51–52, 251–52
birthrates, 23–24, 270n6
in California, 215–18, *217*
census data, racial categories in, 93, 151
characteristics of, 269n1
citizenship for, 162, 170
congressional elections, 184–89, *186, 187, 188*
Congressional Hispanic Caucus, 234, 262
contemporary immigrants and racial expectations, 78–79, 92–93
current status of, 13, 14–15
descriptive representation, 176–77, 179–80, *179*, 181–82, 184–89, *186, 187, 188*, 189–92, *216*, 220–21
discrimination against, 70, 152–53, 261
distinctions between Blacks and, 79–80
diversification and national-origins composition, 24–25, *25*, 92, 111–12, 139, 150–51, 202
educational attainment levels, 160–61, *161*, 170–71
educational opportunities and school segregation, 117–20, *119, 120*, 122–23
in Florida, 218–19
fragmentation of groups, 202
geographic concentrations, 25–27, *26*, 81–82, 92–93, 112, 249
governing coalitions, 200–208, 212–14, *212–13*, 215–18, 220, 262
group consciousness, 150–54
historical racialization experiences, 81–92, 103
household incomes, *121*
housing opportunities and segregation, *110*, 111–13, 115–16, 122–23
immigration, *16*, 19, 20, 23–29, 92, 111, 146, 250

increase in population of, *16*, 18, 19, 20, 23, *24*, 27, 108, 202, 249
individual assimilation, 1–2, 37–38, 40–41, 253–54
interracial housing segregation, 114–15, *114*
labor union activity, 84–85, 206, 223–25
language abilities and linguistic assimilation, 199–200, 212
linked fate, 151
mayoral elections, *179*, 182–84, *183*
median age of, 170
multiracial hierarchy and, 3, 55–56
obstacles to political power, 203–4, 205
occupational status, 161, *161*
panethnicity, 92–93
partisanship, 153, 155–56, 262
pluralism, 37–38, 48–49, 250–51, 254–56, 271nn3–4
and politics, 2–3, 4, 5, 13, 14, 48–49, 52, 54, 58–60, 121–22, *122*, 126–27, 131–32, 144–46, 169–72, 174–77, 212–14, *212–13*, 215–18, 250–58, 261–62, 271nn3–4
public policies for equality of opportunities, 234
racial and ethnic identity of, 28–29, 93, 150–51
racial hierarchy, 62, 260–62
racial inequalities, government involvement to correct, 229, 234
racial isolation of, 118
segregation of, 106
self-identity of, 28–29, 93
sense of closeness to other Latino Americans, 153
social separation of, 40
socioeconomic status of, 120–22, *121, 122, 123*, 158–62, *158, 159, 161*, 170–71, 261
tension between ethnic groups, 205, 208, 250
transformation of culture and politics of United States by, 61
unauthorized immigrants, 24
as voters, 139, 163, 165, *166, 168*, 169–72, 189–92, 244–45, 273n2 (chap. 5)

Latino National Congreso, 139
League of United Latin American Citizens (LULAC), 85, 138, 140
Lee, Wen Ho, 142
liberal politics. *See also* Democratic Party
  race-based politics of, 40
  racial inequalities, government involvement to correct, 227, 229
linked fate, 72–73, 148, 151
literacy tests, 11
Liu, John, 190
Long Beach, 108, *183*, 184
Los Angeles
  Black American descriptive representation, 177
  governing coalitions, 204–6
  housing segregation dissimilarity index, *110*
  immigrant population in, 17, 108, 203–6
  interracial housing segregation, *114*
  Japanese Americans in, treatment during World War II, 99
  labor union activity, 206, 223–25
  mayoral elections, *177, 183,* 184
  political incorporation, 48
  racial equality movements, 12
  tension between ethnic groups, 208
Los Angeles County, 192, 205
Louisiana
  Asian and Pacific Island Americans in, 180
  Black Americans in, *211*
  Latino and Hispanic Americans in, 179, *212*
  one-drop rule for Blackness, 75
  racialization of public policy, 69
  voter-eligible population, composition of, 180
LULAC (League of United Latin American Citizens), 85, 138, 140
lynchings, 75

Madison, James, 45–46
Maine, *211, 212*
Malcolm X, 231
MALDEF (Mexican American Legal Defense and Education Fund), 138, 140, 192
MAPA (Mexican American Political Association), 85
marches and demonstrations. *See* activism, movements, protests, and organizational activity
March on Washington, 9, 10
Marielitos, 91
Marshall, Dale Rogers, 48, 194–95, 200–202, 233, 271n3
Martinez, Matthew, *187*
Maryland, 164, *211, 212*
Massachusetts
  African-origin American population, 21, 22
  Asian American population in, 32
  Black representation and incorporation, *211*
  immigrant population in, 17
  Latino representation and incorporation, *212*
Massey, Douglas S., 104–5
McCarran-Walter Act (Immigration and Nationality Act), 99, 162, 165
median voter and public policy, 221–22, 259, 262, 264, 267
Medicare and Medicaid programs, 231
Meng, Jimmy, 190
Mexican American Legal Defense and Education Fund (MALDEF), 138, 140, 192
Mexican American Political Association (MAPA), 85
Mexican Americans
  activism of, 12, 84, 85, 137–38, 139, 145
  bilingual education, 244
  Chicano Movement, 12, 84, 85
  citizenship for, 82–83, 162
  colonial labor system, 83
  descriptive representation, 192
  diversification of Latino American population, 24–25, *25*
  education for, 85
  geographic concentrations, 92–93, 112, 203
  governing coalitions of, 85, 153

group consciousness, 153
historical racialization experiences, 82–85, 103
housing segregation and opportunities for, 84
immigration statistics, 19
individual assimilation of, 40–41
labor movement and farm workers, 84–85
land owned by, 84
opinions about in California, 217
political empowerment, barriers to, 58–59
racial and ethnic identity of, 87, 153
segregation of, 84
socioeconomic status of, 84
tension between ethnic groups, 205
unauthorized immigrants, 24
violence against, 84
Mexican-American War, 82, 244
Miami
    housing opportunities and segregation, 110, 114, 115
    immigrant population in, 90, 108, 203, 208
    mayoral elections, 183, 184
    tension between ethnic groups, 208
Michigan, 211, 212
Middle Eastern–origin Americans, 18, 51, 70, 206
Midwestern United States, 272–73n3
    immigrant population in, 18
    Latino American population in, 25, 112
    school segregation in, 118, 119–20, 120
Miller, Laura, 183
Million Man March, 135
Mineta, Norman, 183
minimum wage law, 232
Minnesota
    African-origin Americans in, 21, 22
    Black Americans in, 211
    immigrant population in, 18
    Latino and Hispanic Americans in, 212
minority businesses, 12
minority populations, 269n1. See also Asian and Pacific Island Americans;

Black Americans; Latino and Hispanic Americans
    diversity of, 10
    increase in, 10
    political influence of, 2–3
Mississippi, 18, 211, 212
Missouri, 211, 213
Missouri City, Texas, 17
Model Cities Act, 231, 234
model minority, 13, 57, 99–100, 272n8
monocultural America, 226, 227–29
monoculturists, 227–28
Montana, 211, 213
Mosely-Brown, Carol, 177–78
Mountain/Western United States, 18
Mulatto, 72
multicultural America, 228–29
multiculturists, 228
multiracial hierarchy
    Asian and Pacific Island Americans and, 3, 55–56, 57–58
    Black Americans and, 55–56
    concept of, 3, 55–56, 252
    immigrant newcomers and disruption or reinforcement of, 55–56
    Latino and Hispanic Americans and, 55–56
    as national pattern, 51, 55, 59–60
    political implications of, 58–60
    segmented assimilation, 56
    social and political structures and, 38
    triangulated racial order, 57–58

NAACP, 11, 135
NALEO (National Association of Latino Elected Officials), 139, 179
Napolitano, Grace, 187
National Association of Latino Elected Officials (NALEO), 139, 179
National Coalition for Haitian Rights (NCHR), 137
National Conference on Civil Rights, 135, 244
National Council of La Raza (NCLR), 138, 140, 156
National Latino Survey, 93

national politics. *See also* Democratic
Party; partisanship and political
affiliations; Republican Party
nonelected channels to influence,
222–23
political incorporation, 220–22
Native Americans
activism of, 80
characteristics of, 269n1
supposed inferiority of races and discrimination, 70
voting rights and language assistance
for voting process, 165, 244–45, 273n2
(chap. 5)
Native Hawaiians and Other Pacific Islander Americans, 270–71n8. *See also*
Asian and Pacific Island Americans
NCHR (National Coalition for Haitian
Rights), 137
NCLR (National Council of La Raza), 138,
140, 156
Nebraska, 18, *211, 213*
neoconservative politics. *See* conservative
and neoconservative politics
Nevada
African-origin Americans in, *22*
Asian and Pacific Island Americans in,
173
Black Americans in, *211*
immigrant population in, 17, 18
Latino and Hispanic Americans in, *26,
27, 213*
Newark, *110*
newcomers
citizenship for, 69
competition between Blacks and, 80
dual nationalities or citizenships,
61
ethnoracial groups, disruption or reinforcement of, 20, 27–29, 33, 55–56,
59–60, 62, 67, 146
issues and problems of, 146
meaning of race, immigrant's role in
changing, 41, 42
national policies and, 129
Pan-Asian American identity, 101–2
perception of, 1

and politics, 126, 128–29, 131, 133,
174–75, 264–65
racial hierarchy and, 264–65
racialization legacy of, 102–3
segmented assimilation, 56
social contexts for understanding effects of, 104, 122–24
socioeconomic status, effect on, 160
technology and contact with home
country and families, 60–61
transnationalism and, 38, 60–62, 129
New Deal policies, 155, 268
New Hampshire, *211, 213*
New Haven, Connecticut, 47, 48
New Jersey
African-origin Americans in, 21, *22*
Asian and Pacific Island Americans in,
32, *157*
Black Americans in, 20, *211*
immigrant population in, 17
Latino and Hispanic Americans in, 20,
27, *213*
New Mexico
Black Americans in, *211*
Latino and Hispanic Americans in, 27,
81–82, 179, *180, 213*
Mexican Americans in, 83, 84
New Orleans, *180*
Newsome, Gavin, *183*
New York City
Asian and Pacific Island Americans in,
190
Black Americans in, 22–23, 177
Caribbean-origin Americans in, 111
fragmentation of groups in, 202
housing segregation, *110,* 114
immigrant population in, 17, 108,
203–4, 205–8
labor union activity, 206, 224
Latino and Hispanic Americans in, 25
mayoral elections, *183*
Puerto Rican Americans in, 88, 89
racial equality movements, 12
racial politics in, 59
tension between ethnic groups, 206–8
New York State
African-origin Americans in, 21, *22*

Asian and Pacific Island Americans in, 32, 173, 174, 190
Black Americans in, 20, *211*
congressional elections, 185, 187, *188*
immigrant population in, 17, 18
Latino and Hispanic Americans in, 20, 27, 180, 187, *188*, *213*
noncitizen voters, 164
Nicaraguan Americans, 208
Nixon, Richard, 232, 233, 234, 239–40
North Carolina
Black Americans in, *211*
immigrant population in, 18
Latino and Hispanic Americans in, 26, *26*, *213*
North Dakota, *211*, *213*
Northeastern United States, 272–73n3
Latino and Hispanic Americans in, 93, 112, 139–40
racial equality movement, 12
school segregation in, 118, 119–20, *120*, 123
Northwestern United States, 112
Nunes, Devin, *187*

Oakland
housing opportunities and segregation, *110*, *114*, 115
immigrant population in, 108
mayoral elections, *183*
Obama, Barack, 13, 136, 167, 174, 178, 265–68
occupational stratification, 83, 86–87
Ohio, 75, 177, *211*, *213*
Oklahoma
Black Americans in, *211*
immigrant population in, 18
Latino and Hispanic Americans in, *213*
lynchings in, 75
one-drop rule for Blackness, 74–75
Orange County, California, 108, 184
Oregon
Asian and Pacific Island Americans in, 173
Black Americans in, *211*
immigrant population in, 18

Latino and Hispanic Americans in, *26*, *213*
organizational activity. *See* activism, movements, protests, and organizational activity
"Orientals," 100–101. *See also* Asian and Pacific Island Americans
Ortiz, Solomon, *186*
outsiders
impact of recent immigrants on, 126
influence of, 54
national policies and, 129
and politics, 39, 125–29, 131
Ozawa v. United States, 98

Pacific Islander Americans, 270–71n8. *See also* Asian and Pacific Island Americans
Pakistani Americans, *31*, 206
PAN (Priority Africa Network), 137
panethnicity
Asian and Pacific Island Americans, 100–102
Latino and Hispanic Americans, 92–93
partisanship and political affiliations, 154–55
Asian and Pacific Island Americans, 157–58, 173–74, 263
Black Americans, 22–23, 53, 155, 166, 167, 169, 259–60
Chinese Americans, 174
Cuban Americans, 91, 153, 156, 218, 219
in Florida, 219
governing coalitions, 196
immigration issues, opinions about, 217–18
Korean Americans, 174
Latino and Hispanic Americans, 153, 155–56, 262
Puerto Rican Americans, 89
PASSO (Political Association of Spanish Speaking Organizations), 85
Pennsylvania, *211*, *213*
permanent residents, 198–99
Philadelphia, 12, *110*, 177
Philadelphia Plan, 233
Phipps, Susie Guillary, 75

Pilot National Asian American Political
Survey (PNAAPS), 102
Pinderhughes, Dianne, 52–53
Platt Amendment, 90
Plessy v. Ferguson, 80, 116–17
pluralism, political, 2, 3, 45, 250–51
   African-origin Americans, 255–56
   Asian and Pacific Island Americans,
      37–38, 250–51, 254–56
   Black Americans, 37–38, 48, 254–56,
      271n3
   Caribbean-origin Americans, 255–56
   increase in, 5, 49–50, 254–56
   Latino and Hispanic Americans, 37–38,
      48–49, 254–56, 271nn3-4
   optimism about, 254–56
   political incorporation and, 46–50,
      206, 250–51, 257
   racial hierarchy and, 37–38
   racial identity and, 45–47
   social and political structures and, 38
   transnationalism and, 62
   White population, 58–59
PNAAPS (Pilot National Asian American
   Political Survey), 102
Polish Americans, 251
political affiliations. *See* partisanship and
   political affiliations
Political Association of Spanish Speaking
   Organizations (PASSO), 85
political coalitions. *See* governing coalitions
political incorporation, 125
   African-origin Americans, 52
   Asian and Pacific Island Americans, 52,
      54, 250–58, 263–64
   benchmarks of, 3–5, 125–29, 252–58
   benefits of, 128–29, 194
   biracial hierarchy and, 52–54, 251–52
   Black Americans, 48, 52–54, *210–11,*
      250–58, 259–60, 271n3
   Caribbean-origin Americans, 52
   criteria for, 194–95
   encouragement of and support for,
      162–63
   European-origin Americans, 47–48,
      52–53, 251

failure of ethnoracial groups to incorporate, 129, 202
fragmentation of groups and, 202
impact of recent immigrants on, 126,
   129
institutional incorporation, 209–10
integrationist orientation toward,
   128–29
Latino and Hispanic Americans, 48–49,
   52, 54, *212–13,* 250–58, 261–62,
   271nn3–4
national politics, 220–22
Obama and, 265–68
of outsiders, 39, 125–29
pluralism and, 46–50, 206, 250–51,
   257
public employment and, 223
skin color and, 54, 251
transnationalism and, 129
urban politics and, 200–208
political participation. *See also* state politics
   access to, 125, 126–27, 132, 133–34,
      144–46
   activism and, 132, 133–46
   advantages of, 154
   African-origin Americans, 22–23, 270n5
   Asian and Pacific Island Americans, 4,
      5, 32–33, 126–27, 131–32, 144–46,
      172–75, 215–18, 255–56
   as benchmark of incorporation, 3, 4,
      125–27, 252
   Black Americans, 4, 5, 11, 22–23, 126–27,
      131–32, 144–46, 154, 166–69, 174–75,
      209–11, *210–11,* 213–14, 215–18, 255–56,
      270n5
   Caribbean-origin Americans, 22–23
   citizenship and, 162–64
   discrimination, perception of, and,
      152–53
   group consciousness, 132, 147–54
   impact of recent immigrants on, 133,
      174–75, 264–65
   importance of, 4, 131–32
   increase in, 3, 5
   Latino and Hispanic Americans, 4, 5,
      126–27, 131–32, 144–46, 169–72,

174–75, 212–14, *212–13*, 215–18, 255–56, 261–62
obstacles to, 11
racial equality movements and, 12
resources, 132, 134, 146, 147
socioeconomic status and, 132, 158–62
political parties. *See also* Democratic Party; Republican Party
political incorporation in national politics, 220–22
political representation. *See also* descriptive representation
Asian and Pacific Island Americans, 13, 127, 255
as benchmark of incorporation, 3, 4, 125–26, 127, 129, 252
Black Americans, 12, 13, 14, 127, 255
current status of minority populations, 13, 14
disparity between groups, 127
gains in, 176–77
impact of immigrants on, 127, 133, 176, 199
importance of, 4
increase in, 3, 5
Latino and Hispanic Americans, 13, 14, 127, 255
minority population and representative elected officials, 132–33
racial equality movements and, 12
racial hierarchy and, 4
voter dilution, 176
political system. *See also* Democratic Party; Republican Party
access to, 47
barriers to political empowerment, 58–59
Black versus White racial politics, 41–42, 239–40
campaign contributions, 157
in Chicago, 52–53
citizenship requirements, 162–64
influence of outsider groups, 54
openness to groups seeking to influence, 47–48, 222, 271n3
responsiveness to minority voter concerns, 221–22

poll taxes, 11, 165
poverty
Great Society programs, 89
native versus immigrant groups, 105, 121–22, *122*
school segregation and, 120
War on Poverty, 89, 231, 234, 237
Priority Africa Network (PAN), 137
PRLDEF (Puerto Rican Legal Defense and Education Fund), 138, 140
Protest Is Not Enough (Browning, Marshall, and Tabb), 48
protests. *See* activism, movements, protests, and organizational activity
public employment, political incorporation and, 223
public policies
access to redistributive programs, 199
toward Asian immigrants, 94–96
civil rights movement and, 11
discrimination, government involvement to correct, 148, 152
economic equality and policies, 231–33, 235, 238–39, 268, 274n1
equality-of-opportunity programs and policies, 229–36
ethnoracial democracy and, 5–6
ethnoracially egalitarian, as benchmark of incorporation, 3, 4–5, 125–26, 128, 252
failure to adopt, 4–5
impact of immigrants on, 225–26, 240–46
legislative outcomes, minority groups' influence on, 212, 213–14
median voter and, 221–22, 259, 262, 264, 267
monocultural America, 226, 227–29
moral claim to group entitlements, 148
multicultural America, 228–29
national policies, 129
obstacles to political power, 257–58
race relations and, 231–33
racial equality, reversal of agenda for, 236–46
racial equality aspirations of, conflicts about, 226–29

public policies (*continued*)
  racial equality movements, 12, 226
  racial hierarchy and, 69–70, 258, 267–68
  racial inequalities, 5–6, 129, 148, 225–29, 234, 240, 257–58, 259–60, 273n3 (chap. 6)
  Second Reconstruction, 229–36
  social programs, 231–36, 238–39, 241–42
  transnationalism and, 62, 129
  welfare policy, 214, 232, 234, 235, 241
Puerto Rican Americans
  activism of, 12, 89, 137–38, 139, 145
  citizenship for, 86
  colonial labor system, 86–87
  diversification of Latino American population, 24–25, 25
  education for, 87, 88
  employment training and opportunities for, 86–87, 88
  geographic concentrations, 92–93, 112
  governing coalitions of, 88–89
  historical racialization experiences, 85–89
  housing segregation and opportunities for, 87
  immigration statistics, 19
  migration to mainland by, 86
  militant groups, 89
  partisanship, 89
  racial and ethnic identity of, 87
  segregation of, 87
  skin color and, 87
  social justice for, 89
  socioeconomic status of, 87–88
  tension between ethnic groups, 205
Puerto Rican Legal Defense and Education Fund (PRLDEF), 138, 140

racial and ethnic identity
  of African-origin Americans, 149–50
  of Armenian Americans, 98
  of Asian and Pacific Island Americans, 39–40, 97–98, 100–102, 151–52
  of Asian Indian Americans, 98
  of Black Americans, 147–50
  of Caribbean-origin Americans, 149–50
  census data, 71–72, 270n7
  of Chinese Americans, 97–98
  contemporary immigrants and racial expectations, 72–73, 77–80
  ethnic identity, symbolic nature of, 40, 42
  of European-origin Americans, 39–40
  governing coalitions and, 45–47
  group consciousness, 147–54
  individual assimilation and, 39–42
  of Latino and Hispanic Americans, 28–29, 93, 150–51
  meaning of race, immigrant's role in changing, 41, 42
  of Mexican Americans, 87, 153
  monocultural America, 226, 227–29
  pluralism and, 45–47
  political interests and, 39
  of Puerto Rican Americans, 87
  racial slurs and ethnic distinctions, 101
  self-identity of Asian Americans, 100–102
  self-identity of Latino and Hispanic Americans, 28–29, 93
  social acceptance and, 56
  as social construct, 39, 56–57, 67, 98, 271–72nn1–3
  socioeconomic status and, 39, 57
  of Syrian Americans, 98
  triangulated racial order, 57–58
racial balance, 19
racial barriers. *See* racial hierarchy
racial equality
  color line, diminishment of, 41
  commitment to, 222
  current status of movement for, 13, 15
  equality-of-opportunity programs and policies, 229–36
  marches and demonstrations for, 9–10
  March on Washington, 10
  movements with goal of, 12–13, 226
  pessimism about, 40
  public policies to support, conflicts about, 226–29, 236–46
  racial essentialism, 71
racial hierarchy. *See also* biracial hierarchy; multiracial hierarchy

Asian and Pacific Island Americans, 263–64
Black Americans, 259–60
Caribbean-origin Americans and, 62
in Chicago, 52–53
continuation of, 5, 50–51, 198
creation of, 67–71, 271–72nn1–3
elimination of, 5–6
ethnoracial politics and, 65
impact of recent immigrants on, 264–65
individual assimilation and, 37–38, 42
Latino and Hispanic Americans, 62, 260–62
Obama election and, 265–68
pessimism about, 256–58
pluralism and, 37–38
political representation and, 4
public policies and, 69–70, 258, 267–68
transnationalism and, 62
racial inequalities
current status of minority populations, 13–14
government involvement to correct, 148, 226–27, 228–29, 234, 273n3 (chap. 6)
individual assimilation and, 2
political activism against, 80
political incorporation and, 126
public policies and, 69–70, 225–29, 257–58, 259–60
reinforcement of, 129, 240
reversal of, 5–6, 228
racial isolation
of Asian and Pacific Island Americans, 118
of Black Americans, 105, 118
of Latino and Hispanic Americans, 118
in schools, 118
of White population, 118
racial politics, 71
Black versus White, 41–42, 239–40
deracialization of, 46–47
ethnic politics compared to, 53
immigrants' role in changing, 41–42
in New York City, 59
Reagan, Ronald, 167, 234–35, 238–39

redistributive programs, 199
Regime Politics (Stone), 54
religious divisions, 40
Republican Party
anti-immigration politics of, 153, 156
Asian and Pacific Island American voters and, 157–58
Black American voters and, 53, 155, 169
Cuban American voters and, 91, 153, 156, 218, 219
economic policy, 238–39
in Florida, 219
immigration issues, opinions about, 217
national politics and governing coalitions, 220–22
racial equality policies, opposition to, 239, 260
reserve labor force, 83
residential segregation. *See* housing opportunities and segregation
Reyes, Silvestre, *186*
Rhode Island, 27, *211, 213*
Riordan, Richard, *183*
Riverside–San Bernardino, 108, 109, *110*
Rodriquez, Ciro, *186*
Rogers, Reuel, 206–8
Roosevelt, Franklin D., 155, 268
Ros-Letinen, Ileana, *188*
Roybal, Edward, *187*
Roybal-Allard, Lucielle, *187*

SAAVY (South Asian American Voting Youth), 142–43
San Antonio, *114*
Sanchez, Linda, *187*
Sanchez, Loretta, *187*
San Diego, 108, *183, 184*
San Francisco
Asian and Pacific Island Americans in, 172–73, 192
discrimination against Chinese Americans, 94
equality of opportunity, policies to support, 233
housing segregation dissimilarity index, 109, *110*

San Francisco (*continued*)
immigrant population in, 108
mayoral elections, *183*
racial equality movements, 12
White population voters in, 173
San Jose, 17, 108, *183, 184*
school segregation. *See* educational opportunities and school segregation
Second Reconstruction, 229–36
segmented assimilation, 56, 59, 78
segregation. *See also* educational opportunities and school segregation; housing opportunities and segregation
of Asian and Pacific Island Americans, 106
of Black Americans, 52, 76, 105–6
Civil Rights Act and, 11
civil rights movement and, 80
current status of minority populations, 14, 122–24
democracy in America and, 105
disadvantages that accompany, 103
of Japanese Americans, 95
Jim Crow system and, 11, 41
of Latino and Hispanic Americans, 106
laws against, 11, 91
of Mexican Americans, 84
public policies against, 229–31
Puerto Rican Americans, housing patterns, 87
racialization legacy and, 103
role in racialization of American life, 65–66
skin color and, 52
socioeconomic status and, 105
trends in, context for understanding, 106, 107
SEIU (Service Employees International Union), 206, 223
Serreno, Jose, *188*
Service Employees International Union (SEIU), 206, 223
Shaw v. Reno, 191
Sherry, Peter, 48
Sikhs, 94
Slave Codes, 75

slaves
abolition of slavery, 75
census data, racial categories in, 72
diversity of, 73–74
emergence of slave trade, 73
Fifteenth Amendment and, 162, 164
lynchings, 75
political activism, 80
regulation of behavior of, 75
three-fifths compromise, 72
social acceptance, racial identity and, 56
social construct, racial identity as, 39, 56–57, 67–68, 98, 271–72nn1–3
social justice, 89
social movements. *See* activism, movements, protests, and organizational activity
social programs
backlash to, 234–36
changes to and elimination of, 236–46
encouragement of immigration through, 241–42
equality-of-opportunity programs and policies, 229–36
expansion of, 231–34
funding for, 235, 238–39, 241–42
socioeconomic status. *See also* poverty
of African-origin Americans, 159–60, *159*
of Asian and Pacific Island Americans, 33, 57, 120–22, *121, 122,* 123, 158–62, *158, 159*
of Black Americans, 80–81, 105, 120–22, *121, 122,* 123, 158–62, *158, 159*
of Caribbean-origin Americans, 159–60, *159*
class differences, impact of, 60
current status of minority populations, 123
distinctions between Blacks and other immigrant groups, 79–80
household incomes, *121*
individual assimilation and, 206, 250
of Latino and Hispanic Americans, 120–22, *121, 122,* 123, 158–62, *158, 159, 161,* 170–71, 261
of Mexican Americans, 84

political participation and, 132,
158–62
of Puerto Rican Americans, 87–88
racial identity and, 39, 57
school segregation and, 120
segregation and, 105
social acceptance and, 56
voter registration and turnout and, 167,
169, 170–71
of White population, 158, 159, 159
Solis, Hilda, 187
South America–origin Americans, 19,
24–25, 25, 112, 250
South Asian American Voting Youth
(SAAVY), 142–43
South Carolina, 18, 26, 211, 213
South Dakota, 211, 213
Southeastern United States, 18
Southern Christian Leadership Conference, 135
Southern United States, 272–73n3
biracial pattern, 51
Black Americans in, 4, 20
housing segregation and opportuni-
ties, 116
Jim Crow system, 11
Latino and Hispanic Americans in, 20,
25, 26, 112
lynchings in, 75
racial equality movement, 12
school segregation in, 118, 119–20, 120,
123
Southwestern America
Latino and Hispanic Americans in, 25,
81–82, 112, 139–40
multiracial hierarchy and, 3
multiracial pattern, 51, 60
Southwest Voter Registration Education
Project (SVREP), 139
Spanish Americans, 78–79
Spanish American War, 85–86, 89–90
state politics
Asian influence in, 215–18
Black influence in, 209–11, 210–11,
213–14, 215–18
California, governing coalitions in,
215–18, 216

Florida, governing coalitions in, 218–19
immigrant issues, 219–20
initiative process, 215, 216–17
Latino influence in, 212–14, 212–13,
215–18
legislative outcomes, minority groups'
influence on, 212, 213–14
statutory racialization, 69
Stone, Clarence, 54
Suarez, Xavier, 183
suburban communities, 19, 115
SVREP (Southwest Voter Registration
Education Project), 139
Syrian Americans, 98

Tabb, David H., 48, 194–95, 200–202, 233,
271n3
tax codes
Black Americans and, 76–77
census categories and, 72
Foreign Miners License, 94
poll taxes, 11, 165
Puerto Ricans, 86
Tejeda, Frank, 186
Temporary Assistance to Needy Families,
235
Tennessee, 18, 26, 211, 213
Texas
annexation of, 82
Asian and Pacific Island Americans in,
32, 157
Black Americans in, 20
congressional elections, 185–86, 186
immigrant population in, 17
Latino and Hispanic Americans in, 20,
27, 81–82, 180, 185–86, 186, 190, 213
Mexican Americans in, 83
Vietnamese Americans in, 190
Thai Americans, 31
Thind v. United States, 98
Thornburg v. Gingles, 176, 185, 186, 189,
192, 273n4 (chap. 5)
Torres, Esteban, 187
transnationalism
African-origin Americans and, 136,
149–50
Black Americans and, 136

transnationalism (*continued*)
  Caribbean-origin Americans and, 136, 149–50
  Cuban Americans and, 92
  ethnoracial politics and, 38, 60–62, 129
  political incorporation and, 129
  public policies and, 62, 129
  racial hierarchy and, 62
Trinidadian Americans, 78
Tydings-McDuffie Act, 96

unauthorized immigrants, 24, 143–44, 146, 240–41
undocumented immigrants, 199
union activity, 84–85, 206, 223–25, 235, 255
United Farm Workers, 85
United States
  biracial model, 42, 249
  border control and patrols, 241
  demographic makeup of, 15–20, *16*, 33, 107–8, 269–70nn1–3
  transformation of culture and politics by Latino Americans, 61
  triangulated racial order, 57–58
United States Census Bureau
  comparison of data, 270n7
  immigration statistics, 15–19, 269n1 (chap. 1)
  racial categories in census, 71–72, 93, 151, 250
United States Commission on Civil Rights, 244
United States Congress
  Asian and Pacific Island American descriptive representation, 180, *181*, 220–21
  Black American descriptive representation, 177–78, *178*, 220–21
  Congressional Black Caucus, 137, 234, 259
  Congressional Hispanic Caucus, 234, 262
  ethnoracial democracy and, 267–68
  governing coalitions, 196, 220–22
  immigration policy reform hearings, 242
  Latino and Hispanic American de-

scriptive representation, 180, 184–89, *186*, *187*, *188*, 220–21
  Voting Rights Act, 191, 244–45
United States Constitution, amendments to
  Fourteenth Amendment, 176
  Fifteenth Amendment, 162, 164
  Twenty-fourth Amendment, 11
United States Constitution, Latino and Hispanic American descriptive representation, 179
United States Pan-Asian American Chamber of Commerce (USPAACC), 142
urban areas. *See* cities and metropolitan areas
Urban League, 135
USPAACC (United States Pan-Asian American Chamber of Commerce), 142
Utah, 18, 82, *211*, *213*

Velazquez, Nydia, *188*
Vermont, *211*, *213*
Vietnamese Americans
  diversification of Asian American population, 31, *31*, 113
  immigration statistics, 19
  racial slurs and ethnic distinctions, 101
  self-identity of, 102
  voting rights and language assistance for voting process, 190
Vietnam War, 101
Villaraigosa, Antonio, *183*, 205, 224
violence. *See* crime and violence
Virginia, 32, *211*, *213*
voter registration and turnout
  Asian and Pacific Island Americans, 142–43, 157–58, 163, *168*, 172–73, 190–91
  Black Americans, 166–67, *168*
  Cuban Americans, 163
  get-out-the-vote campaigns, 255
  immigrant voter turnout, 163–64
  Latino and Hispanic Americans, 139, 163, *168*, 169–70, 171–72, 190

noncitizen voters, 163–64
obstacles to, 11
political participation and, 132
socioeconomic status and, 167, 169,
170–71
voter-eligible population, composition
of, 165–66, *166*, 169, 180
White population, *168*
voting rights
of Black Americans, 154, 164
civil rights movement and, 80
discrimination and, 164–65, 173, 176,
244–45
for immigrants, 145–46
language assistance for voting process,
165, 190, 244–45, 273n2 (chap. 5)
for noncitizens, 163–64
political participation and, 132
voter dilution, 176
voter-eligible population, composition
of, 165–66, *166*
Voting Rights Act, 11, 128
Asian and Pacific Island Americans
and, 165, 189–93
basis for, 176
Black Americans and, 11, 165, 189–91
civil rights movement after, 135
continuation of benefits of, 235–36
descriptive representation and, 176, 185,
186, 189–93, 273n4 (chap. 5)
effectiveness of, 191
equality of opportunities and race relations, 229–30
impact of, 165
importance of, 164
language assistance for voting process,
165, 190, 244–45, 273n2 (chap. 5)
Latino and Hispanic Americans and,
165, 189–92
limitations of, 192
provisions of, 11, 162, 164–65, 176
renewal of, 189–90
results test, 185, 273n4 (chap. 5)

wage labor, 83
Wallace, George, 239
War on Poverty, 89, 231, 234, 237

Washington
African-origin American population,
21, *22*
Asian and Pacific Island Americans in,
32, 157
Black Americans in, *211*
immigrant population in, 18
Latino and Hispanic Americans in, *26*,
213
Washington, D.C.
Black American descriptive representation, 178
Civil Rights Project, 272–73n3
Haitian march on, 137
housing segregation dissimilarity index, 109, *110*
immigrant population in, 108
March on Washington, 9, 10
mayoral elections, *183*, *184*
Million Man March, 135
Washington, Harold, 53, *183*
Washington, Walter, *183*
WCVI (William C. Velasquez Institute),
139
welfare policy, 214, 232, 234, 235, 241
Western United States, 272–73n3
housing segregation and opportunities, 116
immigrant population in, 18
multiracial hierarchy and, 3
multiracial pattern, 51, 60
racial equality movement, 12
school segregation in, 118, 119–20, *120*,
123
West Indian–origin Americans. *See*
Caribbean-origin Americans
West Virginia, *211*, *213*
White, Bill, *183*
White backlash, 239
White population
Asian Americans as, 97–98
birthrates, 24
Black Americans' status, comparison
to, 149
Black versus White racial politics,
41–42, 239–40
characteristics of, 269n1

White population (*continued*)
  decrease in population percentage of,
    18
  group consciousness, 147
  household incomes, *121*
  housing segregation and opportunities
    for, 104–5
  immigration statistics, *16*
  individual assimilation, 39–40, 51,
    58–59
  interracial sex and marriage, 69–70, 80,
    272n4
  median age of, 170
  multiracial hierarchy and, 3
  pluralism and, 58–59
  poverty and, 121–22, *122*
  racial isolation of, 118
  religious divisions of, 40
  socioeconomic status of, *158*, 159, *159*
  triangulated racial order, 57–58
  as voters, 166, *166*, *168*
  White privilege, 70, 97
Who Governs? (Dahl), 47–48
William C. Velasquez Institute (WCVI),
  139
Wilson, Lionel J., *183*
Wisconsin, *211*, *213*
Wyoming, 75, 82, *211*, *213*

Yarborough, Ralph, 244